City of Djinns

Also by William Dalrymple

In Xanadu

City of Djinns

A YEAR IN DELHI

WILLIAM DALRYMPLE

ILLUSTRATIONS BY
OLIVIA FRASER

HarperCollins*Publishers*

HarperCollins*Publishers*
77–85 Fulham Palace Road,
Hammersmith, London W6 8JB

Published by HarperCollins*Publishers* 1993

1 3 5 7 9 8 6 4 2

A catalogue record for this book is
available from the British Library

ISBN 0 00 215725 X

Set in Linotron Meridien
by Rowland Phototypesetting Ltd
Bury St Edmunds, Suffolk

Printed and bound in Great Britain by
Hartnolls Limited, Bodmin, Cornwall

Acknowledgements

This book, the story of one year in Delhi, has taken nearly four times that long to complete. It has been a long haul and on the way I have incurred debts to a great number of people whom I must now thank.

Firstly, Dominic Arbuthnott, with whom I first explored Delhi as a back-packer nine years ago. Without him I would probably never have come within a thousand miles of India in the first place. Jon Connel and Dominic Lawson both made me their Indian correspondent thus enabling me to return here; both were understanding when the book got in the way of their reports and articles. During that time, Mike Fishwick was a generous (and patient) editor, and Maggie Noach a model agent. During summer breaks in North Berwick, my parents were as long-suffering as ever.

Malcolm and Kathy Fraser let me loose on their wonderful archives: to them, particular thanks.

Salman Haidar took on the Delhi bureaucracy and got me my first residence visa; Sunil and Shalini Sethi provided shelter in Delhi until I found a house of my own. Khuswant Singh shoved me in the right direction at the beginning; he later helped with eunuchs and goddesses. Anil Seal, who taught me a little Indian history at Cambridge, helped me to secure an elusive ticket for the Nehru Memorial Library where I did the research.

Pavan Verma and Satish Jacob showed me some obscure nooks and crannies of the Old City; Dr Yunus Jaffery showed me others, and in addition kept me plied with strong hot tea and improving Sufi anecdotes. Mozaffar Alam helped with the Mughals. Siddarth and Rashmi Singh provided months of hospitality at Rohet Garh where, in a desperate bid for inspiration, I started the manuscript at the desk where Bruce Chatwin wrote *The Songlines*.

Several friends read through the manuscript and made invaluable comments. In Britain: Lucian Taylor, Patrick French, David Gilmour, Edward Whitley, Lucy and John Warrack, Nick and Georgia Coleridge, Fania Stoney, Elizabeth Chatwin, James Holloway, my brother Rob and my parents-in-law, Simon and Jenny Fraser. In India: Sam Miller, Navina Haidar, Tavleen Singh, Javed Abdulla, Manvender Singh, Pavan Verma, Sachin Mulji and Naveen Patnaik.

But my biggest debt by far is, of course, to my wife Olivia. Not only did she twice encourage (or rather order) me to continue when, in black moments, I decided to throw the whole thing in, she also read and edited each day's work, put up with tantrums, picked up the pieces, made encouraging noises, wielded a mean red pen, quite apart from drawing the cover, the wonderful maps and pictures.

This book would, quite literally, never have been completed without her. I dedicate it to Olivia with love and affection and a big hug.

William Dalrymple
6.III.93
New Delhi

PROLOGUE

IT WAS in the citadel of Feroz Shah Kotla that I met my first Sufi.

Pir Sadr-ud-Din had weasel eyes and a beard as tangled as a myna's nest. The mystic sat me down on a carpet, offered me tea, and told me about the djinns.

He said that when the world was new and Allah had created mankind from clay, he also made another race, like us in all things, but fashioned from fire. The djinns were spirits, invisible to the naked eye; to see them you had to fast and pray. For forty-one days, Sadr-ud-Din had sat without eating, half-naked in the foothills of the Himalayas; later, he had spent forty-one days up to his neck in the River Jumna.

One night, asleep in a graveyard, he was visited by the King of the Djinns.

'He was black, as tall as a tree, and he had one eye in the centre of his forehead,' said the Pir. 'The djinn offered me anything I wanted, but every time I refused.'

'Could you show me a djinn?' I asked.

'Certainly,' replied the Pir. 'But you would run away.'

I was only seventeen. After ten years at school in a remote valley in the moors of North Yorkshire, I had quite suddenly found myself in India, in Delhi. From the very beginning I was mesmerized by the great capital, so totally unlike anything I had ever seen before. Delhi, it seemed at first, was full of riches and horrors: it was a labyrinth, a city of palaces, an open gutter, filtered light through a filigree lattice, a landscape of domes, an anarchy, a press of people, a choke of fumes, a whiff of spices.

Moreover the city – so I soon discovered – possessed a bottomless seam of stories: tales receding far beyond history, deep into the cavernous chambers of myth and legend. Friends would moan about the touts on Janpath and head off to the beaches in Goa, but for me Delhi always exerted a stronger spell. I lingered on, and soon found a job in a home for destitutes in the far north of the city.

The nuns gave me a room overlooking a municipal rubbish dump. In the morning I would look out to see the sad regiment of rag-pickers trawling the stinking berms of refuse; overhead, under a copper sky, vultures circled the thermals forming patterns like fragments of glass in a kaleidoscope. In the afternoons, after I had swept the compound and the inmates were safely asleep, I used to slip out and explore. I would take a rickshaw into the innards of the Old City and pass through the narrowing funnel of gullies and lanes, alleys and cul de sacs, feeling the houses close in around me.

In summer I preferred the less claustrophobic avenues of Lutyens's Delhi. Then, under a pulsing sun, I would stroll slowly along the shady rows of neem, tamarind and arjuna, passing the white classical bungalows with their bow fronts and bushes of molten yellow gulmohar.

In both Delhis it was the ruins that fascinated me. However hard the planners tried to create new colonies of gleaming concrete, crumbling tomb towers, old mosques or ancient Islamic colleges – *medresses* – would intrude, appearing suddenly on roundabouts or in municipal gardens, curving the road network and obscuring the fairways of the golf course. New Delhi was not new at all. Its broad avenues encompassed a groaning necropolis, a graveyard of dynasties. Some said there were seven dead cities of Delhi, and that the current one was the eighth; others counted fifteen or twenty-one. All agreed that the crumbling ruins of these towns were without number.

But where Delhi was unique was that, scattered all around the city, there were human ruins too. Somehow different areas of Delhi seemed to have preserved intact different centuries, even different millennia. The Punjabi immigrants were a touchstone to the present day; with their nippy Maruti cars and fascination with all things new, they formed a lifeline to the 1980s. The old majors you would meet strolling in the Lodhi Gardens were pickled perhaps half a century earlier. Their walrus moustaches and Ealing comedy accents hinted that they had somehow got stuck in about 1946. The eunuchs in the Old City, some speaking courtly Urdu, might not have looked so out of place under the dais of the Great Mogul. The *sadhus* at Nigambodh Ghat I imagined as stranded citizens of Indraprastha, the legendary first Delhi of the *Mahabharata*, the great Indian epic.

All the different ages of man were represented in the people of the city. Different millennia co-existed side by side. Minds set in different ages walked the same pavements, drank the same water, returned to the same dust.

But it was not until months later, when I met Pir Sadr-ud-Din, that I learned the secret that kept the city returning to new life. Delhi, said Pir Sadr-ud-Din, was a city of djinns. Though it had been burned by invaders time and time again, millennium after millennium, still the city was rebuilt; each time it rose like a phoenix from the fire. Just as the Hindus believe that a body will be reincarnated over and over again until it becomes perfect, so it seemed Delhi was destined to appear in a new incarnation century after century. The reason for this, said Sadr-ud-Din, was that the djinns loved Delhi so much they could never bear to see it empty or deserted. To this day every house, every street corner was haunted by them. You could not see them, said Sadr-ud-Din, but if you concentrated you would be able to feel them: to hear their whisperings, or even, if you were lucky, to sense their warm breath on your face.

In Delhi I knew I had found a theme for a book: a portrait of a city disjointed in time, a city whose different ages lay suspended side by side as in aspic, a city of djinns.

Five years after I first lived in Delhi I returned, now newly married. Olivia and I arrived in September. We found a small top-floor flat near the Sufi village of Nizamuddin and there set up home.

Our landlady was Mrs Puri.

9

ONE

THE FLAT PERCHED at the top of the house, little more than a lean-to riveted to Mrs Puri's ceiling. The stairwell exuded sticky, airless September heat; the roof was as thin as corrugated iron.

Inside we were greeted by a scene from *Great Expectations*: a thick pall of dust on every surface, a family of sparrows nesting in the blinds and a fleece of old cobwebs – great arbours of spider silk – arching the corner walls. Mrs Puri stood at the doorway, a small, bent figure in a *salwar kameez*.

'The last tenant did not go out much,' she said, prodding the cobwebs with her walking stick. She added: 'He was not a tidy gentleman.' Olivia blew on a cupboard; the dust was so thick you could sign your name in it.

Our landlady, though a grandmother, soon proved herself to be a formidable woman. A Sikh from Lahore, Mrs Puri was expelled from her old home during Partition and in the upheavals of 1947 lost everything. She arrived in Delhi on a bullock cart. Forty-two years later she had made the transition from refugee pauper to Punjabi princess. She was now very rich indeed. She owned houses all over Delhi and had swapped her bullock for a fleet of new Maruti cars, the much coveted replacement for the old Hindustan Ambassador. Mrs Puri also controlled a variety of business interests. These included the Gloriana Finishing School, India's first etiquette college, a unique institution which taught

11

village girls how to use knives and forks, apply lipstick and make polite conversation about the weather.

Mrs Puri had achieved all this through a combination of hard work and good old-fashioned thrift. In the heat of summer she rarely put on the air conditioning. In winter she allowed herself the electric fire for only an hour a day. She recycled the newspapers we threw out; and returning from parties late at night we could see her still sitting up, silhouetted against the window, knitting sweaters for export. 'Sleep is silver,' she would say in explanation, 'but money is gold.'

This was all very admirable, but the hitch, we soon learned, was that she expected her tenants to emulate the disciplines she imposed upon herself. One morning, after only a week in the flat, I turned on the tap to discover that our water had been cut off, so went downstairs to sort out the problem. Mrs Puri had already been up and about for several hours; she had been to the gurdwara, said her prayers and was now busy drinking her morning glass of rice water.

'There is no water in our flat this morning, Mrs Puri.'

'No, Mr William, and I am telling you why.'

'Why, Mrs Puri?'

'You are having guests, Mr William. And always they are going to the lavatory.'

'But why should that affect the water supply?'

'Last night I counted seven flushes,' said Mrs Puri, rapping her stick on the floor. 'So I have cut off the water as protest.'

She paused to let the enormity of our crime sink in.

'Is there any wonder that there is water shortage in our India when you people are making seven flushes in one night?'

Old Mr Puri, her husband, was a magnificent-looking Sikh gentleman with a long white beard and a tin zimmer frame with wheels on the bottom. He always seemed friendly enough – as we passed he would nod politely from his armchair. But when we first took the flat Mrs Puri drew us aside and warned us that her husband had never been, well, quite the same since the riots that followed Mrs Gandhi's death in 1984.

It was a rather heroic story. When some hooligans began to break down the front door, Mr Puri got Ladoo (the name means Sweety), his bearer, to place him directly behind the splintering

12

wood. Uttering a blood-curdling cry, he whipped out his old service revolver and fired the entire magazine through the door. The marauders ran off to attack the taxi rank around the corner and the Puris were saved.

From that day on, however, the old man had become a fervent Sikh nationalist. 'Everyone should have their own home,' he would snort. 'The Muslims have Pakistan. The Hindus have Hindustan. The Punjab is our home. If I was a young man I would join Bhindranwale and fight these Hindu dogs.'

'It is talk only,' Mrs Puri would reply.

'Before I die I will see a free Khalistan.'

'You are daydreaming only. How many years are left?'

'The Punjab is my home.'

'He may have been born in the Punjab,' Mrs Puri would say, turning to me, 'but now he could not go back to village life. He likes flush toilet and Star TV. Everybody likes flush toilet and Star TV. How can you leave these things once you have tasted such luxury?'

Since the riots, Mr Puri had also become intermittently senile. One day he could be perfectly lucid; the next he might suffer from the strangest hallucinations. On these occasions conversations with him took on a somewhat surreal quality:

MR PURI (up the stairs to my flat) Mr William! Get your bloody mules out of my room this minute!

WD But Mr Puri, I don't have any mules.

MR PURI Nonsense! How else could you get your trunks up the stairs?

During our first month in the flat, however, Mr Puri was on his best behaviour. Apart from twice proposing marriage to my wife, he behaved with perfect decorum.

It had been a bad monsoon. Normally in Delhi, September is a month of almost equatorial fertility and the land seems refreshed and newly-washed. But in the year of our arrival, after a parching summer, the rains had lasted for only three weeks. As a result dust was everywhere and the city's trees and flowers all looked as if they had been lightly sprinkled with talcum powder.

13

Nevertheless the air was still sticky with damp-heat, and it was in a cloud of perspiration that we began to unpack and to take in the eccentricities of our flat: the chiming doorbell that played both the Indian national anthem and 'Land of Hope and Glory'; the geyser, which if left on too long, would shoot a fountain of boiling water from an outlet on the roof and bathe the terrace in a scalding shower; the pretty round building just below the garden which we at first took to be a temple, and only later discovered to be the local sewage works.

But perhaps the strangest novelty of coming to live in India — stranger even than Mrs Puri — was getting used to life with a sudden glut of domestic help. Before coming out to Delhi we had lived impecuniously in a tiny student dive in Oxford. Now we had to make the transition to a life where we still had only two rooms, but suddenly found ourselves with more than twice that number of servants. It wasn't that we particularly wanted or needed servants; but, as Mrs Puri soon made quite clear, employing staff was a painful necessity on which the prestige of her household depended.

The night we moved in, we spent our first hours dusting and cleaning before sinking, exhausted, into bed at around 2 a.m. The following morning we were woken at 7.30 sharp by 'Land of Hope and Glory'. Half asleep, I shuffled to the door to find Ladoo, Mr Puri's bearer, waiting outside. He was holding a tray. On the tray were two glasses of milky Indian *chai*.

'*Chota hazari*, sahib,' said Ladoo. Bed tea.

'What a nice gesture,' I said returning to Olivia. 'Mrs Puri has sent us up some tea.'

'I wish she had sent it up two hours later,' said Olivia from beneath her sheets.

I finished the tea and sank down beneath the covers. Ten seconds later the Indian national anthem chimed out. I scrambled out of bed and again opened the door. Outside was a thin man with purple, betel-stained lips. He had a muffler wrapped around his head and, despite the heat, a thick donkey-jacket was buttoned tightly over his torso. I had never seen him before.

'*Mali*,' he said. The gardener.

He bowed, walked past me and made for the kitchen. From the bedroom I could hear him fiddling around, filling a bucket with water

14

then splashing it over the plants on the roof terrace. He knocked discreetly on the bedroom door to indicate he had finished, then disappeared down the stairs. The *mali* was followed first by Murti, the sweeper, then by Prasad, the *dhobi*, and finally by Bahadur, Mrs Puri's Nepali cook. I gave up trying to sleep and went downstairs.

'Mrs Puri,' I said. 'There has been a stream of strange people pouring in and out of my flat since seven-thirty.'

'I know, Mr William,' replied Mrs Puri. 'These people are your servants.'

'But I don't want any servants.'

'Everyone has servants,' said Mrs Puri. 'You must have servants too. This is what these people are for.'

I frowned. 'But must we have so many?'

'Well, you must have a cook and a bearer.'

'We don't need a bearer. And both of us enjoy cooking.'

'In that case you could have one cook-bearer. One man, two jobs. Very modern. Then there is the *mali*, the sweeper, and a *dhobi* for your washing. Also you must be having one driver.' Mrs Puri furrowed her brow. 'It is very important to have good chauffeur,' she said gravely. 'Some pukka fellow with a smart uniform.'

'I haven't got a car. So it's pointless having a driver.'

'But if you have no car and no driver,' said Mrs Puri, 'how will you be getting from place to place?'

Balvinder Singh, son of Punjab Singh, Prince of Taxi Drivers, may your moustache never grow grey! Nor your liver cave in with cirrhosis. Nor your precious Hindustan Ambassador ever again crumple in a collision – like the one we had with the van carrying Mango Frooty Drink.

Although during my first year in Delhi I remember thinking that the traffic had seemed both anarchic and alarming, by my second visit I had come to realize that it was in fact governed by very strict rules. Right of way belongs to the driver of the largest vehicle. Buses give way to heavy trucks, Ambassadors give way to buses, and bicyclists give way to everything except pedestrians. On the road, as in many other aspects of Indian life, Might is Right.

15

Balvinder Singh

Yet Mr Balvinder Singh is an individualist who believes in the importance of asserting himself. While circumstances may force him to defer to buses and lorries, he has never seen the necessity of giving way to the tinny new Maruti vans which, though taller than his Ambassador, are not so heavily built. After all, Mr Singh is a *kshatriya* by caste, a warrior, and like his ancestors he is keen to show that he is afraid of nothing. He disdains such cowardly acts as looking in wing mirrors or using his indicators. His Ambassador is his chariot, his klaxon his sword. Weaving into the oncoming traffic, playing 'chicken' with the other taxis, Balvinder Singh is a Raja of the Road.

Or rather was. One month after our arrival in Delhi, Mr Singh and I had an accident. Taking a road junction with more phlegm than usual, we careered into the Maruti van, impaling it on its bows, so that it bled Mango Frooty Drink all over Mr Singh's bonnet. No one was hurt, and Mr Singh – strangely elated by his 'kill' – took it stoically. 'Mr William,' he said. 'In my life six times have I crashed. And on not one occasion have I ever been killed.'

Although I am devoted to him, Olivia is quick to point out that

16

Mr Singh is in many ways an unattractive character. A Punjabi Sikh, he is the Essex Man of the East. He chews *paan* and spits the betel juice out of the window, leaving a red 'go-fast' stripe along the car's right flank. He utters incoherent whoops of joy as he drives rickshaws on to the pavement or sends a herd of paper boys flying into a ditch. He leaps out of his taxi to urinate at traffic lights, and scratches his groin as he talks. Like Essex Man, he is a lecher. His eyes follow the saris up and down the Delhi avenues; plump Sikh girls riding side-saddle on motorbikes are a particular distraction. Twice a week, when Olivia is not in the car, he offers to drive me to G.B. Road, the Delhi red light district: 'Just looking,' he suggests. 'Delhi ladies very good. Having breasts like mangoes.'

Yet he has his principles. Like his English counterpart, he is a believer in hard work. He finds it hard to understand the beggars who congregate at the lights. 'Why these peoples not working?' he asks. 'They have two arms and two legs. They not handicrafted.'

'Handicrafted?'

'Missing leg perhaps, or only one ear.'

'You mean handicapped?'

'Yes. Handicrafted. Sikh peoples not like this. Sikh peoples working hard, earning money, buying car.'

Ignoring the bus hurtling towards us, he turns around and winks an enormous wink. 'Afterwards Sikh peoples drinking whisky, looking television, eating tandoori chicken and going G.B. Road.'

The house stood looking on to a small square of hot, tropical green: a springy lawn fenced in by a windbreak of champa and ashok trees. The square was the scene for a daily routine of almost Vedic inflexibility.

Early in the morning, under a bald blue sky, the servants would walk plump dachshunds over the grass, or, duties completed, would stand about on the pavements exchanging gossip or playing cards. Then, at about nine o'clock, the morning peace would be broken by a procession of bicycle-powered vendors, each with his own distinctive street-cry: the used-newspaper collector ('Paper-wallah! Paper-wallah! Paper-wallah!') would be followed by the fruit seller

17

('Mangoes! Lychees! Bananas! Papaya!'), the bread boy and the man with the vegetable barrow. My favourite, the cotton-fluffer, whose life revolved around the puffing up of old mattresses, would twang a Jew's harp. On Sunday mornings an acrobat would come with his dancing bear; he had a pair of drums and when he beat them the whole square would miraculously fill with children. Early that afternoon would follow a blind man with an accordion. He would sing hymns and sacred *qawwalis* and sometimes the rich people would send down a servant with a handful of change.

In the late afternoon, a herd of cattle twenty or thirty strong could be seen wandering along the lane at the back of the house. There was never any herder in sight, but they would always rumble slowly past, throwing up clouds of dust. Occasionally they would collide with the household servants wobbling along the back lane on their bicycles, returning from buying groceries in Khan Market. Then followed the brief Indian dusk: a pale Camembert sun sinking down to the treeline; the smell of woodsmoke and dung cooking fires; the last raucous outbursts from the parakeets and the brahminy mynas; the first whirring, humming cicadas.

Later on, lying in bed, you could hear the *chowkidars* stomping around outside, banging their sticks and blowing their whistles. There were never any robberies in our part of New Delhi, and the *chowkidars* were an entirely redundant luxury.

But, as Mrs Puri said, you had to keep up appearances.

Mr Singh also had strong views about appearances.

'You are Britisher,' he said, the very first time I hailed him. 'I know you are a Britisher.'

It was late afternoon at the end of our first week in Delhi. We had just moved in and were beginning the gruelling pilgrimage through Indian government departments that all new arrivals must perform. We were late for an appointment at the Foreigners Regional Registration Office, yet Mr Singh's assertion could not go unquestioned.

'How do you know I'm a Britisher?'

'Because,' said Mr Singh, 'you are not sporting.'

'Actually I am quite sporting,' I replied. 'I go for a run every day, swim in the summer . . .'

'No Britisher is sporting,' said Mr Singh, undaunted.

'Lots of my countrymen are very keen on sport,' I retorted.

'No, no,' said Mr Singh. 'You are not catching me.'

'We are still a force to be reckoned with in the fifteen hundred metres, and sometimes our cricket team . . .'

'No, no,' said Mr Singh. 'Still you are not catching me. You Britishers are not *sporting*.' He twirled the waxed curlicues of his moustache. 'All men should be sporting a moustache, because all ladies are liking too much.'

He indicated that I should get in.

'It is the fashion of our days,' he said, roaring off and narrowly missing a pedestrian.

Mr Singh's taxi stand lay behind the India International Centre, after which it took its name: International Backside Taxis. The stand was run by Punjab Singh, Balvinder's stern and patriarchal father, and manned by Balvinder and his two plump brothers, Gurmuck and Bulwan. There was also a rota of cousins who would fill in during the weekends and at nights. Over the following months we got to know them all well, but it was Balvinder who remained our special friend.

That first week, and the week following it, Balvinder drove Olivia and myself through a merry-go-round of government departments.

Together we paid daily visits to the rotting concrete hulk known as Shastri Bhavan, nerve centre of the Orwellian Indian Ministry of Information and Broadcasting. Here, in the course of nine visits, I deposited four faxes, three telexes, two envelopes of passport photographs (black and white only) and a sheaf of letters from my editor in London, all in an effort to get accredited as a foreign correspondent.

In due course, as the slow wheels of bureaucracy turned, my application did get processed – but not until about a year after the newspaper I represented had ceased publication. Undaunted, to this day Shastri Bhavan still refuses to acknowledge the downfall of the *Sunday Correspondent*, and continues to send its India representative daily press releases detailing the reasons for the decline in the production of Indian pig iron, or celebrating the success of the Fifth International Conference on the Goat (theme: The Goat in Rural Prosperity).

More depressing even than Shastri Bhavan is the headquarters of Mahanagar Telephone Nigam Limited. The Telephone Nigam is India's sole supplier of telecommunications to the outside world. Without the help of the Telephone Nigam one is stranded. This is something every person who works for the organization knows; and around this certainty has been built an empire dedicated to bureaucratic obfuscation, the perpetration of difficulty, the collection of bribes and, perhaps more than anything else, the spinning of great glistening cocoons of red tape.

It was a hot, dusty late September morning when I first entered room 311, home to Mr Ram Lal. Mr Lal was sitting beneath a poster of Mahatma Gandhi on which was written: 'A customer is the most important visitor to our premises. He is not dependent on us, we are dependent on him.'

As if in deliberate subversion of the Mahatma's message, Mr Lal held in his hands the *Times of India*, open at its sports page. The paper formed a barrier between Mr Lal and the asylumful of suppliants who were bobbing up and down in front of him, holding out chits of paper, arching their hands in a gesture of *namaste* or wobbling their turbans from side to side in mute frustration. A Punjabi lady sat weeping in a corner, repeating over and over again: 'But I have a letter from the Minister of State for Communications . . .

but I have a letter . . . a letter . . .' Menials passed silently to and fro through the door, carrying files and sheaves of xeroxes. Behind Mr Lal, placed there for apparently purely decorative purposes, sat a dead computer.

When Mr Lal eventually deigned to lower his paper – which he did with infinite slowness, folding it into perfect quarters – he rang a bell and ordered one of his peons to bring him a cup of tea.

'Right,' he said, looking up for the first time. 'Who's first?'

A hundred hands were raised, but one voice stood out: 'I am.'

The speaker pushed himself forward, holding together his bulging dhoti with one hand. He was an enormously fat man, perhaps seventy years old, with heavy plastic glasses and grey stubble on his chin.

'My name is Sunil Gupta – please call me Sunny.' He strode forward and grabbed Mr Lal by the hand, shaking it with great verve.

'I am a nationalist,' said Mr Gupta. 'A nationalist and a freedom fighter. I am also an independent candidate in the forthcoming municipal elections. My election office will be opposite Western Court, adjacent to the *paan* shop. I want a temporary telephone connection, and would be most grateful if you could expedite.' He stroked his belly. 'Early action would be highly appreciated.'

'Have you already applied for a connection?' asked Mr Lal.

'No, gentleman,' said Sunny Gupta. 'This is what I am doing now.'

'First applications Room 101. Next, please.'

'But,' said Mr Gupta. 'I have to maintain contact with my constituents. I need a phone immediately. I would be very grateful if you would expedite a VVIP connection without delay.'

'Are you a member of the Lok Sabha?'

'No. I . . .'

'In that case you must contact Mr Dharam Vir . . .'

'Gentleman, please listen . . .'

'. . . in Room 101.'

With a great flourish, Mr Gupta pulled a much-pawed piece of paper from his waistcoat pocket. 'Gentleman,' he said. 'Please be looking here. This is my manifesto.'

Across the top of the piece of paper, in huge red letters, was

21

blazoned the slogan: A NATIONALIST TO THE CORE AND A FREEDOM FIGHTER. Mr Gupta straightened his glasses and read from the charter:

'I was a Founder Member cum Chairman of the Religious and Social Institute of India, Patna Branch . . .'

Mr Lal was meanwhile studying the application of the weeping Punjabi lady. He read it twice and, frowning, initialled it at the top right-hand corner: 'See Mr Sharma for countersignature. Room 407.'

The woman broke down in a convulsion of grateful sobs. Beside her Mr Gupta was still in full flood:

'. . . I am ex-member of the Publicity Committee of the All-India Congress I, Bhagalpur division. Ex-Joint Secretary of the Youth Congress Committee, Chote Nagpur, Bihar. I am a poet and a journalist. A war hero from the 1965 Indo-Pak war, Jaisalmer sector . . .'

'Madam,' continued Mr Lal. 'Please make payment with Mr Surwinder Singh, accounts, Room 521.'

'. . . I was the founder editor of *Sari*, the Hindi monthly for women and *Kalidasa*, the biannual literary journal of Patna. I have donated five acres of land for the Chote Nagpur Cow Hospital. Four times I have been jailed by the Britishers for services to Mother Bharat.'

'If you think it is bad now,' said Mr Lal, taking my application. 'You should see this office on Fridays. That's the busiest time.'

I left Mr Lal's office at noon. By four-thirty I had queued inside a total of nine different offices, waiting in each for the magic letter, seal, signature, counter-signature, demand note, restoration order or receipt which would, at some stage in the far distant future, lead to my being granted a telephone.

'Phone will be connected within two months,' said Mr Lal as he shook my hand, the obstacle course completed. 'Two months no problem. Or maybe little longer. Backlog is there.'

Mr Gupta was still sitting at the back of Mr Lal's office. He was quiet now, though still tightly clutching at his election manifesto. I gave him a sympathetic wave as I left.

'To think,' he said, 'that I was in British prison seven times with Gandhiji for this.'

At his desk, Mr Lal had returned to the sports page of the *Times of India*.

Although parts of the city still preserved the ways of the Mughal period or even the early Middle Ages, Delhi was nevertheless changing, and changing fast.

Mr Gupta's world – the cosy world of the Freedom Struggle, of homespun Congress Socialism and the Non-aligned Movement – all of it was going down; driving around New Delhi you could almost feel the old order crumbling as you watched, disappearing under a deluge of Japanese-designed Maruti cars, concrete shopping plazas and high-rise buildings. Satellite dishes now outnumber the domes of the mosques and the spires of the temples. There was suddenly a lot of money about: no longer did the rich go up to Simla for the summer; they closed their apartments and headed off to London or New York.

The most visible change was in the buildings. When I first saw Delhi it was still a low-rise colonial capital, dominated by long avenues of white plaster Lutyens bungalows. The bungalows gave New Delhi its character: shady avenues of jamun and ashupal trees, low red-brick walls gave on to hundreds of rambling white colonial houses with their broken pediments and tall Ionic pillars.

One of my strongest memories from my first visit was sitting in the garden of one of the bungalows, a glass to hand, with my legs raised up on a Bombay Fornicator (one of those wickerwork planter's chairs with extended arms, essential to every colonial veranda). In front lay a lawn dotted with croquet hoops; behind, the white bow-front of one of this century's most inspired residential designs. Over the rooftops there was not a skyscraper to be seen. Yet I was not in some leafy suburb, but in the very centre of New Delhi. Its low-rise townscape was then unique among modern capitals, a last surviving reminder of the town planning of a more elegant age.

Now, perhaps inevitably, it was gradually being destroyed: new structures were fast replacing the bungalows; huge Legoland blocks were going up on all the arterial roads radiating from Connaught

Circus. The seventeenth-century salmon-pink observatory of Rajah Man Singh – the Jantar Mantar – lay dwarfed by the surrounding high-rise towers that seemed purpose-built to obscure its view of the heavens. Over the great ceremonial way which led from Lutyens's Viceroy's House to India Gate now towered a hideous glass and plastic greenhouse called the Meridien Hotel.

Other, still more unsympathetic blocks were already planned. On Kasturba Gandhi Marg (originally Curzon Road) only two of the old Italianate villas still survived, and one of these was in severe disrepair. Its plaster was peeling and its garden lay untended and overgrown. In front of its gate stood a huge sign:

A PROJECT FROM THE HOUSE OF EROS
ULTRAMODERN DELUXE MULTISTOREYED
RESIDENCE APTS.
COMPLETION DATE 1994.

It was said that not one private Lutyens bungalow would survive undemolished by the turn of the century.

There were other changes, too. The damburst of western goods and ideas that were now pouring into India had brought with them an undertow of western morality. Adulterous couples now filled the public gardens; condom advertisements dominated the Delhi skyline. The Indian capital, once the last bastion of the chaperoned virgin, the double-locked bedroom and the arranged marriage, was slowly filling with lovers: whispering, blushing, occasionally holding hands, they loitered beneath flowering trees like figures from a miniature. Delhi was starting to unbutton. After the long Victorian twilight, the sari was beginning to slip.

Other changes in the city were less promising. The roads were becoming clogged; pollution was terrible. Every day the sluggish waters of the Jumna were spiced with some 350 million gallons of raw sewage.

Alongside the rapidly growing wealth of the middle class, there was also a great increase in poverty. Every week, it was said, six thousand penniless migrants poured into Delhi looking for work. You could see them at the traffic lights along Lodhi Road, hands outreached for alms. The *jhuggis* – the vast sackcloth cities in which these people lived – had quadrupled in size since 1984. New *jhuggi* outposts were spreading along the dry drainage ditches, filling the flyovers, sending tentacles up the pavements and the hard shoulders. At night, cooking fires could be seen flickering inside the old Lodhi tombs.

Attitudes were changing too. A subtle hardening seemed to have taken place. In the smart drawing-rooms of Delhi, from where the fate of India's 880 million people was controlled, the middle class seemed to be growing less tolerant; the great Hindu qualities of assimilation and acceptance were no longer highly prized. A mild form of fascism was in fashion: educated people would tell you that it was about time those bloody Muslims were disciplined – that they had been pampered and appeased by the Congress Party for too long, that they were filthy and fanatical, that they bred like rabbits. They should all be put behind bars, hostesses would tell you as they poured you a glass of imported whisky; expulsion was too good for them.

Strangely, in these drawing-rooms, you never heard anyone complain about the Sikhs. But of course it was they and not the Muslims who had most recently suffered the backlash of this hardening, this new intolerance which, like an unstable lump of phosphorus, could quite suddenly burst into flames.

TWO

As WAS HER HABIT, Indira Gandhi had toast and fruit for breakfast. It was 31 October 1984 and the bougainvillaea was in flower.

At 9.15 she stepped out of the portico of her white bungalow, crossed the lawns by the lotus pond, then passed into the dim green shade of the peepul avenue. There she smiled at her Sikh security guard, Sub-Inspector Beant Singh. Singh did not smile back. Instead he pulled out his revolver and shot her in the stomach. His friend, Constable Satwant Singh, then emptied the clip of his sten gun into her.

Today, Mrs Gandhi's house is a shrine dedicated to the former Prime Minister's memory. Busloads of school children trail through, licking ice creams and staring at Mrs Gandhi's rooms, now permanently frozen as they were on the day she died. Her Scrabble set, a signed photograph from Ho Chi Minh ('loving greetings to Indira'), a pair of her knitting needles and her books – an unlikely selection, including Marx, Malraux and *The Diaries of Evelyn Waugh* – all lie behind glass, numbered and catalogued. Outside, in the middle of the avenue, a strangely tasteless memorial stands on the spot where she fell: a bouquet of red glass roses on a frosted crystal plinth, a gift from the people of Czechoslovakia. It is as if it marked the place of her death. But in fact as she lay there, pouring with blood from some twenty bullet wounds, Indira Gandhi was still alive.

An ambulance was waiting outside the gate of her house, as regulations demanded, but, this being Delhi, the driver had disappeared for a tea break. So Indira's daughter-in-law, Sonia Gandhi, bundled the Prime Minister into the back of a decrepit Hindustan Ambassador, and together they drove the three miles to the All-India Medical Institute.

Indira was probably dead on arrival, but it was not until one o'clock that the news was broken to the waiting world. The effect was immediate. When the crowds learned that their leader had been assassinated, and that a Sikh was responsible, the thin ice of Delhi's tenuous peace was shattered. The mourners wanted blood. Grabbing sticks and stones and whatever else came to hand, they set off looking for Sikhs.

In those days Mr and Mrs Puri had a house beside the Medical Institute. They were thus the very first Sikh family to receive the attentions of the mob. Mrs Puri had just finished her lunch – as usual, dal, two vegetables and one hot aloo paratha – and was deep in her customary post-prandial knit, when she looked up from her woollies, peered out of her window and noticed three hundred emotional thugs massing around her garden gate and chanting: '*Khoon ka badla khoon*'– blood for blood, blood for blood, blood for blood.

'They were very *jungli* peoples – not from good castes. So I told Ladoo to lock the door and stop them from coming in,' Mrs Puri remembers. 'We could hear them talking about us. They said: "These people are Sikhs. Let us kill them." Then they began to throw some stones and broke all the glasses. We switched off the lights and pretended no one was at home. We thought we would be killed. But first we wanted to kill some of them. You see actually we are *kshatriyas*, from the warrior caste. My blood was boiling and I very much wanted to give them good. But they were standing outside only. What could I do?'

The mob smashed every window in the house, burned the Puris' car and incinerated their son's motorbike. Then they attacked the front door. Luckily, Mr Puri was on the other side, leaning forward on his zimmer frame, armed to the teeth. He fired three times through the door with his old revolver and the mob fled. As they did so, old Mr Puri got Ladoo to kick open the door, then fired the rest of the round after them.

Three hours later, cruising in his taxi, Balvinder Singh passed

Green Park, an area not far from the Medical Institute, when he encountered another mob. They surrounded the taxi and pelted it with stones. Balvinder was unhurt, but his front windscreen was shattered. He swore a few choice Punjabi obscenities, then returned quickly to his taxi stand. The next day, despite growing unrest, Balvinder and his brothers decided to return to work. For an hour they sat on their charpoys looking nervously out on to the empty streets before agreeing the moment had come to hide the cars and shut up the stand. At five past eleven they received a phone call. It warned them that the nearby Sujan Singh Park gurdwara was burning and that a large lynch mob was closing in on them. Leaving everything, they hastily set off to their house across the Jumna, twelve cousins in a convoy of three taxis.

They were nearing one of the bridges over the river when they were flagged down by a police patrol. The policemen told them that there were riots on the far side and that it was not safe to proceed. Punjab Singh, Balvinder's father, said that there were riots on the near side too, and that it was impossible to go back. Moreover, they could not leave their wives and children without protection. The police let them through. For five minutes they drove without difficulty. Then, as they neared Laxmi Nagar, they ran into a road block. A crowd had placed a burning truck across part of the road and were massing behind it with an armoury of clubs and

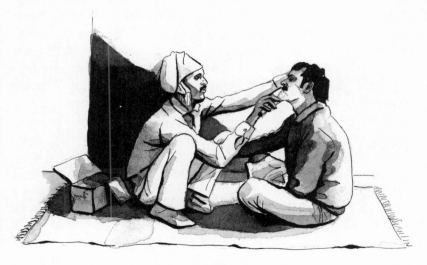

29

iron bars. The first two cars, containing Punjab, Balvinder and two of his brothers, swerved around the truck and made it through. The third taxi, containing three of Punjab's young nephews, was attacked and stopped. The boys were pulled out of the cars, beaten with the rods, doused with kerosene and set alight.

That night, from their roof, Balvinder and his family could see fires burning all over Delhi. To save themselves from the fate of their cousins the brothers decided to cut their hair and shave off their beards; the first time they had ever done so. Punjab reminded them of their religion and tried to stop them; afterwards, in atonement, he refused to eat for a whole week.

In the meantime, the Singhs also took more concrete steps to protect themselves. The family lived in an entirely Sikh area – a taxi drivers' colony – and the residents quickly armed themselves with *kirpans* (Sikh ceremonial swords) and formed makeshift vigilante forces to defend their narrow alleys. Preferring to concentrate on less resolutely guarded areas, the mobs left them in peace. For four days they lived under siege. Then the army was deployed; and as quickly as they had appeared, the rioters vanished.

Balvinder had lost three cousins in the riots. There were other, smaller losses too: Bulwan, Balvinder's elder brother who lived slightly apart from the others, had his house burned to the ground; he had left it and taken shelter with his brothers. Everything he owned was destroyed. Over at the International Backside, the taxi stand's shack was broken into; its primus, telephone and three rope-strung charpoys were all stolen. Someone had also discovered Balvinder's hidden taxi and ran off with the back seat, the battery and the taxi meter. Yet compared to many other families of Sikhs in the capital, Balvinder Singh's family were extremely lucky.

Trilokpuri is the dumping ground for Delhi's poor.

It was constructed on a piece of waste land on the far side of the Jumna during the Emergency of 1975. It was intended to house the squatters whom Sanjay Gandhi evicted from their makeshift shelters on the pavements of Central Delhi; the area remains probably the most desperately poor neighbourhood in the whole city. During 1984 it was here, well away from the spying eyes of the journalists, the diplomats and the middle classes, that the worst massacres took place: of the 2150 Sikhs murdered in the capital during the three days of rioting, the great majority were killed here.

It was a warm, early October afternoon when I set off to see Trilokpuri. I had never been across the Jumna before and did not know what to expect. Balvinder Singh drove past the battlements of the Old Fort of Humayun, over the Ring Road and headed on across the lower Jumna bridge – exactly the route that he and his cousins had taken in October 1984.

Across the bridge, quite suddenly everything changed. If you took Lutyens's city to be the eighth city of Delhi, we had crossed zones into a ninth, a sort of counter-Delhi: a Metropolis of the Poor. Here there were no tree-lined avenues, few advertising hoardings, still fewer cars. We passed alongside a rubbish dump crawling with rag-pickers. Thin chickens pecked around a litter of sagging roadside shacks. Women palmed buffalo-dung into chapattis of cooking fuel. Over everything hung a choking grey smog: fly-ash from a nearby power station. Here for the first time you got an impression of a fact which Delhi seemed almost purpose-built to hide: that the city is the capital not just of a resurgent regional power, formerly the jewel in Britain's Imperial crown, but that it is also the chief metropolis of a desperately poor Third World country; a country whose affluent middle class is still outnumbered four or five to one by the impoverished rural masses.

When the outside world first discovered the Trilokpuri massacres, long after the rioters had disappeared, it was Block 32 that dominated the headlines. Dogs were found fighting over piles of purple human entrails. Charred and roasted bodies lay in great heaps in the gullies; kerosene fumes still hung heavy in the air. Piles of hair, cut from the Sikhs before they were burned alive, lay on the verandas. Hacked-off limbs clogged the gutters.

Yet, as the journalists soon discovered, it was difficult to find anyone who admitted to being present during the madness. Everyone was vague and noncommittal: the killers were men from outside; we were asleep; we saw nothing. Trying to find witnesses or

31

survivors proved no easier five years later. I passed from block to block. What had once been a largely Sikh area was now entirely Hindu. The Sikhs had all moved, I was told. No, none of us were there at the time. We were visiting our villages when it happened. No, no one had seen anything. And the men sat cross-legged on their charpoys, gravely shaking their heads from side to side.

It was Balvinder who, while chatting in a *chai* shop, discovered that there was one solitary Sikh family left, in Block 30. They had been there at the time, he said, and had survived by hiding in a hole. Moreover, they were also witnesses; through a small chink they had seen everything.

Sohan Singh Sandhu was an old man in a cream-coloured *salwar kameez*. He had the bushiest eyebrows I have ever seen: they seemed to join with his mutton-chop whiskers and full, Babylonian beard so as to give the impression of a face peeping out through thick undergrowth. He sat cross-legged on a rope bed, backed by a frieze of Sikh holy pictures: icons of beards and swords and haloes filled the wall. Sohan Singh Sandhu was the *granthi* (reader) of the local gurdwara. He gave us his card, and while we settled ourselves down on his charpoy he shouted through to the kitchen, telling his wife – whom we had not yet seen – to bring us some tea.

His family had originally lived in a pukka house in Shastri Nagar, on the rich bank of the Jumna. But in 1975, during the Emergency, bulldozers flattened their home; they were given half an hour to move their valuables. According to the police, the demolitions were necessary to make way for a line of new electricity pylons, but the last time he had visited the site of his old house the land was still lying vacant. Much later they had received a plot in Trilokpuri, along with a government loan to cover building materials. His three sons and he had built the house with their own hands. It wasn't a bad area, he said. A little out of the way, but quite tolerable. And their neighbours, who had suffered the same evictions as they, had always been friendly.

The troubles began quite suddenly on 1 November 1984. They had been anxiously listening to the news on the radio when a Sikh boy came running down the gully shouting that a mob, four or five thousand strong, was massing nearby.

'About 150 of us assembled on the waste land at the edge of the block,' said Sandhu. 'The mob stoned us and we stoned them back. It was during the stoning that my son was hit.'

He pointed to a charpoy in a dark corner of the room. There, so silent that we had failed to notice him, lay a boy of about my own age. Like his father he had a full, uncut beard and a powerful physique. But he was behaving oddly. Although he could obviously hear that we were talking about him he still lay on his back on the rope bed, admiring himself in a rickshaw wing-mirror that he held in his hand.

'He had bad head injuries,' said his father quietly. 'Now he has some mental problem.'

The boy ignored us and continued to stare at the mirror. As we watched, his face suddenly suffused with child-like happiness, and still looking at the mirror he burst into a fit of high-pitched giggles. His father frowned and looked away.

'After the stone throwing had been going on for two hours the police suddenly intervened. They escorted the mob away, then returned and collected all our weapons: they took all our *lathis* (sticks) and *kirpans* (swords); they even took away the stones and the bricks that were lying around our houses. They said: "There is a curfew. Lock yourselves up." When we had followed their instructions and retreated inside our houses, they let the mob loose.'

Groups of forty or fifty thugs descended on a single gully, flailing around them with their iron bars: 'They would knock on a door. If it wasn't opened they'd beat it down. Sometimes, when people had managed to barricade themselves in, they would climb up on the roof, break open the ceiling and pour in kerosene. Then they would burn everyone inside alive.'

'They used our own kerosene,' said Sandhu's wife, appearing now with the tray of tea. She gave us each a glass and sat down on the bed beside her husband. 'They stole it from us then used it to murder us.'

'Once they shouted: "Send out the men and we won't harm them." A couple of doors opened and some of our neighbours gave themselves up. They took them away. It was only later that we discovered they had taken them to the edge of the block, made them drink kerosene then set them alight.'

33

'How did you manage to escape?' I asked.

'Look,' said Sandhu. And getting up from the charpoy he pulled back a drape which covered the top of one wall. Behind lay a tiny cubby-hole filled with a metal trunk and two packing-cases laid end to end. 'Ranjit,' he indicated the son still lying in the corner, 'Ranjit and I hid in there for three days.'

'But you couldn't possibly have fitted,' I said.

'We managed,' replied Sandhu. 'There was no other choice.'

'Did they never think of looking behind the drapes?' I asked.

'We scattered all our jewellery and valuables at the front of the house. Most of the mob were interested only in looting. They took the jewellery and forgot about us.' Sandhu smiled: 'Once one of their leaders – a local Congress politician – came inside and rebuked them: "You are just looting," he said. "You should be killing." He flicked back the drape and saw our attic but we had placed the cases and mattresses in front of us. He said: "It is too small. Nobody can hide there."

'That was the worst moment. I whispered to Ranjit: "Do not be afraid. It will be a quick pain, then it will be over." And I told him that he was a Sikh and that he must be brave. I said: "They have to kill you. When the moment comes do not beg them for your life."'

'You were very lucky,' I said.

'I was,' replied Sandhu. 'But my other two sons were less fortunate. On the second day they were discovered hiding in the shop of some Hindu friends. The mob burned the shop. Then they put rubber tyres around the necks of my sons, doused them with petrol and burned them too.'

The old man was sitting cross-legged beside his wife. His voice was lowered yet he spoke almost matter-of-factly. Up to that point he had hardly mentioned his other two sons at all.

'God is behind every act,' he said. 'There must have been something wrong that we did in the past.'

'Yet you were spared.'

'It was not our turn,' he replied. 'That was why we were saved.' He shrugged and pointed to the ceiling: 'He is the one who saves.'

There was a halt in the conversation. There was nothing more to say.

Sandhu brought out an album of old photographs: the two dead boys – formal black and white studio photographs, two youths in turbans staring straight at the camera, one with heavy plastic glasses, the other with a slight squint; a shot of the wreckage in the house after the looting – clothes strewn everywhere, smashed crockery, a half-burned charpoy; a snap of a smashed-up autorickshaw, a lump of buckled metal with a frosted windscreen.

'That was Ranjit's,' said his father. 'He used to be a driver.'

For a few seconds no one spoke. Then I asked: 'Aren't you frightened it might happen again?'

'No: now we are no longer worried. I am still the *granthi* of the gurdwara. I give *langoor* (food) to the poor Hindus; the rich Hindus give us offerings. These wounds are healed now.'

'But isn't it upsetting to stay on in the same street? To live where your children were murdered?'

'Personally I would like to leave. To return to the Punjab. It is my wife who wishes to stay. She says: "This is where my children used to eat, to sleep, to play, to laugh . . ."'

'I feel they are still here,' said Mrs Sandhu. 'They built this house with their hands. They fitted the bricks and the mud.' She shook her head. 'Since they died not for one day have I left this place. I will die here.'

On the bed in the corner, her one surviving son suddenly broke out laughing again. We all turned towards him. He was still staring at himself in the wing-mirror of his old rickshaw.

Delhi had many failings, but I had never felt it was a violent city. In all the time I had spent in the dark *mohallas* (quarters) of the old walled city I had never once felt threatened. There were no areas that I felt uneasy to visit after sunset. Instead I had always found Delhi-wallahs, particularly the poor, remarkable for their gentleness and elaborate courtesy. Wherever we went, complete strangers would invite Olivia and me to sit and talk and share a glass of tea with them. To one brought up on a diet of starchy English reserve this habitual kindness of the Delhi-wallah was as touching as it was strange.

Yet as Balvinder and Sandhu could witness, when provoked the inhabitants of this mild town could rise up and commit acts of extreme brutality. Men would avert their eyes as next door neighbours were burned alive or disembowelled. The same people who would invite you to share their last plate of food could, with equal spontaneity, lose control and run amok. Then, with equal ease they could return to their bazaars and shops, factories and offices and carry on as if nothing had happened. It was difficult to understand.

Moreover, despite Delhi's historic reputation as the most cultured town in India, the city's history was punctuated with many such flashes of terrible, orgiastic violence. It was not just invaders who put the people of Delhi to the sword. During the Middle Ages and throughout the long Mughal twilight the town was continually rent with bloody riots, even small civil wars. Out of the first twelve Sultans, only two died peacefully in their beds; the rest were killed, usually in a horrible manner and almost always by their courtiers or subjects. Invaders like Timur the Lame were able to storm the high walls of the city only because the inhabitants were already busy cutting each others' throats. The death toll from bazaar disputes such as the eighteenth-century Shoe Sellers' Riot could run into tens of thousands.

The last great conflagration was Partition. In the dying days of the British Raj, when the subcontinent was split into Muslim-only Pakistan and Hindu-majority India, twelve million people were made refugees. Hordes of non-Muslims – Sikhs and Hindus – fled their ancestral villages in Pakistan; India's displaced Muslims struck out in the opposite direction. It was the greatest migration the modern world had ever seen. Yet again Delhi was consigned to the flames. Following some of the worst rioting in its history, nearly half of its ancient Muslim population – the descendants of the people who had erected the Qutab Minar and lined the streets to cheer the Great Mogul – packed their bags and headed off to a new country. Their place was taken by refugees from the Western Punjab, among them Mr and Mrs Puri and Punjab Singh. Delhi was transformed from a small administrative capital of 900,000 people to a Punjabi-speaking metropolis half the size of London.

Of the two peoples who had ruled Delhi during the previous thousand years, the British disappeared completely while the

Indian Muslims were reduced to an impoverished minority. In the space of a few months, the face of the city was probably changed more radically than at any other time since the Muslims first came to India, a millennium before.

THREE

'OUR VILLAGE was famous for its sweets,' said Punjab Singh. 'People would come for miles to taste the jalebis our sweet-wallahs prepared. There were none better in the whole of the Punjab.'

We were sitting on a charpoy at International Backside Taxi Stand. For weeks I had been begging Balvinder's father to tell me the story of how he had come to Delhi in 1947. A stern and sombre man, Punjab would always knit his eyebrows and change the subject. It was as if Partition were a closed subject, something embarrassing that shouldn't be raised in polite conversation.

It was only after a particularly persistent bout of badgering, in which Balvinder took my side, that Punjab had agreed to relent. But once started, he soon got into the swing of his story.

'Samundra was a small and beautiful village in District Lyallpur,' he said. 'It was one of the most lovely parts of the whole of the Punjab. We had a good climate and very fertile land. The village stood within the ruins of an old fort and was surrounded on four sides by high walls. It was like this.'

With his hands, the old man built four castle walls. From the details that he sketched with his fingers you could see he remembered every bastion, every battlement, each loophole.

'Our village was all Sikh apart from a few Hindu sweepers. Our neighbours were Mahommedan peoples. We owned most of the land but before 1947 we lived like brothers. There were no differences between us . . .' Punjab stroked his beard. He smiled as he recalled his childhood.

'On the 15th of August 1947 the Government announced Partition. We were not afraid. We had heard about the idea of Pakistan, but we thought it would make no difference to us. We realized a Mahommedan government would take over from the Britishers. But in our Punjab governments often come and go. Usually such things make no difference to the poor man in his village.

'Then, quite suddenly, on the 10th of September, we got a message from the Deputy Commissioner in Lyallpur. It said: "You people cannot stay. You must leave your house and your village and go to India." Everyone was miserable but what could we do? All the villagers began loading their goods into bullock carts. The old men were especially sad: they had lived their whole lives in the village. But we were young and could not understand why our grandfathers were crying.

'In the villages round about the Mahommedans heard we were being forced to move. Many came and said: "You must stay, do not go," but others were thinking dirty thoughts. They wanted to take our possessions.

'At about six or seven o'clock on the morning we were due to leave, too many Muslim peoples – perhaps five or six thousand – suddenly appeared outside our fort, waving their swords and calling us dogs and infidels. The watchmen shut the gates. Inside, there were only nine hundred of us, including old women and childrens. We had no weapons. We thought we would be killed.

'Then the *Pradhan* [head] of the Sweet-Makers said: "We have no guns but we have our pans and our sugar and our water. Let us make jalebis for our Muslim friends." Some of our people thought that the Sweet-Maker had gone mad, and they shook their heads and tore the bristles from their beards. They said: "This is crazy man. The Mahommedan peoples will not go away when they taste our delicious jalebis. Instead they will come inside and kill us." These old men were very sad and went off to the gurdwara to say their prayers.

'But the Sweet-Maker took his assistants up on to the battlements and he built a big fire. He boiled the water in a pan and he added the sugar. He stirred the mixture until it was thick and flies were buzzing all around. He told the other *mithai*-wallahs to take their pans and to make jalebis over the other three gates. His assistants did as he said.

'Down below, the Mahommedans had a tree trunk and were running with it against the great gates of the fort, but the gates still held. Eventually the mixture was ready, and the *Pradhan* shouted down: "You like our jalebis?" and he tilted his pan over the parapet. The boiling sugar poured over the wicked Muslims and they were all burned alive.'

Punjab beamed a bright smile: 'All day and all night these dirty Mahommedans tried to find a way to enter the fort, but whenever they tried to get near the gates the sweet-makers gave them a taste of our celebrated jalebis. Then, some time about two a.m. the second night, our peoples saw headlights coming towards us across the fields. It was the British army. They had seen the fires of the sweet-makers burning on the battlements and had come to investigate. The convoy was led by an English colonel. He fired six shots into the air and the Mahommedan fellows ran off into the night as if their Shaitan [satan] was after them.

'The next day the English colonel evacuated us in his trucks. We were only able to take one small bag each, and we had to leave all our carts and goats and sheep and buffalo and oxen. This made us very sad, but at least we were alive. The colonel took us to Amritsar and from there we caught the train to Delhi. Ah! To me Delhi was a wonderful town. I was amazed by all the beautiful cars in the streets. All the Mahommedan tonga-wallahs had gone to Pakistan, so I decided to become a taxi-wallah. This is the job I have been doing ever since.

'After that day, for good luck, my brother Kulwinder began to make jalebis. He still has a shop in Begampur and I have heard some people say that he makes the best jalebis in all of Delhi . . .'

I had been living in Delhi for some months before I began to realize quite how many of the people I met every day were Partition refugees. Even the most well-established Delhi figures – newspaper

41

editors, successful businessmen, powerful politicians – had tales to tell of childhoods broken in two, of long journeys on foot over the Punjab plains, of houses left behind, of sisters kidnapped or raped: the ghastly but familiar litany of Partition horrors.

The Puris' story was fairly typical. Before Partition they had a large town house in Lahore. When the riots came they packed a couple of suitcases, bought their bullock cart and headed off towards Delhi. Their possessions they left locked up in the *haveli*, guarded by Muslim servants. Like the Palestinians a year later, they expected to come back within a few months when peace had been restored. Like the Palestinians, they never returned.

On arrival in Delhi they found a gutted house in Subzi Mandi, the vegetable bazaar of the Old City. It had belonged to a Muslim family that had fled weeks before. The Puris simply installed a new door and moved in. There were still killings, and occasionally stray bullets ricocheted around the bazaar, but gradually the Puris began to find their feet.

'We acquired slowly by slowly,' Mrs Puri remembers. 'My husband started a business making and selling small houses. I knitted woollens. At first it was very hard.'

After a year of carrying water in leaky buckets, the house was connected to the water mains; later the Puris got electricity installed. By 1949 they had a fan; by 1956 a fridge. In the late 1960s the Puris moved to a smart new house in South Extension. They had arrived.

We heard the same story repeated over and over again. Even the most innocuous of our neighbours, we discovered, had extraordinary tales of 1947: chartered accountants could tell tales of single-handedly fighting off baying mobs; men from grey government ministries would emerge as the heroes of bloody street battles. Everything these people now possessed was built up by their own hard labour over the last few years.

Mr Seth, our next door neighbour, was a retired official in the Indian Railways. A safari-suited civil servant, he was polite, timid and anonymous. After passing out of Walton Railway Training School, Seth's first posting came in 1946: he was made Assistant Ticket Inspector at Sheikhapura near Lahore. One year later there came the great divide and Mr Seth, a Hindu, found himself on the wrong side of the border. The killing had started. Sikhs and Hindus stopped trains carrying refugees to Pakistan and killed all the Muslims. Muslims stopped trains going to India and killed all the Sikhs and Hindus.

'Every train from India that passed our station was totally smashed,' remembers Mr Seth. 'Women, children, old, young: all were killed. Blood was pouring from the bogies [carriages].'

Then one day, a refugee train from Rawalpindi under the custody of the Gurkhas passed through Sheikhapura. Nervous of being attacked by Muslims, the Gurkhas – all Hindus – let off a barrage of shots through the train windows. A stray bullet hit the wife of the Muslim station master. The station master, unhinged with grief, tried to shoot the only Hindu in the station – his Assistant Ticket Inspector, Mr Seth. He missed. But Mr Seth realized that the moment had come to flee Pakistan. He jumped off the platform and ran down the line towards India. There, a little later, he was ambushed by a party of Muslims heading in the opposite direction. They took everything he owned, including his shoes, his shirt and his trousers.

'I travelled barefoot down the lines having only a knicker,' said Mr Seth. 'Four times I escaped death. Four times! I arrived at Amritsar station at midnight, and got a new uniform from the station master. The next day I reported for duty at nine a.m. exactly.'

'What happened then?'

'Promotion!' said Mr Seth, beaming a red betel-nut smile. 'I became Commercial Accountant bracket Parcel Clerk, Booking Clerk, Goods Clerk etcetera unbracket. Later I was transferred to Delhi and was given a temporary house in Lodhi Colony. It was previously owned by a Muslim. I was told he had been shot dead on the veranda.'

The violence totally gutted many of the poorer parts of Delhi, but even the very richest districts were affected. While shoppers looked on, Hindu mobs looted the smart Muslim tailors and boutiques in Connaught Place; passers-by then stepped over the murdered shopkeepers and helped themselves to the unguarded stocks of lipstick, handbags and bottles of face cream. In Lodhi Colony, Sikh bands burst into the white Lutyens bungalows belonging to senior Muslim civil servants and slaughtered anyone they found at home.

In some areas of the Old City, particularly around Turkman Gate and the Jama Masjid, the Muslims armed themselves with mortars and heavy machine guns. From their strongpoints in the narrow alleyways they defied not only the rioters but also the Indian Army. Many of the Muslim families who remain in Delhi today survived by barricading themselves into these heavily defended warrens.

Meanwhile, refugees poured into India: '300,000 Sikh and Hindu refugees are currently moving into the country,' stated one small page three report in a 1947 edition of the *Hindustan Times*. 'Near Amritsar 150,000 people are spread 60 miles along the road. It is perhaps the greatest caravan in human history.' It was this steady stream of Punjabi refugees who, despite the great exodus of Muslims, still managed to swell the capital's population from 918,000 in 1941 to 1,800,000 in 1951. The newspaper stories were illustrated with pictures showing the dead lying like a thick carpet on New Delhi Railway Station. Other photographs depicted the refugee camps on the ridge, the white tent cities in which Punjab Singh had stayed on his arrival. There were also shots of some fire-blackened and gutted houses standing in the rubble of the Subzi Mandi. It was in a house such as this that Mr and Mrs Puri had taken shelter for their first months in their new city.

The more I read, the more it became clear that the events of 1947 were the key to understanding modern Delhi. The reports highlighted the city's central paradox: that Delhi, one of the oldest towns in the world, was inhabited by a population most of whose roots in the ancient city soil stretched back only forty years. This explained why Delhi, the grandest of grand old aristocratic dowagers, tended to behave today like a *nouveau-riche* heiress: all show and vulgarity and conspicuous consumption. It was a style most unbecoming for a lady of her age and lineage; moreover it jarred with everything one knew about her sophistication and culture.

This paradox also exposed the principal tensions in the city. The old Urdu-speaking élite who had inhabited Delhi for centuries – both Hindu and Muslim – had traditionally looked down on the Punjabis as boorish yeoman farmers. With their folk memories of the *mushairas* (levees) of the old Mughal court and the *mehfils* (liter-

44

ary evenings) of the great Delhi poets, with their pride in the subtlety and perfection of Delhi Urdu and Delhi cooking, they could never reconcile themselves to the hardworking but (in their eyes) essentially uncivilized Punjabi colonizers. It was as if Blooms-bury were made to absorb a deluge of mud-booted Yorkshire farmers. To these people, of course, Mrs Puri's finishing school was the ultimate presumption: a Punjabi immigrant using western textbooks to teach etiquette to Delhi-wallahs – and this in a city which for centuries had regarded itself as the last word in refine-ment and courtly behaviour.

In their turn, the Punjabis despised the old Delhi-wallahs as effeminate, slothful and degenerate: 'Maybe these Delhi people are not always lazy,' Punjab Singh once said to me. 'But they are not too active either. Punjabi people are good at earning money and also at spending it. They enjoy life. Delhi peoples are greedy and mean. They expect to live well, but never they are working for it.'

Today the two worlds, Mughal Old Delhi and Punjabi New Delhi, mix but rarely. Each keeps to itself, each absolutely certain of its superiority over the other. Even on common festivals such as Dusshera, in Delhi traditionally celebrated by the Hindu and Mus-lim communities without distinction, entirely separate ceremonies are now held, one set around the Red Fort and the Ram Lila Grounds of Old Delhi, the other in the parks and gardens of Punjabi residential colonies south of Lutyens's city.

Despite all that politicians of both faiths have done to create a division between Hindu and Muslim, from the early days of the Muslim League to the recent sudden rise of the Hindu fundamental-ist Bharatiya Janata Party or BJP, in Delhi that communal chasm is still far less marked than the gap separating the Old Delhi-wallah from the Punjabi immigrant.

Dusshera is the Hindu feast celebrating the victory of Lord Ram over the demon Ravanna; the feast also marks the incipient victory of the cool season over summer's heat.

According to the legend, Ravanna kidnapped Sita, Ram's bride, and carried her off to Lanka, his island fortress. There he tried a number of strategies to enrol her into his splendid harem. But with the help of Hanuman, the Monkey God, Ram leaped across the straits to Lanka, rescued Sita, and after an epic struggle lopped off all ten of the demon's heads.

For the last two weeks of September, in the Delhi parks and maidans, huge wickerwork effigies of Ravanna and his two monstrous brothers, Meghnath and Kumbhakaran, were being erected: workmen clung like sparrows to rickety bamboo scaffolding, busily hammering noses and ears into place. On the feast day, amid a flurry of celebrations, all the effigies were to be burned.

The day of Dusshera – hot, dusty and humid – burned out into a fine warm evening. A Delhi journalist friend had invited Olivia and me to celebrate the festival with him in South Extension. Together we walked to a park near his house. Ravanna was a giant corn dolly 120 feet high, dressed in bright pink pyjamas. He was held upright by six straining guy-ropes. In some of the big gardens in Old Delhi whole circles of hell had been erected – ten or eleven demons, Ravanna's whole family, all lined up in menacing rows, black moustaches curled – but our friend was very proud of his single pink devil, and there was no denying that he was a very fine demon indeed.

Beside Ravanna's ankles a marquee had been erected, and in it a band of Goan boys were playing songs from recent Hindi movies. We took a seat and listened to a number called 'Ding Dong' – apparently a great hit a few months before. A plump man in a dhoti passed a collection plate around.

Then, to the great excitement of the two hundred children present, the sun set and the pyrotechnics began. Some Roman candles spluttered between Ravanna's legs. A volley of rockets arched above his shoulders. With a small pirouette, the plump man in the dhoti took a burning torch and touched both Ravanna's feet. A slow blue flame licked up his legs and hovered around his waist. Suddenly his pink pyjama top took light; and in a trice the whole effigy was in flames. We could feel the heat like a furnace in our faces. Then a canister of Chinese crackers secreted in Ravanna's chest blew up with a deafening roar. The crowds cheered; and a full moon rose over the demon's smouldering carcass.

That October was a season of strange and fiery sunsets: great

46

twilight infernos blazing in the heavens. Sometimes, just as the sun was going down, the evening fumes would mingle with the dung fires of the *jhuggi*-dwellers to form a perfectly straight sheet of mist along Lodhi Road. Beyond, the thick and dusty air would turn weird, unnatural colours in the gloaming: vivid, luminous mauves; dark, dingy crimsons; deep, bloody reds. Once I saw the great onion dome of Safdarjang's Tomb illuminated by a beam from the doomed sun. The light remained constant for less than a minute, but it picked out the great Mughal tomb with an unearthly brightness, spot-lit against an abattoir sky.

Compared with the months before the temperature was suddenly quite bearable. Up in the high Himalayas the first snows had begun to fall and cool winds were blowing down, quenching the fires of the plains. Though it was still very warm, the bottled-up irritations, suppressed during the previous six months of white heat, came bubbling out in a burst of righteous indignation. Delhi suddenly blossomed with little encampments: every traffic island had someone fasting to death; every day a new pressure group would march on Parliament. You could see them trotting along in a great crocodile, banners held aloft, or else sitting sweating under canopies in Rajpath: there were the teachers and the Tibetans, the blood donors and the dog owners; once, to Balvinder Singh's delight, there was even a delegation of prostitutes from G.B. Road. All the sit-ins, walk-outs and protest marches were remarkably good-humoured; even the hunger strikers seemed strangely to be enjoying themselves.

It was now cool enough for Olivia to go out painting in the mornings. Every day she would get up at eight and disappear with her brushes and her watercolours. She had given up her place at art school to come out to Delhi and she was determined to make the most of the opportunity. For the rest of the cold season she toured Old Delhi's *kuchas* and *mohallas* sketching the people, the buildings and the ruins. Some days she would not return until dusk.

The new season also brought about changes downstairs in the Puri household. From the middle of October, Mr Puri embarked on his winter routine of taking a morning walk around the square below the house. Though the square was only half the size of a football pitch, getting Mr Puri around it was quite an operation, and a new servant was contracted to oversee the business of his daily perambulation. He was a tiny Nepali boy, clearly not a day older than eight. I said as much to Mrs Puri.

'He is nineteen,' she replied.

'But he is only three and a half feet tall.'

'He is Nepali,' said Mrs Puri. 'Nepali people are small.'

'But he has no beard. His voice hasn't broken. He should be at primary school.'

Mrs Puri considered this. 'They have bad food in Nepal,' she explained. She wobbled her head: 'In a year, when he has eaten our nutritious dal and rice, he will double in size. Then he will have a moustache and maybe a beard also.'

Every day the boy, Nickoo, performed the tricky task of winding a new white turban around Mr Puri's head and winching the cantankerous old man down the stairs. He then had to push Mr Puri around the square – the old man all the time raving or propositioning passers-by – before pushing him back up again. There was no doubt, however, that Mr Puri clearly enjoyed the whole thing enormously. His spirits rose in anticipation of his daily treat, and if crossed while on tour he could be positively frisky.

'Good morning, Mr Puri,' Olivia once ventured on meeting him and Nickoo half-way around the square.

'My darling, my sweetheart,' replied Mr Puri, somewhat unexpectedly. 'Be my wife.'

'You've picked the wrong girl, Mr Puri,' replied Olivia, marching off, brushes in hand.

This put-down, like the others before it, failed to put Mr Puri off the scent, although he did initiate enquiries, through Nickoo, as to whether Olivia and I really were married. In the meantime he continued to shoot around the flat on his zimmer, chasing Olivia if ever she ventured downstairs to borrow some milk. Finally he got caught.

One day Olivia was standing in the doorway chatting to Mrs Puri when Mr Puri appeared at the bottom of the stairs. He had just returned from his morning walk and did not realize his wife was the other side of the door.

'My sweetheart: are you damsel or madam?' he asked.

Olivia turned round to see Mr Puri advancing towards her.

'This man,' he said pointing to Nickoo, 'says you are madam. I say you are damsel.'

Mrs Puri flung open the door and fired a burst of rapid-shot Punjabi at her husband. Then she turned to Olivia.

'He means you are married now so you are "madam",' she said, glowering at her husband, 'while before you were "damsel".'

'Are you damsel or madam?' repeated Mr Puri, undaunted, grabbing hold of Nickoo and propelling himself upwards towards Olivia.

Olivia held up her wedding ring like garlic to a vampire. 'Mr Puri,' she said. 'I am madam.'

That October I often accompanied Olivia on her expeditions into the alleys of Old Delhi, once Shahjehanabad, the capital of the Empire of the Great Mogul. It was an area I had always loved, but there was no denying that it had fallen on hard times. The Old City had been built at the very apex of Delhi's fortunes and had been in slow decline virtually from the moment of its completion. The final and most dramatic wrecking of its fortunes had, however, taken place in 1947.

Just as Partition resulted in prosperity and growth for the new Delhi, it led to impoverishment and stagnation for the old. The fabulous city which hypnotized the world travellers of the seventeenth and eighteenth centuries, the home of the great poets Mir, Zauq and Ghalib; the city of nautch girls and courtesans; the seat of the Emperor, the Shadow of God, the Refuge of the World, became a ghetto, a poor relation embarrassingly tacked on to the metropolis to its south. Since 1947 the Old City has survived only by becoming one enormous storehouse for North India's wholesale goods; one by one the old palaces and mansions have been converted into godowns (warehouses) and stores. It has become more remarkable for its junk markets and car parts bazaars than for any fraying beauty or last lingering hints of sophistication. The crafts and skills developed over the centuries for the tastes of the old Urdu-speaking Delhi élite either adjusted to the less sophisticated Punjabi market, or simply died out.

Near the Ajmeri Gate lies the old Cobblers' Bazaar. Most of the Muslim shoemakers who worked here fled to Karachi in 1947, and today the Punjabis who replaced them sell mostly locks and chains and hardware. But a few of the old shopkeepers remain, and among them is the shop of Shamim and Ali Akbar Khan. Despite the position of their workshop, the father of Shamim and Ali was no cobbler; he was one of the most famous calligraphers in Delhi. Shamim continues his father's trade and still lives by producing beautifully inscribed title deeds, wills and marriage documents.

I met Shamim in a *chai* shop outside the Ajmeri Gate mosque. He was a tall and elegant man in his early fifties, dressed in an immaculate *sherwani* frock coat and a tall lambskin cap. He had high cheekbones, fair skin, and narrow, almond-shaped eyes that hinted at a Central Asian ancestry. On his chin he sported a neat goatee beard. He sat down beside me at a table in the rear of the shop and over a glass of *masala* tea we began to talk.

'My forebears were writers at the Mughal court,' said Shamim. 'And before that we were calligraphers in Samarkand. My family have always been in this business.'

'And you illuminate your documents in exactly the way your father taught you?'

'My father was a very accomplished man. He knew the *shikastah* script as well as the *nastaliq*; he could write both Persian and Urdu. I learned only the *nastaliq*. Slowly the skills are dying. Today there are only two other calligraphers in Delhi and they are of inferior quality.'

Shamim called the *chai*-boy over and asked for the bill. When it finally came he totted it up, checking all the figures in a slightly pedantic manner.

'Today most of the work is in Hindi,' he said. 'Because of this there is little demand for our skills.'

'Can you not learn the Hindi script?' I asked.

'I know it. But with the change from Urdu has come a loss of prestige. Earlier it was a highly respected job that few people were qualified to perform: you had to be familiar with Islamic law, had to know the old Delhi customs, and most of all you had to be a talented calligrapher. Now I am just a clerk; most of the work is done quickly on typewriters.'

He downed the rest of the tea in a single swallow and swirled the dregs around in his glass: 'It is because of the newcomers. They have a very different culture; they have no interest in fine calligraphy.'

We walked together through the jostling crowds to his office; and while we walked he told me about Ali. With his share of the inheritance, the raffish younger brother had, it seemed, started some sort of shady photography studio at the front of the shop.

'My brother cannot write in Urdu,' said Shamim. 'Like many of the young men he has no knowledge of his own culture. Only he is interested in photography.' The calligrapher's face set in a deep frown. 'Ali got involved with men of very bad character,' he whispered. ''Photography was the only way we could divert his attention from even worse occupations. Still I am very ashamed. How can you explain these pictures?'

We had arrived at the shop – little more than a small cavity in the street-frontage – and Shamim was pointing to a frieze of pin-ups cut from Indian magazines. It was quite a collection: voluptuous actresses lying scantily-clad on tiger-skins, topless white girls posing on the beaches of Goa, a selection of portly Egyptian belly-dancers covered with earrings and bracelets; diamonds flashed from the folds around their belly-buttons. Beyond the counter in the studio I could see Ali taking passport photographs with a new Japanese camera. He was dressed in cream-coloured slacks and a polyester shirt.

'These pictures are the concern of my brother,' whispered Shamim, still grimacing at the pin-ups. 'They are not my business. But because of them I cannot invite to this office any of my religious-minded relatives. Because of these pictures no good Muslim will come near this shop. It is all most unIslamic.'

'Maybe in time Ali will take them down,' I said.

'Maybe,' agreed Shamim. 'When men are young they are getting involved in photography, beer-drinking and nudity. But,' he continued, 'when they are older they return to Islam.'

'When people get older they decide to wear the long beard and to look very pious,' said Ali. He had come over to the counter and overheard the end of our conversation. 'But people do not change. I know several men who look like Shamim – with beards and *sherwani* – yet they run brothels in G.B. Road.'

Shamim frowned, but Ali had not finished.

'The problem with people around here is narrow thinking,' he said airily. 'They are not broadminded. They are not reading magazines from Bombay. They do not know what is happening in the world.'

'You obviously read a lot of Bombay magazines,' I replied, pointing at the pin-ups.

'You like them?'

'I'm not sure about the Egyptian ladies.'

'I put them up to attract the customers,' replied Ali. 'My brother is unhappy with me only because I am doing much better business than he. Today no one wants a calligrapher. Even in a town like Delhi.'

Ali stepped out on to the pavement and made a disdainful gesture out over the street: 'Look! This city is now so dirty. Everything is old and falling down. Why should I stay in a place like this? One day I will leave and go to Bombay. Delhi is finished.'

A black silk bundle walked into the shop accompanied by her heavily bearded husband. The man talked to Ali and all three headed off into the curtained booth reserved for taking passport pictures of women in *chador*.

'This family were clients of my father's,' said Shamim, trying to explain why any decent Muslim families would dream of using his brother's services.

'Don't your father's old customers support you too?' I asked.

'There was much bloodshed in this area in 1947,' replied Shamim. 'Most of my father's customers are either dead or living in Karachi. The old Delhi-wallahs continue to come here, but now they are so few.'

'So your skill will die?'

'My son does not want to learn the trade. He wants to become a businessman or to join some modern profession.'

'But you will carry on?'

Shamim's face fell. '*Inshallah* I will continue,' he replied. 'There is no money in it – but this is my craft, the craft of my fathers.'

He said: 'I must be loyal to it.'

Since I had first explored the labyrinths of Shahjehanabad five years previously, I had read some of the descriptions of the area penned by the seventeenth-century writers and poets: 'Its towers are the resting place of the sun,' wrote Chandar Bhan Brahman in 1648. 'Its avenues are so full of pleasure that its lanes are like the roads of paradise.' 'It is like a Garden of Eden that is populated,' echoed Ghulam Mohammed Khan. 'It is the foundation of the eighth heaven.' 'It is the seat of Empire . . . the centre of the great circle of Islam . . .'

For all the Old City's considerable charm, it was impossible to reconcile the earthly paradise praised by the poets with the

53

melancholy slum that today squatted within the crumbling Mughal walls. Even allowing for the conventions of Persian hyperbole (and for the fact that most of the writers were professional flatterers – sycophancy being throughout history the pervasive vice of the ambitious Delhi-wallah), the chasm between the two visions seemed unbridgeable.

The greatest disappointment was Chandni Chowk. In the poems and travelogues, the Moonlight Bazaar is praised as a kind of Oriental Faubourg St Honoré, renowned for its wide avenues, its elegant caravanserais and its fabulous Mughal gardens. Having read the descriptions of this great boulevard, once the finest in all Islam, as you sit on your rickshaw and head on into the labyrinth you still half-expect to find its shops full of jasper and sardonynx for the Mughal builders, mother-of-pearl inlay for the *pietra dura* craftsmen; you expect to see strings of Bactrian camels from Kashgar and logs of cinnamon from Madagascar, merchants from Ferghana, and Khemer girl concubines from beyond the Irrawady; perhaps even a rare breed of turkey from the New World or a zebra to fill the Imperial menagerie and amuse the Emperor.

But instead, as you sit stranded in a traffic jam, half-choked by rickshaw fumes and the ammonia-stink of the municipal urinals, you see around you a sad vista of collapsing shop fronts and broken balustrades, tatty warehouses roofed with corrugated iron and patched with rusting duckboards. The canal which ran down the centre of the bazaar has been filled in; the trees have been uprooted. All is tarnished, fraying at the edges. On the pavement, a Brahminy cow illicitly munches vegetables from the sack of a vendor; a Muslim ear-cleaner squats outside the Sis Ganj gurdwara and peers down the orifices of a Sikh *nihang* (gurdwara guard). A man grabs your arm and stage-whispers: 'Sahib, you want carpets hashish smack brown sugar change money blue film sexy ladies no problem!'

Another vendor waves some cheap plastic trinkets in your face. 'Hello, my dear,' he says. 'You want?'

His brother joins the scrum, his arms full of posters: 'Whatyouwant? I have everything! Guru Gobind Singh, Alpine meadow scene, Arnold Swartznegger, two little kittens, Saddam Hussein, Lord Shiva, Charlie Chaplin . . .'

A crowd gathers.

'Your mother country?'

'This lady your wife?'

'How many childrens?'

The gridlock tightens; it is time to jettison the stationary rickshaw and beat a retreat.

Turkman Gate on the south of the Old City is less crowded, but even more depressing. The area is named after an eleventh-century Turkoman nomad who turned Sufi and built his hermitage here; but the Punjabis who moved here in 1947 have confused the name, and it is now known as Truckman Gate after the lorry drivers who come to eat in the roadside restaurants.

The streets here are narrow and full of goats being fattened for Bakri Id. Pack-donkeys trot past carrying saddlebags full of rubble. As you pass into the Sita Ram bazaar and take in the grand old gateways tumbling down on either side of you, you begin to realize what has happened here. The same walls that now form the rickety *paan* shops and dirty godowns once supported sprawling mansions and the lovely Delhi courtyard houses known as *havelis*. You can see it for yourself: the slum was once a city of palaces.

In Shahjehanabad the town houses were so planned that a plain façade, decorated only with an elaborate gatehouse, would pass into a courtyard; off this courtyard would lead small pleasure gardens, the zenanas (harems), a guardhouse or a miniature mosque, the *haveli* library and the customary *shish mahal* or glass palace. The *haveli* was a world within a world, self-contained and totally hidden from the view of the casual passer-by. Now, however, while many of the great gatehouses survive, they are hollow fanfares announcing nothing. You pass through a great arch and find yourself in a rubble-filled car-park where once irrigation runnels bubbled. The *shish mahals* are unrecognizable, partitioned up into small factories and workshops; metal shutters turn zenana screens into locked store rooms; the gardens have disappeared under concrete. Only the odd arcade of pillars or a half-buried fragment of finely-carved late Mughal ornament indicates what once existed here.

The desolation is even sadder when a *haveli* is associated with a

55

known piece of history. At the end of the Sita Ram Bazaar stands the Haksar Haveli. Here, little more than seventy years ago, India's first Prime Minister, Jawaharlal Nehru, married his wife Kamla. The house belonged to one of the most distinguished of the Kashmiri Pandit families in Delhi, the Haksars, and was famed for its size and magnificence. The gatehouse survives still as a witness to this grandeur: with its Dholpur sandstone façade, its delicate *jharokha* balconies and its fine fish-tail mouldings it is still a magnificent sight. But the interior is a gutted ruin. Through the locked grille you can see the desolation: collapsed rafters now act as a sort of walkway for the cook who squats in the rubble frying his samosas; the cellars are gradually overflowing with his kitchen refuse and old potato peelings. Cusped sandstone arches are buried up to their capitals in rubble; vaults hang suspended in a litter of disintegrating brickwork. No one seems to care. It is as if the people of Delhi had washed their hands of the fine old mansions of the Old City in their enthusiasm to move into the concrete bunkers of the New.

There *is* still continuity here, a few surviving traditions, some lingering beauty, but you have to look quite hard to find it.

One day in late October, Olivia and I stumbled across Ali Manzil, the home of Begum Hamida Sultan. It was one of the last *havelis* still occupied in the old style. A narrow passageway led from the gatehouse into a shady courtyard planted with neem and mulberries; the open space was flanked by a pair of wooden balconies latticed as intricately as a lace ruff. Ahead lay an arcade of cusped Shahjehani arches. This was recently the house of the former Indian President Fakhruddin Ali Ahmed and so was saved from the rapid eclipse that had blacked out many similar households. Yet even here, the inevitable decay had set in. The outer courtyard had recently been destroyed and its space given over for shops. The balconies were collapsing, the paint was flaking. The veranda lay unswept.

Begum Hamida Sultan sat with her silent younger sister at a large teak table. She was dressed in tatty cotton pyjamas. She was old and frail, with white hair and narrow wrists, but she sat bolt upright, as if still animated by some lingering, defiant pride of her Mughal blood. She had fair skin, but her fine aristocratic face – obviously once very beautiful – was now lined with frown-marks.

'I am sorry,' she said, indicating the litter on the floor and the unswept dust. 'We have no servants. The last one died two years ago.'

As girls, she said, she and her sister used to be driven from Ali Manzil to Queen Mary's School in a horse-drawn landau. In those days the house was full of writers, musicians, politicians and poets; you needed to have an appointment to be let into even the outer courtyard.

'We had fifty visitors a day. Now . . .' Her voice tailed off. 'It was Partition that destroyed our Delhi.'

'Can you remember it?' I asked.

'We were in Shillong. When we returned we found the house had been ransacked. The cook had run away. The gardener had been killed. Of my relations, the Loharus, only the Nawab [of Pataudi] was left. Everyone else had fled to Pakistan.'

She shook her head. 'I loved Delhi. But now Delhi is dead.'

57

'What do you mean?' I asked.

'Hardly any of the original inhabitants are left. The outsiders have taken over. Even our language is dead.'

'But many people in Delhi still speak Urdu.'

'Urdu is an aristocratic language. It was not the language of the working classes. Those who are left – the artisans – speak *Karkhana* [factory] Urdu. The Urdu of the poets is dead.'

An emaciated cat which had been mewing hungrily at the Begum's feet jumped up on to the table. Flirtatiously it smoothed itself against her bony fingers. The Begum brushed it away.

'Partition was a total catastrophe for Delhi,' she said. 'Those who were left behind are in misery. Those who were uprooted are in misery. The Peace of Delhi is gone. Now it is all gone.'

Olivia asked whether we could come back and visit her again, and whether she needed anything from New Delhi.

'I do not need anything,' replied the Begum haughtily. 'Do not come back.' She paused; then added huskily, almost in a whisper: 'I just want to be forgotten.'

The best impression of the Shahjehanabad of Hamida Sultan – of the city that was destroyed in 1947 – can be found not in photographs or pictures, nor even in the jaded memories of the survivors, but in a slim first novel published to some critical acclaim in 1940. Although the brilliance of *Twilight in Delhi* by Ahmed Ali was immediately recognized by both E.M. Forster and Virginia Woolf, most copies of the book were lost when the warehouse of the Hogarth Press was destroyed during the Blitz. There was no reprint, and the book was overlooked first during the trauma of the Second World War, then in the holocaust of Partition. Only now with the recent publication of a paperback has the book begun to receive the recognition it deserved. For although (until recently) forgotten even in the city it immortalized, *Twilight in Delhi* is not only a very fine novel, it is also an irreplaceable record of the vanished life and culture of pre-war Delhi. Written only seven years before the catastrophe of 1947, its gloomy tone and pessimistic title were more visionary than Ahmed Ali could ever have imagined.

The novel follows the fortunes of a traditional Muslim family living in a *haveli* very like Ali Manzil. At the opening of the book a cloud is looming over the house: the patriarch, an old Mughal named Mir Nihal, disapproves of his son courting a low-born girl named Bilqeece. As the love of Ashgar and Bilqeece first grows, blossoms, then decays, the whole dying world of Shahjehanabad is evoked: the pigeon-fliers and the poets, the alchemists and the Sufis, the beggars and the tradesmen.

Beyond Kashmiri Gate the British usurp the mantle of the Mughal emperors, enforcing their authority but rarely deigning to mix with the ordinary Delhi-wallahs. The First World War and the influenza epidemic strike down the young; vultures circle ominously overhead. Yet inside the walls of the *havelis* and the lattice screens of the zenana, life goes on as it always did. Births follow upon marriages, love affairs decay, middle age gives way to crumbling senility – but all the time the stories and traditions are passed on:

'Cover your head, daughter, or some evil spirit may harm you . . .'

'If you put a broom under the leg of a bed, the wind-storm abates . . .'

'When a dust storm blows it means the djinns are going to celebrate a marriage . . .'

Up on the roof the men discuss the different breeds of racing pigeon: the *golays* that fly low over the roofs, but in a perfectly straight line; the fast and high flying *Kabuli kabooter*; or the slow but beautiful fan-tailed *nisarays*. Elsewhere, the fakirs and alchemists discuss the herbs and rituals which can turn tin into molten gold; and they talk in hushed voices of the alchemist's vital ingredient, the luminous flower called 'Lamp of the Night' which at dusk flickers like a firefly on the parched hillsides of Rajputana.

Twilight in Delhi survived Partition to represent the life of Old Delhi to a new readership today, but what, I wondered, had happened to its author? My edition of the book gave no clue; and I scanned the bookshops in vain to find other, later works by the same hand. It was a Delhi publisher friend who told me that Ali was in fact still alive, now an old man living in obscurity in Karachi. This only made it more intriguing: why would anyone who so

59

obviously loved Delhi with a passion opt to leave it? And why had he not gone on to write other even better books?

Karachi seemed to hold the key to many of the unanswered questions of 1947. Not only did the city contain some 200,000 refugees who had fled from Delhi to Pakistan in the upheavals of that year, it also contained their most distinguished chronicler. The moment had come for me to visit Karachi for myself.

In Delhi I had been given an introduction to Shanulhaq Haqqee, a pipe-smoking Urdu poet and the direct descendant of Abdul Haq, a famous literary figure at the court of Shah Jehan. Shanulhaq fled from Delhi in 1947. He left to escape the rioting and meant to return as soon as order was re-established. He was never allowed to except much later, for a week, as a tourist from a foreign country. It was almost exactly seven hundred years since the first of his line arrived in Delhi from Turkestan to fight in the Deccani wars of the thirteenth-century Sultan, Ala-ud-Din Khalji.

Shanulhaq was the only person I had been able to find who was actually a friend of Ahmed Ali. 'Ali doesn't mix much,' a Pakistani friend had told me. 'He never really fitted in in Karachi.' 'He's a bit abrupt,' said someone else. 'You know . . . rather bitter.'

Shanulhaq Haqqee offered to drive me over to see Ahmed Ali the evening of my arrival. But first, he said, I should come and meet some other Delhi exiles. He would expect me at his house in time for tea.

The exiles – now elderly and respectable figures – sat sipping jasmine tea from porcelain cups while they nibbled pakoras and cucumber sandwiches. On the wall hung a faded sepia photograph of Shanulhaq's family in their *haveli* near the Ajmeri Gate around 1912; beside it hung another of a very small boy dressed in late Mughal court dress: a brocaded *sherwani*, baggy white pyjamas, and on his head, a tiny red fez. It was Shanulhaq as an infant.

'Of course Karachi Urdu is really pure Delhi Urdu,' explained a judge, biting a pakora. 'Now that they have Sanskritized all the dialects in India, this is the last place you can hear it spoken.'

Outside, you could hear the dull drone of the Karachi traffic. The city kept reminding me of the Gulf: the new motorways, the glossy high-rise buildings, the Japanese cars. But when you talked to the exiles it was the Palestinians who came to mind. Each one treasured his childhood memories like a title-deed. Each one knew by heart the stories of the catastrophe, the massacres and the exodus; the forty-year-old tales of exile flowed from everyone's lips like new gossip. Each one talked about the old city as if it remained unchanged since the day they had departed.

'Have you ever been to Gulli Churiwallan?' asked the judge, referring to a dirty ghetto now full of decaying warehouses. 'The *havelis* there are the most magnificent in all Delhi. The stonework, the fountains . . .'

It reminded me of a conversation I had had two years before in a camp near Ramallah on the West Bank. Did I know the orange groves at Biddya near Jaffa, Usamah had asked me. They grew the best oranges in Palestine at Biddya, he said. As a boy he could remember creeping in and shinning up the trees and the juice running down his face afterwards . . . How could I tell him that his orange groves now lay under one of the ugliest suburbs of Tel Aviv?

'Have you been to Burns Road?' asked a civil servant's wife, breaking into my thoughts. 'It's just around the corner from your hotel. All the sweetmeat vendors from the Delhi Jama Masjid set up their stalls there. Sometimes I just go there to listen. I sit in a *dhaba* and close my eyes and then there is a whiff of shammi kebab and I think: Ah! The smell of my childhood.'

'Do they still teach Ghalib in the schools?' asked the newsreader, referring to the great Urdu poet. 'Or is it just Kalidasa and the *Ramayana*?'

'I bet no one even knows who Ghalib is in Delhi these days,' said the judge. 'They probably think he's a cricketer.'

Later, Shanulhaq drove me slowly through the streets of Karachi. As we went, he pointed out the shops which had once filled the streets of Delhi: the English Boot House, once of Connaught Place; Abdul Khaliq, the famous sweet-seller of Chandni Chowk; Nihari's, the kebab-wallah from the steps of the Delhi Jama Masjid. He pointed out how such and such an area still preserved the

61

distinctive idiom or the distinctive cut of *kurta* pyjamas unique to such and such an area of Delhi.

Even the streets were like a Delhi Dictionary of Biography. While the roads of modern Delhi are named after a dubious collection of twentieth-century politicians – Archbishop Makarios Marg, Tito Marg and so on – the streets of Karachi are named after the great Delhi-wallahs of history: to get to Ahmed Ali we passed through a litany of Delhi sufis and sultans, poets and philosophers, before turning left into Amir Khusroe Drive.

Ahmed Ali was there to meet us. He wore severe black-rimmed glasses above which sprouted a pair of thin grey eyebrows. He slurred his consonants and had the slightly limp wrist and effete manner of one who modelled himself on a Bloomsbury original. His hair was the colour of wood-ash. For a man once seen as a champion of Delhi's culture, a bulwark of eastern civilization against the seepage of western influence, Ahmed Ali now cut an unexpectedly English figure: with his clipped accent and tweed jacket with old leather elbow-patches he could have passed off successfully as a clubland character from a Noël Coward play.

But despite his comfortable, well-to-do appearance Ahmed Ali was an angry man. Over the hours I spent with him, he spluttered and spat like a well-warmed frying pan. The first occasion was when I inadvertently mentioned that he was now a citizen of Pakistan.

'Poppycock! Balderdash!' he said. 'I was always against Jinnah. Never had any interest in Pakistan.'

'Steady on,' said Shanulhaq.

'The devil!' said Ali. 'Pakistan is not a country. Never was. It's a damn hotchpotch. It's not your country or my country.' He was shouting at Shanulhaq now. 'It's the country of a damn bunch of feudal lords . . . robbers, bloody murderers, kidnappers . . .'

The outburst spluttered out into silence.

'But,' I ventured. 'Didn't you opt for Pakistan? Surely you could have stayed in Delhi had you wanted to.'

There was another explosion.

'*I* opted for Pakistan? I did not! I was the Visiting Professor in Nanking when the blasted Partition took place. The bloody swine of Hindus wouldn't let me go back home so . . .'

'What do you mean?'

'I went and saw the Indian ambassador in Peking. Bloody . . . bloody swine said I couldn't return. Said it was a question of Hindu against Muslim and that there was nothing he could do. I was caught in China and had nowhere to go.'

'Careful,' said Shanulhaq, seeing the state his friend had worked himself up into.

'So how did you end up in Karachi?' I asked.

'When my salary in Nanking was stopped I found my way to some friends in Hong Kong. They put me on an amphibious plane to Karachi. Where else could I have gone if I couldn't go back to Delhi?'

Ali had ceased to quiver with rage and was now merely very cross.

'I never opted for Pakistan,' he said, gradually regaining his poise. 'The civilization I belong to – the civilization of Delhi – came into being through the mingling of two different cultures, Hindu and Muslim. That civilization flourished for one thousand years undisturbed until certain people came along and denied that that great mingling had taken place.'

'Views like that can hardly have made you popular here.'

'They never accepted me in Pakistan, damn it. I have been weeded out. They don't publish my books. They have deleted my name. When copies of *Twilight in Delhi* arrived at the Karachi customs from India, they sent them back: said the book was about the "forbidden" city across the border. They implied the culture was foreign and subversive. Ha!'

'In that case can't you go back to Delhi? Couldn't you re-apply for Indian citizenship?'

'Now no country is my country,' said Ali. 'Delhi is dead; the city that was . . . the language . . . the culture. Everything I knew is finished.'

'It's true,' said Shanulhaq. 'I went back thirteen years after Partition. Already everything was different. I stayed in a new hotel – the Ambassador – which I only later realized had been built on top of a graveyard where several of my friends were buried. In my *mohalla* everyone used to know me, but suddenly I was a stranger. My *haveli* was split into ten parts and occupied by Punjabis. My wife's house had become a temple. Delhi was no longer the abode

63

of the Delhi-wallah. Even the walls had changed. It was very depressing.'

'Before Partition it was a unique city,' said Ali. 'Although it was already very poor, still it preserved its high culture. That high culture filtered down even to the streets, everyone was part of it: even the milk-wallahs could quote Mir and Dagh . . .'

'The prostitutes would sing Persian songs and recite Hafiz . . .'

'They may not have been able to read and write but they could remember the poets . . .'

'And the language,' said Shanulhaq. 'You cannot conceive how chaste Delhi Urdu was . . .'

'And how rich,' added Ali. 'Every *mohalla* had its own expressions; the language used by our ladies was quite distinct from that used by the men. Now the language has shrunk. So many words are lost.'

We talked for an hour about the Delhi of their childhood and youth. We talked of the eunuchs and the sufis and the pigeons and the poets; of the monsoon picnics in Mehrauli and the djinn who fell in love with Ahmed Ali's aunt. We talked of the sweetmeat shops which stayed open until three in the morning, the sorcerers who could cast spells over a whole *mohalla*, the possessed woman who used to run vertically up the zenana walls, and the miraculous cures effected by Hakim Ajmal Khan. The old men swam together through great oceans of nostalgia before finally coming ashore on a strand of melancholy.

'But all of that is no more,' said Ali. 'All that made Delhi special has been uprooted and dispersed.'

'Now it is a carcass without a soul,' said Shanulhaq.

'I am a fossil,' said Ali. 'And Shanulhaq is on his way to becoming a fossil.'

'But nevertheless,' I insisted. 'If you both loved Delhi so much wouldn't you like to see it just one more time?'

'I will never see that town again,' said Ali. 'Once I was invited to give some lectures in Australia. There was some mechanical fault and the plane was diverted to Delhi. The plane landed but I refused to get out. I said: "I am not getting out. I don't have to. You call your damned Chairman. But I'm not putting my foot on that soil which was sacred to me and which has been desecrated."

'They got the entire staff of the airport there to get me out, but I didn't move. How could I? How could I revisit that which was once mine and which was now no longer mine? When they asked why I was behaving as I was, I simply sat in my seat and quoted Mir Taqi Mir at them:

> What matters it, O breeze,
> If now has come the spring
> When I have lost them both
> The garden and my nest?'

'What happened?' I asked.

'The swine were all Punjabis,' said Ali. 'Tell you the truth, I don't think they could understand a bloody word I said.'

FOUR

MY FIRST ACTION on returning from Karachi was to retrieve from the Delhi Customs Shed my computer, printer, ghetto blaster and precious electric kettle. How they got there is a long and harrowing story.

Five days before, I had arrived at Delhi International Airport in good time for the Karachi flight. Getting thus far had taken a week of hard work, for in Delhi the simple matter of leaving the country can turn into some sort of mediaeval penitential exercise. For four days I spent my waking hours pacing the corridors of Hans Bhavan, headquarters of the Immigration Authorities, in the quest for exit permits; waited patiently in a queue outside the Pakistani Embassy Visa Section in search of an entry permit; then underwent five long, dull hours sitting in the Air India office while their ticketing computer lay disembowelled on the desk, undergoing emergency surgery at the hands of a computer 'expert'.

As I strode through Immigration on the way to Customs, I congratulated myself on having got everything achieved: I had a boarding pass and a seat number; the tickets were in my hand; the appropriate stamps were in my passport. Proudly I handed it to the customs officer:

OFFICER (leafing through passport) Good day, sahib. I am thinking you are new in our India.

WD Yes. I've just moved here.

OFFICER But now you are planning to leave?

WD (cheerily) That's right. Not for long though!

OFFICER (suddenly severe) When you arrived in our India, I am thinking you brought in one computer, one printer, one piece cassette recorder and one Swan electric kettle.

WD That's very clever of you. Oh, I see! (The truth dawns) Your colleagues wrote them in the back of my passport when I arrived.

OFFICER Sahib, I do not understand. You are planning to leave our India but I am not seeing one computer, one printer (reads out list from passport).

WD (nervous now) No – but I'm not going for long. I won't be needing the kettle. I'm going to be staying in a hotel. Ha! Ha!

OFFICER Ha! Ha! But sahib. You cannot leave India without your computer and other assorted import items.

WD Why not?

OFFICER This is regulation.

WD But this is absurd.

OFFICER (wobbling head) Yes, sahib. This is regulation.

WD But I'm only going for five days.

OFFICER This has no relevance, sahib. One day, one year it is same thing only.

WD (losing cool) Do you understand? I AM ONLY GOING AWAY FOR FIVE DAYS. My things are all at home. Of course I won't bring my bloody kettle with me when I go away for a short trip. Any more than bring my fridge, my pots and pans or my air conditioning unit.

OFFICER Sahib – you are having imported air conditioning unit?

WD (backtracking fast) No, no. It was just a figure of speech . . .

OFFICER Sahib. Point is this. Maybe you have broken number one tip-top most important regulation and have sold your kettle or one piece cassette recorder.

WD (desperate) I promise you I haven't sold anything. They are all in my flat. Please, I just want to go to Karachi.

OFFICER Sahib. I cannot see your items. So I cannot let you go.

It took twenty minutes of wrangling, pleading, cajoling and threats before we patched up a compromise. I would rush home and bring my 'assorted items' to the airport. I would show them to the officer.

68

He would hold them as surety for my return. When I got back they would be returned.

On my return from Karachi the officer, Mr Prakash Jat, was true to his word. He was waiting for me, items safely secreted in his customs pound. I handed over the receipt.

'You are lucky man,' said Mr Jat. 'We are breaking all regulations letting you out of India without your items.' Then he added: 'By the way, much am I liking your [reads from label] Discoblast Cassette Recorder with Anti-Woof and Flutter Function.'

Mr Jat gave my cassette recorder a loving caress, held it in his hands and admired its sleek lines and sturdy build. Then, casting a shady look on either side, he added in a lowered voice: 'Sahib, you are wanting to sell? I give you good price.'

Outside, I was both pleased and surprised to see Balvinder Singh waiting for me. I say surprised because during the weeks prior to my departure, Balvinder had been playing truant. It had all begun in the middle of October when Balvinder was thrown out of his house by his wife and he had been forced to take refuge with the whores on G.B. Road. My friend feigned a lack of interest in his domestic drama — 'No problem, Mr William. Paying forty-fifty rupees, spending whole night. Too much fun, everyone too much happy' — but despite this bravado, as the month progressed Balvinder Singh began to show distinct signs of wear and tear. Absent from International Backside most of the morning, he would appear still unshaven in the early afternoon. No longer would he point out pretty girls in the street with a cheerful 'You like, Mr William?' More ominously, he began to discharge himself from duty promptly at five-thirty and head off at some speed towards the Khan Market Beer Shop.

Balvinder's preferred tipple had always been a strong local brand called German Beer, whose large litre bottles were distinguished by the enormous swastika which decorated their labels. Balvinder had always been apt to down a litre or two of German Beer an evening, but through October his intake rose dramatically. Over the month empty beer bottles piled up in the taxi, so that every time we turned a corner a monumental crash of broken glass would be heard in the boot.

'I am having some breakable items in my dickie,' Balvinder would explain, a touch shamefaced.

Whether it was his spending on German Beer or Rajasthani whores that landed him in debt, one day towards the end of October Balvinder confronted me and asked whether he could borrow one thousand rupees. His creditors were after him, he said. A month earlier he had borrowed money from a friend, a local *gunda*; now the *gunda* was threatening to perform some impromptu surgery unless he could pay up. It all sounded a bit of a tall story, but I lent Balvinder the money. The next day he disappeared to the Punjab.

Now, a month later, the upsets seemed forgotten and he cheerily handed back all the money he owed. When I asked my friend about his *gunda* and his debts he just shrugged.

'Big man, big problem,' he said. 'Small man, small problem.'

'What do you mean, Balvinder?'

'Rajiv Gandhi has big problem, Balvinder Singh has small problem.'

What he actually meant, I later discovered, was that his father, Punjab Singh, had bailed him out of trouble in exchange for a promise of future good behaviour. It lasted about a fortnight. In the meantime, for the first couple of weeks of November, Olivia and I enjoyed the new-leaf, clean-shaven, fresh-smelling Balvinder and the novel sensation of riding in a taxi that didn't reek of brewery.

Two days after I returned from Karachi, I called Balvinder and asked him to take me up to Coronation Park.

When I first came to Delhi I had expected to find much that was familiar. I knew that India had been influenced by England since the Elizabethan period, and that the country had been forcibly shackled to Britain, first in the form of the East India Company, then the British Crown, for nearly two hundred years.

Moreover, in the mid-1980s, Britain was in the grip of a Raj revival. The British public wallowed in a nostalgic vision of the Raj as some sort of extended colonial soap opera — *Upstairs, Downstairs* writ large over the plains of Asia. *The Jewel in the Crown* was being shown on television, and the correspondence columns of *The Times* were full of complaints from old India hands about the alleged inaccuracies in Attenborough's *Gandhi*. Academic presses were churning out books on the buildings of the Empire while the Booker shortlist could be counted on to include at least two books whose plot revolved around the Raj: *The Siege of Krishnapur*, *Heat and Dust*, *Staying On* and *Midnight's Children* had all been winners in recent years.

Such was the enthusiasm at home for things Imperial Indian that I had assumed that India would be similarly obsessed with things Imperial British. Nothing, of course, could have been further from the truth. Instead, visiting the subcontinent less than forty years after the last sahib set sail back to Britain, I was intrigued by the degree to which India had managed to shed its colonial baggage. True, people spoke English, played cricket and voted in Westminster-style elections. Nevertheless, far from encountering the familiar, I was astonished how little evidence remained of two centuries of colonial rule. In the conversation of my Indian contemporaries, the British Empire was referred to in much the same way as I referred to the Roman Empire. For all the fond imaginings of the British, as far as the modern Delhi-wallah was concerned, the Empire was ancient history, an age impossibly remote from our own.

Nowhere was this distance clearer than at Coronation Park. The park stands on the site of the three great Delhi Durbars, the ceremonial climaxes of the entire Imperial pageant. Today, as Balvinder and I discovered after a long search, the site lies far north of the northernmost suburb of Old Delhi, stranded now amid a great flooded wilderness. As the eye sweeps over the plain, it seems a flat and uninteresting expanse, so level that a single bullock cart inching its way across the land appears as tall as some towering temple chariot. Then, to one side of the horizon, erupting suddenly from the marshy flatlands, there appears a vast marble image, an Indian Ozymandias.

The statue is sixty feet tall, a king enthroned with orb and sceptre; around him stands a crescent of stone acolytes, an ossified court marooned in an Arthurian wasteland of swamp, mud and camel-thorn. Creepers tangle through the folds in the robes; grass greens the Crown Imperial. At first it is possible to mistake the Ozymandias-image for a displaced Egyptian Pharaoh or a lost Roman Emperor. Only on closer examination does it become clear that it is George V, the King Emperor, surrounded by his viceroys.

The statue originally surmounted the central roundabout of New Delhi, the climax of the Kingsway (now Rajpath). It was hauled into retirement soon after Independence and now stands forgotten and unloved, an unwanted reminder of a period few Indians look back to with any nostalgia. Although the statue is only sixty years old, the world it came from seems as distant as that of Rameses II.

Perhaps it is language, the spoken word, which is the greatest indication of the distance travelled since 1947.

The English spoken by Indians – Hinglish – has of course followed its own idiosyncratic journey since the guardians of its purity returned home. Like American English, likewise emancipated by Britain's colonial retreat, it has developed its own grammatical rules, its own syntax and its own vocabulary.

One of the great pleasures of our life in India has always been being woken on the dot of 7.30 every morning by Ladoo bearing 'bed tea' and the *Times of India*. The news is inevitably depressing stuff ('400 Killed in Tamil Train Crash', '150 Garrotted by Assam Separatists' and so on), yet somehow the jaunty *Times of India* prose always manages to raise the tone from one of grim tragedy. There may have been a train crash, but at least the Chief Minister has *air-dashed* to the scene. Ten *convented* (convent-educated) girls may have been gang-raped in the Punjab, but thousands of students have staged a *bandh* (strike) and a *dharna* (protest) against such *eve-teasing* (much nicer than the bland Americanese 'sexual harassment'). And so what if the protesters were then *lathi* (truncheon) charged by police *jawans* (constables)? In the *Times of India* such miscreants are always *charge-sheeted* in the end.

My favourite item is, however, the daily *condoling*. If the *Times* is to be believed, Indian politicians like nothing better than a quick condole; and certainly barely a day passes without a picture of, say, the Chief Minister of Haryana condoling Mrs Parvati Chaudhuri over the death of Mr Devi Chaudhuri, the director-general of All-India Widgets. Indeed, condoling shows every sign of becoming a growth industry. If a businessman has died but is not considered important enough to be condoled by the Chief Minister, it is becoming fashionable for his business colleagues to take out an illustrated advertisement and condole him themselves. The language of these advertisements tends to be even more inspired than that of the *Times* news columns. In my diary, I copied down this example from a November 1989 issue:

SAD DEMISE

With profound grief we have to condole the untimely passing of our beloved general manager MISTER DEEPAK

73

MEHTA, thirty four years, who left us for heavenly abode
in tragic circumstances (beaten to death with bedpost). Condole presented by bereft of Mehta Agencies (Private)
Limited.

Perhaps the most striking testament to the sea-change in Indian
English in the forty years since Independence lies not in what has
survived – and been strangely, wonderfully mutated – but in what
has died and completely disappeared.

The best guide to such linguistic dodos is *Hobson Jobson: A Glossary
of Anglo-Indian Colloquial Words and Phrases*, originally published by
John Murray in 1903. The book was written as a guide to those
words which had passed from Sanskrit, Urdu, Persian and Arabic
into English, and the list is certainly extraordinary: every time you
wear *pyjamas* or a *cummerbund*; if ever you sit on the *veranda* of
your *bungalow* reading the *pundits* in the newspapers or eat a stick
of *candy*; indeed even if you are haunted by *ghouls* or have your
cash stolen by *thugs* – then you are using a branch of English that
could never have developed but for the trading and colonizing
activities of the East India Company.

Yet perhaps the most interesting aspect of *Hobson Jobson* is how
many of its words and phrases are stone cold dead, now utterly
incomprehensible to a modern reader. In 1903 an Englishman
could praise a cheroot as 'being the real cheese' (from the Hindi
chiz, meaning thing) or claim his horse was the 'best goont in Tibet'
(from the Hindi *gunth*, meaning a pony); and whether he was in
the middle of some *shikar* (sport) relaxing with his friends in their
chummery (bachelor quarters) or whoring with his *rum-johny* (mistress, from the Hindi *ramjani*, a dancing girl) he might reasonably
expect to be understood.

Half of *Hobson Jobson* is filled with these dead phrases: linguistic
relics of a world so distant and strange that it is difficult to believe
that these words were still current in our own century. Yet clearly,
in 1903, if a *Jack* (sepoy) did anything wrong he could expect to
receive some pretty foul *galee* (abuse); if he were unlucky his *chopper*
(thatched hut) might fall down in the *mangoes* (April showers); and
if he forgot his *goglet* (water bottle) on parade he might well have
been thrown out of the regiment for good.

To us, the vocabulary of the Raj now seems absurd, distant and comical, like the pretensions of the rotting statues in Coronation Park. Yet many who actually spoke this language are still alive in England. For them, the world of *Hobson Jobson* is less linguistic archaeology than the stuff of fraying memory.

Before I went to India I went to Cambridge to see a friend of my grandmother. Between the twenties and the forties, Iris Portal's youth had been spent in that colonial Delhi that now seemed so impossibly dated. I wanted to hear what she remembered.

It was the last weekend of summer. Over the flat steppe of East Anglia tractors were beginning to plough the great wide plains of fenland stubble. A sharp wind gusted in from the coast; cloud-shadows drifted fast over the fields. On the Backs, the trees were just beginning to turn.

'Welcome to my rabbit hutch,' said Iris. 'It's not very big, but I flatter myself that it's quite colourful.'

She was an alert and well-preserved old lady: owlish and intelligent. Her grey hair was fashionably cut and her voice was attractively dry and husky. Iris's family had been Cambridge dons and although she had broken out and married into the army, there was still something residually academic in her measured gaze.

She sat deep in an armchair in her over-heated flat in a sheltered housing complex off the M11. Outside, beyond the car park, you could see the pavements and housing estates of suburban Girton. But inside, a small fragment of another world had been faithfully recreated. All around, the bookshelves were full of the great Imperial classics – Todd, Kipling, Fanny Parkes and Emily Eden – some riddled with the boreholes of bookish white ants. On one wall hung a small oil of houseboats on the Dal Lake; on another, a print of the Mughal Emperor Muhammed Shah Rangilla in the Red Fort. Beside it was an old map of 1930s Delhi.

Somehow the pictures and the books – and especially the dusty, old-buckram, yellow-paged library-scent of the books – succeeded in giving the thoroughly modern flat a faint whiff of the Edwardian, a distant hint of the hill-station bungalow.

'You must give my love to dear old Delhi,' said Iris. 'Ah! Even now when I close my eyes I see . . .' For a minute she left the sentence incomplete, then: 'Pots of chrysanthemums!' she said quite suddenly. 'Rows and rows of chrysanthemums in little red pots! That's what I remember best. Those and the ruins: riding out through the bazaars and out into the country. The Qutab Minar and moonlight picnics in Hauz Khas – a place we all thought was madly romantic. The tombs everywhere all tumbling down and black buck and peacocks and monkeys . . . Is it still like that?'

'Up to a point,' I said.

'Dear, dear, dear old Delhi,' she said. 'How I envy you living there.'

She smiled a contented smile and rearranged herself in the armchair.

'So,' I ventured. 'You were born in Delhi?'

'No, no, no.' Iris closed her eyes and drew a deep breath. 'Certainly not. I was born in Simla in 1905 in a house called Newstead. It was immediately behind Snowdon, the Commander-in-Chief's house. Curzon was then the Viceroy and Kitchener the Commander-in-Chief.'

Now she had mentioned Simla, I remembered that in the biography of Iris's brother, the great Rab Butler, I had seen a sepia photograph of the two of them at a children's party in the Simla Viceregal Lodge. In the image you could clearly see Iris's plump little face peeping out from a Victorian cocoon of taffeta and white silk.

'So you spent your childhood in Simla?'

'No. I only spent the first five summers of my life in Simla,' she said, correcting me again. 'Then I was brought back to England. I went to school in a madhouse on the beach of Sandgate under the Folkestone cliffs. It was a sort of avant-garde Bedales-type place. Perfectly horrible. We were supposed to be a Greek Republic. We made our own rules, wore aesthetic uniforms and I don't know what else.'

'Did you miss India?'

'I thought of nothing else. India was home.' She shrugged her shoulders. 'All I wanted was India, a horse of my own and a dashing cavalry escort. When my mother and I arrived back in Bombay we *immediately* caught the train up to Delhi. I remember vividly the joy of coming in the driveway and seeing all those rows and rows of chrysanthemums in their pots and thinking: "Ah! I'm back!"

'Everything was as I remembered it. My father's bearer, Gokhul, was a little fatter than before. He had been with my father since he was a boy and was now a rather grand figure: he used to walk around with a great brass badge on his front. Otherwise everything was unchanged.'

Iris spoke slowly and precisely as if making a mental effort to relay her memories with absolute accuracy.

'It was . . . 1922, I suppose. The Government of India was in Delhi by that time, waiting for New Delhi to be completed. We were all living in the Civil Lines [of Old Delhi]. There was no Secretariat and all the Government offices were in Nissen huts. But the officials' bungalows were all in beautiful gardens. You know how things grow in Delhi. The jacarandas . . .'

'Had you come out to work?' I asked.

'No, no. My life was extremely frivolous. I had been very high-brow at school. No one ever talked about anything except Browning. But in Delhi people would have been horrified if they discovered you read *poetry*. The English in India were not a very cultured lot. The atmosphere was too giddy: it was all riding, picnics, clubs, dances, dashing young men and beautiful polo players . . .' She smiled. 'Looking back of course, the whole set-up was very odd. There was such snobbery. Everyone was graded off into sections. One would never have dreamt of going anywhere with someone from the Public Works Department . . .' She blinked with mock horror.

'The most snobbish event of all was the polo, though the Delhi Hunt was rather wonderful in its own way. All the Viceregal staff – who were usually rather interesting and attractive – came out in their Ratcatcher – black coats and so on: in Ooty everyone wore pink, but in Delhi it was only the whippers-in and the master who were allowed to. It was taken very seriously. The hounds – rather dapper ones – were imported from England. I used to get up before dawn and motor down to the Qutab Minar in my father's T-model Ford. A *syce* would have been sent down the night before with the pony. Then, as soon as the sun rose, we would gallop about this dry countryside chasing after the jackals.

77

'But much more worthwhile than hunting the poor old jackal was going hawking with Umer Hyat Khan of the Tiwana clan. I expect you know all about him. He was a big landowner from the Northern Punjab: rather like a Highland laird. Umer Hyat was a member of the first legislative assembly and whenever the Assembly was in session he would come down to Delhi with his horses, his hawks and his hounds . . . Before dawn we would canter over the Jumna by the Bridge of Boats. The horses were sent ahead. There were all these splendid tribesmen with hawks on their wrists and greyhounds straining on the leash. We rode out like a medi-aeval company. When the hounds had stirred up the hares, the hawks were let fly.

'After I had been in Delhi for a while I began to sober up a little. My father set me down at a table to learn Urdu with a bearded *Munshi*. Soon afterwards I met Sir John Thompson at a big dinner at Viceregal Lodge. He was Commissioner for Delhi and an old friend of my father. A very intelligent man: he could speak several Indian languages, understood Sanskrit and so on. He said to me: "What do you do with yourself all day?" and I replied: "I sleep late because I've been to a party then I go for a ride and . . ." He said, a little severely: "Has it never occurred to you to study Indian history?" I said "No" and he replied: "I'll lend you a book on the history of Delhi. You read that and see if it doesn't inspire you to look around" – which indeed it did.

'From that moment onwards, wherever I went, I was poking my nose about, looking at the ruins. Most afternoons I used to ride down to the Purana Qila – I loved the Purana Qila – and sit at the top of the Sher Mandal thinking of poor old Humayun tripping down those stairs and killing himself. I always used to come down very carefully. Of course it was all so lonely then. Humayun's Tomb was absolutely out in the blue. It was open land, strewn with tumbledown tombs and the rubble of ages. Beyond the plains were dotted with black buck and peacocks. You could ride anywhere . . .'

'So this was all before Lutyens's Delhi went up?' I interrupted.

'Well, I suppose the building was just about beginning.'

'Did you ever meet the man himself?'

'Who? Lutyens? Oh yes. He was a great friend of my parents.'

'What was he like?'

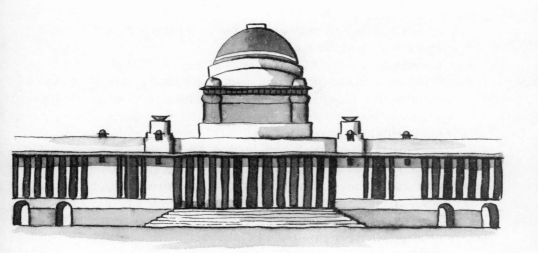

The Viceroy's House

'Well, he was very taken with my mother. Because my father's name was Monty, he used to call her Carlo. That was typical Lutyens. Always making these rather childish jokes.

'He took me around Viceroy's House when it was only two to three feet high. What I will always remember was going to one of the staff bungalows. He said: "Look – I planned this with a central space in the middle and eight doors leading off." Some of these doors just led into housemaid's cupboards. "I thought it would be terribly funny," said old Lutyens – he was absolutely thrilled with this, "that if people had had too much to drink at a big party, they'd come home and they wouldn't know which was their door. They'd all end up in the cupboards."'

Iris frowned. 'He was such a silly man. But of course I greatly admire his work. I love New Delhi. I always thought it was so much better than Washington. And you know, people forget that that magnificent city of Delhi was built on such a flimsy basis – both human and material. There was no proper scaffolding or any of the equipment that they have now: no cranes or mechanical things to help with the lifting of weights . . . I can remember seeing them, these little wizened people carrying great hods of bricks and vast bags of cement. There were myriads of them: climbing up rickety bamboo ladders tied together with string, and all of it getting more precarious as it got higher . . .

'Of course, people of my father's generation hated the whole thing. He and my uncle Harcourt thought it was frightfully extravagant, and that those lakhs of money could have been far better used elsewhere. Moreover they always felt that the prophecy – whoever builds a new city in Delhi will lose it – would come true. If ever anybody raised the subject of New Delhi my father would always quote the Persian couplet in a most gloomy voice. And of course it did come true. Whoever has built a new city in Delhi has always lost it: the Pandava brethren, Prithviraj Chauhan, Feroz Shah Tughluk, Shah Jehan . . . They all built new cities and they all lost them. We were no exception.'

I could see Iris was tiring. It was now dark outside and I knew I was soon going to have to leave her. But before I went I wanted to ask one last question.

'In retrospect,' I said. 'Do you think British rule was justified?'

Iris mulled over the question before answering.

'Well, at the time we certainly didn't think of ourselves as wicked imperialists,' she said, answering slowly. 'Of course not. But you see, although people of my generation were very keen on Gandhi and Indian Independence, we were still very careless. We didn't give much thought to the question of what on earth we were doing to that country and its people.

'That said, I can't forget the sacrifices made by the "wicked" imperialists over the centuries – the graves, so many very young, the friends I have had, and what good people many of them were.

'But on balance I think you must never take land away from a people. A people's land has a mystique. You can go and possibly order them about for a bit, perhaps introduce some new ideas, build a few good buildings, but then in the end you must go away and die in Cheltenham.' Iris sighed. 'And that, of course, is exactly what we did.'

I walked around Lutyens's Delhi that November, thinking of Iris. It seemed incredible that someone who had been taken around the foundations of the Viceroy's House – now the President's Palace – by Lutyens himself could still be alive and well. The buildings appeared so solid, so timeless, so ancient. It was like meeting someone who had been taken around the Parthenon by Pericles.

To best appreciate New Delhi I used to walk to it from the Old City. Leaving behind the press and confusion of Shahjehanabad – the noise and the heat, the rickshaws and the barrow-boys, the incense and the sewer-stink – I would find myself suddenly in a gridiron of wide avenues and open boulevards, a scheme as ordered and inevitable as a Bach fugue. Suddenly the roads would be empty and the air clean. There was no dust, no heat: all was shaded, green and cool. Ahead, at the end of the avenue, rose the great *chattri* which once held the statue of George V. Arriving there at the end of the green tunnel, I would turn a right angle and see the cinnamon sky stretching out ahead, no longer veiled by a *burqa* of buildings or trees. It was like coming up for air.

This was Rajpath – once the Kingsway – one of the great ceremonial ways of the world. It was planned as an Imperial Champs Elysées – complete with India Gate, its own butter-coloured Arc de Triomphe. But it was far wider, far greener, far more magnificent than anything comparable in Europe. On either side ran wide lawns giving on to fountains and straight avenues of eucalyptus and casuarina. Beyond, canals running parallel to the road reflected the surroundings with mirror-like fidelity.

Ahead, high on Raisina Hill, crowning an almost infinite perspective, rose a silhouette of domes, towers and cupolas. As I drew near, Herbert Baker's two Secretariats would rise precipitously out of the plain, their projecting porticoes flanking the hemispheric dome of the Viceroy's House. East fused with West. Round arches and classical Greek colonnades were balanced by latticework stone screens and a ripple of helmet-like *chattris*. At the very centre of the complex, the resolution of every perspective in New Delhi, stood Lutyens's staggering neo-Buddhist dome.

However many times I revisited the complex, I would always be amazed by the brilliantly orchestrated flirtation of light and shade – the dim colonnades offset by massive walls of sun-blasted masonry. Yet the most startling conceit of all lay in the use of colour: the play of the two different shades of pink Agra sandstone;

one pale and creamy; the other a much darker burnt crimson. The two different colours were carefully arranged, the darker at the bottom as if it was somehow heavier, yet with the two contrasting tones blending as effortlessly into one another as they once did in the quarry.

It was superb. In the dusk, as the sun sank behind the great dome of the Viceroy's House, the whole vista would turn the colour of attar of roses. I would realize then, without hesitation, that I was looking at one of the greatest marriages of architecture and urban planning ever to have left the drawing board.

Nevertheless, the more often I came and looked, the more I felt a nagging reservation. This had less to do with aesthetics than with comparisons with other massive schemes of roughly similar date that the complex brought to mind. Then one evening, as I proceeded up the cutting and emerged to find Baker's Secretariats terminating in the wide portico of the Viceroy's House, with this great imperial mass of masonry towering all around me I suddenly realized where I had seen something similar, something equally vast, equally dwarfing, before: Nuremberg.

In its monstrous, almost megalomaniac scale, in its perfect symmetry and arrogant presumption, there was a distant but distinct echo of something Fascist or even Nazi about the great acropolis of Imperial Delhi. Certainly it is far more beautiful than anything Hitler and Mussolini ever raised: Lutyens, after all, was a far, far greater architect than Albert Speer. Yet the comparison still seemed reasonable. For, despite their very many, very great differences, Imperial India, Fascist Italy and Nazi Germany all belonged to comparable worlds. All were to different extents authoritarian; all made much of magnificent display; all were built on a myth of racial superiority and buttressed in the last resort by force. In the ceremonial buildings of all three, it was an impression of the might and power of the Imperial State that the architects aimed above all to convey.

To do so they used the same architectural vocabulary: great expanses of marble, a stripped-down classicism, a fondness for long colonnades and a love of Imperial heraldic devices: elephants' heads, lions couchant, massive eagles with outstretched wings. Of course, much of the similarity is due to the fact that Speer and

Lutyens were commissioned to build monuments of state at roughly the same time. Moreover, Speer appears to have drawn on Lutyens's experience and style. Yet there can be no doubt that New Delhi was very deliberately built as an expression of the unconquerable might of the Raj. As Lord Stamfordham, Private Secretary to George V, wrote in a letter articulating the King Emperor's views on his new capital: 'We must let [the Indian] see for the first time the power of Western civilization . . .'

In New Delhi, as in Fascist Milan or Nazi Berlin, the individual is lost; the scale is not human, but super-human; not national, but super-national: it is, in a word, Imperial. The impression of the architect as bully receives confirmation in the inscription that Lutyens ordered to be raised above the great recessed *ivan* gateway of the Secretariats.

For those who like to believe in the essential benevolence of the British Empire it is a depressing discovery, for it must be one of the most patronizing inscriptions ever raised in a public place:

LIBERTY WILL NOT DESCEND TO A PEOPLE;
A PEOPLE MUST RAISE THEMSELVES TO LIBERTY;
IT IS A BLESSING WHICH MUST BE EARNED
BEFORE IT CAN BE ENJOYED.

I had brought out to Delhi with me a copy of the collected letters of Lutyens. One evening in November I sat in the shade of the *chattris* beside the two Secretariats, facing down the Rajpath towards India Gate and reading through them. As I did so, I tried to bring the creator of Imperial Delhi into focus in my own mind.

The picture that the letters give of their author is a mixed one. There are certainly elements of the joker and buffoon that Iris had described: Lutyens incessantly doodles on the writing paper, turning the P & O crests on successive letterheads into a tiger, a man with a turban and an elephant. His first action after arriving in India is to play a game of musical chairs ('Mrs Brodie who weighs 20 stone or more was the most energetic of the party and broke two chairs entirely [amid] many a scrimmage and wild shriek . . .').

Later, on seeing the hideous government buildings of Simla, Lutyens writes that they are 'a piece of pure folly such as only Englishmen can achieve: if one were told the monkeys had built them one would have said what wonderful monkeys, they must be shot in case they do it again.'

This playfulness is balanced by ample evidence of Lutyens's tenacity and stubbornness; a stubbornness which in the end saved New Delhi from both the aesthetic whims of successive philistine Viceroys – Lord Hardinge was determined to build the entire scheme in the Indian version of Victorian mock-Gothic, the horrible Indo-Saracenic style – and from the cost-cutting penny-pinching interference of the civil servants.

But the letters also confirmed my hunch concerning Lutyens's autocratic tendencies. Like some other of his English contemporaries, he was clearly disillusioned with Parliamentary democracy and found in the Raj what he regarded as an ideal – an enlightened despotism: 'I am awfully impressed by the Civil Service,' he wrote to his wife, early on in his Indian travels. 'I wish they would abolish the House of Commons and all representative government and start the system in England.' Later, in a moment of fury with a negligent workman, he expressed his opinion that the Empire's subjects 'ought to be reduced to slavery and not given the rights of man at all . . .'

Yet perhaps the overwhelming surprise of the letters is Lutyens's extraordinary intolerance and dislike of all things Indian. Even by the standards of the time, the letters reveal him to be a bigot, though the impression is one of bumbling insularity rather than jack-booted malevolence. Indians are invariably referred to as 'blacks', 'blackamoors', 'natives' or even 'niggers'. They are 'dark and ill-smelling', their food is 'very strange and frightening' and they 'do not improve with acquaintance'. The helpers in his architect's office he describes as 'odd people with odd names who do those things that bore the white man'. On another occasion he writes of the 'sly slime of the Eastern mind' and 'the very low intelligence of the natives'. 'I do not think it possible for the Indians and whites to mix freely', he concludes. 'They are very, very different and I cannot admit them on the same plane as myself.'

Considering that Lutyens managed to fuse Eastern and Western aesthetics more successfully than any other artist since the anonymous sculptors of Gandhara (who produced their Indo-Hellenic Buddhas in the wake of Alexander the Great), his dislike of Indian art and architecture is particularly surprising: 'Moghul architecture is cumbrous ill-constructed building,' he writes in one letter. 'It is essentially the building style of children [and] very tiresome to the Western intelligence.' At one stage, after visiting Agra, he is grudgingly forced to admit that 'some of the work is lovely', but he attributes these qualities to an (imaginary) Italian influence.

In the end one is left with the same paradox confronted by lovers of Wagner: how could someone with such objectionable views and so insular a vision have managed to produce such breathtaking works of art? Here was a man capable of building some of the most beautiful structures created in the modern world, but whose prejudices blinded him to the beauty of the Taj Mahal; a man who could fuse the best of East and West while denying that the Eastern elements in his own buildings were beautiful.

Authoritarian regimes tend to leave the most solid souvenirs; art has a strange way of thriving under autocracy. Only the vanity of an Empire — an Empire emancipated from democratic constraints, totally self-confident in its own judgement and still, despite everything, assured of its own superiority — could have produced Lutyens's Delhi.

Pandit Nehru wrote: 'New Delhi is the visible symbol of British power, with all its ostentation and wasteful extravagance.' He was right, of course, but that is only half the story. It is also the finest architectural artefact created by the British Empire, and preferable in every way to Nehru's disastrous commission of a hideous new city by Le Corbusier at Chandigarh. Chandigarh is now an urban disaster, a monument to stained concrete and discredited modernism; but Imperial Delhi is now more admired and loved than perhaps ever before. Nevertheless, in its patronizing and authoritarian after-taste, Lutyens's New Delhi remains as much a monument to the British Empire's failings as to its genius.

That month I began to make enquiries to try and track down British stayers-on from Imperial Delhi. For a while I failed to come up with anything: those few who had chosen to remain after 1947 seemed to have either died or recently emigrated. But for the transitory diplomatic community, the British had totally disappeared from Delhi.

Then, in mid-November, I was told about two old English ladies who now lived in the mountains above Simla. They had moved to the hills in the sixties, I was told, but before then they had spent their working lives in Delhi. If I wanted reminiscences of Imperial Delhi, said my informer, then Phyllis and Edith Haxby were exactly what I was looking for. In the event, when I flew up to see them, the two old ladies produced few Delhi memories. But their attitudes gave a sad insight into the fate of those Britons who not so long ago had dominated Raj Delhi, and who had opted to stay on in India after the Empire which created them had dissolved.

Their house had once been quite grand – a rambling half-timbered affair with a wide veranda and cusped Swiss gables. But the Haxbys' estate had clearly fallen on hard times. A lint of withered spiders' webs hung from the beams of the veranda. Only thin, peeling strips of burnt sienna indicated that the house had ever been painted. A tangle of thorns had overcome the near-side of the building and docks and ragwort grew from between the paving stones of the path.

At first I thought no one was at home. But after ten minutes of knocking on doors and peering through windows, I was rewarded with the sight of one of the sisters hobbling across her sitting-room. She undid the multiple bolts of the door and slumped down in one of the wickerwork chairs of the veranda.

'And who are you?' she asked.

I explained, and to make conversation complimented her on the view from her front door.

'It may be beautiful to you,' she said abruptly. 'But it's not beautiful to us. We want to go back home.'

Phyllis Haxby was a frail old woman with mottled brown skin and thin, toothpick legs. Her tweed skirt was extravagantly darned and her thick brown stockings were shredded with a jigsaw of tears and ladders.

'We want to sell up,' she continued. 'We've been through a very bad time. There are prostitutes living all over the place, making life hell for us. They say we're English and shouldn't be here. After seventy-eight years!'

Phyllis grunted angrily and began rapping on the front door with her stick: 'Edith! Edith! There's a boy here to see us. Says he's British. He wants to know about Delhi.'

Then she turned around and began talking to me in a stage whisper: 'She had a fall today. The prostitutes put dope down the chimney. It makes her want to sleep. She fell on the fender — bleeding from eight a.m. until after lunch. They're trying to drive us out, you see.'

'It's not just dope down the chimney,' said Edith, who had at this point appeared at the door. 'They come through the floorboards at night.'

'Through the floorboards? Are you sure?' I asked.

'Of course I'm sure. When we're asleep they put stuff in our eyes to make us go blind. Every day my sight gets a little worse. You've no idea what we've gone through.'

'You know something,' said Phyllis, leaning forward towards me and continuing to speak in her conspiratorial stage whisper. 'They're all *Jews*. All of 'em. They're as fair as lilies but they wear these brown masks to pass off as natives. They've been persecuting us for twenty years.'

'Thirty years, Phyllis.'

'Since Partition, in fact.'

'But we're not going to give in, are we, darling? We're not going to cut and run.'

At this point the drizzle which had followed me to the bungalow turned into a downpour. The water dripped through the roof of the veranda and we decided to move inside. From the sitting-room I could see the half-lit bedroom. To one side of the bed was an upturned chest of drawers, on the other an inverted ironing board.

'That's to stop the Jewish prostitutes from coming in through the floorboards,' said Phyllis, seeing where I was looking.

'But they still come down the chimney,' said Edith.

'Oh — they'll do anything to drive us out. They've even started

87

to watch us bathe. They peer through the window as if we were some sort of ha'penny peep show.'

We arranged ourselves around a table and Phyllis poured the tea.

'Just look at my hands shake,' she said.

'It's the prostitutes' dope,' said Edith.

'Makes me shake like a Quaker and dribble like a dog. I used to be hale and hearty, too.'

'Very hale and hearty, my sister. Those prostitutes should be shot on sight.'

The two sisters fussed around with their teacups, trying to spoon in the sugar and the powdered milk before their shakes sprinkled the stuff over the table. At length, when this was achieved and they had relaxed, I turned the conversation towards their memories of Delhi in the old days.

'Oh it was such fun. We were young and blond and had admirers. The Delhi season lasted from October until March. At night we went to dances and drank champagne – real champagne – and by day we would sit outside and watch the soldiers riding past, four abreast. Those were the days.'

'But my God have things changed. Imagine – I now do my own sweeping . . .'

'. . . and the cooking and the cleaning and the laundry. Us – Colonel's daughters.'

'Our father was the Colonel of the 23rd Punjabis. I told the grocery boy last week. The Twenty-Thirds! He couldn't believe such people lived in such . . . in such . . .'

'Simplicity,' said Edith.

'Exactly,' said Phyllis. 'Simplicity. You know, Mr Dalrymple, you people today can have no idea what India was like before. It was . . . just like England.'

'Shut up, darling! The prostitutes – they'll report us. They've got microphones. Speak softly.'

'I will not. The wickedness! Tell them to go to the devil.'

The two sisters sipped angrily at their tea. They were silent for a second, and I again tried to turn the conversation back towards Delhi.

'Did you ever meet Lutyens?' I asked.

Phyllis wasn't listening: 'And you know the worst thing. Those Jewish prostitutes. They tried to . . .'

'Don't Phyllis.'

'I will. You can't gag a Haxby of Haxby. They tried to put us in a madhouse. We went out for a walk and they started to drag us down the road. And I said: "This isn't the way home."'

'Damn cheek. A colonel's daughter.'

'The warders were very nice to us. We stayed there for two weeks. Then a young police officer came and said: "Who put you here?" He went to the I.G. – the Inspector General – and by four o'clock we were back here. The I.G. ordered us to be brought home. All the other inmates were very jealous.'

'I'll say.'

'Imagine putting two elderly people in a madhouse. Those prostitutes – they're from Baghdad, you see. They were able to do it because they have a money-minting machine and were able to bribe the inspectors.'

'They use us as a respectable cover for their operations. That's why we're going to leave this place – as soon as we can sell the house. We've had enough of Simla.'

'More than enough. We've had an offer for one lakh rupees [about £2000] from this man. If we can find someone to give us two lakhs we'll be off home.'

'We thought we'd try Ooty first. Get a taxi to Delhi . . .'

'Dear old Delhi.'

'. . . then a flight to Coimbatore, then a car up to the Nilgiris.'

'It used to be lovely in Ooty. Just like England.'

'But if we have no luck there we thought we'd try Wales. With two lakhs you could get a nice house in Wales I'd have thought.'

Looking at my watch I saw it was time to leave: my train back was leaving in less than an hour. I got up, said my goodbyes, and promised to send them the English brassieres and stockings they had asked for – they seemed to have trouble with domestic Indian brands: 'Indian women have the strangest shaped breasts,' explained Edith.

Both of the sisters heaved themselves up and saw me to the door. But just as I was setting off down the garden path, Phyllis called me back. I thought that maybe she had finally remembered some forgotten snippet of Delhi gossip.

'One last thing,' she said, clenching my hand in her claw-like grip. 'Just watch out.'

'What do you mean?' I asked, surprised.

'Look after yourself,' she said earnestly. 'Don't drink anything strange — or anything bitter. Watch out for the smell of bitter almonds. The Jews will all be after you now — after you've tried to help the Haxbys. You won't be safe anywhere.'

I thanked her again and opened the wicket gate. As I closed it, I heard her shouting behind me.

'Take it,' she called, 'from a colonel's daughter.'

FIVE

IN NOVEMBER, on the first night of the new moon of Kartika, Delhi celebrates Diwali, the Hindu Festival of Lights.

In the markets trestles go up selling little clay lamps and mountains of honey-soaked Bengali sweets. Postmen, telephone engineers and *chowkidars* tour the streets, knocking on doors and asking politely for their Diwali *baksheesh*. (Balvinder Singh, it must be said, opted for a more confrontational approach: 'Mr William, tomorrow is holiday. Today you give me 200 rupees extra.')

Every night during the week leading up to the festival the sky reverberates with a crescendo of thunderflash and fireworks. The pyrotechnics culminate in an ear-splitting, blitz-like barrage the night of Diwali itself. That evening every Hindu and Sikh house in Delhi is lit up with a blaze of candles; even the *jhuggi*-dwellers place one small nightlight outside their corrugated-iron doors. You can smell the thick cordite-smoke of the fireworks billowing in over the kitchen spices and the scent of dung fires.

Although it is a Hindu festival, many Muslims join in too; over centuries of co-existence the holidays of the two faiths have long become confused and mingled. On my way back from the Lodhi Gardens at dusk I saw two heavily-bearded men bowed in prayer on a small masonry dais by the roadside. Though it lay beside a path I walked along every day I had never previously noticed the tomb, hidden as it was by a thick covering of weeds and thorns.

The two men had cleared the undergrowth, covered their heads

91

with pocket handkerchiefs, and were now busy placing a series of little oil lamps over its breadth; on the raised grave marker they hung a garland of marigolds. I asked the men whom the tomb commemorated. They replied that it belonged to Khwaja Nazir-ud-Din, a great Sufi from the time of the Emperor Akbar.

'Are you imams?' I asked.

'No, no,' replied one of the men, lighting another low, wide oil lamp of prehistoric design. 'We are working for Electricity Board.'

More comprehensible celebrations were being conducted around the square outside our house. Mrs Puri's numberless grandchildren were scattered outside her gate throwing sparklers and Catherine wheels at each other. Next door, Mr Seth was letting off a volley of roman candles for the benefit of a gathering of portly-looking retired railway officials.

My landlady, however, refused to have anything to do with such extravagance. 'Actually these fireworks are too costly,' she explained when I met her on the stairs. 'Money is not for burning.'

Mrs Puri, it emerged, adhered to a characteristically monetary interpretation of the Diwali festival. Most Hindus agree that Diwali marks the triumphant return of Ram and Sita to their north Indian capital, Ayodhya, following their successful war against Ravanna in Lanka; hence the festival's date, some three weeks after the victory commemorated at Dusshera. But Mrs Puri would have none of it.

'Mr William,' she said. 'You must understand that Diwali is a very important night for us.'

'Why is that, Mrs Puri?'

'Diwali is not about burning money,' said my landlady, her eyes glinting. 'It is about accumulating it.'

'Oh?'

'Diwali is the festival of Laxmi, the Goddess of Wealth,' explained Mrs Puri. 'If we light candles and leave our front door open, on this night Laxmi will come into our house and count all our moneys.'

'Why does she do that?' I asked, intrigued by the idea of Laxmi parking her lotus outside the gate and paying a visit in her avatar as divine auditor.

'Actually Laxmi likes too much hard work,' replied Mrs Puri. 'If we have said our prayers to Laxmi – performed the money *puja* –

93

we believe Laxmi will reward us by doubling all our savings.'

'But I thought the festival celebrated the return of Ram and Sita . . .'

'No, no,' said Mrs Puri very firmly. 'That is for poor people only.'

Diwali saw the last great burst of the autumnal exuberance unleashed a month earlier at Dusshera. Within a month of the last Diwali rocket vanishing into the Delhi skies, the city seemed to curl its tail between its legs and disappear into a state of semi-hibernation for the duration of the cold season.

The brief but bitter Delhi winter came as suddenly as an undertaker: dark-clad, soft-footed, unannounced and unwelcomed. There is no snow in Delhi – the winters are too dry – but white winds from the snow peaks still sweep down the slopes, freezing the plains of the Punjab and shattering the brittle buds, before raking through the streets of the capital and brushing the narrow Delhi alleyways clear of people. The Delhi-wallahs withdraw into themselves. They lift up their knees to their chins and pull their heavy Kashmiri blankets tightly around. Over their heads they wind thick woollen mufflers. If you look into the dark of the road-side restaurant-shacks you see only the whites of their eyes peering out into the cold.

The sky is grey, the air is grey, and the dull, cold greyness seeps into the ground, the stones and the buildings. The only colours are the red and yellow silk flags flying over the new Muslim graves in Nizamuddin. The trees in the gardens stand shrouded in a thin wrap of mist. In Old Delhi, the goats fattening for slaughter huddle together under sackcloth coats; some are given old cardigans to wear, with their front legs fitted through the sleeves. Winter smoke winds slowly out of the chimneys; bonfires crackle outside the *jhuggi* clusters. As you look through the window panes you can see winter lying curled like a cobra across the land.

Olivia now spent her mornings in the warmth of our flat; it was too cold and misty to paint until the sun had reached its zenith at midday. If she ventured out she would return early, before a sudden dusk brought to a close the brief winter afternoon. Brisk evenings were followed by cold nights. We muffled ourselves in our new shawls – we had not considered packing jerseys or overcoats when we set off to India – and sat warming ourselves in front of the heaters. My reading was mostly historical. I had become fascinated with that period of Delhi's history known as the Twilight. It was an epoch whose dark melancholy perfectly reflected the cold, misty scenes outside our own windows.

The Twilight is bounded by two of the greatest disasters in Delhi's history: the Persian massacres of 1739 and the equally vicious hangings and killings which followed the British recapture of Delhi after the 1857 Indian Mutiny.

The first massacre took place in the wake of an unexpected invasion of India by the Persian ruler, Nadir Shah. At Karnal in the Punjab the newly-crowned Shah defeated the Mughal army and advanced rapidly on Delhi. He encamped at the Shalimar Gardens, five miles north of the city. Having been invited into Delhi by the nervous populace, Nadir Shah ordered the massacre after a group of Delhi-wallahs attacked and killed 900 of his soldiers in a bazaar brawl. At the end of a single day's slaughter 150,000 of the city's citizens lay dead.

Nadir Shah's massacre exacerbated the decline of the Mughal Empire which had been steadily contracting since the death of Aurangzeb, the last Great Mogul, in 1707. By the end of the eighteenth century Delhi, shorn of the empire which gave it life, had sunk into a state of impotent dotage. The aristocracy tried to maintain the life-style and civilization of the empire, but in a ruined and impoverished city raped and violated by a succession of invaders. The destruction created a mood conducive to elegy, and the great Urdu writers made the most of the opportunity. 'There is no house from where the jackal's cry cannot be heard,' wrote Sauda. 'The mosques at evening are unlit and deserted. In the once beautiful gardens, the grass grows waist-high around fallen pillars and the ruined arches. Not even a lamp of clay now burns where once the chandeliers blazed with light . . .'

On the throne in the Hall of Audience in the Qila-i-Mualla, the

Exalted Fort, sat the Emperor Shah Alam. He was a brave, cultured and intelligent old man, still tall and commanding, his dark complexion offset by a short white beard. He spoke four languages and maintained a harem of five hundred women; but for all this, he was sightless – years before, his eyes had been gouged out by Ghulam Qadir, an Afghan marauder whom he had once kept as his catamite. Like some symbol of the city over which he presided, Shah Alam was a blind emperor ruling from a ruined palace.

At his court, the elaborate etiquette of Mughal society was scrupulously maintained; poetry, music and the arts flourished. But beneath the surface lustre, all was rotten. Servants prised precious stones from the *pietra dura* inlay on the walls to sell in Chandni Chowk. The old court costumes were threadbare; the plaster was peeling. Mountains of rubbish accumulated in the city streets and amid the delicate pavilions of the Exalted Palace.

Unable to see the decay around him, Shah Alam still could not escape its stench.

With Iris Portal and the Haxby sisters I had heard the testimonies of the last British in Delhi. Now, in the cold of early December I visited the chilly Delhi libraries searching for the accounts of the first English to penetrate the city's walls in the late eighteenth century.

The most detailed of the early descriptions was that written by Lieutenant William Franklin. Franklin had been sent to Delhi by the directors of the East India Company to survey the then unknown heartlands of the empire of the Great Mogul. Franklin's account of his discoveries, published in Calcutta in the 1795 *Asiatick Researches* (the journal of the newly founded Royal Asiatic Society) painted a melancholy picture of the once-great capital.

Franklin had approached the city on horseback from the northwest. His first glimpse was of a landscape littered with crumbling ruins: 'The environs are crowded with the remains of spacious gardens and the country-houses of the nobility,' he wrote in his report. 'The prospect towards Delhi, as far as the eye can reach, is covered with the remains of gardens, pavilions, mosques and burying places. The environs of this once magnificent and celebrated

96

city appear now nothing more than a shapeless heap of ruins . . .' Inside the city walls, the decay was equally apparent. Shacks had been erected in the middle of the grandest streets of Delhi 'so that it is only with difficulty [that] a person can discover their former situation'. The bazaars were 'indifferently furnished' and their commerce 'very trifling'.

Most dramatic of all were the crumbling remains of the vast palaces of the *omrahs* (great nobles) of the empire. Though now in ruins and often occupied by squatters, it was still possible to see their extraordinary size and grandeur; that of Qamar-al-Din Khan 'occupied the whole length of one side of a considerable street'. Franklin was impressed:

> All these palaces are surrounded with high walls and take up a considerable space of ground. Their entrances are through lofty arched gateways, at the top of which are the galleries for music; before each is a spacious court for the elephants, horses and attendants . . . All of the palaces [once] had gardens with stone reservoirs and fountains in the centre . . . Each palace was likewise provided with a handsome set of baths and a *teh khana* [a set of domed marble cool-rooms] underground . . .

Other travellers were equally amazed by the size of these palaces. Another Englishman, James Forbes, arrived in Shahjehanabad a few months later to find that the Emperor had arranged for him to be quartered in the crumbling palace of Safdar Jung, once the most magnificent private palace in the city. Having explored the enormous edifice in which he and his companions had spent their first night, Forbes suddenly realized that their lodgings represented only a fraction of the whole palace.

'In the evening, on taking a more complete view of this Mogul mansion, [we] were surprised to find the apartments just mentioned formed only a very small part of this immense pile, which occupied six squares corresponding with that in which we immediately resided. Its magnitude,' he concluded, 'exceeded [that of] any of the palaces belonging to the nobility in Europe.'

There was stabling and accommodation for five thousand mounted troops; beyond stretched extensive gardens and large bathing tanks paved with white marble. All the ceilings were constructed from carved wood and were magnificently painted, giving the whole a 'peculiar light and airy appearance'. The harem apartments were lined with looking-glass, while in the marble expanse of the *teh khana*, three fountains were set within arches to 'cool the atmosphere when the ladies were there assembled, such places being generally appropriated to the pleasures of the voluptuous Mogul and his favourites in the harem.'

Franklin published his account of the Mughal capital in 1795. Eight years later, following a British victory at the Battle of Delhi, a permanent British Resident was installed within the ruins of another palace, a little to the north of the Red Fort. Just as Delhi was no longer the focal point of India – like the rest of India, it now looked nervously over its shoulder to British Calcutta – so within the city the focus shifted from the Red Fort to the British Residency. As the first half of the nineteenth century progressed and the power and arrogance of the British grew, so the Resident came to act less and less like ambassador to the Great Mogul, and more and more like the Mogul's paymaster and overlord.

Nevertheless the Emperor continued to hold court as he had always done, and at first the charade of Mughal power was maintained with the express approval of the British residents. These early residents were a series of sympathetic and slightly eccentric Scotsmen, whose love and respect for India was reflected by their adoption of Indian modes of dress and Indian ways of living.

The first, Sir David Ochterlony, set the tone. With his fondness for hookahs and nautch girls and Indian costumes, Ochterlony was decidedly different from the normal run of starch-shirted, stiff-lipped *burra sahibs*. Although known to the common peoples as 'Loony Akhtar' (or Crazy Star), when in the capital he liked to be addressed by his proper Mughal title, Nasir-ud-Daula (Defender of the State), and to live the life of a Mughal gentleman. Every evening all thirteen of his Indian wives used to process around Delhi behind their husband, each on the back of her own elephant.

Yet perhaps the most fascinating of all the British in Delhi was not Ochterlony but another Scot, William Fraser, a young Persian scholar from Inverness. In 1805, Fraser was sent up to Delhi from Calcutta where he had just won a gold medal at the Company's

Fort William College. He was to be the Resident's Assistant; it was his first job.

Within a few years, Fraser had changed beyond all recognition from the callow youth who left Calcutta on a steam boat heading nervously upstream along the jungly banks of the Ganges. Given responsibility for subjugating the unruly brigand-country around Delhi – living continually on the move and under canvas, isolated from his compatriots, commanding his own private force of Indian auxiliaries – Fraser gradually turned into a great bear of a man. Like Mr Kurtz in Conrad's *Heart of Darkness*, he saw himself as a European potentate ruling in a pagan wilderness; like Kurtz, he would brook no challenge to his authority. Like Kurtz, many considered him insane.

He pruned his moustaches in the Rajput manner and fathered 'as many children as the King of Persia' from his harem of Indian wives. His favourite relaxation was hunting the Asian lion, often on foot with a spear. He had 'a perfect monomania for fighting' and would always throw up his usual duties as an East India Company servant whenever a war broke out in the subcontinent. While he slept, his bodyguard of Indian tribals would unroll their mattresses and sleep around his couch.

Fraser's enemies, like the Resident Charles Metcalfe, had serious reservations about him. 'He is masterly and self-willed to so great a degree that no power can be entrusted to him without some risk of it being abused,' Metcalfe wrote in a confidential report to the Governor General in Calcutta. Yet Fraser was no brute. A more brilliant scholar than Metcalfe, he was a metaphysician and a philosopher. He loved to discuss ancient Sanskrit texts and he composed Persian couplets as a form of relaxation. He was the first European to take a serious interest in the ruins of Delhi. He befriended and helped Ghalib, the greatest of all Urdu poets; along with his brother James he commissioned the Fraser Album, the finest collection of Company paintings ever executed.

Fraser remains a strange and enigmatic figure – misanthropic, antisocial and difficult to fathom – part severe Highland warrior, part Brahminized philosopher, part Conradian madman. He was also, as chance would have it, a forebear and kinsman of my wife, Olivia. Moreover, Moniack House, his remote Highland home, was still in the hands of her Fraser cousins; and every year for a fortnight, Olivia's family hired it from them for their summer holidays.

The house was like a memory of childhood, or a dream. There were long, dimly lit passages ending in locked doors. On the walls hung dark family portraits and old, early nineteenth-century prints of the Himalayas. Outside, the long, formal Georgian façade was framed by shallow pilasters and overhung with virginia creeper. Inside it was dark, with the grey Scottish light filtering in through the weathered skylights or partially obscured windows. In the evenings, when the temperature dropped, everyone gathered around the blazing log fire in the kitchen.

It was the end of August, the best season: that high, clear, sharp early Highland autumn which suddenly sweeps in while the rest of the country is still enjoying late summer. The harvest is collected; the fields are empty. The landscape appears deserted: there are no people and no sounds, but for the occasional cackle of a cock-pheasant breaking cover in the woods.

In the month before we first went out to Delhi, Olivia and I spent ten days relaxing at Moniack. As we were preparing to leave the house for Inverness station, I went to say goodbye to our landlord, Malcolm Fraser. I found him practising his reels in the basement. I thanked him, and happened to mention that I was soon planning to visit Register House in Edinburgh to see if any of William Fraser's Indian letters had survived there.

'There are some letters,' he said. 'But you won't find them in Edinburgh.'

'Why not?' I asked.

'Because,' said Malcolm, 'they're all upstairs in the library.'

Leaving Malcolm to his piano, I ran straight upstairs. The library lay at the top of the house, immediately beside the room where I had been sleeping. I had passed it several times every day, but the door was always locked and I had never thought to look inside. Now a quick search revealed the key to be hidden in the dust above the doorframe. The wards creaked, and at a slight press the door swung open.

Inside it was pitch dark. The windows were shuttered. It seemed as if the thick, musty smell of buckram and old leather had hung undisturbed in the library air for centuries. When my eyes had begun to adjust to the light, I saw that the walls were covered with mahogany cabinets full of old leather-bound books; the remaining space was filled with woodcuts of eighteenth-century Highland lairds, including one without a head which was labelled *Lord Lovat's Ghost*. Around the room, among piles of lumber, stood a great mountain of shoe boxes. I walked in and lifted the lid of the topmost box.

There were piles of letters, bound up in separate groups of ten or fifteen. The epistles were written on thick parchment in a wild early nineteenth-century scrawl. The writer had used his old quill pen the way a conductor uses his baton. There were frequent underlinings and a jungle of exclamation marks. The elaborate downstroke curlicues kept getting caught in mid-flourish and scratching the parchment. Taking a letter directly under the lamp and looking more closely, I was just able to decipher the erratic copperplate:

> Dehlee 20 March 1806.
> My dear father and mother,
> Yesterday the memory of the gallant and victorious Nelson was drunk with enthusiasm in the capital of Hindustan . . .

The other boxes and the chests revealed the complete correspondence of Fraser and his four brothers: several volumes of diaries and more than a thousand letters, all written from in or around Delhi. Alongside the Fraser letters lay a whole archive of other material about Twilight Delhi: letters from the various British Residents and other Delhi characters such as Colonel James Skinner, the founder of the legendary Skinner's Horse. There was also a series of notes from some of the great travellers of the period: Victor Jacquemont, the pioneering French botanist, and William Moorcroft, the self-appointed British spy who penetrated Central Asia to play some of the opening moves in the Great Game.

The entire archive had been rediscovered by Malcolm a few years earlier languishing in the Moniack cellar; it lay inside a trunk marked, in large letters:

THE PAPERS IN THIS BOX
ARE TO BE STORED AS CAREFULLY AS POSSIBLE.
THEY ARE OF GREAT INTEREST.

Beneath the letters lay the book subsequently known as the Fraser Album. The album contained a series of superb Company paintings – vignettes of early nineteenth-century Delhi life, and portraits of the Frasers' staff, soldiers and friends. The pictures were drawn by Delhi artists to commissions from William and his elder brother James. Malcolm Fraser later sold most of these paintings at Sotheby's, and after their importance had become clear, the art historians Toby Falk and Mildred Archer had worked through much of the Moniack archive looking for material relating to the pictures. But as a historical source for Twilight Delhi the Moniack letters were still virgin material. I had spent three summer holidays in the house, yet it was only by an accident that I found the treasure trove that had been sitting all the time less than ten yards from my bedroom.

That same afternoon I postponed my flight to India and got Malcolm's permission to trawl methodically through his great-great-great-uncle's letters. I spent the following fortnight cloistered in the Moniack library, holding in my hands letters written in the British Residency in Shahjehanabad at a time when Delhi was the Empire's North-West Frontier – a remote and dangerous outpost, flying the only Union Jack between Bengal and the British Embassy in Moscow. The letters were all addressed to William's father, Edward Satchwell Fraser. As I read, I pictured him sitting down to read them at the same old desk in the same dark Moniack library where I was sitting, 183 years later.

In the late eighteenth century, Northern Scotland was still suffering from the pillage of the Highlands that followed the defeat of Bonny Prince Charlie at Culloden in 1745. Moniack lay only a few miles away from the site of the battle, and the Frasers had fought in it on the losing side. Their lands lay on poor and marshy ground (Moniack actually means 'little bog' in Gaelic). There was no prospect for industry in the area. Like many Scots landowners the Frasers found that if they were to pay off their debts and maintain themselves in their cold, echoing houses there was no alternative but to send the younger sons out to make their fortunes in the colonies.

William Fraser's grandfather, James Fraser, had worked in India as a young man and on his return had sat in the Moniack library writing the first history in English of the Persian marauder, Nadir Shah. Forty years later, as the debts at Moniack mounted, Edward Satchwell Fraser was forced to revive his father's Indian connections. One by one William and his four brothers all received postings in the subcontinent; one by one they caught a ship to Edinburgh, where they had their portraits painted by Raeburn, before continuing their journey on to London and the waiting ship in East India Dock. Of the five who left for the subcontinent, only one ever made it back to Moniack.

After leaving Calcutta in June 1805, William's steamer up the Ganges finally terminated at Allahabad, a last British outpost. The remaining stretch of the journey to Delhi was overland through some 400 miles of the most anarchic country in India. 'On the road I passed several parties of armed men whom I knew to be plunderers,' William later wrote to his father. 'I always passed any who I met at a very quick pace . . . They generally keep about 100 yards [away] and fire with their matchlocks and are so expert that your only chance is in moving about to avoid their fire or riding straight upon them with your pistol. I talk of them when mounted; footmen robbers never show themselves but fire from some ambush.'

Nights were worse. The servants were kept constantly on the alert until dawn for fear of losing both horses and baggage to footpads and thugs. It was a ragged and exhausted party which, several weeks later, entered the Turkman Gate of Shahjehanabad and headed for the Residency. William rode into the compound, mounted the steps, and breakfasted with Ochterlony, 'six months and a day since I left Calcutta'.

Delhi cannot have been very different from the grand but

103

crumbling slum described by Forbes and Franklin; yet for all its decay the city soon cast its spell on William. Its remoteness must have been perfectly familiar to anyone brought up in eighteenth-century Inverness, while its literary and historical associations must have appealed to the prize-winning Orientalist. 'My situation is as desirable as any one I could hold,' William wrote in his first letter home, 'nor should I care if I lived here during the whole period of my sojournment in India.'

It was a prophetic letter. In the course of a career lasting thirty years, William refused all appointments which would take him away from the city. Like many other Britons after him, William had become completely hypnotized by the great capital.

His early letters gave detailed descriptions of the court of Shah Alam and the palaces of the preceding dynasties which lay scattered among the ruins to the south of the city. William's duties – attending the Mughal court, hearing petitions at the Residency, establishing the Delhi criminal courts – seem to have been flexible enough to allow him to pursue his growing interest in Delhi's history.

'The business of my situation generally takes up five hours [a day],' he explained to his parents. '[Afterwards] I read and study with pleasure the [local] languages. They are the chief source of my amusement, [although] Delhi affords much [other] food besides. Learned natives there are a few, and [they] in poverty, but those I have met with are real treasures. I am also making a collection of good oriental manuscripts.'

The miniatures William gathered in Delhi are probably the group now known as the Emperor's (or Kevorkian) Album which today forms the core of the oriental manuscript collection of the Metropolitan Museum in New York. The bound book which contained these miniatures was discovered in a Scottish antique shop in 1929 by Jack Rolfe, an American tourist. He bought the book for less than £100 and resold it in Sotheby's a few months later for £10,500. The album is now recognized as one of the finest collections of Imperial Mughal manuscripts in existence and today each leaf from its folios would be worth at least a six-figure sum.

Whether or not the Emperor's Album is his collection, William's artistic interests went far beyond the stockpiling of manuscripts.

'I wish to ascertain historically,' he wrote, 'the account of every remarkable place or monument of antiquity, or building erected in commemoration of singular acts of whatever nature. The traditional accounts I receive from natives are generally absurd or contradictory. I must first know how they obtained credence, and then search for the origins of the story . . .'

In later years, few would deny that Fraser knew the people and country in and around Delhi better than any other Briton. According to the French botanist Victor Jacquemont, 'his mode of life has made him more familiar, perhaps than any other European, with the customs and ideas of the native inhabitants. He has, I think, a real and profound understanding of their inner life.' Even Fraser's enemy, the resident Charles Metcalfe, admitted that William had no 'difficulty dealing with the highest order of natives, with some of [whom] he has been more intimate than most Europeans.'

Yet it was less his intellectual and linguistic gifts than his devil-may-care bravery which moulded William's career. A few years after his arrival, Fraser was forced to abandon his sedentary pursuits in the city in favour of a nomadic life-style around its periphery. Since Mughal authority had collapsed, the hinterland of the capital had become the refuge of robbers and brigands who occupied the crumbling tombs to the south and the decaying Mughal gardens to the north. They made the city unsafe after dark and travel outside the walls impossible, even in broad daylight, without a large armed escort. Fraser had suffered from the brigands on his ride from Allahabad; now he was given the job of flushing them out from their nests and replacing their terror with his own.

William raised and trained a force of irregular cavalry. There are several pictures of his men in the Fraser Album. They are shown both as recruits fresh from the villages with their naked torsos and homespun dhotis and later as fully equipped cavalrymen in Fraser's service. He dressed them not in contemporary Company red coats, but in a theatrical uniform of old-fashioned Napoleonic inspiration, with gleaming cavalry boots, brocaded doublets, and cummerbunds striped gold and scarlet; the uniform was topped with a tall brown busby. Strapped across the chest of each man is a silver plate bearing a hart's head, the Fraser crest.

Fraser's force often faced serious opposition – squadrons of

Mahratta cavalry were still at large in the Delhi plains – and soon William's letters home had begun to assume a tone of chilling nonchalance. 'I never saw a Mahratta yet whom I would dread to meet single handed,' he wrote in June 1806:

The other day I had an opportunity of seeing how they would fight. Two or three rebellious villages within the district of Dehli we were obliged to cut up, and besides storming the villages, we had to disperse parties [of Mahratta cavalry] who came to their assistance. They advance gradually, firing their matchlocks till within one hundred yards, when they sling them over their shoulder with a belt and take to the sword and spear. If you have a pistol the matter is easily settled, and you shoot them just when within the length of their spears.

Although such skirmishing earned him 'two fine sabre cuts on the arms, a wound in the back from a pike, and an arrow in the neck which almost killed him' such warfare seems to have greatly excited William. According to his friend Jacquemont, 'to him the most keenly pleasurable emotion is that aroused by danger: such is the explanation of what people call his madness.' Certainly his letters of 1806–7 are full of remarks about his well-being and contentment: 'My health is robust and uninterruptedly good, which I owe to constant exercise and stout temperance. I seldom have but one meal in the day and never exceed two glasses of Madeira. For occasional recreation I keep horses & hawks and borrow an elephant when I wish to shoot.'

Fraser had taken on the customs and dress of the Indians from the very beginning of his residence in the subcontinent. An early picture shows him sitting in a long Indian robe, a sash around his waist, while on his head he sports a curious Scottish tam o'shanter. One of his first notes home thanks his parents for a letter, using a turn of phrase that could rarely have been heard before on the Beauly Firth – 'to use a Persian hyperbole,' he wrote, 'was [your letter] divided into a thousand parts, my double tongued pen could not obey my heart in expressing and writing one of them.' But now, isolated in the wilds of Haryana, controlling an area the size

106

of Wales with only his Mewatti bodyguards for company, Fraser began to 'go native' with a vengeance.

In eighteenth-century India such behaviour was the norm among the more intelligent and open-minded of the Company's servants. But by 1810, the days of the Brahminized Englishmen had long passed and in the more severe and self-righteous atmosphere of nineteenth-century Calcutta such eccentricities had become far from fashionable. When Lady Nugent, the wife of the British Commander-in-Chief, visited Delhi, she was genuinely shocked to discover that Fraser had given up eating pork and beef and had grown a thick Rajput beard. She thought Fraser was as much 'Hindoo as Christian' and felt it necessary to remind him sharply 'of the religion [he] was brought up to'.

Rumours about William's strange ways soon reached Bengal, where his younger brother Aleck was studying at Fort William College. 'I have heard several funny stories of William's whimsical disposition,' Aleck wrote home towards the end of 1808. 'In the district of Mewat [immediately west of Delhi], which he was stationed in, to civilize it, he built a fort and called it "Fraser Ghur" in which he maintained 1000 seypoys of his own raising and disciplining. There he lived like a Nawab, being [as] absolute in his domain as Bonaparte in France. [It is said that] long residence so distant from the principal European stations has made William half a Hindoostanee.'

Later, when Aleck was sent to join his brother in Delhi, he found William unrecognizable: 'His countenance is certainly materially altered. He is [now] iron in constitution and bodily force . . . his chest is wonderfully broad and round, his limbs full and well-turned . . .' Nor was the change merely physical. At the time, Aleck's letters home were full of cheerful remarks about how well he and his brother were getting on. There are only occasional hints that William had become 'proud, fiery and impetuous' and 'too fond of exposing himself to danger'. Only much later, in the private confession that Aleck wrote as he was dying, did he tell the truth. William, he wrote, had become wild, manic and obsessive, a different man to the brother he had known in Scotland: 'He would not either talk, or shoot or read with me . . . this hurt my pride so much that a considerable coldness took place between us.'

107

Elsewhere in his letters Aleck complains of William's 'excessive rashness': 'frequently he has ridden, unarmed saving a sword, into crowds of desperadoes whose only chance was to fight to the last – and this although he had plenty of soldiers with him,' and also of his 'too great attachment to, and trust in, the natives of this country; and a fondness for their customs'.

Perceptions of India had changed dramatically in the few years that separated William's and Aleck's respective training in Calcutta, and on his arrival in Delhi, Aleck brought with him the new set of more imperious racial prejudices. From his point of view, William and his friend, Charles Seton, were both 'romantically fond of pleasing the natives' and he was 'offended by the concessions in respect, and almost servility' that he was expected to pay to the Mughal princes. No less odd, to Aleck's eyes, was the strange retinue with which his brother went about. It was very different from anything that had ever been seen in Inverness – and yet there were some lingering similarities. 'He is surrounded by Goojurs,' wrote Aleck,

> formerly Barbarians, now like [Scottish] Highlanders; independent to equals, fiery and impetuous, but faithful and obedient . . . When Willie civilized the wild inhabitants of the region [around] Dehlie, he took hostages from the chief inhabitants of the most turbulent districts as security for the good conduct of the rest.
>
> The most ferocious have become the most faithful. These men – formerly robbers and perhaps murderers, certainly the relations of such – now sleep by our couches and would at any time risk their lives for us.

Aleck went on to list William's staff. Apart from the Mewatti bodyguards, there was a set of Muslim table servants, ten palanquin bearers (who also cleaned William's shoes), four tent-men, a dog keeper, three water carriers, an elephant driver and his assistants, the cook and his staff, two washermen, two tailors, two errand boys and a barber; in addition there was a groom and a grass cutter attached to each of William's five horses and seven camels. The total must have added up to about seventy household servants.

William's irregular cavalry may have numbered ten or twenty times this many again.

One thing neither Aleck nor William wrote home about was the latter's harem. According to Jacquemont, Fraser had 'six or seven legitimate wives' who all lived together 'some 50 leagues from Delhi and do as they like'. His children were without number but were all 'Hindus and Muslims according to the religion and caste of their mamas and are shepherds, peasants, mountaineers etc, according to the occupation of their mother's families.'

A picture of William's chief wife survives in the Fraser Album. It shows a tall and exquisite Indian woman, dressed in a slight close-fitting bodice and a long pleated Rajasthani skirt. Her torso is swathed in a *jamevar* shawl, her hair is worn loose, and her arms are steeled with torcs and tribal bracelets. Her slippers have up-curled toes. Beside her stands a single boy, aged perhaps six years old. Although he is dressed in Mughal court pyjamas, there is a distinctly European look to his features. The inscription, in Persian, reads simply: 'Amiban, a Jat woman of Rania, the chosen one of Fraser Sahib, whose delicate beauty was beyond compare . . .'

While William Fraser was touring the area around Delhi, the British Residency in Shahjehanabad was his base and headquarters. Here, on his return from his expeditions he would dine with the Resident, catch up on the political news and watch performances by Delhi's celebrated dancing girls. The building, I had been told, still survived in Old Delhi as a warehouse for the Archaeological Survey of India. One day in early December, as a foggy winter morning turned into an unexpectedly bright afternoon, Olivia and I decided to go out and see for ourselves what was left of the building.

The Residency stands today in one of the most depressing and impoverished parts of Old Delhi. Even sixty years ago, Lothian Road had been a smart shopping area, but the flight of the middle class to Lutyens's New Delhi had left the area to the cycle rickshaw men and the beggars. Now, while we wandered around trying to establish the whereabouts of the Residency, we passed on the pavement the sad detritus of Delhi's development: huddled couples

crouching on sackcloth beneath the railway arches; rag-pickers bringing in their bulging hessian bags of rubbish for weighing; long lines of donkey-jacketed cobblers and filthy roadside shoe-blacks.

Amid the squalor, the old ochre-coloured mansion was immediately recognizable. It lay behind a high wall, surrounded by a wind-break of ancient neem and ashok trees. Its front was formed by a flat colonnade of Ionic pillars which supported a partly-collapsed architrave. Wickerwork slats were fitted between the pillars, and a small flight of steps led up, through a shady veranda, to the front door.

Although the mansion has survived virtually in its entirety, it has fallen on hard times. Rubbish and dirt spilled into the Residency compound from the fly-blown streets outside. Scaffolding propped up one side of the main façade. The space in front of the mansion – the place where Fraser's troops would have paraded, where the Resident's carriage would have jolted to a halt after audiences in the Red Fort – was left neglected by the civil servants who now occupied the building.

At the rear of the mansion, where once the Residency gardens sloped down to a terrace overlooking the Jumna waterfront, a new concrete block, an engineering college, had been erected. Discarded stoves, an old lawnmower and piles of kitchen rubbish lay scattered around the old orchards. Monkeys scampered about the debris. Saddened by the decay and neglect, we began to turn away from the building when, out of the corner of my eye, I spotted something which made me stop. At the back of the Residency, the plaster-covered British masonry rested on a plinth not of brick, as elsewhere in the building, but of mottled pink Agra sandstone. The stonework was broken by a line of cusped Mughal blind-arches. The work was unmistakably from the period of Shah Jehan.

Although the building was locked and deserted, it was still possible to peer in through the old Residency windows. What lay within confirmed the hint given by the plinth. Behind the classical façade lay the earlier frontage of a Mughal pavilion: a double row of blind arches leading up to a central portal. The entire building was erected on the foundations of a much earlier mansion. It all made sense: when the Emperor gave the British the ruins of the library of Dara Shukoh, Shah Jehan's eldest son, they saw no need to knock down the existing work and start afresh; instead they merely erected a classical façade over a Mughal substructure. It was just like Ochterlony: in public establishing the British presence; but inside, in private, living the life of a Nawab.

I remembered the famous miniature of Ochterlony hosting an evening's entertainment at the Residency. He is dressed in full Indian costume, and reclines on a carpet, leaning back against a spread of pillows and bolsters. To one side stands a servant with a fly-whisk; on the other stands Ochterlony's elaborate glass hubble-bubble. Above, from the picture rail, the Resident's Scottish ancestors – kilted and plumed colonels from Highland regiments, grimacing ladies in stiff white taffeta dresses – peer down disapprovingly at the group of nautch girls swirling immodestly below them. Ochterlony, however, looks delighted. The picture summed up the period, to my mind perhaps the most attractive interlude in the whole long story of the British in India. There is a quality of the naughty schoolboy about Ochterlony and his contemporaries in Delhi: away from the disapproving gaze of the Calcutta memsahibs they gather their harems and smoke their hookahs; there is none of the depressing arrogance or self-righteousness that infects the tone of so much of Raj history.

In the background of the Ochterlony miniature you can see a double doorway topped by a half-moon fan window; outside, the branches of a large tree announce the Residency gardens. The doorway, the window and the tree remain, but inside, everything has changed. Dusty filing cabinets stand where the nautch girls once danced. Doors hang loose on their hinges. Everywhere paint and plaster is peeling. So total is the transformation that it is difficult now, even with the aid of the miniature, to people the empty corridors with the bustling Company servants, glittering Mughal *omrahs* (noblemen) and celebrated courtesans. To aid the imagination, I got out my copies of the Fraser letters and diaries that I had brought with me.

By the time William's elder brother James came to Delhi in 1815, the Residency had come to form the centre of the city's society.

James was particularly intrigued by the endless round of nautches that the Resident hosted, and he frequently wrote about them in his diary: '[The nautch girls] were very fair – and their dresses very rich. Some sang extremely well . . . This morning,' he adds, '[I] am lying late from the effects of the nautch . . .'

Occasionally guests would bring their own musicians to dinner with them. The most accomplished band in Delhi belonged to the Begum Sumroe, a Kashmiri dancing girl who converted to Christianity, married two European mercenary-adventurers in succession and inherited from one of them a small principality at Sardhana near Meerut, to the north of Delhi.

'The Begum today dined at the residency,' wrote James in his diary on 24 August, 'and we had her band to play to us – this consisting of four or five singing men who play on different instruments – the sitar, the tambour – and sing well. They sang God save The King, taught them by an English officer, and the Marseillaise hymn [taught] by a French officer. The words were kept so well that I could hardly have known that they were foreigners had I kept from looking at them. They also sang many fine Persian and Hindoostanee airs.'

There were other diversions too. There was a table for 'billyards', and at one stage the Residency dining-room was enlivened by the presence of a pair of Asian lion cubs. Soon after their arrival, Aleck wrote home about them in a state of great excitement: 'These animals have only been known to us since our conquest of Hurriana in 1809 . . . [The cubs are] as large as a common spaniel, and yet quite tame. They played about Seton's dining room with perfect good humour, and were not surly unless much teazed.'

As the British tightened their grip on North India, the Residency staff grew quickly to keep pace with the work. Moreover, numbers at Residency entertainments could increasingly be supplemented by the small but curious European community which had settled in the Civil Lines, the European suburb which was beginning to take shape immediately north of Shahjehanabad.

This community consisted of men like Dr Ross ('short and corpulent and very ugly . . . a shocking bad doctor'), whose three standard prescriptions were leeches, senna packed in dirty 'black beer bottles and huge pills sent in a rough wooden box'; or Dr Sprengler, the Principal of the new Delhi College, whose wife ('worthy but common') used to hide her husband's trousers to prevent him going out in the evening and leaving her alone. Most of the new residents, however, were Scots. 'Would you suppose it?' wrote Aleck at this time. 'We usually sit down 16 or 18 at the Residency table, of whom near a half, sometimes more, are always Scotsmen – about a quarter Irish, the rest English. The Irish do not always maintain their proportion – the Scotch seldom fail.'

Increasingly, however, William was not among the diners. Not only did he prefer to be on the move with his troops in the wilds of Haryana or fighting the Gurkhas in the hills above Gangotri, he also found Metcalfe and the bores of the European community intolerable. When in Delhi, he was happy to mix freely with his friends from the Mughal aristocracy, but the likes of Dr Sprengler's wife were not for him.

'He is a thinker,' wrote Jacquemont in his memoir, 'who finds nothing but solitude in that exchange of words without ideas which is dignified by the name of conversation in the society of this land.'

I met Norah Nicholson in 1984, the first time I lived in Delhi.

Norah was an old lady with white hair and narrow wrists and she lived in an old shack. On my way to and from the Mother Teresa Home I would sometimes look in and have a cup of tea with her. Even then I remember thinking she was like a survivor from a different age. But it was only later that I was able to place her definitively in my mind as a sort of living fossil of the Twilight, a Civil Lines eccentric who really should have shared a bungalow with Dr Ross or Mrs Sprengler, rather than spend her old age in a tatty shack behind the Old Secretariat.

'But you see there was nothing I could do,' she would say. 'They cut off my pension and I found I couldn't afford to rent even quite basic chambers. So I ended up here, with my books, furniture, two packing cases and a grand piano – all under this tree.'

Not, of course, that she ever complained. 'It would be a perfectly nice place to live,' she would insist, 'if it weren't for the cobra. He's taken to having his afternoon snooze under my bed. Every day I spray his hole with Flit [insecticide] but it never seems to bother him. Then there are those damned pigs which come and nose around my larder. They belong to the Anglo-Indians over the road.' There was an enormous crash behind us.

'And it would be nice if the roof was a bit stronger. Then the peacocks wouldn't keep falling through. I don't mind during the day, but I hate waking up at night to find a peacock in bed with me.'

It was always slightly difficult to establish the truth about Norah Nicholson. She claimed to be a great-niece of Brigadier General John Nicholson, 'the Lion of the Punjab', who was killed in the storming of Delhi in 1857 but who was still worshipped long afterwards as a hero by the British and as a god by a Punjabi sect called the Nikalsini.

Although the British High Commission quietly insisted that she was an Anglo-Indian and so ineligible for automatic British citizenship, Norah would have none of it. She maintained that she was a full-blooded Englishwoman, was once a great friend of Lady Mountbatten, and that she had briefly been the nanny of Rajiv and Sanjay Gandhi. What was absolutely certain was that she had never been to Britain, had no living relations there, and that in her old age she had fallen on hard times in a quite spectacular manner.

In 1960 some bureaucratic tangle had led to her being thrown out of her government lodgings and, as she would proudly tell you, she had refused to pull any strings to save herself.

'I am an Englishwoman with a little pride,' she would say. 'I'm not one of these people to take advantage and I never like to force myself on anyone.'

She would gather herself up, and with a slight nod of her head give you one of her knowing looks: 'Nevertheless all my friends did help. They clubbed together and bought me some tin sheets, while *dear* Sir Robert, the High Commissioner, contributed some plywood. *Darling* Indira [Gandhi] gave me a new tarpaulin. I had such a lovely time putting it all together.'

Norah was very independent, and hated above all to be patronized. If ever you sounded over-concerned about her in the cold or during a monsoon, she would quickly bring you up short.

'Young man, I'll have you know that actually I have a very nice

115

life here. It may get a little bit wet during the rains, but normally it's lovely to live out with my Creator and his creatures.' She would point to the menagerie around her: 'I have four dogs to look after me and a fluctuating number of cats. I think there are twelve at the moment. Then I've got my peahens, partridges and babbler-birds . . .'

Only if you pressed her about the future would she eventually admit to some anxieties.

'My only fear is that they will throw me off my little plot. I've been here twenty-four years and have applied for the land, but they ignore me because I refuse to give them a bribe. The boy wants my camera, but I'm damned if I'm going to pander to their corruption. There is no law and order and still less justice since the British left.'

'Have they ever tried to evict you?'

'They have a go every so often. In 1968 they came around and I set the dogs on them. Then the following year they tried to make me pay dog tax. They didn't know that I spoke Hindustani and this fellow – thought he was being so clever – said to his friend: "If she doesn't pay tomorrow we'll come along and shoot the dogs."

'I waited until they had finished and then said, in Hindustani: "If you try to shoot my dogs, you'll have to shoot me first and before you do that I'll have your throats cut and your bodies in the Jumna . . ." That was 1969 and no one has bothered me about dog tax since.'

'So you don't have any bother with the authorities any more?'

'Well there was one incident. In 1975, during the Emergency, they were trying to clear up Delhi. All the dirty work was being done by this nasty young Indian police captain. He was beating people up and burning down their houses. Well, one day I was in the queue for milk when the young officer came up and broke the queue. I was jolly well not going to put up with this. So I told him that he should go to the back and that he had no right to queue-barge.

'All my neighbours were terrified. They said: "This man will do you in." Anyway, the next day, just as they said, he came around here. Those Anglo-Indians next door barricaded themselves into their houses and turned off the lights. But I said: "How are you?"

and gave him a cup of tea and some Patience Strong tracts. They were on Christianity and how to love people. After that he was very nice to me and came back the following month for more books. You see, William, it's all in the way you approach people . . .'

I had this conversation with Norah in June 1984. When I returned to Delhi five years later, I went straight up to her little plot of land to look for her. But there was no sign of her and her shack had been dismantled.

'Are you looking for Norah?' asked a voice from behind me.

I turned round. It was Norah's Anglo-Indian neighbour.

'Yes,' I said. 'Where is she?'

'She's dead, I'm afraid,' he replied. 'She's been dead and buried a while now. The monsoon before last.'

'What happened?' I asked.

'It was her cobra,' he said matter-of-factly. 'He finally got her. She'd given up trying to gas him out and had begun feeding him bowls of milk.'

'What?'

'We all tried to reason with her, but she wouldn't listen. She kept repeating that cobras were God's creatures too.' The man shrugged his shoulders. 'We found her the next day. My wife went over straight away because we knew something was up.'

'How?' I asked.

'It was her dogs,' said the man. 'They were howling like the end of the world had come.'

Norah was dead, but that month as I explored the area around the Residency, I found many other characters who seemed, like her, to be bits of stranded flotsam left over from the Delhi of William Fraser.

A little to the south of the Residency compound lay the old Magazine, the British arsenal blown up in the Mutiny. Beside that, tucked away off the main road, lay the original British cemetery. I had expected the graveyard to be as dirty and neglected as the Residency, but was surprised to find it spotlessly clean. It did not take long to work out why. The graveyard had become a rather smart housing estate. The marble grave slabs were kept scrubbed until they shone; the Palladian chamber tombs had been restored and rebuilt. Washing was strung up between obelisks and television aerials were attached to the higher crosses.

Many of the pavement-wallahs and *jhuggi*-dwellers in Delhi complain of police protection rackets, so I asked one of the men in the graveyard whether they had had any trouble.

'Good heavens, no,' he replied in a clipped Anglo-Indian accent. 'They can't harm us. We're all Christians here.'

'I am sorry,' I said, seeing that I had caused offence.

'It's our churchyard,' continued the man, straightening his tie. 'The Andrews family has been here for three generations. These Hindus don't like Christian monuments so we are guarding it. You will have tea?'

Tea was brought and we settled down on the grave of a British auditor-general. A plate of Indian sweets and a wedding album was brought out from beneath a slab.

'Since I retired from the railways in 1985 I've turned my hand to a little gardening,' continued Mr Andrews. 'Now we try to grow most of our own vegetables here. And that was my poultry farm.'

He pointed at the marble cot at my feet, once the tomb of a Colonel Nixon from County Tyrone. A makeshift wire mesh had been strung from the corners, but the grave was empty of all chickens.

'We've eaten all the hens,' he explained, seeing my glance. 'Now I plan to keep fishes in there.'

Mr Andrews told us about his visit to Scotland with the 1948 All-India hockey team. He liked Inverness, he said, though he thought it a little cold. Then he asked Olivia what we were doing in Old Delhi. She explained about our trip to the Residency and he tut-tutted when she mentioned about the neglect of the building.

'The trouble with these people,' he said, 'is that they have no sense of history.'

As we were talking, an amazingly chic woman stepped out of one of the larger tombs and strutted past us, swinging her leather shoulder bag.

118

'That's my niece,' said Mr Andrews proudly. 'She's an estate agent.'

We returned to our flat to find Mr Puri, wrapped up as if for the Antarctic, berating Nickoo, his unfortunate Nepali servant. The two of them were standing in the middle of the road near the house, surrounded by a crowd of curious passers-by. Nickoo, it emerged, had been taking Mr Puri on his daily constitutional when the old man had suddenly begun raving:

MR PURI (waving his stick) This man's a bloody scoundrel.

NICKOO I am good boy.

WD He's a good boy, Mr Puri.

MR PURI Nonsense! He's from the sweeper caste.

OLIVIA He's still a good boy.

MR PURI Madam. We are kshatriyas. We are warriors. We fought the British. We fought the Pathans. Now we fight the Hindus.

WD I'm sure there's no need to fight Nickoo.

MR PURI No need! This sweeper is a bloody scoundrel! Take him back to Britain with you! Let him look after your bloody mules!

WD But Mr Puri. I've told you before. I don't have any mules. Here or in England.

MR PURI Nonsense! All Britishers have mules. How else did you Britishers defeat our great Sikh armies? How else did you come to rule our India?

As December progressed, the mercury continued to sink. It was as if a grey shadow had fallen over the town.

Although the winter temperatures were much warmer than those at home in Scotland, the cold seemed every bit as severe because the Delhi houses were so ill-equipped to deal with it. Designed to fight the heat, they proved spectacularly useless at fending off the cold. They never had central heating or open fires. In our *barsati*, in the absence of radiators or a fireplace, we were forced to go out and buy a great battery of bar heaters to keep

119

ourselves warm. We kept them burning most of the day, and took it in turns to replace the fuses when, as happened with exciting frequency, Mrs Puri's antiquated electrics blew up with a fantastic blue flash.

Over at International Backside, Balvinder Singh decided it was now too cold to shave in the mornings, and began to grow back the beard he had shaved off in 1984. Punjab, his father, was delighted. But because of the cold, we now saw rather less of our friends than usual. In fact by mid-December, we began to consider it rather a triumph if ever we succeeded in summoning a taxi from International Backside, especially after sunset. In the hot season, the night shift at the stand would always lie out under the stars on their charpoys. Unable to sleep, they would appear at our door within minutes of us ringing for them. But in winter Balvinder and his brothers retreated into their taxis, under mountains of old blankets, and greatly disliked answering the telephone which lay outside, six freezing feet away in the taxi-stand tent. On the rare occasions we did manage to rouse one of the brothers that winter, we were treated to a ride in a taxi sweetly scented with sleeping Sikh.

On those winter nights, Delhi took on an eerily deserted aspect. Occasionally there would be a *chowkidar* outside some rich man's house, wrapped and muffled as if on the Retreat from Moscow. Otherwise, as the milky-white fog swirled through the avenues of the city, you would see only ghostly herds of cows patrolling the broad boulevards. Turning a corner, the coils of mist would suddenly part to reveal forty or fifty head of cattle, their eyes shining red in the taxi headlights, plodding resolutely north in a long line.

During his first winter in Delhi, Aleck Fraser was also surprised by the temperature. 'It is now the cold weather,' he wrote home on 3 January 1811. 'So cold that I am glad to be in my bed until 8 a.m. in the morning . . .' (this from a man who usually rose at five-thirty).

Aleck had moved in with his elder brother William, and was now living surrounded by William's vast household, supplemented at any moment by crowds of petitioners and favour-seekers. Aleck's letters frequently express his impatience with the number of people milling around his house: '[I am writing this letter] in a room

120

like a thoroughfare; a dozen people and half a dozen languages resounding in my ear all the time . . . Willie has not since my arrival been for one hour free from the interruptions of natives . . . From morning until night he is troubled by these tiresome visits and forced to keep up a conversation . . . the weather, personal and mutual flattery, perhaps horses and cattle make up the common subjects.'

Not only was the house packed with William's curious retinue; it was also unconventionally furnished.

'William's room was a curiosity,' wrote James Fraser when he visited the house in 1815, 'tygres skins, caps of tygres heads, saddle cloths of ditto, quantities of saddlery, matchlocks, bows and arrows, quivers, belts, armours, guncases . . . Persian books and Indian curiosities of all sorts filled up the place. I shall certainly seize hold of some of these things and convey them from India to Inverness.'

Much of the clutter did make it back to Moniack, including William's extraordinary collection of Mughal weaponry. But as I read James's description, I realized that I had no idea where the strange bungalow had stood and whether, like the Residency, anything of it had survived. Searching again through my copies of the Fraser correspondence, I eventually found the answer to the first question in a letter of Aleck's in which he quite accurately sketches the whereabouts of the house:

'It is now nine o'clock evening, and I am sitting by a fine fire in our house, on the bank of a branch of the Jumna. The main branch is within sight of the windows; and beyond it stretch the plains of the Doab. A little down the river, or rather this little branch of it, lies the grand palace of Shah Jehan, and across the stream, connected by a bridge (a very fine one) the frowning Bastille of Dehli, called Selim Gurh.'

Piecing together details from several different letters, it was possible to pinpoint pretty accurately where the house must have stood. Marking the area on a map of Old Delhi, I got Balvinder Singh to drive me slowly up along the Ring Road, which today follows the old course of the river. We passed the salmon-coloured curtain wall of the Red Fort and curved around the great bastions of Selim Gurh. We crossed under the British railway bridge which replaced the earlier Mughal structure described by Aleck. The road led on, past the remains of the British Residency and continued along the line of the ramparts for another three or four minutes. Then, quite suddenly, I saw what I knew immediately must be the building.

It stood high above the city walls, now partially obscured by a recent flyover, a single-storey bungalow of exactly the right period. The building now supported a curious melon-shaped dome which even from a distance looked like a later addition. Far below, on the wall beneath the ramparts, you could see the blocked-up arch of the old water gate. Through this the occupants would once have been able to reach their own jetty on the Jumna, and from there take a barge downstream to the Red Fort or beyond to Agra and the Taj. Turning left through the old city walls we soon found the bungalow down a lane near St James's Church. So far everything had proved deliciously easy. This being Delhi, I knew the state of affairs could not continue. It didn't.

As a notice at the gate prominently announced, the bungalow was now the Office of the Chief Engineer of the Northern Railways Board (Construction Department), Government of India. Presumably suspecting me of being a Pakistani agent intent on sabotage – the famous Foreign Hand invoked by Indian politicians to explain all manner of Indian disasters from train crashes and burst water mains to late monsoons and lost test matches – the heavily armed guards at the gate refused even to let me set foot within the gates. It took an entirely separate visit the following evening as the Chief Engineer was leaving his office before I was able to ambush Mr Raj Prashad and arrange a third visit when Olivia and I were (finally) to be allowed to see inside the premises.

At the time arranged, we turned up at the now familiar gates. In our hands we held our written invitation from Mr Prashad. The guards grudgingly escorted us – at gunpoint – down the drive. As we drew near, we were able to take in the house properly for the first time. Two entirely separate structures seemed to have been joined together to form the building as it stood today.

In the first block, a porte-cochère gave on to a low rectangular building flanked by four octagonal corner turrets. Although much altered in a late Victorian Indo-Saracenic style – perhaps after damage in the Indian Mutiny – the building seemed originally to have been a gatehouse. Then came the later dome chamber. Beyond that

122

stood the second and larger of the two original structures, the Fraser bungalow, with its bow-fronted veranda facing back on to the Jumna waterfront. It was here that Aleck must have sat looking down the river, smoking his hookah while he scribbled the letters I had read in Moniack.

After we had toured the building, we sat in Mr Prashad's office sipping sweet Indian tea and discussing the merits of the 'famous Railway Engineering Institute of Watford', where Mr Prashad had once attended a course. During our conversation, it emerged that Mr Prashad had actually been responsible for saving the house from destruction ten years previously. After some bad subsidence, the department had been ordered to destroy Fraser's house and build a modern office block on the site. Mr Prashad had persuaded his superiors to keep the existing building, but the most difficult part of the whole business, he maintained, had been getting the authorities to spend money to save and restore the old basement which was causing the subsidence in the first place.

Several ideas clicked into place. When I had first read through the Fraser correspondence, I had noticed that the letters – generally full of observations about the passage of the seasons – were curiously mute about the terrible heat inside Delhi houses during the summer. From my own experience of the hot season, I knew this to be an extraordinary omission. Even with the use of an electric ceiling fan, the Delhi summer is pure torture; it is inevitably the first thing every letter writer mentions when he puts pen to paper. How could William and Aleck have written as they did, I had wondered, unless like the Mughals, they had built themselves a *tykhana* (underground cool room) to keep themselves sane? In one letter Aleck ambiguously remarks how in the hot season it is best to spend as much time as possible inside 'a cool house'. By this did he mean a *tykhana*? And was it possible that the basement described by Mr Prashad was the remains of such a structure?

Mr Prashad pressed a bell on his old mahogany desk and a few minutes later an old moustachioed janitor appeared, furiously clanking a ringful of keys. He led us outside to a small wooden shed with a corrugated iron roof, like a sentry box or an outdoor lavatory. The janitor turned the key in the lock; the door swung open to reveal a steep flight of steps disappearing deep down into

123

the ground. He turned on his flashlight and led the way into the darkness. The steps were narrow, damp and slippery. Water dripped from the ceiling, generating soft growths of strange yellow lichens on the steps and on the walls. The temperature sank lower, and I began to regret that I had not wrapped up more warmly.

The plaster on the walls had long since flaked off, and as we descended you could see that the brickwork was changing. The large and solid British bricks which indicated Residency-period work gave way to the smaller and more delicate bricks favoured by Mughal builders. Within a few seconds of reaching the bottom the janitor's flashlight fell on a moulding that was unmistakably of Shah Jehan's period.

The underground passage reached a T-junction. Bowing our heads under a low, cusped Mughal arch, we entered an anteroom which in turn led into a large, echoing underground chamber. The air was old and used and smelt of damp rot. Roots spiralled down from the roof like curvilinear stalactites. It was pitch dark, but as the flashlight passed over the walls you could see that its surface was decorated with beautiful ogee-shaped arched niches. Although it was difficult to see clearly, in some of the arches you could faintly make out traces of Mughal murals, perhaps originally of flowers inside filigree vases.

We picked our way through the puddles to the far end of the room, stepping carefully to avoid any lurking snakes. Here a passage led off to two further shallow-domed chambers of identical size and shape. The only sound in the whole underground complex was our own breathing and the echoing drip-drip-drip of falling water. When we spoke, we found ourselves whispering as if in a church, or a graveyard.

We retraced our way back to the steps and took a left turn. The vaulted passageway led on ten feet, then split in three directions. One route headed off east in the direction of the Jumna waterfront, presumably to the blocked-up water gate we had seen from the road. Another headed off west as if to run under St James's Church. The third headed south, in the direction of the Red Fort. All three underground passages had been walled up during the recent 'restoration', a precaution, Mr Prasad later explained, against 'the ever-present terrorist threat'.

It took little research to work out what we had stumbled across. The 'basement' Mr Prasad had saved from destruction seems in fact to have been the largest and best preserved Mughal *tykhana* to have survived in Delhi up to the present day; it is also perhaps the most important piece of domestic architecture from Shah Jehan's Delhi to have survived anywhere outside the Red Fort. Yet, as my enquiries soon made clear, no one apart from the Railway Engineering Department seemed to be aware of its existence.

But what was a seventeenth-century Mughal *tykhana* doing under Fraser's house in the first place? According to the records, the Jumna waterfront near the Kashmiri Gate was known in the 1650s to have been the site of the palace of Ali Mardan Khan, Shah Jehan's senior general and one of the most important *omrahs* in the Mughal Empire at the peak of its power. In 1803, when the British first came to Delhi, just as the Resident was given the remains of the Palace of Dara Shukoh, so – although it is not recorded in any of the sources – the Deputy Resident must have been given the palace of Ali Mardan Khan, the crumbling remains of the next most important property in Shahjehanabad. But rather than building his house around the shell of the old Mughal structure as Ochterlony had done, Fraser seems to have made a clean break with the past and razed the ruins of Ali Mardan Khan's palace, preserving only the vast *tykhana* which ran underneath it. In the course of Mr Prashad's restoration, much of the marble was covered with concrete while steel girders were raised to prop up some of the arches. Yet it is still easy to see how the subterranean chambers must once have been cool and inviting, especially during the terrible heat of midsummer.

Yet perhaps the most intriguing aspect of the whole affair is the matter of the three vaulted passages leading away from the *tykhana*. Delhi is alive with legends of secret passages – there are old wives' tales of underground ways linking Feroz Shah Kotla with the Ridge and of others passing from under the Qutab Minar to Tughlukabad – but the passages underneath Fraser's House are, as far as I know, the first substantial remains of anything of this sort to have come to light.

Was the passage heading towards the Red Fort some sort of Imperial Mughal escape route linking the royal apartments in the

Fort, the library of Dara Shukoh and the palace of Ali Mardan Khan? Did the branch heading off underneath St James's Church pass outside the city walls to safety? Or did the passages merely lead to other now lost suites of rooms in the *tykhana*? This last option seems the least likely explanation because, according to Mr Prashad, the narrow vaulted passages extended on underground as far as any of his workmen had dared to follow them.

Today the passages are only blocked with a small plug of concrete; it should not be difficult to remove that plug and investigate what lies beyond. The problem would be to motivate India's impoverished and bureaucratic Archaeological Survey to take an interest in the matter. As Mr Prashad explained when we were leaving: 'You see actually in India today no one is thinking too much about these old historical places. India is a developing country. Our people are looking to the future only.'

Facing the entrance gates of William Fraser's bungalow, directly across what was then an open park, stood the *haveli* of Colonel James Skinner, the legendary founder of Skinner's Horse. Like Ochterlony, Skinner had received a title from the Mogul Emperor: Nasir-ud-Dowlah Colonel James Skinner Bahadur Ghalib Jang. Nevertheless, Skinner was always known to Delhi-wallahs simply as Sikander Sahib: to the people of the capital he was a reincarnation of Alexander the Great.

Skinner's irregular cavalry – into which William's personal army was eventually absorbed – enabled the East India Company to secure great chunks of North India for the Union Jack. With their scarlet turbans, silver-edged girdles, black shields and bright yellow tunics, Skinner's cavalrymen were, according to Bishop Heber, 'the most showy and picturesque cavaliers I have seen'. Moreover, another contemporary wrote that they were 'reckoned, by all the English in this part of the country, [to be] the most useful and trusty, as well as the boldest body of men in India.'

But Skinner was more than some starchy military caricature: he was also an engaging companion, an entertaining conversationalist, a builder of churches, temples and mosques, and the host of some

126

of the most magnificent nautches ever held in the Indian capital. 'I have seldom met a man who on so short an acquaintance gained so much on the heart and goodwill as this man,' wrote James Fraser soon after their first meeting in 1815. 'He has seen a great deal and run many risks and consequently has much anecdote and many adventures to relate . . . yet there is the most total absence of all affectation, pretention, pride or vanity.'

Skinner and William Fraser were best friends, business partners and brothers-in-arms. Fraser became the second-in-command of Skinner's Horse while Skinner joined Fraser and another Mughal nobleman, Ahmed Baksh Khan, in a partnership which imported stallions from Afghanistan and TransOxiana for sale in the Delhi bazaars. The ruins of the stud farm which Skinner built for the business, complete with its wonderful baroque gatehouse – all fluted columns and Corinthian capitals – still survive two miles to the south of Skinner's country estate at Hansi, north-west of Delhi.

In the National Army Museum in London there is a picture of Skinner and Fraser, the latter heavily bearded, sitting side by side on their favourite chargers. They are dressed in full regimental doublet and busby; behind them Skinner's Horse can be seen performing complicated training exercises in the Hansi plains. These same exercises greatly impressed James Fraser when he saw them being performed on the outskirts of Delhi in 1815.

> This morning we went out to see Skinner's Horse practice their matchlocks at full speed – and as no bottle was forthcoming I put down my hat to be fired at and consequently got several shot holes in it, which has made it worse than it was . . . The practice was really wonderful . . . these men have been known not uncommonly to shoot a hare coming at them at speed . . . [They have] galloped along with her [the hare] and loaded their guns [on horseback] and killed her. This really is having command of seat, hand and eye.

But even more entertaining than watching Skinner's Horse was chatting with Skinner himself. As James recorded in his diary later the same week:

> Skinner arrived and afterwards we had a dish of the usual conversation relating battles and sieges and accidents . . .

127

Skinner is really an enchanting fellow, and the number of anecdotes he has, and the knowledge which may be obtained of native manners and character, is very great . . . Skinner, Ferguson and I practised with the Bow and Arrow – at which the former excels; afterwards we all dined together.

Skinner's father, the Scottish mercenary Hercules Skinner, was the son of a former Provost of Montrose. When James Skinner raised his cavalry regiment he had the Skinner clan emblem – the bloody hand – tattooed on the bellies of his Hindu recruits. But Skinner had Indian as well as Scottish blood in his veins; his mother was a Rajput princess (known to her Scottish in-laws as Jeannie), and according to Fraser, in his looks Skinner was 'quite a Moor, not a negro, but a Desdemona Moor, a Moor of Venice'. It was this mixed racial inheritance that determined Skinner's career.

By 1792 it had already become impossible for anyone with even one Indian parent to receive a commission in the East India Company army. So, although he had been brought up in an English school in British Calcutta, the eighteen-year-old James Skinner was forced to leave westernized Bengal and accept service in the army of the Company's principal rivals in India.

During the course of the eighteenth century, the Hindu Mahratta confederacy had extended its power over much of the subcontinent, from the fastness of the Deccan to the borders of the fertile Punjab. One reason for the Mahrattas' success had been their skilful use of European and Eurasian mercenaries. Skinner was quickly welcomed into their ranks and before long was even permitted to raise his own irregular cavalry force.

For seven years he fought a series of battles in Rajasthan and Haryana using military techniques that were virtually unchanged since mediaeval times. Although one of Skinner's cousins was, at the same time, founding the modern Bombay Chamber of Commerce, two hundred miles away in the deserts of North-West India, the rhythms of warfare followed much the same course as they did in the campaigns depicted in the miniatures of the great Mughal manuscripts: sieges of Chittor and the vast forts of Rajputana were interspersed with intrigues, ambushes and charges of heavily armoured cavalry.

Reading Skinner's *Military Memoirs*, you sometimes become confused as to which century Skinner is describing. One of Skinner's typical anecdotes relates how, in the Battle of Malpura, his regiment managed to kill the richly caparisoned war elephant of the Maharaja of Jaipur. Seeing this the Maharajah's massed troops fled in panic, leaving Skinner's Horse to plunder the camp. 'I marched into the encampment,' wrote Skinner. 'It was the largest and best I had ever seen but was totally deserted. Here were the most beautiful tents, and large bazaars, filled with everything imaginable . . . The Rajah's wooden bungalow was covered with embroidery and crimson velvet. I entered and saw nothing but gold and silver.' The scene has echoes of the Crusades; yet the setting is the nineteenth, not the twelfth century.

Skinner's spectacular career in the ranks of the Mahrattas was, however, brought to an abrupt close. In 1803 the great Confederacy prepared to take on the British. Despite their proven loyalty, Skinner and the other Anglo-Indians in the Mahrattas' service were summarily dismissed and given only twenty-four hours to quit Mahratta territory. Just as Skinner's mixed blood had barred him from the Company army, so the same disability came to block his career in the ranks of their rivals; his birth acted, as James Fraser put it, 'like a two-edged blade, made to cut both ways against him'. Although Skinner's Horse was still ineligible to join the British army, Lord Lake, the British Commander in North India, eventually permitted the troop to fight as an irregular unit under the Company flag. Their job was to act as mounted guerrillas: to scout ahead of the main force; to harass a retreating enemy; to cut supply lines and to perform covert operations behind Mahratta lines.

In the years that followed there were several humiliating rebuffs by the British establishment: Skinner's estates, given to him by the Mahrattas, were revoked; his pay and rank were limited; the size of his regiment cut by a third. It was only much later, after a series of astonishing victories over the Sikhs and the Gurkhas, that Skinner's Horse was officially absorbed into the Company army and Skinner made a Lieutenant Colonel and a Companion of the Bath.

William Fraser remained the regiment's second-in-command, and appropriately it was William's brother James who edited and

129

translated (from their original Persian) Skinner's *Military Memoirs*. James also looked after Skinner's children in the holidays when they came to Edinburgh to receive their education. Yet even here Skinner was to be humiliated. On his return home James married his cousin, Jane Tytler. Brought up entirely in Scotland, Jane had no love for or interest in India and she certainly did not want her house full of Skinner's 'half-castes'.

The message got back to Delhi. In his last letter to Moniack, Skinner thanked his friend for looking after his 'poor black children', but adds that James should not go to see them again as he knew James's wife harboured 'a great aversion to children of that description'. Seeking comfort in religion, Skinner wrote that he could now only trust in 'Him who gave them birth, where I hope black or white will not make much difference before His presence.'

Even in the home of his closest friend, Skinner was unable to escape the growing colour prejudice of the British.

In the Spanish Americas it was military heroes of mixed Indian and colonial parentage – men like Bolivar – who came to dominate and rule the colonies. But India was different. As Skinner's career demonstrated, Hindus and British were both too proud of their blood for 'half-castes' ever to be really successful. As the nineteenth century progressed, such horrible prejudice only increased. Any hint of 'black blood' brought out the worst of Victorian bigotry, and in Delhi, Skinner's children became the butt of snide British jokes.

'The whole [Skinner] family was a marvellous revelation to anyone fresh from England,' wrote Emily Bayley sometime in the 1870s. '[They] were very dark in complexion and spoke English with an extraordinary accent . . . although they looked upon themselves as English people and held a prominent position in Delhi society, they had very little education and were more native than English in their ways . . .

'[Joe Skinner] was a marvellous creation . . . his visiting dress consisted of a green coat with gilt buttons, claret coloured trousers, patent leather boots, white waistcoat and necktie. He always carried a gold-mounted Malacca cane and talked of the time when he was in the Guards, though he has never been out of India . . . [His] children are named after the Royal Family, but are all black.'

The Skinners remained in Delhi, filling first the pews, then the graveyard of St James's, the great mustard-coloured church which Sikander Sahib built late in his life next to his *haveli* in Shahjehanabad.

The Skinners at least had some place in Delhi society, but year by year things only became more difficult for most other Anglo-Indians. Increasingly they came to suffer the worst racial prejudices of both Indians and British: the Indians refused to mix with them; and despite their fierce and unwavering loyalty to the Union Jack, the English rigidly excluded them from their clubs and drawing-rooms. Behind their backs they were cruelly ridiculed as 'chee-chees', 'Blackie Whities' or 'Chutney Marys'. They were given the railways and the telegraphs to look after and achieved some modest prosperity, but they remained effectively ostracized by both rulers and ruled. As Independence approached, an idea was mooted for an Eurasian homeland – a kind of Anglo-Indian Israel – in the Chote Nagpur hills in southern Bihar; but the scheme never came to anything and MacLuskie Ganj, the putative Tel Aviv of the home-land, today lies desolate and impoverished, little more than a run-down and outsize old folks' home.

Realizing there was no longer any secure place for them in India, the Anglo-Indians emigrated en masse. Some 25,000 made new homes in America, Canada and Australia, where their hockey team, the Harlequins, gained brief celebrity. Many more emigrated to England. There, 'back home', their distinct character became lost in the post-war melting pot; some, like Engelbert Humperdinck (born Gerald Dorsey from Madras) and Cliff Richard (born Harry Webb, the son of an Anglo-Indian train driver from Lucknow) became famous – though not until they had thrown away their old names and identities like a set of unwanted and unfashionable clothes.

The rump who had remained in India – the optimistic, the old or the nostalgic – stayed on in the face of some Indian resentment, and an increasing degree of poverty. The younger generation, especially the girls, tended to intermarry and were able to blend

St James's Church

in; but others, particularly the older ones, found it hard to change their ways.

I heard about two households of retired Anglo-Indians in Old Delhi. As chance would have it, their bungalows lay in a small back street only a stone's throw away from the site of the great neo-classical mansion Skinner built for himself during the twilight of the Mughals, the Anglo-Indian's forgotten heyday.

'It was the lavatories that did it. They were the final straw.'

'That's right. The lavatories.'

'They put in Indian ones.'

'His daughter and my son. Our own children.'

'You've got to draw the line somewhere.'

'That you have.'

'There's not one of those Indian lavatories you can sit on properly.'

'And one thing I'll never do is squat on my haunches.'

'Never.'

132

'Not on my haunches.'

'You've got to draw the line somewhere.'

Henry Smith and Bert Brown were sitting outside on Mr Brown's veranda when I went to see them. Despite the incipient evening chill, they were both sipping cold ginger beer. Mr Brown made it himself, with a Boots kit brought back by his son Thomas from a trip to England.

Mr Smith and Mr Brown are related now, by marriage: Mr Smith's Thomas is married to Mr Brown's Edith. Driven out by their children's plumbing, they have taken shelter side by side in two old-fashioned English-style bungalows. During the day they tend their gardens, pruning their roses and straightening the hollyhocks. Each evening they meet for a drink on Mr Brown's veranda. There they talk about the steam trains they used to drive between Lucknow and Calcutta.

'I always say you can't beat a train for seeing a country,' said Mr Jones removing his heavy black glasses and cleaning them on the bottom edge of his shirt.

'Aye, that's right,' agreed Mr Smith. 'Up on the fender. There's nothing like it.'

'It was a good healthy life on the railways. Plenty of fresh air.'

'Have you visited the Taj Mahal?' asked Mr Smith turning to me. 'That's a lovely place, the Taj Mahal.'

'Up on the fender you get to know a place,' continued Mr Brown.

'The languages,' said Mr Smith, 'the people, the habits . . .'

'And they're a fascinating people, the Indians. I'll say that for them.'

'I've always had friendly relations with them, mind. It's their country. That's what my father always used to say.'

'That's right. The Indians are a nice people. Provided you treat them as human beings.'

'Treat them as you would expect to be treated. That's my motto.'

'But they never could drive trains, in my experience. Those new diesel ones perhaps. But not the old steam trains.'

'A bit too laz . . . sleepy, some of them Indian drivers. With all due respect.'

'You have to be awake on a steam train.'

'Always something to do. Never time to be idle.'

133

'That's where we came in. The Anglo-Indians. The locomotives were our responsibility. If anything went wrong we could mend it. Do it up and get it moving.'

I asked Mr Smith and Mr Brown whether they had ever wanted to emigrate, but they both shook their heads.

'My brothers are both in England,' said Mr Smith. 'The eldest went in 1953 and the youngest followed in '63. Still I said: "No. I am not going."'

'But if your brothers have all gone . . .'

'This is my home,' said Mr Smith. 'I grew up here. I'm happier here than what I would've been had I gone anywhere foreign.'

'Do the Indians accept that this is your home?'

'Sometimes the people this side are inclined to be a bit rough,' said Mr Brown. 'They never tell us: "Go back home to England." They're just not always that friendly.'

'There's this fellah in the market gets nasty sometimes,' said Mr Smith. 'I just say: "My roots are deeper here than what yours are. Don't look at my skin. Look at my heart."'

'That shuts them up,' said Mr Brown, chuckling. 'Oooh. That shuts them up good and proper.'

'You see we're not Britishers,' said Mr Smith. 'We're something different.'

'Of course we sing the British songs: Daisy Daisy . . .'

'. . . Apple Blossom Time . . .'

'. . . When Irish Eyes are Smiling . . .'

'. . . Bless Them All . . .'

'All the old songs. And we wear the English clothes. Speak the English language. But we're different. England's not our home . . .'

'. . . though our people have done very well for themselves over there,' added Mr Smith proudly. 'Done better in their exams than the English, some of them.'

'And then there's that Clifford Richards from Lucknow. Very popular singer at the moment I'm told.'

'I knew his uncle,' said Mr Smith. 'Old Pete Webb. A very spiritual man he was. Knew the Bible like he'd written it himself.'

As we were talking, Mr Brown spotted a large rhesus monkey moving stealthily towards the fruit bowl on the table between us.

'Get on! Out! Bloody animal.'

Mr Smith heaved himself up from his chair and threw a pebble at the intruder. The monkey loped off, into Mr Brown's hollyhocks.

'Never trust a monkey. That's what my father used to say.'

'It's because of that Hindu temple down the road,' explained Mr Brown. 'They've started giving their monkeys bananas. Now they all want them.'

'He's coming back. This fellah's after something. He's after these plantains.'

'In British times they used to export the monkeys for laboratory experiments,' said Mr Brown with a sigh. 'But they worship them now.'

Marion and Joe Fowler live in a similar bungalow nearby. They have a front room and a back room, and in the back room stand their two single beds, side by side. On the wall above, hanging from a peg, is a picture of the Queen from The Royal Family Calendar of 1977. Marion sat in the front room in a canary yellow dress clearly modelled on that of her sovereign.

'We got that calendar from UK,' said Marion. 'On our visit.'

'Very picturesque is England,' said Joe. 'It was our first visit, but we both felt quite at home there.'

'They eat all the food we like. All the recipes we were taught by our parents.'

'Steaks.'

'Old English stew.'

'Mixed fruit pudding. Apple crumble.'

'None of this curry and rice.'

'The dish I like is that Kentucky Fried Chicken,' said Joe Fowler. 'It's a very popular dish over there, that Kentucky Fried Chicken is. A delightful dish.'

'And the shops! Ooh! They've got everything in the shops in England. Even special food for diabetics . . .'

'A diabetic is our Marion.'

'. . . Diabetic jam. And a variety of diabetic chocolates with soft and hard centres.'

We talked about their visit to the promised land. Joe and Marion's eldest daughter Elizabeth moved there in 1973 ('although of course we called her Betty in those days'). Now she was living in a detached house in Surrey. Two years previously, when she had saved up enough, Elizabeth sent her parents a return ticket with British Airways.

'They treat everyone the same in England. Not like here.'

'Of course we expected it to be a nice place. A little drizzle and rain perhaps but . . . nice.'

'Ye oldy England. That's what they called it in the brochure.'

'But to be honest with you we were a bit surprised to see so many Indians there. After we had our visas refused twice.'

'The second time we applied for citizenship we really thought we'd make it. We were fully prepared to go. Then we had to unpack all over again.'

'All her people and all my people are over there. But when we applied they said: "No. You're Indians. You have to stay here."'

'It was that Mrs Thatcher. She never liked the Anglo-Indians. She made it very hard for us. All her rules and regulations.'

'Colour prejudice. That's what it was. Colour prejudice pure and simple.'

'Yet she let the Indians in.'

'We did feel it about the Indians,' said Marion. 'There weren't so many in Stratford on Avon. Or in Surrey. But in London! There's more of them on that London Underground than there are in Delhi.'

'When we saw that we felt very let down. They played us dirty, the British. I don't mind saying that.'

'After they left in 1947 it became very hard for us.'

'It was impossible to find a job. If you did go for a job the Indians would put some high degree of obstacle in your way. We lost all the high positions in the posts and the telegraphs.'

'And the railways.'

'Our status went down. Right down.'

'They should have made provisions for us. We'd served them all our days.'

'We ran their railways and their mines. We sang in their canteens. You've probably never heard of Tony Brent, the singer?'

'I don't think so.'

136

'You'd be too young,' said Marion. 'Tony Brent: "The Singing Engineer" they called him. He had a wonderful voice, Tony Brent did. He was one of our boys – from Bombay.'

'Very popular was Tony Brent.'

'And handsome! I'd say. Used to give me quite a flutter when I was a girl at Kolar Gold Fields.'

'I was in the Auxiliary Force – like the TA,' said Joe, changing the subject. 'Served the British for forty years. A loyal citizen of Her Majesty. Never sympathized with the Congress. Not for one day.'

'And then they give them Indians the visas to run all those ruddy grocery stores – and tell us we must stay here. It doesn't seem just.'

Outside darkness had fallen. Joe turned on the bedside light. It was suddenly very cold.

'It was born and bred in us that the British Empire would last for ever. They promised us that they would stay.'

'It was quite a shock in 1947 when they suddenly said they would hand over to the Indians. We never thought they'd do *that*.'

'Them Indians should have got their freedom. I'm not saying they shouldn't. They were giving freedom to all sorts of countries. But before the British went, they should have made sure that there was some sort of guarantee we'd be looked after.'

'After they went, the young all emigrated . . .'

'. . . to Australia mostly . . .'

'. . . and the UK.'

A long silence followed. Somewhere a clock chimed, Big Ben chimes. I got up; Joe saw me out.

'I still worry for Marion,' he said as we stood by the taxi. 'When I die I don't know what will happen to her. She's twenty years younger than me. She'll be left on her own. She doesn't know a word of any Indian language.' He shrugged his shoulders, helpless.

We shook hands. As I got back into Balvinder Singh's taxi, Joe saluted his old Auxiliary Force salute.

'Long live Her Majesty the Queen,' said Joe.

The taxi pulled away. In the car's headlights, I could see the nightjars swooping down after the moths.

137

During the 1830s and 1840s the new increasingly racist and puritanical attitudes which had made Skinner's life so painful were beginning to spread. The world which William Fraser and Ochterlony knew – the world of the Scottish Nawabs with their Indian harems and Mughal wardrobes – was passing.

If Ochterlony symbolized the beginning of the period, so Sir Thomas Metcalfe (the nephew of William's old enemy Sir Charles Metcalfe) represented its close. A fastidious Englishman, he would have blanched at even the thought of a 'native' mistress. Indeed so refined were his feelings, according to his daughter Emily Bayley, that he could not bear to see women eat cheese. Moreover he believed that if the fair sex insisted on eating oranges or mangoes, they should at least do so in the privacy of their own bathrooms.

He would never have dreamt of dressing as Ochterlony had. Instead, he arranged that his London tailors, Pulford of St James's Street, should regularly send out to Delhi a chest of sober but fashionable English clothes. A trunk of the latest English books was likewise dispatched twice every year. His one concession to Indian taste was to smoke a silver hookah. This he did every day after breakfast, for exactly thirty minutes. If ever one of his servants failed to perform properly and efficiently his appointed duty, Metcalfe would call for a pair of white kid gloves. These he would pick up from their silver salver and pull on over his long white fingers. Then, 'with solemn dignity', having lectured the servant on his failing, he 'proceeded to pinch gently but firmly the ear of the culprit, and then let him go – a reprimand that was entirely efficacious'.

As the nineteenth century progressed, Delhi gradually began to fill with stiff-lipped English families whose attitudes and prejudices mirrored those of Sir Thomas. Passing through the city in 1838, Fanny Eden, sister of the Governor-General Lord Auckland, described the European community as undistinguished 'in any way, except perhaps that the female part of it are addicted to black mittens of their own making, with large brassy-looking bracelets over them'. Although Fraser was fond of remarking that these people 'had no rational conversation' he did every so often dine at the Residency, and very occasionally managed to find there a stimulating companion.

The most interesting was certainly Lady Hood, an aristocratic tomboy whom Fraser had taken lion-hunting in 1814. Fraser's letters to Lady Hood are a strange testament to his odd mixture of machismo and donnishness. In one letter of 1817, having boasted of his hunting prowess ('I have killed seven lions lately, five with the spear'), Fraser goes on to discuss his somewhat idiosyncratic personal faith. His beliefs seem to have had as much in common with Hinduism as they did with Christianity; certainly, he appears to have dropped conventional monotheism in favour of a more universal metaphysical philosophy.

The mid-nineteenth century was the Golden Age of starched evangelicalism, and unorthodox beliefs such as Fraser's, however unformed, were neither general nor popular; people like Lady Hood who could appreciate such enquiring open-mindedness were rare. It must have been partly this intellectual isolation that led Fraser to sink into bouts of depression; and increasingly his letters home were filled with thick fogs of gloom and homesickness. 'Fifteen years in India is equal to twenty five in Europe', he wrote from Hansi in 1817. 'Indian scenes and subjects get gradually stale . . . war and politics are both very near their end and India proves daily less interesting . . . I think there is much greater chance of getting buried than married in India.'

Nor can Fraser's mood have been improved by what appears to have been an embarrassing bout of gonorrhoea. There is only one reference to this affliction in the Moniack archive, but the message seems pretty unambiguous. In a letter addressed to William, one of his colleagues remarks: 'I do not understand what kind of a affliction of the loins you can have to render mercury beneficial. You have, I dare say, been flourishing your genitals over and above that which nature requires . . .'

But much more serious for William's mental health were the series of family tragedies that befell him after he had been living in Delhi for some ten years.

In the hot July of 1812, the fourth of the Fraser brothers, Edward, arrived in Delhi and promptly moved in with William and Aleck. He had been there only a few weeks when he began to show symptoms of unusual listlessness. It was Aleck who first noticed that something was wrong. 'Towards the end of August,' he wrote

139

in his logbook, 'I began to be uneasy at observing a certain languor in him which rendered him indifferent to the little excursions of curiosity and pleasure that were sometimes proposed . . . I grew more and more uneasy, and being regularly all day absent at the court used to be in the evenings sometimes struck with the lassitude that appeared in Edward. He omitted his morning exercise – and addicted himself to sedentary amusements . . . music, with a little reading.'

One day in early September, Edward was in the bungalow garden overlooking the Jumna, lazily pruning the orange trees. William was away bathing at the ghats two miles upstream; Aleck was busy with his legal work inside the house: 'I was suddenly alarmed by a servant who told me Edward was spitting blood. Running out I found that in stooping to prune a tree, he had been seized with this alarming symptom. In about an hour it stopped; and he declared himself much relieved by it. The quantity of blood effused was small – perhaps a wine glass full in all, pure and florid.'

The doctor was called. He said there was no cause for worry and prescribed digitalis, abstinence from wine and a vegetarian diet. He told Edward to rest.

'For several days after his saliva continued to be tinged with blood, but his cough was better, and he was, or thought himself, much better on the whole. About four days after this occurrence, Edward, without telling us, went out to breakfast with the Commanding Officer of our troops on guard in the Palace [the Red Fort]. There, unfortunately, he was tempted to walk about, and up several staircases, viewing the curiosities of the Palace, so little was he aware of the state he was in. On his return, however, he was again attacked by the spitting of blood, which recurred in small quantity the day after.'

The doctor was again called; this time he admitted the symptoms looked very like incipient consumption and advised that Edward should be taken immediately to Calcutta and from there 'to sea'. Aleck volunteered to escort Edward, and the following day they set off on the long journey to Allahabad and thence down the Ganges to Calcutta, the capital of British India. On the way Edward's health continued to deteriorate and his haemorrhages became more frequent. Nevertheless, Aleck pressed on. He booked a passage on a boat to St Helena and carried the invalid on board. When the brothers arrived at the island, Edward was clearly dying. A week later, on 25 April 1813, Edward had a final violent attack of blood-spitting and expired, 'quite peacefully', a couple of hours later.

Aleck was broken and exhausted. He wearily arranged for his little brother's burial and mailed a long, sad account of Edward's final hours back to Moniack. Then, packing up his things, he set sail back to Calcutta, alone. It was on this return journey that he noticed that his own saliva had started to become very slightly tinged with blood. A week later he had his first bloody coughing fit. Realizing immediately what this probably meant, he began to scribble an *apologia* in his logbook:

> Conceiving myself to be at this moment in a state that, although susceptible to recovery, is more likely to terminate in an early death, I have an inclination to commit to paper while I still have adequate strength to the task, an account of my life, my character, and of the principles or passions that have chiefly influenced my actions – as they appear to myself.
>
> I have always thought it would be a real blessing to mankind if everyone, forsaking dissimulation, were to exhibit himself and his sentiments to the world without disguise . . . my life has been undistinguished and unhonoured; I know, and am indifferent to, the oblivion that will surely follow my death. It is but a slight mortification to [now] confess my views, my follies, my weaknesses and my errors, while the benefit or amusement that might accrue to my near relations and friends is a full compensation. Should such advantage accrue, it may procure to the memory of the weak but harmless author a momentary tribute of compassion and regard.

Aleck went on to confess his own laziness at college, what he saw as his essential selfishness and frivolity, and to describe the friction between him and William when they shared a house in Delhi:

> I had expected much pleasure from the society of a brother whom I had not seen for seven years. I was disappointed.

141

All my pursuits were [too] trifling and frivolous [for William]. Even my reading, when I read, was of the slightest kind. My brother's whole mind was devoted to business. A sober morning's ride (our horses at a walk) was succeeded by a long day of business, or silence. It was only with his servants that he [William] ever chatted or joked.

Most surprising of all was Aleck's confession of his lack of language skills, and how this affected his duties as supreme judge of the new Delhi courts:

In this situation I reaped the bitter fruits of my idleness at college. I was continually at a loss. Every petition, every record, was in the Persian language, of which I was almost totally ignorant. The language of Delhi and its vicinity differed so materially from that to which I had been accustomed that I could not understand one word in five spoken by witnesses.

Aleck continued to scribble his confession as he limped back to Delhi along the same route he had taken with Edward the previous year. Eventually he became too weak and too confused to continue. Carried as far as Jokhoulee (on the outskirts of Delhi) on a palanquin, he was deemed too ill to continue and was nursed in a roadside tent by his eldest brother James. After a long and painful illness, 'his emaciation so great that there is hardly enough to cover bones and sinews', Aleck finally died there on 3 June 1816.

'His sufferings for some days before his death were very great and immediately preceeding it they were distressing beyond description,' wrote James in his diary. '[But] at last his pulse ceased to play and the breathing stopped. Only the corps remained before us. Such was the end of my beloved brother Aleck.'

Together, William and James closed Aleck's eyes and washed his body: 'About six o'clock we wrapped it up in a piece of bedding and carried it ourselves to the grave. There we restored it to its native clay.'

Whether through uneasy conscience or genuine grief, it was William, who for so long had ignored and humiliated Aleck, who took the death most severely. In his diary, James described William's rapid deterioration: 'Poor William has been terribly shocked by this day's blow, and from the time the grave was filled up and the few people who attended gone, he sat at its head or lay on the ground along its side the whole day, weeping and groaning most bitterly.'

Days later, he was still ordering larger and larger doses of laudanum.

In the years that followed, William Fraser continued to maintain his distance from the other Europeans in Delhi. 'He hates the grimmace and chatter of society,' wrote James, 'and to hear his wild talk would rather be removed to the family of the Usbecks, to Siberia or some other part of Tartary [where man remains in what] he considers an unsophisticated and noble state.'

To this end William travelled in the Himalayas, both on business with Skinner, fighting the Gurkhas, and on his own, for pleasure: one of the greatest draws of the Indian hills was what William saw as their great likeness to the Invernessshire he remembered from his childhood. 'We now bound China and Tartary,' he wrote to Lady Hood in 1817, 'and live in a climate very like Scotland . . . I can go and lie down under the oak, birch, larch, elm or gather strawberries and raspberries as at home.'

When in Delhi, William devoted himself to constructing a massive country house outside the city walls. The house – a kind of Palladian villa with odd Scotch Baronial features – stood on the summit of the hogsback ridge which straddled the north-west outskirts of Old Delhi, high above the Roshanara Gardens and the Sadar Bazaar.

In his letters to his father William was understandably reticent about the project; after all, for many years to come it would suck up the funds he was supposed to be sending home to Moniack. Moreover, the house anchored William in Delhi more firmly than ever – at exactly the time when his age and experience was bringing him offers of more lucrative postings elsewhere in India. For both these reasons, William only mentioned his building project once, and then very briefly in an aside. 'I [now] go back to Dehlee,' he wrote on 23 September 1819 from Skinner's house in Hansi, 'where

I have built a large white house on top of a hill, from the top of which I am getting a large view of Dehlee.'

Victor Jacquemont, as usual, is more forthcoming. In one of his letters to his father in Paris he describes how he is staying in 'Monsieur Fraser's enormous house, a sort of Gothic fort which has been built at great expense on the very spot where Timur once pitched his tent during the seige of Delhi . . .' Fraser's 'fort' later became known as Hindu Rao's House (after its subsequent owner) and, although it was badly shelled during the 1857 uprising, the central part of it survives today as the core of the Hindu Rao Hospital.

In 1820, James Fraser, having conceived a plan to return home overland via Persia, Mesopotamia and the Ottoman Levant, visited Delhi for one last time. On 11 November he and William said a final goodbye to each other at a camp near the Qutab Minar.

> William is not a man to shew his feelings however keen, nor to give way to common forms on such occasions. We got up – he gave me his hand & said 'Well Good Bye – take care of yourself'– gripping it hard – but I did not speak – I did not trust myself – I took one look – probably I shall see him no more – & quitted the tent. Such things do not do to be often felt, particularly when there is no means of giving way to feelings – but for very long I have not been able to relieve these by tears on any such occasion. Suffocation may come but tears not.
>
> The Nawab [Ahmed Baksh Khan, William's business partner and friend] & I mounted & set forward leaving my brother in the tent – I have requested Skinner to tell me how he is & how he bears my departure, for though it is not death he knows as I do too, how many chances there are of our ever again meeting.

William stayed on in Delhi for another thirteen years and in 1833 finally got the job he had coveted for three decades, the Delhi Residency. But it was the winning of this position that finally brought about his own downfall.

In 1834, on the death of his old friend Ahmed Baksh Khan, Fraser, as Resident, became officially involved in the violent inheritance dispute which broke out between the Nawab's sons. In the course of this controversy, Fraser forcibly ejected from his house his own ward, Khan's eldest child, Shams-ud-Din, a raffish Mughal nobleman who had started the dispute by seizing his younger brothers' share of the family property.

As well as humiliating Shams-ud-Din by ejecting him without an audience, there were persistent rumours circulating in Delhi – rumours still remembered to this day in the bazaars of the Old City – that Fraser had added insult to injury by making improper overtures to Sham-ud-Din's sister. To a young Mughal nobleman, brought up in the strict courtly etiquette of the Red Fort, this sort of behaviour was an unforgivable insult. Shams-ud-Din had not only lost face; he had been dishonoured by his own guardian. He left Delhi immediately, returned to his Haryana estates and there began to plot revenge.

Three months later, on 22 March 1835, the young Emily Bayley was at home in Metcalfe House, north of the Civil Lines. It was late on a Sunday evening. Emily and her brother George were sitting with their mother in the bay drawing-room: 'The whole house was still and hushed as only an Indian house can be, when suddenly there were sounds of great stir among the servants, and my Father came hurriedly into the room where we were sitting and announced Mr Fraser's death, and that he was going out to enquire into the murder.

'How well I remember clinging to my Mother,' Emily wrote later, 'and her horror at the news – and our childlike fears for our father's safety, because if Mr Fraser had been murdered, perhaps Papa would be killed too! We heard the carriage drive rapidly away and we sat by our mother who was silent, and remained there until Father's return.'

Holding flaming torches in front of them, Metcalfe's runners led him up on to the Ridge where William's body still lay on the steps of his vast Gothic house.

According to witnesses, Fraser had been returning from an evening's entertainment at the house of his friend the Maharaja of Kishengarh. Just before he reached the turning into his house a single figure who had been riding in front of him slowed down. He allowed William to come level, then from point-blank range fired a single shot from his sawn-off blunderbuss. Metcalfe, with his customary precision, noticed that the slugs had entered the right-hand side of Fraser's body; 'two had perforated as far as the outer skin of the opposite side,' while one had passed 'quite through'. 'Death,' concluded Metcalfe, '[had] instantly ensued.'

Thanks to some extraordinary detective work the murder was soon solved. Metcalfe and his assistant sleuth, John Lawrence, noticed that, mysteriously, none of the tracks on the road seemed to lead in the direction that the assailant had fled. But a search of a *haveli* belonging to friends of Shams-ud-Din Khan revealed a horse whose shoes had recently been reversed – exactly the trick used by Dick Turpin to outwit his trackers. Within the *haveli* were discovered incriminating letters between the assassin and Shams-ud-Din. A month later, after another accomplice had turned King's Evidence, the case was complete. Khan and his henchman were tried and publicly executed.

William's body, originally hastily buried in the British cemetery near the Residency, was exhumed and reburied in a great white tomb built by James Skinner at great expense in the churchyard of St James's Church. The design, suitably enough, had a European form, but its substance, Mughal marble inlay, was wholly Indian. The epitaph, written by James Skinner, read as follows:

THE REMAINS

INTERRED BENEATH THIS MONUMENT

WERE ONCE ANIMATED

BY AS BRAVE AND SINCERE

A SOUL

AS WAS EVER VOUCHSAFED TO MAN

BY HIS

CREATOR.

A BROTHER IN FRIENDSHIP

HAS CAUSED IT TO BE ERECTED

THAT WHEN HIS OWN FRAME IS DUST

IT MAY REMAIN

AS A

MEMORIAL

FOR THOSE WHO CAN PARTICIPATE IN LAMENTING
THE SUDDEN AND MELANCHOLY LOSS
OF ONE
DEAR TO HIM AS LIFE
WILLIAM FRASER
DIED 22ND MARCH 1835

Twenty-two years later the period was brought to a bloody close by the uprising of 1857.

The hopes of a happy fusion of British and Indian culture, promised during the Twilight, were forgotten in the massacres which initiated and the hangings which followed the Indian Mutiny. The recapture of Delhi by the British on 14 September 1857 led to the wholesale destruction of great areas of the city. The Red Fort was plundered and much of it razed to the ground; what remained of one of the world's most beautiful palaces became a grey British barracks. It was only by a hair's-breadth that the great Mughal Jama Masjid was saved from similar destruction and the city spared the planned replacement, a hideous Victorian Gothic cathedral.

Three thousand Delhi-wallahs were tried and executed – either hanged, shot or blown from the mouths of cannon – on the flimsiest evidence. British soldiers bribed the hangmen to keep the condemned men 'a long time hanging, as they like to see the criminal's dance a "Pandy's hornpipe" as they termed the dying struggles of the accused'. The last Emperor was sent off to exile in Rangoon in a bullock cart; the princes, his children, were all shot. The inhabitants of the city were turned out of the gates to starve in the countryside outside; and even after the city's Hindus were allowed to return, Muslims remained banned for two whole years. The finest mosques were sold off to Hindu bankers for use as bakeries and stables.

The behaviour of the British in the weeks following the capture of the city is extraordinary to read. It is as if in victory all the most horrible characteristics of the English character – philistinism, narrow-mindedness, bigotry, vengefulness – suddenly surfaced all at once. The account of Hugh Chichester, who visited Delhi at this time, is not at all untypical:

> There are several mosques in the city most beautiful to look at. But I should like to see them all destroyed. The rascally brutes desecrated our churches and graveyards and I do not think we should have any regard for their stinking religion. One was always supposed to take one's shoes off before going to visit one of these mosques, or to have an interview with the King. But these little affairs we drop now. I have seen the old Pig of a king. He is a very old man, and just like an old *khitmutgar* [waiter].

Similar sentiments were expressed in verse and even hymns. 'Avenge O Lord Thy Slaughtered Saints' (a pastiche of a sonnet by Milton) was published the same month in the *Civil and Military Gazette*; the author develops a theme which was becoming increasingly common in the second half of the nineteenth century – that God was really an Englishman, and subduing the rebellious heathen was his own special work:

> And England now avenge their wrongs,
> By vengeance deep and dire,
> Cut out this canker with the sword,
> And burn it out with fire,
> Destroy these traitor legions,
> hang every Pariah-hound,
> And hunt them down to death,
> in all the hills and cities round.

Years later the city had yet to recover. In 1861 the poet Ghalib, who had earlier written that he felt the death of Fraser 'like a father', now bemoaned the fall of his own people and the desecration of the city he loved: 'Helpless I watch the wives and children of aristocrats literally begging from door to door. One must have a heart of steel to witness the contemporary scene . . . the moon-faced Begums of the Red Fort wandering around the streets in filthy clothes, ragged pyjamas and broken shoes.'

Even today, stories about British atrocities in the aftermath of the Mutiny are current. In Karachi, Ahmed Ali told me how he vividly remembered his grandmother describing in hushed tones how she was thrown out of her *haveli* and forced to take shelter in a tomb to the south of the city; later a pair of British 'Tommies' found her hiding there. They pulled off her chador and stripped her naked in their search for the jewels they supposed she was hiding from them. Up to then she had never once left the family zenana or revealed even her face to anyone except her maid.

Yet, perversely, the British remembered the siege and capture of Delhi as one of the great moments of the Empire, one of the golden bulwarks of the Raj which, along with Plassy and Seringapatam, had established Britannia's rule over the Indian waves. Places associated with the Mutiny were preserved and became popular late Victorian tourist attractions. Monuments were erected all over the subcontinent commemorating massacres and last stands. The most important of these is the Delhi Mutiny Memorial, erected on the site of the British Camp on the Ridge. A strange, displaced Gothic spire, illegitimate first cousin to the Albert Memorial, it still stands today above the swirl of domes, rooftops and bazaar shacks that is Old Delhi. The original British inscriptions commemorating the siege and capture of the City remain, though they are now complemented by another plaque which intends to set the record right:

> THE 'ENEMY' OF THE INSCRIPTIONS ON THIS MONUMENT WERE THOSE WHO ROSE AGAINST COLONIAL RULE AND FOUGHT BRAVELY FOR NATIONAL LIBERATION IN 1857. IN MEMORY OF THE HEROISM OF THESE IMMORTAL MARTYRS FOR INDIAN FREEDOM, THIS PLAQUE WAS UNVEILED ON THE 25TH ANNIVERSARY OF THE NATION'S ATTAINMENT OF FREEDOM, 28TH AUGUST 1972.

But the most striking thing is not either of the two inscriptions; it is the statistical tables raised by the British to commemorate the Mutiny's casualties. Each of the monument's eight sides has one of these tables, set in a little Gothic trefoil. Against a list of the engagements fought in 1857 are three columns: KILLED,

WOUNDED and MISSING; each of the results are then, inevitably, divided into NATIVE and EUROPEAN. The cold and exact set of mind which could reduce the human casualties of a bloody war to the level of bowling averages was a world away from the attitudes of Ochterlony and William Fraser. The Twilight was finished; the sun had finally sunk.

Yet, ironically, the Memorial stands only a few feet from the great white house which William Fraser laboured throughout the early years of the century to build. One monument with its Mughal borrowings and position determined by Timur's camp represents what the Raj might have been. The Mutiny memorial represents – crudely and distastefully – what was.

SIX

DECEMBER ENDED as it had begun, both bleak and cold.

On New Year's night the poor huddled in primeval groups under the flyovers. You could see them squatting on their hams silhouetted around bonfires; sometimes one of the figures would throw a lump of dried buffalo-dung on to the flames. Nearby, in Golf Links and Chanakyapuri, the rich were celebrating. As midnight drew near, they burst balloons, popped champagne corks and tore around Delhi honking the horns of their new Marutis. At the traffic lights, as outstretched palms were thrust through open car windows, the two worlds briefly met.

That night we went to a party given by a magazine editor. Outside the house, alongside the usual mêlée of Marutis, stood a line of imported Mercedes – the ultimate mark of arrival for a *nouveau-riche* Punjabi businessman – and a few white ministerial Ambassadors distinguished by their little red roof beacons. Inside we were greeted by the sight of a gaggle of top-heavy Sikhs energetically bopping around the hall to 1970s disco music; beautiful Hindu ladies lilted delicately from side to side trying to avoid stepping on each other's saris. Liveried bearers carried trays of kebabs around the room. On the walls, spotlights illuminated sensuous Hindu sculptures torn from the brackets of ruined temples.

At the other Delhi parties we had been to – mostly boring official events – it had been a struggle to avoid getting cornered by some grey under-secretary from the Ministry of Fertilizer Distribution.

Mosque at Safdarjung's Tomb

But the tone and guest list at this party was very different; here it seemed were the elusive Delhi *jeunesse dorée*. Pearl chokers glittered on every female neck; huge diamonds flashed in the strobe lights.

The disc-jockey put on Earth, Wind and Fire and Olivia was whisked away by a young columnist from Amritsar; I was left talking to a rather bulbous Congress MP.

'You are British?' he asked.

I nodded.

'Did you go to Eton?'

'No.'

'How sad,' he replied, moving quickly away.

As I walked forlornly around on my own, I could hear fragments of different conversations wafting over the music:

'She thought she was getting a millionaire. What she *did* get was five children and two poodles . . .'

'Actually I think they are saying she was an air hostess before she met her husband, *ya*? It was case of trolley to lolly.'

'. . . The children are one thing. But imagine having to take on those disgusting poodles . . .'

'I really don't know where His Highness is. Bapji *swore* he would be here before twelve.'

'. . . at least her husband bought her a nice little boutique in Hauz Khas Village. But you should see her new collection. Oh! So vulgar . . .'

'. . . Ya, Rohit is *so* talented. Really he is Delhi's Yves St Laurent.'

Most of the guests seemed to be either journalists, politicians, or fashion designers, the three occupations most favoured by the nascent New Delhi chattering class. The different cliques stood together in their separate groups, talking shop: the ethnic collection of the new Paris-trained designer; the likely winners in the next cabinet reshuffle; the latest chapter in the interminable Bofors corruption scandal. Only the Sikh men seemed to have other things on their mind as, twirling their moustaches, they downed great tumblers of whisky and tried to lure the prettiest girls on to the dance floor. Around the room the chatterers were still gossiping:

'*Acha*. It's true: his grandfather had *one hundred* vintage cars. He drove whichever one happened to match his cuff-links.'

'Rajiv looks *really* sexy in his *shahtoosh*, *ya*? But Sonia — so

153

awkward. Really she is just some common bricklayer's daughter.'

'Bubbles is nothing but a little tart. You should have seen her at Neemrana . . . clinging chiffon or some wet sari . . . straight out of the *worst* kind of *masala* movie . . .'

'Did you see Bina at the horse show? Even that Chanel suit she got in Paris can't disguise all the weight she's put on. And she used to be so pretty . . .'

At midnight everyone joined hands and tried to sing 'Auld Lang Syne', but despite a spattering of British diplomats, only a pair of Indian army generals knew the words. The Sikhs bounced off the dance floor, dripping with sweat, and joined in. After the toasts and handshakes, the socialites opened their diaries and began to swap telephone numbers and lunch dates. Then, en masse, they embraced and staggered off towards their waiting cars and frozen drivers.

'It's the drivers that run this town,' muttered one politician as he tripped off into the driveway. 'I was at a party last week. Half-way through one driver came in and said that the Minister for Human Resources had spent half an hour longer than he had agreed.'

'No!' replied his friend. 'What happened?'

'Imagine it. The Minister actually apologized and left without an argument . . .'

'Servants these days! They are less reliable even than the telephones.'

'Unless you give them *paan*, cigarettes and seven days' notice, they won't do a thing.'

'I *ask* you. What *is* our India coming to?'

Mrs Puri did not see the New Year in, but the following day she celebrated the event in her own inimitable fashion.

Soon after we had finished our New Year's lunch, we heard the familiar sound of the Indian National Anthem chiming defiantly around the flat. I opened the door to find Mrs Puri standing to attention outside. As I let her in, she put on her best funeral face.

'Mr William, Mrs William,' she said. 'Have you been reading our *Hindustan Times*?'

'Yes,' we replied, noncommittally.

'In that case you will know that the rupee is in a parlous state.'

Mrs Puri went on to describe, at some length, the trials and

154

tribulations currently being faced by the Bombay Stock Exchange.

'In short,' she concluded, 'our Indian economy is far from tip-top condition.'

'But, Mrs Puri,' we protested, having heard this all several times before. 'Indian industry is going from strength to strength.'

'Ah, you are kind, Mr William. But sadly things are very dire in our India.' She paused and shook her head: 'I'm afraid I am forced to put up your rent.'

There followed protracted negotiations; and it was not until weeks later that we settled on a permanent arrangement that satisfied everyone. Our rent, in pounds sterling, was to be sent monthly to Mrs Puri's bank account in deepest Ludhiana. The amount was to be fixed for one year. Fluctuations in the value of the pound were, however, to be made up in Marks and Spencer underwear which we would get our friends to mail out from Britain.

'You must understand,' explained Mrs Puri, 'that we are not having your Marks and Spencer lingerie in India.'

'No,' we replied, embarrassed. 'Of course not.'

'Our Indian lingerie is most unsatisfactory.'

'Why is that?' Olivia asked.

'In India we are having no good viscose. Here we are having only cotton and silks. For quality modern undergarments you are needing viscose.' Mrs Puri tapped her stick triumphantly on the ground.

'Actually, Mr William, I think you have no head for business,' she said with unexpected frankness as we shook hands on the deal. 'Really this arrangement is most satisfactory for me.'

Although the early mornings and evenings remained grey and foggy, the afternoons at the beginning of January became increasingly warm and bright. In the gardens there appeared the first signs of spring: leaf-buds reappeared on the bougainvillaea and the poinsettias burst into flower.

One day, inspired by the balmy weather, I decided to go and see the great onion-domed tomb of Safdarjung, the last really great Mughal building to be built in India. It was a landmark I had passed a thousand times and yet had never properly explored. From my reading, however, I knew a little about its occupant. Safdarjung was a Persian nobleman from Nishapur in Iranian Khorasan. In the late seventeenth century he came to India, gained a prominent post in the Imperial army and married into the Mughal aristocracy; a few years later he succeeded his father-in-law as Nawab (Governor) of Oudh.

Safdarjung interested me because his life seemed to encapsulate perfectly the intriguing but cataclysmic half-century that linked the Mughal high noon at the close of the seventeenth century with the decay and disintegration of the Twilight fifty years later. When Safdarjung arrived from Persia, Aurangzeb was still Emperor and Delhi was still the richest, most magnificent and most populous city between Istanbul and Edo (Tokyo); with its two million inhabitants it was far larger than either London or Paris. Its army was invincible; its palaces unparalleled; the domes of its many mosques quite literally glittered with gold. By the time of Safdarjung's death, the Persian Nadir Shah had been and gone, carrying with him the accumulated riches of eight generations of Empire. Three Emperors had been murdered (one was, in addition, first blinded with a hot needle); the mother of one ruler was strangled and the father of another forced off a precipice on his elephant. Delhi, the great capital, was left a city of gutted ruins.

To be Emperor during this period was a highly dangerous undertaking. The longest surviving sovereign of the age, the Emperor Muhammed Shah (called *Rangila*, or the Colourful), survived by the simple ruse of giving up any pretence of ruling: in the morning he watched partridge and elephant fights; in the afternoon he was entertained by jugglers, ventriloquists, mime artists and conjurers. Politics he wisely left to his scheming advisers.

While the empire was being gradually reduced to a fraction of its former size, the court gave itself over to pleasure and sensuality. As the aristocracy gradually lost all interest in war and soldiering, they diverted their remaining funds into frequenting courtesans, patronizing poets, holding *mehfils* (literary evenings) and constructing pavilions and pleasure gardens. Music, writing and nautch dancing all flourished; the old military aristocracy complained that it was now sitar and sarangi players, not generals and cavalrymen, who were rewarded with honours and estates. Poets were so highly esteemed that it was said that a Delhi-wallah visiting a friend in another part of India would always take with him as a present not jewels or hookahs or fine weapons but a few of Mir Taqi Mir's new verses copied on to a single sheet of paper. A new *ghazal* (love lyric) by one of the great Delhi poets was considered the most desirable gift that any civilized host could wish for.

While Muhammed Shah and his circle busied themselves with amusement, Safdarjung consolidated his position. From his palace in Lucknow, the Nawab governed a province which stretched from Bengal through the rich plains of North India to the Doab. It was the most fertile land in India; Delhi was far away and the hold of the Emperors was becoming ever weaker. Safdarjung was the richest and most powerful man in India; in all but name he had become an independent ruler. On the death of Muhammed Shah, Safdarjung moved in to take over. He seized the post of Vizier (Prime Minister) and within weeks Muhammed Shah's ineffectual successor had been effectively excluded from all decisions; he remained a figurehead, left to console himself with drink, opium and his harem.

Eventually, however, Safdarjung overplayed his hand. His arrogance and bullying alienated the Imperial family; and in their desperation they called in the armies of the Hindu Mahratta Confederacy from the Deccan to help rid them of their troublesome Vizier. In the Civil War that followed, as rival armies from all over India converged on Delhi, Safdarjung was finally driven out of the capital. He returned only in death when his son begged permission to build his father's tomb in the waste land to the southwest of Shahjehanabad.

The tomb stands today as a telling memorial to the period. Most obviously, it demonstrates the strained circumstances of the age. Compared to the purity of the Taj Mahal — the spotless white marble, the unfussy shapes, the perfectly balanced design — Safdarjung's tomb with its bulbous dome and stained sandstone walls seems somehow flawed and degenerate. Every schoolchild the world over knows the profile of the Taj, and in so far as Safdarjung's tomb is different, it at first sight looks wrong: its lines look somehow faulty, naggingly incorrect.

Moreover, the tomb has an unmistakably threadbare quality to it. As the traditional Delhi quarries near Agra were no longer controlled by the Mughals – the road between Delhi and Agra was usually blocked by wild and hostile Jat tribesmen – the builders were forced to strip other Delhi tombs in order to gather the material for Safdarjung's memorial. Half-way through the construction, the marble appears to have run out. Prominent strips of inlay were left unfinished; awkward patches of pink sandstone intrude into the glistening white of the dome. The effect is like a courtier in a tatty second-hand livery: the intention grand, but the actual impression tawdry, almost ridiculous.

Nevertheless, the longer you look, the more the qualities and character of the tomb become apparent and the clearer it is that the architect was not simply trying to imitate the Taj and failing. He had another, quite different aesthetic he was aiming to achieve – a sort of blowzy Mughal rococo. His design was the product of another age with very different, more eccentric tastes. The tomb shows how the aesthetes of the age of Safdarjung liked their gateways to be as ornately sculpted as their prose was purple; how they preferred their onion domes to be overextended and tapered; how they thought the interior of a tomb incomplete unless covered with a rococo riot of elaborate plasterwork.

For anyone used to the chaste purity of the Taj, it is here in the interior that the biggest surprises lie: inside, the capitals have turned almost into cabbages as they curve and curl in vegetable convulsions. They throw up stamens and tendrils past the stalactite *murqanas* and squinches, gripping and voluting towards the floral boss of the low inner dome. Even the pillars have taken root and become living things, blossoming into lotus filials at the base, cusping around the voussoirs of the arch, erupting out into little *jharokha* balconies at the top. The spirit is fecund, Bacchanalian, almost orgiastic.

Like some elderly courtesan, the tomb tries to mask its imperfections beneath thick layers of make-up; its excesses of ornament are worn like over-applied rouge. Even the little mosque to the side of the gatehouse has a whiff of degeneracy about it: its three domes are flirtatiously striped like the flared pyjama bottoms of a nautch girl; there is something fundamentally voluptuous in its buxom curves and poise.

Despite its sad little economies, Safdarjung's tomb exudes the flavour of an age not so much decaying miserably into impoverished anonymity as one whoring and drinking itself into extinction. The building tells a story of drunken laughter as the pillars of empire collapsed in a cloud of dust and masonry; and afterwards, of dancing in the ruins.

If poetry, music and elephant fights were the preferred amusements of the court, the humbler folk of the age of Safdarjung had their partridges. Again and again in the letters and diaries of the period there are references to both partridge and elephant fights; they also feature prominently in the miniature illustrations of late Mughal manuscripts.

Both sports were clearly popular and well-established traditions; but when I asked my Indian friends about their survival in modern Delhi, they all shook their heads. As far as any of them knew, the last elephant fights had taken place around the turn of the century in the princely states of Rajputana; and as for partridge fights, said my friends, those sorts of Mughal traditions had all died out at Partition. I might find the odd partridge fight surviving in Lahore or somewhere in Pakistan, they thought, but not in Delhi.

It was Balvinder Singh who one day in late January suddenly announced, quite unprompted, that he would not be on duty on Sunday as he and his father Punjab Singh were going to watch what he called a 'bird challenge'. The fights apparently took place every Sunday morning in a Muslim cemetery in Old Delhi: '*Bahot acha* event *hai*,' said Balvinder. 'All very good birds fighting, very good money making, all very happy people enjoying.'

I asked whether I could come along too; and Balvinder agreed.

The following Sunday at six in the morning the three of us set off from International Backside into the thick early morning mist. As we neared the cemetery, the streets began to fill with people, all heading in the same direction. Some were carrying bulky packages

159

covered with thick quilted cloths. Every so often one of the packages would let out a loud squawk.

The cemetery lay within a high walled enclosure at the back of the Old Delhi Idgah. Despite the early hour, the arched gateway into the cemetery was already jammed with *chai* wallahs and snack sellers trying to push their barrows through the narrow entrance. On the far side a crowd of two or three hundred people had already gathered: craggy old Muslims with long beards and mountainous turbans; small Hindu shopkeepers in blue striped *lungis*; Kashmiri pandits in long frock coats and Congress hats.

The crowd milled around chatting and exchanging tips, hawking and spitting, slurping tea and placing bets. As the partridge enthusiasts pottered about, three elderly men tried to clear a space in the centre of the cemetery. They strutted around, sombre and authoritative, clearly in charge of the proceedings. These, explained Balvinder in his (characteristically loud) stage whisper, were the *khalifas*, the headmen of the partridge fights.

'Very big men,' said Balvinder approvingly.

'How do you become a *khalifa*?' I asked.

'Experience and market value,' said Punjab.

'You must be very good fighter,' added Balvinder, 'and you must have too many *titar* (partridges). This man here has one hundred fighting birds . . .'

The *khalifa* whom Balvinder had pointed out came up and introduced himself. He was a very old man; he had blacked his eyelids with collyrium and his teeth and upper lip were heavily stained with *paan*. His name was Azar Khalifa and he lived in Sarai Khalil in the Churi Wallan Gulli of the Old City.

'We *khalifas* live for the bird challenge,' he said. 'We have no other occupation.'

Azar and Punjab Singh agreed that Delhi was the best place to see the partridge challenge in the whole of the subcontinent. 'I have seen the partridge fights of Lucknow, Jaipur and Peshawar,' said Azar. 'But never have I seen anything like the fights in Delhi. *Khalifas* come here from all over India and Pakistan to participate.'

Some of Azar Khalifa's partridges were fighting in the match that day, and the old man showed us his birds. From behind the headstone of an old Muslim grave he produced an oblong parcel

160

trussed up in flowery chintz. Unbuckling the fastenings, he removed the wraps and uncovered a wickerwork cage. Inside, separated by a dividing trellis, were two fine plump partridges.

'This one lady. This one gent,' explained Balvinder.

The birds responded with a loud cry of 'Ti-lo! Ti-lo!'

Of the two birds, the male was the more beautiful. It had superb black markings as precise and perfect as a Bewick wood engraving running down its spine; lighter, more downy plumage covered its chest. Half-way along the back of the lower legs you could see the vicious spur with which the birds fought.

'I feed my birds on milk, almonds and sugar cane,' said Azar, sticking his finger through the cage and tickling the female under its neck. 'The males I train every day so that they can jump and run without feeling too much tired.'

As we talked there was a shout from one of the other *khalifas*; the first fight was about to begin.

Azar called me over and with a flourish sat me down on a plastic deckchair at the front of the ring of spectators. The open space in the middle had been carefully brushed and in its centre squatted two men about five feet apart; by their sides stood two cages, each containing a pair of birds. The spectators – now arranged in two ranks, those at the front squatting, those behind standing upright – hurriedly finished placing their bets. A hush fell on the graveyard.

At a signal from Azar, the two contestants unhitched the front gate of the cage; the two cock partridges strutted out. As they did so, their mates began to squawk in alarm and encouragement. The males responded by puffing up their chests and circling slowly towards each other. Again the hens shrieked 'Ti-lo! Ti-lo!' and again the males drew closer to one another.

Then, quite suddenly, one of the two cocks lost his nerve. He turned and rushed back towards the cage; but finding the gate barred, he skittered off towards the nearest group of spectators, hotly pursued by his enemy. At the edge of the ring the cock took off, flying up amid a shower of feathers into the lower branches of a nearby tree. There he remained, shrieking 'Ti-lo!', his chest heaving up and down in fright. The rival male, meanwhile, strutted around the deserted lady partridge in ill-disguised triumph. The hen averted her head.

This first short fight obviously disappointed the connoisseurs in the audience. Balvinder shook his head at me across the ring: 'This one very weakling bird,' he shouted. 'This one very weakling.'

Money was exchanged, the two contestants shook hands, and their place in the ring was taken by a second pair of fighters: a

Rajput with a handlebar moustache, and a small but fierce-looking Muslim who sported a bushy black beard. To my eyes the new pair of partridges were indistinguishable from any of the other birds I had seen that day, but the rest of the audience clearly thought otherwise. A murmur of approval passed through the crowd; Balvinder got out his wallet and handed two 100-rupee notes to his neighbour.

At another signal from Azar Khalifa the two gates were pulled back and again the cocks ran out. This time there was no bluffing. Encouraged by the raucous shrieks of their mates, the two birds rushed at each other. Handlebar's bird, which was the lighter of the two, gave the Muslim's bird a vicious switch across its forehead; the darker bird responded by ripping at its rival's throat. The two then fenced at each other with their beaks, each parrying the other's thrust. A frisson went around the crowd: this was more like it. Despite the violence, the blood and the cloud of feathers, I was surprised to find it strangely thrilling to watch: it was like a miniature gladiator contest.

The two birds had now broken loose from each other and withdrawn to the vicinity of their respective cages. Then Handlebar's cock suddenly jumped into the air, flew the distance that separated it from its rival and came down on the darker bird with its neck arched and talons open. The spurs ripped at the Muslim's bird and drew blood on its back, just above the wing. The bird rolled over, but on righting itself managed to give its attacker a sharp peck on its wing tip as it tried to escape. Then, scampering up behind Handlebar's bird it grabbed its rival by the neck, gripped, and forced it down on to its side. The first bird lay pinioned there for four or five seconds before it managed to break free and fly off.

Handlebar's mate had meanwhile broken out in a kind of partridge death-wail. The cry was taken up by the loser of the previous fight who was still watching the new contest from his tree. Soon the whole graveyard was alive with the squawking of excited partridges.

The action had also electrified the crowd who were pressing in on the ring despite the best efforts of the *khalifas* to keep them all back. Someone knocked over the tray of a *chai* wallah and there were loud oaths from the squatting men over whom the tea had fallen. But the incident was soon forgotten. The Muslim's bird had gone back on to the offensive, swooping down with its spurs and ripping a great gash along its enemy's cheek. It followed the attack up with a vicious peck just above the other bird's beak. Handlebar's bird looked stunned for a second then withdrew backwards towards its mate.

The ring which had originally been twenty feet across was now little wider than seven or eight feet; the squatters were now standing and getting in everyone else's view. In the middle, Handlebar was looking extremely agitated. Although the rules laid down that he could not directly intervene he hissed at the hen who dutifully shrieked out a loud distress call. This checked her mate's retreat and the bird turned around to face the Muslim's partridge with his back against her cage.

The proximity to his hen seemed to bring the cock new resolution. For a few seconds the two birds stood facing each other, chests fully extended; then Handlebar's bird flew at its rival with a new and sudden violence. He dealt the Muslim's bird a glancing blow with the hook of his beak, then rose up, wings arched, and fell heavily on the lighter bird's head. As he hopped out of reach he again cut the darker bird with his spurs.

The reprisal never came. The Muslim's bird slowly righted itself, got unsteadily to its feet, then limped off through the legs of the crowd. There was a great cheer from the spectators. Balvinder jumped up and down, punched the air, then promptly confronted the man with whom he had made the bet. The latter grudgingly handed over a stash of notes. All around the ring wallets were being slapped open and shut; fingers were being angrily pointed. Everywhere arguments were breaking out between debtors and creditors, winners and losers. The outsider had clearly won.

Suddenly there was a cry from the gateway; and the *khalifas* started ushering everyone to one side. All the spectators frowned.

'What's happening?' I asked Punjab, who had come up beside me.

'This *khalifa* is saying one dead body is coming. We must leave the graveyard for an hour.'

'Now?'

Having described the main shrines and Sufi festivals and mystics, Khan goes on to list the city's secular personalities: the nobles, the musicians and the great *femmes fatales*. These figures range from Azam Khan, 'one of the chief nobles of the Empire' whose principal claim to fame is his vast harem and his insatiable appetites ('a pederast, he is also fond of beautiful girls . . . whenever he is informed of the availability of a lad or a fine wench he endeavours to be the buyer'); through Taqi, 'one of the famous eunuchs and the ringleader of the conjurors of Hindustan' ('his house is the abode of delicate beauties, some as fair as the dawn while others are as dark as volatile passion'); to great musicians such as the blind drummer Shah Nawaz who played his own stomach as if it was a *tabla* drum; or the disgusting Surkhi, a glutton who 'snored and expectorated loudly' but whose horrible habits were overlooked by his hosts because of the unique beauty of his voice ('as melodious as a nightingale'), his brilliant mimicry and his ready wit.

Best of all were the dancers and courtesans – beautiful women like Ad Begum whose speciality was to appear naked at parties, but so cleverly painted that no one noticed: 'she decorates her legs with beautiful drawings in the style of pyjamas instead of actually wearing them; in place of the cuffs she draws flowers and petals in ink exactly as found in the finest cloth of Rum.'

The most famous of the courtesans was Nur Bai, whose popularity was such that every night the elephants of the great amirs completely blocked the narrow lanes outside her house. Even the greatest nobles could only gain admittance by sending in presents of large sums of money: 'whosoever gets enamoured of her gets sucked into the whirlpool of her demands,' writes Dargah Quli Khan, 'and brings ruin upon himself and his house. Many people have become paupers after their association with her but the pleasure of her company can only be had as long as one is in possession of riches to bestow on her.' Meeting Nur Bai was clearly one of the highlights of Khan's visit to Delhi and at the end of his description he quietly drops in the fact that he 'had the good fortune of spending some time in her company . . .'

But if it was the courtesans that captured Dargah Quli Khan's imagination, his real admiration was reserved for the Delhi poets. One of the most interesting descriptions in the *Muraqqa'* is of the

167

famous *mehfils*, the literary or musical evenings for which the city was then renowned. 'Although Hazeen [a Persian Sufi] leads a life of purity and charm, there is always a large crowd gathered in his house,' wrote Khan. 'In the evening, the courtyard of his house is swept and sprinkled with rosewater and colourful carpets are spread out on a raised platform. The great poets then start the recitation of their work. Hazeen's verses make the audience ecstatic and inspire them to polish their own skills.'

Other *mehfils*, however, attracted crowds for non-literary reasons:

> [The poet Miran] is humble, well-mannered and hospitable. [But] he is also a connoisseur in the art of attracting charming new faces . . . As a result Miran's *mehfils* always attract the beautiful and their lovers. Dancers begin to assemble from morning onwards . . . A large number of pretty young lads are lured to the show including both Hindu and Muslim catamites. Good looking women gather in such large numbers that the mere sight of them appeases the appetite, although [of course] for the lecherous this does not suffice.

Khan was in Delhi in 1739, during the Persian invasion, and he witnessed the bloody massacre when Nadir Shah's soldiers went berserk and massacred 150,000 Delhi-wallahs. In most histories the massacre is said to mark the end of Mughal Delhi's greatness, yet Khan clearly sees the invasion as only a temporary setback for the city. Certainly it dimmed the brightness of some of the *mehfils* – one noble was forced to 'lay his capital at the feet of the Emperor' during the invasion and afterwards his *mehfils* are described as 'subdued' – but there is no indication that Khan regarded the invasion as the end of an era; only with hindsight would that become clear. Instead, despite writing soon after Nadir Shah had returned to Persia, the overwhelming impression that Khan tries to convey is still of a bawdy city of joy, a place remarkable for its wild parties, its lively celebrations and orgiastic festivals.

It is, of course, an image of the city very far removed from the way most Delhi people conceive of their home today. Modern Delhi is thought of either as a city of grey bureaucracy, or as the metropolis of hard-working, *nouveau-riche* Punjabis. It is rarely spoken of as a lively city, and never as a promiscuous one. Yet, as I discovered that December, the bawdiness of Safdar Jung's Delhi does survive, kept alive by one particular group of Delhi-wallahs.

You can still find them in the dark gullies of the Old City – if you know where to look.

Turkman Gate lies on the southern edge of Old Delhi. Most of the ancient city walls were pulled down twenty years ago and the gate now stands alone on a traffic island like a great beached whale washed up on the edge of the city.

One morning in mid-January I jumped over the railings and climbed up to the parapet of the gate. It was a little before dawn; the Old City was just getting up. Sweepers raked the dirt and dung away from the front of stalls; a muezzin called from the minaret of a nearby mosque; *chai* wallahs pulled their blankets closer around them and lit their burners to boil the first tea saucepan of the day. It was still very cold.

I waited for a full hour before I caught a glimpse of the sight that I had come to see. Just as the sun was rising, a solitary bicycle rickshaw jolted out of the labyrinth of the Old City and trundled underneath the gate. Inside were three figures. They were clad in brightly coloured silks and muslins, flowing saris edged in glittering gold brocade. They were heavily made up, with painted cheeks and scarlet lipstick; each of their noses was pierced with a single diamond stud. They were dressed for the nautch, dressed as women, yet they were not women. Even at a distance of twenty yards I could see that their physiognomy was very different from the delicate features of Indian girls. Their faces were too strong, their arms were too thick, their shoulders were wrong. They smoked. Physically, they resembled painted men, yet they were not men. Like Dargah Quli Khan's friend Taqi, the figures in the rickshaw were all eunuchs.

Eunuchs were once common over the width of Eurasia. They are fleetingly referred to in ancient Assyrian and Babylonian stelae and became popular as servants – and as passive sexual playthings – in the degenerate days of the later Roman Empire. In the Muslim world their impotence made them perfect harem guards and they

169

rose to power as chamberlains, governors and even generals. They were slaves in Anglo-Saxon England and survived in Italy well into the nineteenth century, singing castrato roles in opera as well as in the Vatican Sistine choir.

Yet today eunuchs have apparently died out everywhere except in the subcontinent. Here they are still not uncommon figures in the poorer parts of the larger cities. In all there are thought to be some three-quarters of a million of them surviving. Modern Indian eunuchs dress as women and arrive uninvited at weddings and birth celebrations. They dance and sing and make bawdy jokes. From the poor they extract money in payment for the good luck and fecundity that their blessings are supposed to impart. From the rich they take larger sums by threatening to strip naked unless paid to leave; terrified middle-class party-givers will give them anything as long as they go quickly. They are volatile, vulgar and can sometimes be violent.

Yet despite their frequent appearances in public, very little is actually known about the Indian eunuchs. They are fiercely secretive and of their own choice inhabit a dim world of ambiguity and half-truths. They trust no one, and hate being questioned about their lives; if they are pressed, at best they will slam their doors in your face. Only occasionally does a scandal – a stabbing during a territorial dispute or rumours of a forcible castration – throw them into the headlines and into the clear light of day.

For ten days after that first sighting from the top of the Turkman Gate, I trawled the teeming alleys of Old Delhi, trying to identify the houses of the eunuchs and attempting to persuade one of them to talk to me. Sometimes I would receive a monosyllabic answer to a question, but generally my enquiries were met with either blank silences or, more often, with graphic expletives.

One fruitless morning, after an unusually rude dismissal from a eunuch's house, I retired dispirited to a nearby *dhaba* for a cup of *chai*. There I finally decided to throw in my efforts at making contact with the Delhi eunuchs; it was taking up a lot of time and there was still no hint of a breakthrough: after ten days I still knew as little about them as I had when I had begun. While I was sitting there, sipping my glass of hot, sweet Indian tea, I was approached by a shifty-looking man who asked me whether I could help him;

he had seen me with my camera; could I help him mend his? I had nothing better to do, so I agreed to try. He led me to his house and in a few minutes I had diagnosed the trouble – a flat battery. Zakir thanked me and then quietly revealed that he had been watching me for several days. He knew what I was looking for; and he indicated that he might be able to help.

He was, he said, a jeweller. His family had always been Delhi jewellers – his ancestors had served the Mughal emperors and before them the Delhi Sultans. At the court they had made the jewellery for the Imperial eunuchs. When the British evicted the Mughals from the Red Fort in 1857, some of the court eunuchs had come to live nearby, a few minutes' walk from the Turkman Gate. There his family had continued to serve them. He said that he had known all the local eunuchs since his childhood, and that he still made all their jewellery. I had helped him, he said, now it was his obligation to help me. He instructed me to meet him the next day at the Turkman Gate, soon after dawn. He would see what he could do.

I was there on time, and Zakir was true to his word. He led me through the narrow alleys of the Old City until we came to a lane barely two feet wide. At the end of the lane, round a chicken-leg turn lay a large *haveli* of the late Mughal period. He knocked three times, and the door swung open.

Like most things in Delhi, the curious position of the eunuchs in Indian society can be explained by the head-on collision of two very different traditions, one Muslim, one Hindu.

Hijras (eunuchs) are referred to in the very earliest of Hindu texts, the Vedas, written in the second millennium BC. Here castration was seen as a degrading punishment meted out only to the very lowest in society. An Untouchable who was caught urinating near a Brahmin could be castrated, as could any lower-caste Hindu who had sex with a Brahmin woman. The act of castration brought the criminal to a level even lower than the Untouchables. By the time of the *Mahabharata*, one thousand years later, the position of eunuchs had improved very little. To be a eunuch was a curse;

171

even the sight of them was defiling to a Brahmin. No one was allowed to accept alms from them, no one was allowed to consume food prepared by them, they were excluded from all sacrifices. As a solitary concession, non-Brahmins were permitted to watch them dance.

The position of eunuchs in Islam was always very different. Although the Prophet Muhammad forbade castration, eunuchs were always common in Muslim society and because of their sterility were considered free of the taint of sexuality. They were thus especially suitable to guard sacred relics and great sanctuaries. The shirt of Muhammad in Cairo was guarded by eunuchs, as was the Great Mosque in Mecca. Pilgrims – *hajjis* – would kiss the eunuchs' hands on their way to the see the Ka'ba, the most holy shrine in all Islam.

Dedicated courtiers, undistracted by families, they soon rose to powerful positions, first in Mameluk Egypt, then in Ottoman Turkey, but most prominently of all in Mughal India. 'The kings, princes, queens and princesses place great confidence in these people,' wrote the Italian traveller Niccolao Manucchi. 'All people of quality have eunuchs in their service and all the other officials, servants and slaves are bound to account to the eunuchs for all they do.' As officials and as singers, dancers and conjurors they were still prominent figures in Safdar Jung's Delhi; according to Dargah Quli Khan, Taqi was a favourite of the Emperor and had 'access to His Majesty's private apartments'.

When the Mughal court was disbanded, Muslim *hijras* were exposed for the first time to the other, Hindu, tradition of eunuchry. In typical Delhi fashion the two traditions merged, and the *hijras* became subject to a very Indian compromise.

To give birth to a hermaphrodite is still considered by simple Indians to be one of the most terrible curses that can befall a woman. At the same time the blessing of a *hijra* is considered to be unusually potent. It can make a barren woman fertile. It can scare off malevolent djinns. It can nullify the evil eye. In the streets *hijras* are jeered at, sometimes even pelted with rubbish. Yet at a poor family's most crucial and most public celebrations, at a marriage or at the birth of a male child, the absence of a *hijra* would almost invalidate the whole ceremony. The eunuchs themselves have aided the merging of the two traditions. They no longer guard harems; instead, as in the *Mahabharata*, they dance for a living. They no longer dress like men as they did in the Mughal court; instead they deck themselves in jewellery and cosmetics and wear saris. Nevertheless, they retain many of the characteristics of their courtly forebears.

Manucchi gives a rather patronizing description of characteristics and temperaments of the eunuchs of Mughal times. 'Among the qualities of this sort of animal is their extreme covetousness in collecting gold, silver, diamonds and pearls,' he writes. 'They are afraid to spend money even when it is necessary, fond of receiving, niggardly in giving. Nevertheless they are anxious to appear well dressed. They are foul in speech and fond of silly stories. Yet among Mohammedans they are the strictest observers of the faith.'

Manucchi obviously disliked the Delhi eunuchs: 'They are baboons,' he wrote, 'insolent, licentious baboons.' Anyone who comes across them casually today can easily see why he was so rude. Yet you do not have to spend very long with them to appreciate how India, then as now, has turned them into what they are, how it has brutalized them and forced them to anaesthetize their own sensibilities.

Thrown out of their homes, rejected by their families, they come together for protection. In the streets they affect the manners of a pantomime dame to gain attention: they pinch men's buttocks, purposely make buffoons of themselves, but are quick to take offence. With little possibility of much fulfilment in this world, they look to the next; they are for ever visiting temples and mosques (for this they are required to revert to their male clothes) and going on pilgrimage to Hindu and Muslim shrines over the subcontinent. In this strange mix of piety and bawdiness, they directly recall the world of Dargah Quli Khan and the *Muraqqa'-e-Dehli*.

The house was a late Mughal *haveli* off Gulli Mr Shiv Prasad. A pretty young eunuch in a canary-yellow silk sari led Zakir and me through a vaulted passageway and out into a small courtyard.

Under a wooden veranda lay a spread of carpets and divans.

173

Sprawled over them were two more eunuchs; one was staring at herself in a mirror, applying lipstick, the other was combing her hair. Nearby sat two effeminate-looking men; there was also a baby in a cradle. Despite the early hour, the eunuchs were all dressed and painted as if they were about to go out to a late-night nautch. They greeted Zakir warmly, but frowned at me.

'Who's the *gora* [white]?' asked one.

'This is my friend Mr William,' said Zakir. 'He's a writer.'

'Why have you brought him here?'

'He would like to meet you all.'

'You know we can't talk to any outsiders,' replied the *hijra*, 'unless Chaman Guruji gives us permission.'

'And she won't,' said the other *hijra*, pouting defiantly at me. 'She doesn't like *goras*.'

'Where is Chaman?' asked Zakir.

'Upstairs. She's sick.'

We climbed the rickety wooden stairs that led up to a balcony; as we did so, one of the eunuchs blew a kiss at me and the others burst out laughing. At the top of the stairs, Zakir knocked at the door. A gruff voice commanded us to enter.

As we stepped through the portal, we left the late Mughal *haveli* behind and entered a very different world: inside we were confronted by a gleaming pink boudoir that could have been the dressing-room of a 1950s Hollywood film star. Mirror-glass tiles covered the end walls and the ceiling; pink plastic carnations peeped out of brass vases; cut-out pictures of actors and actresses were pasted into a frieze over a glass bookcase filled with Hindi videos. The pink chintz curtains matched the pink chintz bedspread; underneath it, prostrate yet fully dressed in a woman's blouse and man's dhoti, sprawled the figure of Chaman, the guru of the household.

Chaman's fingernails were brightly painted and her hair was long and straggly; she had huge sagging breasts. Yet her face with its heavy jowls, hangover eyes and early-morning stubble was entirely that of a man. As we entered the bloated face nodded us a silent greeting.

'Chamanji,' said Zakir. 'You are unwell?'

'I'm dying,' said Chaman. Then, groaning: 'Oh! The pain!'

'What is wrong with you Chamanji?' asked Zakir.

Chaman Guru

'Nothing works any more. This body . . .'

'Is it your knees again?'

'My knees. And my teeth. And my breathing.'

'Have you seen a doctor?'

'I had an injection yesterday. For the asthma. It's like trying to breathe through a thick *chador*.'

Chaman held up the pink bedspread against her mouth to demonstrate what she meant.

'I'm in pain, I'm probably dying, and all my little *chelas* [disciples] are leaving me. I had seven, now only three are left to look after their old mother. Remember Maya? She went off last month and married a boy from Pakistan. Promised she would come and see me, but you know what these little *chelas* are like . . .' Chaman suddenly began to look rather sad. 'I can't even *see* properly any more. And as for my teeth . . .'

'What's happened to your teeth?' asked Zakir.

'I had them all out last month. Got new ones put in. Look.'

175

Chaman pulled out her dentures and flourished them at us. As she did so she seemed to notice me for the first time.

'Who's your *gora*, Zakir?'

'This is my friend, Mr William.'

I smiled. Chaman frowned.

'Is he your boyfriend?'

'No,' said Zakir. 'He's married. To a girl.'

Chaman wrinkled up her nose in disgust.

'He has brought you a present, Chamanji,' continued Zakir.

From the bottom of my pocket I produced a silver *ta'wiz*, the Sufi charm Zakir had suggested I purchase as a gift for Chaman. I handed it to the guru. A fat hand shot out from the covers and snatched it from me.

'Who gave you this?' asked Chaman.

'Pir Hassan Naqshbandi,' I said.

'Naqshbandi, eh?'

Chaman bit the corner of the *ta'wiz*. This seemed to satisfy her as to its authenticity.

'It will make you well again,' I said hopefully.

'Nothing will make me well again.' The old eunuch fixed me with a sharp eye. 'Are you American? From the land of Hollywood?'

'No. I'm British.'

'From London?'

'From Scotland.'

'You know Sean Connery? I read in a magazine that he was from Scotland.'

'You're right. He is.'

'In the old times we *hijras* used to be like your zero zero seven. We were called *khwaja saras*, not *hijras*. We used to live in the king's house. In those days we never danced. Our job was to listen and tell things to the king. We were just like your Sean Connery.'

Somehow I couldn't imagine Chaman and her household taking on Goldfinger or seducing Ursula Andress, but I let this pass.

'I love the movies,' continued Chaman. 'When I was a girl I wanted to be an actress. Look!'

From the bedside table Chaman produced a black and white photograph. It showed a beautiful, heavy-boned girl in a European dress. She had heavily rouged lips and painted eyebrows. A velvet

176

choker was tied around her neck; massive gold earrings hung from her lobes. The tone was sub-Garbo; only the *tikka* mark between the eyebrows gave away that the image was Indian.

'That was me when I was twenty-five,' said Chaman. 'I was beautiful, no?'

'Unique,' I said.

Chaman blushed with pleasure: 'You mean it?'

After the breakthrough with Chaman it still took two months of regular visits with Zakir before I got to know the other eunuchs properly.

I used to arrive early in the morning before the household had left on their rounds. They would always be busy putting on their make-up and brushing their hair. Often there would be some drama: Razia, the loudest and most ebullient of Chaman's *chelas* would be wringing her hands and weeping because her new boy-friend had gone off to Ajmer or because Chaman had called her a tart or because her pet goat had gone missing; she always suspected her neighbours were planning to slaughter it.

Another source of worry was the baby girl that Panna, another of Chaman's *chelas*, had adopted; if ever it wheezed or coughed or refused its food, Panna would work herself up into an opera of agitation. The only *hijra* who always kept her calm was Vimla, the prettiest and quietest of Chaman's *chelas*. She was in charge of the kitchen and by seven in the morning would be busy chopping up chillies and onions ready for lunch.

Razia, Panna and Vimla were all very different – in their back-grounds, their characters, and their looks. Razia was the most unlikely of the three. A Kashmiri Muslim, she claimed to have been to the Doon School (the Indian Eton) and to have completed a Master's degree in English at Bombay University. I was never able to establish whether she was telling the truth – virtually all the *hijras* I talked to shrouded the facts of their lives in a thick wrap of fantasies – but she was certainly from a middle-class background and spoke fluent English.

'I became a *hijra* very late – in my mid-twenties – after my

177

mother died,' she once said. 'I was born with a body that was masculine but my heart was always feminine. I never fitted in anywhere, but now I feel good with these people.'

'Was it very difficult when you first joined the *hijras*?' I asked.

'When I arrived it was very strange. Everyone lived together; there was no privacy. The six other *chelas* were all illiterate and came from villages. Before I used to be a real reader; but here there was not one book in the house. None of them even read a newspaper. But Chaman was very protective and supportive; it was as if I was still living with my mother.'

She added: 'Sometimes I wanted desperately to go home, to see my sisters. Once I went all the way home – but I never went in. I just looked in the window then went away.'

'Did the other eunuchs accept you?' I asked. 'Didn't they mind your posh background?'

'Not at all. Thanks to Chaman they were kind to me. Besides I was useful to them. I was able to talk English and to read and write. We are all happy together. Sometimes when I see Panna with her baby I wish I was a woman and had a husband and a child. But Chaman doesn't like us to have partners. She doesn't like men in the house – at least not corrupt men. She's very jealous of her daughters.'

Panna, Razia's friend, was a very different creature. She was a very large *hijra*: nearly six feet tall. Her face was covered with the scars of smallpox and she had a huge protruding belly; a shadow of light stubble flecked her chin. She would never have won a beauty contest. But she was one of the shyest of all the *hijras* I met, and one of the most gentle; her life revolved entirely around the baby she had just adopted. Her story emerged only after I had got to know her very well.

It seems that Panna was born asexual – with no visible sexual characteristics – into a poor family who lived in a village near Varanasi. When Panna was just twenty days old, the village midwife disclosed that she was neither male nor female, that she was a *hijra*. The news spread like wildfire. Panna's mother, fearing the consequences, left the village with the baby and went to stay with a cousin fifty kilometres away.

'In the village, my deformity had become the sole topic of conversation,' Panna told me. 'The rest of my family were ostracized. It was said that we were cursed. The following day a relative came to the village and said that my mother had died of shock soon after reaching her cousin's house.

'I was brought back along with the body of my mother. The death did not move the village. Instead they sent a message to Chaman, who used to visit the village every so often. The curse on the village had to be removed. Chaman came with two *chelas* and took me away. I grew up to be the *chela* of Chaman, and Chaman became my guru.

'Being a *hijra* was the only possibility for me; there was no other career I could have pursued with the body that was given to me at birth. Sometimes I used to be lonely and unhappy, but now with the baby my life is complete. Now I don't care what people say: at times I look at the child and I am so happy I can't sleep at night. When she is older I will send the child to a good girls' school and see that she is taught English. Maybe one day she will be beautiful and become a model or film star.'

Panna is unusual in that she was born asexual. The vast majority of eunuchs, and almost all those I met, were born physically male. In Europe they would probably describe themselves as transsexuals and have a full sex change. But in India the technology for this does not exist. The only choice is between a brutal – and extremely dangerous – village castration, or, for those who can afford it, a course in hormone pills followed by an anaesthetized operation. The operation is illegal in India, but there are several doctors who, for a fee, are willing to take the risk.

Vimla, the most feminine-looking of the eunuchs, did not have the money for an operation and voluntarily underwent a village castration. The son of a Jat farmer outside Delhi, by the age of thirteen she was already refusing to work in the fields, saying that she felt more like a woman than a man. 'I was sure that I did not have a place in either male or female worlds,' she told me. 'My body was that of a man but deep down I had the heart of a woman. At puberty I started thinking of myself as a *hijra*.

'One day a *hijra* named Benazir came to my village. She was very beautiful and I fell in love with her. When I was on my own I would feel sad and would not eat properly. Only when Benazir

179

returned did I feel happy. My family began to suspect that I was in love, but they did not know with whom. But in the village people who had seen Benazir and me together began to gossip.'

A lucrative marriage settlement that Vimla's family were negotiating fell through as rumours began to spread. In frustration and shame, Vimla's father beat her up. The following day Vimla ran away to Delhi to look for Benazir.

'For days I searched for my Benazir, but I did not have an address or know the name of her guru. I knew no one in Delhi and had no money. I had to sleep on the pavements and beg for money. Occasionally I got a free meal from the *pirzadas* [officials] at the shrine of Khwaja Nizamuddin, but often I would go to bed hungry.'

Eventually Vimla met and was adopted by Chaman Guru.

'In those days Chaman was very rich and beautiful. She became my guru and gave me lots of beautiful saris and gold bangles. I started to wear women's clothes and to put on make-up. The following year I was taken to a village in the Punjab. I was dosed with opium and a string was tied around my equipment. Then the whole lot was cut off.

'I knew it would be very painful and dangerous, but I got cut so that no one would taunt me any more. After I was cut all my male blood flowed away and with it went my manhood. Before I was neither one thing nor the other. Now I am a *hijra*. I am not man or woman. I am from a different sex.'

I once asked Vimla if she ever missed family life.

'We *are* a family,' she said. 'A *chela* must obey her guru like a bride obeys her mother-in-law. We *chelas* must work hard, do the cooking inside the house, and most of the dancing outside. We have an obligation to look after our guru when she grows old, just like we would look after our own mother. In return, when we first become *hijras* Chaman Guru teaches us *chelas* the ways of the eunuchs.'

The longer I spent with the eunuchs, the more it became clear that the whole system was highly structured, both within the household and outside it. Just as every household of eunuchs has

180

its strict rules within its walls, so each household also has a well defined 'parish' where its members are allowed to operate. Violations – poaching in another household's area – is referred to a special council of eunuchs from all over India and Pakistan which meets once a year.

There is even a Central School of Dance for the *hijras*. It occupies a shady campus dotted with bushes of purple bougainvillaea in Panipat, fifty kilometres to the north of Delhi. Here Prem Hijra, a bad-tempered old eunuch with a bun and beady black eyes, offers courses in dancing (folk, Bharat Natyam, Arab belly dancing or disco) and singing (traditional, *ghazals* or modern film songs) to new recruits. She also runs refresher courses for those who want to perfect a particular style of dancing or learn the latest film songs.

'She's very strict,' Vimla once told me, 'But they say that in her youth she was the best dancer in North India.'

I pressed Vimla to show me her dancing and eventually, after first consulting with Chaman, she invited me to join the household on their rounds, or 'going on tolly' as they call it. Every household of eunuchs has a network of informers – sweepers, *dhobis*, midwives – who report back the imminent births and marriages in their district. Every day, before setting out on tolly, the guru of the household prepares a detailed itinerary of addresses to be visited, and the eunuchs adhere strictly to this list.

We set off at seven in the morning after a particularly frantic bout of making-up: all three *hijras* cleaned their teeth with neem twigs, smudged on great quantities of lipstick and dusted their faces with blusher. Then we all took a convoy of rickshaws to Lajpath Nagar, in south Delhi. (Balvinder Singh, in a fit of unusual prudishness, had long since refused to come on my trips to see the eunuchs in Old Delhi: 'Mr William. These *hijras* are very bad and very dirty ladies,' he had said the first time I tried to give Razia a lift in his car. 'Too much bad and too much dirty.' Since then he had declared himself busy whenever I rang and asked for a taxi to take me to the Turkman Gate.)

At Lajpath Nagar we met up with two musicians, a pair of elderly men, one of whom played a harmonium, the other a pair of tabla drums. After a quick breakfast we set off to the first address on the list. As they walked along the streets, the eunuchs clapped their

181

hands and made bawdy jokes, behaving quite differently from the way they did inside their Turkman Gate *haveli*. Vimla in particular underwent a radical character change. Sweet, shy and doe-eyed at home, she would rush up to complete strangers in the street, grapple with her skirts and shout: 'Sardarji! You with the beard! Give me money or else I'll flash!'

The first house on the list was a small ground-floor flat belonging to a carpenter. The eunuchs piled into the entrance hall, the musicians started up the music and Vimla led the dancing by stamping her foot and ringing her little anklet bells. Things were just getting going when a neighbour appeared. Yes, she said, there had just been a birth in the house, but the family had gone to stay with cousins in Haryana; there was now no one at home. Disconsolately, we got back into the rickshaws and set off to the next address.

This was a far larger, middle-class house a few blocks away. Here there had been a marriage three days before, and the bride had just been brought to her new house that morning. The old men started up the music and the eunuchs began to dance. A crowd of beggar children gathered to watch beyond the garden wall, but from the house itself there was no response. After a while a toothless old woman peered nervously round the door and smiled. Then she went back inside again.

Meanwhile Panna, despite her bulk, was putting on a fine display. She wobbled her head one way, wobbled her bottom the other, all the while singing an Urdu verse which Zakir translated as follows:

> God bless you,
> You are very sweet,
> You are very lovely,
> God will give you long life.

This classy poetry appeared to do the trick. People began piling out of the house: two daughters-in-law, several small children, some unmarried daughters, two old grandfathers and the new bridegroom. The new bride, required by Hindu etiquette to be blushingly coy for several weeks after her marriage, cowered beyond the open window, twitching the lace curtain. Vimla now took centre-stage, while Panna grabbed an unwilling daughter-in-law and whirled her around in a waltz for a few steps.

As Vimla pirouetted, pulling her sari over her head in a parody of the Dance of the Seven Veils, Chaman Guru put down the cymbals and got down to the serious business of collecting money. The grandfathers both put fifty-rupee notes in the plate, while one of the daughters-in-law presented Chaman with the traditional gift of a plate of flour. But this clearly was not enough as far as Chaman was concerned. She signalled to Panna to carry on singing. A few more fifty-rupee notes were offered, but again Chaman shook her head. Eventually, as the song wound on to its thirtieth verse, the bridegroom presented Chaman with 1000 rupees (about £25). Bowing and scraping, the eunuchs withdrew.

It was a strangely farcical routine, and must be extremely tedious to enact day after day. But when society closes off all other opportunities there are only two choices for the eunuchs: dancing and prostitution. Of these, going on tolly is probably preferable – and possibly more lucrative.

I was always struck by the eunuchs' lack of bitterness. Through no fault of their own, through deformity or genetic accident, they found themselves marginalized by Indian society, turned into something half-way between a talisman and an object of ridicule. Yet in their own terms they seem fairly content with their lives, and they do not rail against the fate that has left them with this role. In the rickshaw on the way back from that morning's tolly I asked Vimla whether she would like to be reborn as a *hijra* in her next life. She considered for a while before answering.

'Do you have any choice how God makes you?' she answered eventually. 'I pray for our welfare in this life. But the next? It is in the gods' hands.'

Dr Jaffery

SEVEN

THE WINTER RAINS arrived promptly at the end of January.

During the last week of the month Olivia and I had gone to stay outside Delhi, in a fort just over the Rajasthani border. The day before our return, as we looked out over the battlements, we saw a succession of thick black clouds driving slowly in over the sand flats and camel grass. By the end of the afternoon the clouds had thickened into solid curtain walls of charcoal cumulus. They blotted out the sun and cast a dark shadow over the land.

The next day we returned to Delhi to find that the storm had broken. The clouds were scudding low over the rooftops; it was pouring with rain and the streets were flooded. In the Old City, Muslim women were dragging their *chadors* like wet black crows. Gusts of rain lashed down the narrow alleys; rickshaws sluiced through the water, more like boats than bicycles. It was no day to be out, but I had an appointment to keep. I had arranged to see Dr Yunus Jaffery, a historian and an archetypal Old Delhi-wallah. His ancestors had been Persian tutors at the Red Fort; today, Dr Jaffery pursued exactly the same career in Zakir Hussain College on the margins of Old Delhi. His rooms were in the original college, the Ghazi-ud-Din Medresse, a seventeenth-century Mughal building just outside the Ajmeri Gate.

Balvinder Singh dropped me outside during a brief pause in the rain. A low Mughal gateway led on into a wet and glistening flagstone courtyard; it was deserted but for a solitary pupil running

185

late towards his class. The flagstones were slippery and so hollowed-out by three centuries of passing feet that along some of the walk-ways the puddles had coalesced into shallow canals. The courtyard was bounded by a range of cloisters two storeys high. Classrooms filled the ground-floor rooms. On the first floor, leading off a covered balcony, were the chambers of the fellows and scholars. The arcades were broken on three sides by vaulted gateways, and on the fourth, the principal axis, by a red sandstone mosque. Before the mosque, filling both sides of the cloister garth, was a garden of healing herbs and shrubs.

I climbed a narrow staircase leading to the first floor balcony. Outside the scholars' rooms sat a line of bearded old men busily correcting specimens of Arabic calligraphy. Dr Jaffery's room was the last on the corridor.

The door opened to reveal a gaunt, clean-shaven man. He wore white Mughal pyjamas whose trouser-bottoms, wide and slightly flared, were cut in the style once favoured by eighteenth-century Delhi gallants. On his head he sported a thin white mosque-cap. Heavy black glasses perched on the bridge of his nose, but the effect was not severe. Something in Dr Jaffery's big bare feet and the awkward way he held himself gave the impression of a slightly shambolic, absent-minded individual: '*Asalam alekum,*' he said. 'Welcome.' Then, looking behind me, he added: 'Ah! The rains . . . Spring has arrived.'

Dr Jaffery's domed room was small and square and dark. Light-ning from the storm had cut off the electricity and the cell was illuminated by a bronze dish filled with flickering candles. The shadows from the candlelight darted back and forth across the shallow whitewashed dome. Persian books were stacked in dis-ordered piles; in the corner glistened a big brass samovar incised with Islamic decoration. The scene of the Sufi scholar in his room was straight out of a detail from the *Anvar-i Suhayli* – or indeed any of the illuminated Mughal manuscript books – and I said this to Dr Jaffery. 'My nieces also tell me I live in the Mughal age,' he replied. 'But they – I think – mean it as a criticism. You would like tea?'

Dr Jaffery blew on the coals at the bottom of his samovar, then placed two cupfuls of buffalo milk in the top of the urn. Soon

186

the milk was bubbling above the flame. While he fiddled with his samovar, Dr Jaffery told me about his work.

For the previous three years he had been busy transcribing the forgotten and unpublished portions of the *Shah Jehan Nama*, the court chronicle of Shah Jehan. He had converted the often illegible manuscript into clear Persian typescript; this had then been translated into English by a team of Persian scholars in America. The manuscript, originally compiled by Shah Jehan's fawning court historian Inayat Khan, told the story of the apex of Mughal power, the golden age when most of India, all of Pakistan and great chunks of Afghanistan were ruled from the Red Fort in Delhi. It was an age of unparalleled prosperity: the empire was at peace and trade was flourishing. The reconquest of the Mughals' original homeland – trans-Oxianan Central Asia – seemed imminent. In the ateliers of the palace the artists Govardhan, Bichitr and Abul Hasan were illuminating the finest of the great Mughal manuscript books; in Agra, the gleaming white dome of the Taj Mahal was being raised on its plinth above the River Jumna.

The book which contained the fruits of Dr Jaffery's labours was about to be published. Now Dr Jaffery was beginning to transcribe a forgotten text about Shah Jehan's childhood. The manuscript had just been discovered in the uncatalogued recesses of the British Museum; it was exciting work, said the doctor, but difficult: the manuscript was badly damaged and as he had not the money to go to London he was having to work from a smudged xerox copy. The new transcription absorbed his waking hours; but, despite the difficulties, he said he was making slow progress.

'As the great Sa'di once put it: "The Arab horse speeds fast, but although the camel plods slowly, it goes both by day and night."'

As we chatted about Shah Jehan, Dr Jaffery brought out a plate of rich Iranian sweets from an arched recess; he handed them to me and asked: 'Would you not like to learn classical Persian?'

'I would love to,' I answered. 'But at the moment I'm having enough difficulty trying to master Hindustani.'

'You are sure?' asked Dr Jaffery, breaking one of the sweets in two. 'Learning Persian would give you access to some great treasures. I would not charge you for lessons. I am half a dervish:

187

money means nothing to me. All I ask is that you work hard.'

Dr Jaffery said that very few people in Delhi now wanted to study classical Persian, the language which, like French in Imperial Russia, had for centuries been the first tongue of every educated Delhi-wallah. 'No one has any interest in the classics today,' he said. 'If they read at all, they read trash from America. They have no idea what they are missing. The jackal thinks he has feasted on the buffalo when in fact he has just eaten the eyes, entrails and testicles rejected by the lion.'

I said: 'That must upset you.'

'It makes no difference,' replied Dr Jaffery. 'This generation does not have the soul to appreciate the wisdom of Ferdowsi or Jalaludin Rumi. As Sa'di said: "If a diamond falls in the dirt it is still a diamond, yet even if dust ascends all the way to heaven it remains without value."'

I loved the way Dr Jaffery spoke in parables; for all his eccentricities, like some ancient sage his conversation was dotted with pearls of real wisdom. After the banalities of life with Balvinder Singh and Mrs Puri, Dr Jaffery's words were profound and reassuring. As he told little aphorisms from Rumi or the anecdotes of Ferdowsi's *Shah Nama* – the Mughal Emperors' favourite storybook – his gentle voice soothed away the irritations of modern Delhi. But overlaying the gentle wisdom there always lay a thin patina of bitterness.

'Today Old Delhi is nothing but a dustbin,' he said, sipping at his tea. 'Those who can, have houses outside the walled city. Only the poor man who has no shelter comes to live here. Today there are no longer any educated men in the old city. I am a stranger in my own home.' He shook his head. 'All the learning, all the manners have gone. Everything is so crude now. I have told you I am half a dervish. My own ways are not polished. But compared to most people in this city . . .'

'What do you mean?'

'Here everyone has forgotten the old courtesies. For example . . . in the old days a man of my standing would never have gone to the shops; everything would be sent to his house: grain, chillies, cotton, cloth. Once every six months the shopkeeper would come and pay his regards. He would not dare ask for money; instead it would be up to the gentleman to raise the matter and to give payment when he deemed suitable. If ever he did go to the bazaar he would expect the shopkeepers to stand up when he entered . . .

'All these things have gone now. People see the educated man living in poverty and realize that learning is useless; they decide it is better to remain ignorant. To the sick man sweet water tastes bitter in the mouth.'

'But don't your pupils get good jobs? And doesn't their success encourage others?'

'No. They are all Muslims. There is no future for them in modern India. Most become *gundas* or smugglers.'

'Is learning Persian a good training for smuggling?'

'No, although some of them become very successful at this business. One of my pupils was Nazir. Now he is a big gambler, the Chief of the Prostitutes. But before he was one of my best pupils . . .'

At that moment, the cry of the muezzin outside broke the evening calm. Dr Jaffery rustled around the room, picking up books and looking behind cushions for his mosque cap before remembering that he was already wearing it. Muttering apologies he slipped on his sandals and stumbled out. 'Can you wait for five minutes?' he asked. 'I must go and say my evening prayers.'

From the balcony I watched the stream of figures in white pyjamas rushing through the pelting rain to the shelter of the mosque. Through the cloudburst I could see the old men laying out their prayer carpets under the arches, then, on a signal from the mullah, a line of bottoms rose and fell in time to the distant cries of 'Allah hu-Akbar!'

Five minutes later, when Dr Jaffery returned, he again put a cupful of milk on the samovar and we talked a little about his home life.

'The death of my eldest brother in 1978 was the most important event in my life,' he said. 'From my boyhood, I always wanted to live in a secluded place, to live like a Sufi. But since my brother's death it has been my duty to care for my two nieces. I cannot now become a full dervish; or at least not until my nieces are educated and married. Until then their well-being must be my first concern.'

'And after that?'

'Afterwards I want to go on *haj*, to visit Mecca. Then I will retire to some ruined mosque, repair it, and busy myself with my studies.'

189

'But if you wish to retire can't you find some other member of your family to look after your nieces for you?'

'My elder brothers were killed at Partition,' said Jaffery. 'My elder sister is also a victim of those times. To this day she still hears the voices of guns. You may be sitting with her one evening, quite peacefully, when suddenly she will stand up and say: "Listen! Guns! They are coming from that side!"

'In fact it was only by a miracle that my sister and I survived at all: we took shelter with our youngest brother in the Jama Masjid area. Had we been at the house of my parents we would have shared the fate of the rest of the family . . .' Dr Jaffery broke off.

'Go on,' I said.

'My parents lived in an area that had always been traditionally Hindu. During Partition they went into hiding, and for a fortnight their good Hindu friends brought them food and water. But one day they were betrayed; a mob came in the night and burned the house down. We learned later that the traitor was a neighbour of my father's. My father had helped him financially. This was how the man repaid him . . .' Dr Jaffery shook his head. 'In this city,' he said, 'culture and civilization have always been very thin dresses. It does not take much for that dress to be torn off and for what lies beneath to be revealed.'

In all of Delhi's history, at no period was that thin dress of civilization more beautiful – or more deceptively woven – than during the first half of the seventeenth century, during the Golden Age of Shah Jehan.

In public the actions of the Emperor and his court were governed by a rigid code of courtliness, as subtle and elaborate as the interlaced borders the Mughal artists painted around their miniatures. But for all this fine façade, in private the ambitions of the Mughal Emperors knew no moral limitations: without scruple they would murder their brothers, poison their sisters or starve their fathers. The courtly ceremonial acted as a veil around the naked reality of Mughal politics; it was a mask which deliberately disguised the brutality and coarseness that lay hidden beneath.

190

Despite the great volume of material that existed on the Mughals, I had always found them difficult to visualize. Their architecture, their courtliness, their ceremony were famous – but, like a profile miniature portrait, the result was one-dimensional: the jewels, the fineness of the turbans, the swirling details of the drapery – all were more lovingly and clearly drawn than the man inside; the sitter's thoughts and feelings, his character and emotions remain relatively opaque: unfathomed and incomprehensible.

It was Dr Jaffery who told me about two contemporary travel books which rescued the Mughals from being suffocated beneath landslides of silk, diamonds and lapis lazuli – Bernier's *Travels in the Mogul Empire* and Manucci's *Mogul India*. Unlike the sycophantic official court chronicles – the *Shah Jehan Nama* that Dr Jaffery had spent so long transcribing – the accounts of the two European travellers were packed with reams of malicious bazaar gossip. The two books may thus have been peppered with little fictions, but no sharper or livelier pictures of Mughal Delhi, with all its scandals, dramas and intrigues, have come down to us. In the mornings I used to sit out in the warm sun of our terrace and read the travellers' descriptions of the Delhi they knew from their visits at the very apex of the Mughal Empire.

The two authors were very different men. François Bernier was an aristocratic and highly educated French doctor who came to Delhi in 1658; he soon became sought-after as a physician by the Imperial family and the Mughal nobility. In his writings he comes across as wonderfully French – proud and arrogant, a gourmand and an aesthete, an admirer of female beauty; he was also a terrific scandalmonger. Bernier constantly contrasts Mughal India and seventeenth-century France: the Jumna compares favourably with the Loire, he thinks; adultery is easier in Paris than it is in Delhi: 'in France it only excites merriment, but in this part of the world there are few instances where it is not followed by some dreadful and tragical catastrophe.' But Indian *naan*, he regrets, can never ever be compared to a good Parisian *baguette*:

Bakers are numerous, but their ovens are unlike our own and very defective. The bread, therefore, is neither well made nor properly baked, [although] that sold in the Fort

191

is tolerably good. In its composition the bakers are not sparing of fresh butter, milk and eggs; but though it be raised it has a burned taste, and is too much like cake. It is never to be compared to the *Pain de Gonesse*, and other delicious varieties to be met with in Paris.

For all his fopperies, Bernier was very much the educated European of the early Enlightenment: he knew his classics, was a firm believer in Reason, and had no patience with 'ridiculous errors and strange superstitions'. In particular, like Macaulay two centuries later, he had little time for the Brahmins and their Sanskrit learning:

> They believe that the world is flat and triangular; that it is composed of seven distinct habitations . . . and that each is surrounded by its own peculiar sea; that one sea is of milk; another of sugar; a third of butter; a fourth of wine; and so on . . . [also that] the whole of this world is supported on the heads of a number of elephants whose occasional motion is the cause of earthquakes. If the renowned sciences of the ancient Indian sages consisted of all these extravagant follies, mankind has indeed been deceived in the exalted opinion it has long entertained of their wisdom.

Nevertheless Bernier was cautiously appreciative of most aspects of India and was one of the very first apologists for Mughal culture against the growing arrogance of its European visitors. 'I have sometimes been astonished to hear the contemptuous manner in which Europeans in the Indies speak of [Mughal architecture],' he writes, adding of the Delhi Jama Masjid: 'I grant that this building is not constructed according to those rules of architecture which we seem to think ought to be implicitly followed; yet I can see no fault that offends taste. I am satisfied that even in Paris a church erected after the model of this temple would be admired, were it only for its singular style of architecture, and its extraordinary appearance.'

What most terrified Bernier was the notion that his long stay in India would rob him of his cultivated Parisian sensibilities. This fear reached its climax when he saw the Taj Mahal: 'The last time I saw Tage Mehale's mausoleum I was in the company of a French merchant who, like myself, thought that this extraordinary fabric could not be sufficiently admired. I did not venture to express my

192

Jama Masjid

opinion, fearing that my taste might have become corrupted by my long residence in the Indies; but since my companion had recently come from France, it was quite a relief to hear him say that he had seen nothing in Europe quite so bold and majestic.'

Niccolao Manucci, Bernier's slightly younger Italian contemporary, had no such aesthetic qualms. Manucci was the son of a Venetian trader who, aged fourteen, had run away from home as a stowaway on a merchant ship. After crossing the Middle East, he came to India to seek employment as an artilleryman in the Mughal army. A self-confessed con-artist and charlatan, he used his 'nimbleness of wit' to set himself up as a quack doctor and an exorcist. In his memoirs he revels in the audacity of the fraud he pulled off:

Not only was I famed as a doctor, but it was rumoured I had the power of expelling demons from the bodies of the possessed. Once some Mahommedans were at my house, consulting me about their complaints when night came on . . . In the middle of our talk I began to speak as if to some demon, telling him to hold his tongue and not interrupt my talk, and let me serve these gentlemen for it was already late. Then I resumed my conversation with the Mahommedans. But they now had only half their souls left in their bodies, and spoke in trembling tones. I made use of their terror for my own amusement, and raising my voice still more, I shouted at him whom I assumed to be present, lying invisible in some corner . . . They were unable to speak a word out of fright . . .

Being credulous in matters of sorcery, they began to put it about that the Frank doctor not only had the power of expelling demons but had dominion over them. This was enough to make many come, and among them they brought before me many women who pretended to be possessed (as is their habit when they want to leave their houses to meet with their lovers) and it was hoped that I could deal with them. The usual treatment was bullying, tricks, emetics and evil-smelling fumigation with filthy things. Nor did I desist until the patients were worn out, and said that now the devil had fled. In this manner I restored many to their senses, with great increase in reputation, and still greater diversion for myself.

Manucci's account of Mughal India is as full of gossip as Bernier's, but the precarious manner in which he chose to live his life meant that his book has rather more action in it: rather than fussing about the relative merits of Parisian and Mughal architecture, he fights as an artilleryman in the Mughal civil war, has his caravan ambushed by bandits, battles with a pressgang and is finally besieged in a fort on an island in the Indus.

With their two very different viewpoints – one the angst-struck French intellectual, the other the ex-con and hard-nosed Venetian man of action – Bernier and Manucci colour in the gilded outlines

194

provided by the Mughals' own court chronicles and their miniature paintings. The picture that thus emerges of the tensions and jealousies in the Imperial family has a grand, almost Shakespearean feel to it: the Emperor Shah Jehan governs the Mughal Empire through its period of greatest magnificence. He moves the court from Agra to Delhi and builds the Red Fort in the centre of the new Shahjehanabad. But then, despite the gloss given by the court flatterers, the unspoken tensions in the palace eventually build up into a civil war which topples the old order. The characters in the drama – some good, but flawed and naïve, others utterly evil and ruthless – are classic Renaissance types. Like King Lear, Shah Jehan in his old age misplays his hand and is defeated by his ungrateful children. Yet his collapse is partly his own fault: it is the flaws in Shah Jehan's own character – his pride, his sexual gluttony and the unjust way in which he handles his children – that lead to his downfall.

'After the death of his beloved Queen Taj Mahal,' wrote Manucci, 'Shah Jehan selected in Hindustan the city of Dihli in order to build there a new city as his capital. He gave it the name Shahjehanabad – that is to say, "Built by Shah Jehan". He expended large sums in the construction of this city, and in the foundations he ordered several decapitated criminals to be placed as a sign of sacrifice.'

Shah Jehan was forty-seven when he decided to move his court from Agra to Delhi. He had just lost his wife; his children were now grown up. The building of a new city was the middle-aged Emperor's bid for immortality.

Shah Jehan had himself come to power twelve years earlier after a bloody civil war. He had been the able but ruthless third son; to seize the throne he had had to rebel against his father and murder his two elder brothers, their two children, and two male cousins. Yet while Shah Jehan was capable of bouts of cold-blooded brutality, he was still the most aesthetically sensitive of all the Mughals. As a boy of fifteen he had impressed his father, the Emperor Jehangir, with the taste he demonstrated in redesigning the Imperial apartments in Kabul. As the young Emperor he had rebuilt the Red Fort in Agra in a new architectural style that he had himself helped to develop. Then, on his wife's death, he had built the Taj Mahal, arguably the most perfect building in all Islam.

Before her death Mumtaz Mahal had borne Shah Jehan fourteen children; of these, four sons and three daughters survived to adulthood. The eldest was Dara Shukoh – the Glory of Darius. Contemporary miniatures show that Dara bore a striking resemblance to his father; he had the same deep-set almond eyes, the same straight, narrow nose and long, full beard, although in some pictures he appears to have been slightly darker and more petite than Shah Jehan. Like the Emperor he was luxurious in his tastes and refined in his sensibilities. He preferred life at court to the hardships of campaigning; he liked to deck himself in strings of precious stones and belts studded with priceless gems; he wore clothes of the finest silk and from each ear lobe he hung a single pearl of remarkable size.

Nevertheless Dara was no indolent voluptuary: he had an enquiring mind and enjoyed the company of sages, Sufis and *sannyasin* (wandering ascetics). He had the Hindu *Upanishads*, the *Bhagavad Gita* and the *Yoga-Vashishta* translated into Persian and himself composed religious and mystical treatises. The most remarkable was the *Majmua-ul-Baharain* ('The Mingling of the Two Oceans'), a comparative study of Hinduism and Islam which emphasized the compatibility of the two faiths and the common source of their divine revelations. In an age when even the most liberal of Mughal Emperors used to demolish Hindu temples, this was both a brave and novel work; but some considered Dara's views not just unusual but actually heretical. In private, many of the more orthodox Muslim nobles furrowed their brows and wondered how the crown prince could possibly declare, as one noble put it, 'infidelity and Islam to be twin brothers'.

Manucci, who was employed in Dara Shukoh's artillery, portrays his patron as a flawed hero, brave and generous but constantly in danger of being outwitted by his wily opponents:

> Prince Dara was a man of dignified manners, of a comely countenance, polite in conversation, ready and gracious of speech, of extraordinary liberality, kindly and compassion-

ate, but over-confident in his opinion of himself, considering himself competent in all things and having no need of advisers. Indeed, he despised those who gave him counsel.

Prince Aurangzeb, Shah Jehan's third son, was a very different character from his elder brother. As tough and warlike as Dara was civilized and courtly, he cloaked his ambition in a robe of holy simplicity, affecting the ways of a Muslim dervish. A master of deceit, he learned how to sow distrust and dissent within the ranks of his enemies. He controlled an efficient network of spies: nothing could be said in Delhi without Aurangzeb coming to hear of it. Moreover, he knew the art of poisoning with subtle toxins. Manucci was wary of him, fearing and disliking him in equal proportions:

> Although Aurangzeb was held to be bold and valiant, he was capable of great dissimulation and hypocrisy. Pretending to be an ascetic, he slept while in the field on a mat of straw that he had himself woven . . . He ate food that cost little and let it be known that he underwent severe penances and fasting. All the same, under cover of these pretences he led in secret a jolly life of it. His intercourse was with certain holy men addicted to sorcery, who instructed him how to bring over to his side as many friends as he could with witchcraft and soft speeches. He was so subtle as to deceive even the quickest witted people.

One person whom Aurangzeb never deceived was his father. From an early age, Shah Jehan made it clear that he did not care for his third son, and instead increasingly lavished attention on the more amiable Dara Shukoh. Dara he kept at court, showered with favours and titles, while Aurangzeb was sent to the empire's southernmost border, the unruly Deccan.

All the cards seemed to be stacked against Aurangzeb, but he had one key advantage: the support of his sister Roshanara. Just as Aurangzeb was angered by Shah Jehan's obvious preference for Dara, so Roshanara was alienated by the affection lavished on her more attractive sister Jahanara Begum. After the death of Mumtaz Mahal, Jahanara had been given charge of the Imperial harem. Bazaar rumour had it that her closeness to Shah Jehan went beyond merely normal filial affection; after all, as Bernier put it: 'it would

197

have been unjust to deny the King the privilege of gathering fruit from the tree he himself had planted.'

As Jahanara's influence increased, so did the jealousy and resentment of her younger sister. Like Aurangzeb, Roshanara grew bitter and vengeful, a Regan or a Goneril to Jahanara's Cordelia. She became a tireless champion of Aurangzeb's interests, making little secret of her hatred for Dara and Jahanara. Like Aurangzeb, she controlled a network of spies which she used to keep her brother well in touch with developments in the court. Like Aurangzeb she grew bitter and heartless. It was rumoured that she was also a poisoner and a witch. Yet she remains for the modern reader perhaps the most intriguing member of the entire family.

When Shah Jehan moved the court from Agra to the new city of Shahjehanabad in 1648, it was Jahanara Begum who built the Chandni Chowk, the principal avenue of the Old City. Half-way down the boulevard she built a vast caravanserai which, before it was destroyed in 1857, was regularly described by visitors to Delhi as the most magnificent building outside the fort. Manucci, not normally responsive to architecture, dwells at length on its paintings, gardens and lakes, while Bernier pays it his ultimate tribute of recommending the construction of something similar in France.

Roshanara Begum, with her less magnificent resources, was unable to contribute anything quite so ambitious. Nevertheless, she did put up the money for the construction of Roshanara Bagh, a pleasure garden on the far outskirts of Shahjehanabad. Today the garden is still there, although it has long since been absorbed into the sprawling outskirts of the town. It lies a little beyond Sabzi Mandi (the Old Delhi vegetable market), immediately beside a huge lorry park. It is not a beautiful part of the town, and the lush green of the tropical gardens – long lawns, flower beds and eucalyptus and casuarina avenues – comes as a welcome surprise in the midst of all the dirt and poverty.

The lawns are filled with the usual odd-ball cast of characters who like to congregate in Indian parks: little boys playing cricket in the dry water channels; a lost-looking village goatherd with his flock; picnicking Punjabi families with their tiffin-tins; loving couples reclining against trees; a saffron-robed Hindu ascetic sitting cross-legged on the grass; a pair of elderly bent-backed colonels with identical walking sticks. In the middle of all these people stands a single Mughal pavilion, low and rectangular and finely proportioned, of similar design to those in the Red Fort. The pavilion stands three arches broad; four domed *chattris* punctuate the corners. Inside, a rectangle of delicately latticed *jali* screens gives on to the brick-built central chamber.

It was once a beautiful building, but in decay now looks both tatty and sad. It is often the way with Mughal ruins: while the more primitive forts which preceded them still have an aura of power as they rise solid and impregnable from the burning plains, the silky refinement expressed in Mughal architecture turns, in decay, to something approaching seediness.

It is difficult to visualize now, but it must have been within this pavilion that the young Roshanara consulted her spies as she reclined on carpets beside the gently bubbling irrigation runnels. Sadly there is no description of the Princess at this period; the only proper account of Roshanara to survive dates from very late on in her life; it was written by Bernier, who saw the Princess's marvellous train on its way from Delhi – perhaps from this garden – to Kashmir to escape the summer heat:

> Stretch imagination to its utmost limits and you can conceive no exhibition more grand and imposing than Roshanara Begum, mounted on a stupendous *Pegu* elephant and seated in a large latticed *howdah* covered with a silken tent, blazing with gold and azure, followed by other elephants with howdahs nearly as resplendent as her own, all filled with ladies attached to her household . . .
>
> In front of Roshanara's litter, which was open, sat a young, well-dressed female slave, with a peacock's tail in her hand, brushing away the dust and keeping off the flies from the Princess . . . Close to the Princess's elephant are the chief eunuchs, richly adorned and finely mounted, each with a wand of office in his hand. Besides these are several [more] eunuchs on horseback, accompanied by a multitude of lackeys on foot, who advance a great way before the Princess, for the purpose of clearing the road before them . . .

There is something very impressive of state and royalty in the march of these sixty or more elephants; and if I had not regarded this display of magnificence with a sort of philosophical indifference, I should have been apt to be carried away by such flights of imagination as inspire most Indian poets.

Once the winter rains have passed, Delhi experiences two months of weather so perfect and blissful that they almost compensate for the climatic extremes of the other ten months of the year. The skies are blue, the days are warm, and all is right with the world.

That February, Delhi seemed like a paradise. Olivia and I filled the garden on our roof terraces with palms and lilies and hollyhocks and we wove bougainvillaea through the trellising. The plants which seemed to have died during the winter's cold – the snapdragon, the hibiscus and the frangipani – miraculously sprang back to life and back into bloom. The smells began to change: the woodsmoke and the sweet smell of the dung fires gave way to the heady scent of Indian *champa* and the first bittersweet whiffs of China orange blossom.

From the old Mughal bird market in front of the Jama Masjid, Shah Jehan's great Friday Mosque, we bought three pairs of small lorikeets and two large white cockateels. We got a bamboo-wallah to build them two cages and hung them from hooks on the veranda. We fixed red clay pots to the sides to encourage the birds to breed.

Certainly, the other birds in Delhi seemed to be thinking of little else. In the top of a drainpipe next to our sitting-room, two sparrows were frantically building a nest. More springtime activity took place on the tin top of the defunct air conditioning unit that Mrs Puri had left attached to our bedroom wall. There, every morning soon after dawn, two pigeons performed an elaborate and very noisy mating dance. Though the unit had long since given up any pretence of cooling the room, it did turn out to have a curious talent for magnifying the pigeons' footfalls so that their tap dance rang out like a drum-roll at six every morning. Olivia, who likes her sleep, soon developed a great loathing for our morning visitors, but all her efforts to drive them away and apart had little success, and spectacularly failed to calm the passions of the energetically copulating birds.

Mrs Puri celebrated the coming of spring in an uncharacteristically spendthrift manner: she threw a small thanksgiving party. Her eldest son had caught pneumonia on a business trip to America and had been extremely ill. His recovery, Mrs Puri believed, was due to the personal intervention of Guru Nanak, the sixteenth-century founder of the Sikhs. To thank her guru for this kind gesture, she invited a group of four Sikh priests from her gurdwara to come and say some prayers in her garden.

A tent of dyed homespun was erected out in front, while some caterers got busy preparing Punjabi specialities over a clay oven at the back of the house. At nine o'clock four thickly-bearded priests appeared holding an enormous bound copy of the Sikh scriptures, the *Guru Granth Sahib*. They reverently built a small shrine for the book in one of Mrs Puri's flowerbeds. Soon the garden was filled with the sound of sacred hymns and odes in praise of Guru Nanak.

Guests – all Sikhs – began to appear from around the nearby houses and, after greeting Mrs Puri, quietly took their place cross-legged in ranks on the ground. Mr Puri was wheeled out and trussed up on a chair near the shrine. On condition that we both covered our heads, Olivia and I were invited to watch the proceedings from the rear of the crowd. For an hour the guests sat patiently listening; then everybody got up and, with the air of people who have been thinking of little else for some time, demolished the *langoor* (free food) which was waiting for them at the rear of the house.

That evening Mrs Puri remarked to me that none of the considerable expense of the party would have been necessary if members of her family did not insist on leaving the Punjab and pursuing business ventures Abroad. Mrs Puri has always made it clear that she does not like Abroad. Once you leave the bosom of Mother India, she points out, you always find a disturbing ignorance as to the proper preparation of dal and rice as well as an infuriating lack of gurdwaras in which to say your morning prayers. She makes a point of reading out loud items from her newspaper, the *Hindustan Times*, which demonstrate to her satisfaction the old Indian view

201

that Wogs begin at Kabul and that civilization stops on the banks of the Indus.

This is very inconvenient for Mrs Puri, as a great number of her close relations have emigrated. She seems resigned to her brother, Teg Bahadur, becoming a Mountie in Canada, but is very worried by her daughter Rupinder, who emigrated to America while still unmarried. 'Rupinder may be working in America,' Mrs Puri would tell her friends at their monthly kitty parties, 'but she is loving only our Punjab. When she comes back, we will find her a wealthy Sikh husband from a good family.'

'I'm sure there are lots of nice Sikh boys out there,' I once remarked. This went down very badly.

'These American Sikhs we do not want,' said Mrs Puri emphatically. 'Like the Sikhs in your Southall, they are *jungli* Sikhs. They are not educated peoples.'

'Some of them must be educated.'

'Maybe,' said Mrs Puri, coming to the point, 'but they are not from good families. They are villagers.'

'Not any more. The Southall Sikhs are often very successful businessmen.'

'Mr William,' said Mrs Puri drawing a deep breath. 'We are Puris. Outside India there are not Sikhs of our caste.'

With Rupinder's modesty threatened by hordes of lower-caste villagers, Mrs Puri had eventually realized where her duty lay. Painful though it was, she declared that the time would soon come when she would feel it necessary to inspect America for herself. She would hire a Buick and a Sikh driver from a good family, and see the States in the style to which she was accustomed. But she was not looking forward to the trip.

'America is not a traditional country like India,' she said. 'There is no morality there. But I have heard it said that parts of the Rocky Mountains are quite like our Simla.'

Then, just as we had begun to enjoy the blissful peace and calm of spring, the wedding season reached its climax. Overnight, everything changed.

India remains, even in the cities, one of the most superstitious countries in the world. The educated Indian businessman will consult an astrologer as readily as the illiterate villager; and no occasion, except perhaps the birth of a child, necessitates the consulting of astrologers quite so urgently as a marriage. Not only do horoscopes determine the suitability of a partner for an arranged marriage, even the date that the couple should be joined is left to the astrologer's discretion. There is no tradition of marrying on a Saturday in India; a marriage takes place only when the heavens revolve into the most auspicious configuration.

In Delhi, marriages take place over the entire length of the cold season. Nevertheless, since many astrologers seem to agree that a single phase of the spring moon is the most auspicious of the year, it is quite a normal occurrence for half the year's weddings to take place within the space of a single fortnight around Holi, the spring festival. In the fight for tents and caterers that follows, the bride's family is often forced to resort to blackmail and bribery; sometimes even to violence.

Yet the inconvenience of this system is felt far beyond the immediate families involved. All Delhi is thrown out of gear by the chaos. One night the black spring sky may be quiet and peaceful, empty but for the cicadas. The next, the heavens are lit up with flashing neon lights, while from all sides come the bashings and screechings of Indian brass bands. The noise of heavily amplified Hindi movie music can be heard until well after two or three in the morning.

After you have finally dropped off, sometime after three a.m., you can generally snatch a couple of hours' sleep before the next round of jollities begins soon after dawn. Around eight o'clock the sound of distant brass bands can again be heard wafting in through the bedroom windows. Slowly but inexorably the band draws nearer. Half an hour later, blowing as loudly as they can, the band halts three doors from your own. The groom has come to collect his bride. Why this ceremony has to take place so early in the morning has never been explained to me, but it appears to be as essential a part of the nuptials as the Hindi movie music the night before.

The days are little better. One morning, reeling from lack of sleep,

I set off to Khan Market to buy something for my headache, only to find the roads were clogged with white Ambassadors dressed up as Christmas trees. Above one windscreen – although almost totally obscured beneath creepers of gold and silver tinsel – was blazoned the legend: SUNIL AND NALINI CONJOINED 20 FEBRU-ARY. Ahead, jamming the traffic into long impatient queues, was a procession consisting of the groom sitting on a white stallion, and clutching in front of him a small boy, an empty marriage *rath* (chariot), a brass band, twenty rogues carrying portable striplights and, bringing up the rear, a scattering of eunuchs, dancing around, soliciting money and flashing at passers-by.

Trying to get out of the traffic jam, I took a short cut down a back lane but found that it was blocked by a large wedding tent helpfully erected across the full width of the road. At this stage I gave up, went back home and retired to a half-darkened room to read the paper. Even here, however, the marriage season intruded. It was a Sunday, and half the paper was packed with marriage advertisements.

For most Indian families a marriage is as much a business proposition as a romantic affair of the heart, and perhaps for this reason many of the advertisments sound as if they are marketing objects rather than advertising potential spouses:

> WANTED: Kayastha match for employed ordinance factory beautiful, slim, wheatish Ghari double, convented, well versed in household affairs, adaptable.

Some of the adverts, like western lonely hearts columns, are slightly sad:

> WANTED: Handicapped girl, caste no bar, for handicapped blind Bengali boy. Lost parents at a young age; lame in one leg. Able to move around with limp.

Some are embarrassing:

> WANTED: Life companion for 28 year old, good-looking boy, well settled in decent job, suffering from sexual disorder, i.e acute premature ejaculation. Girl should either be suffering from same disease or is not interested in sex otherwise.

A few defy credibility:

> Alliance invited for innocent, beautiful, charming, compassionate, sober, soft-spoken and good natured divorcee.

But my favourites are definitely the ambitious Punjabi boys out for what they can get:

> WANTED: very beautiful, fair, slim, charming, educated, well-connected Green Card holder for very handsome, athletic, energetic and elegant Jat Sikh boy of high ideology. BA and yoga practitioner. Working hard in excellent position in Gurgaon factory. Send photograph and horoscope.

The Indian marriage advertisements are in fact a British invention, a hangover from the period when highly educated and thoroughly eligible ICS officers would spend their youths in remote postings in the jungles of Central India. There they had little hope of meeting, wooing or wedding even the most hideous and unsuitable Englishwomen. For these people the marriage adverts acted as a kind of mail-order lifeline: from deepest Nagpur or Ujjain, a young man's credentials could be easily brought before the eyes of an anxious Mama in Chelsea or Kensington.

Yet, like so many other Raj survivals, the marriage adverts have been mutated out of all recognition from their understated British originals. Today the tone of so many of these adverts is so unashamedly boastful – full of triumphs in beauty competitions, prizes won and degrees achieved – that I often wondered whether these perfect matches are all they claim to be. For this reason my eye was caught one day by a small box-ad at the bottom of the column:

BHARAT DETECTIVE AGENCY
MARRIAGE FRAUD A SPECIALITY.

A telephone call confirmed my suspicions. Mr Pavan Aggarwal, an ex-paratrooper, specializes in investigating the truth behind the adverts – usually by the simple expedient of sending one of his agents to the groom or bride's home village.

'I was trained to see behind enemy lines,' Mr Aggarwal told me, 'and I am knowing how to observe properly.'

'What sort of thing do you look for?' I asked.

'I will check anything – see if boy is knowing too many girls or girl is watching too many Hindi films and not pursuing her studies,' replied Mr Aggarwal. He added: 'I am even checking-out mothers-in-law.'

One of the most evocative passages in Dr Jaffery's transcription of the *Shah Jehan Nama* is the part which describes Dara Shukoh's wedding.

The marriage of Dara to his distant cousin Nadira Begum took place on 11 February 1633, a year after the death of Dara's mother, Mumtaz Mahal. On the day before the marriage, the preliminary ceremony of *hina-bandi* was held: 'Numerous fireworks were ignited along the banks of the Jumna . . . and the vast number of candles, lamps, torches and lanterns [that were lit made] the surface of the earth rival the starry expanses of heaven.' Precious robes were distributed to guests, and *paan* and sweetmeats offered to the attendant nobility. Finally Dara's hands were placed behind the covering curtain of the harem where they were dyed red with henna by the ladies within.

The next day at noon, Aurangzeb and the other young princes escorted Dara through the palace to the Forty Pillared Hall of Public Audience. In the copy of the *Shah Jehan Nama* now in Windsor Castle there is a fine miniature painting by Murar illustrating the scene: all the princes are dripping with gems and strings of pearls; the youthful Dara, a downy moustache now covering his upper lip, leads his brothers into the great audience hall sitting on a black stallion. He fills the centre of the picture; Aurangzeb and his other brothers, on white horses, are relegated to the picture's margin.

After Shah Jehan had loaded his son with precious wedding gifts – 'a superb robe of honour, a jewelled dagger with incised floral ornament, a sword and a belt studded with gems, a rosary of pearls', two fine horses and a pair of war elephants – and the gifts had been displayed and admired, the festivities began:

By His Majesty's command, the gardens beneath the Royal Chambers and boats floating upon the Jumna were illumi-

206

nated with lamps and fireworks; music and singing were kept with spirit [from noon until nine o'clock at night] . . . when the propitious moment for the nuptials finally arrived. Qazi Muhammed Aslam was summoned and he read the marriage service in the sublime presence, fixing the bride's *mihr* [jointure fee in case the marriage were later dissolved] at five *lakhs* of rupees. At the conclusion of the ceremony, shouts of congratulation rose from earth to heaven and the sound of kettle drums of joy rent the skies.

Having read (and heard) so much about Delhi marriages, I was pleased at the very end of February actually to receive an invitation to one under the door. The card read as follows:

Mr and Mrs Shahiduddin Postman
request the pleasure of your company
on the auspicious occasion
of the marriage of their daughter

Saheena
with Mr B. Khan
(son of Mr M. Khan)
At their residence:
No. 11 Village Shahpur Jat
(Near DDA Water Tank.)

Mr Shahiduddin Postman was a familiar figure at the house: every morning after delivering our mail he would squat outside the front gate, smoking a *bidi* with the *mali*, a man to whom he bore a certain resemblance. Both gentlemen were lean, sharp-eyed characters with a highly developed taste for *baksheesh*; and both liked to dress up, whatever the heat, in their thick serge uniforms: the *mali* in his blue gardener's donkey-jacket with its shining brass buttons, Mr Shahiduddin Postman in his official Indian Postal Service khaki.

We had only really talked to Mr Postman on the regular occasions – Dusshera, Diwali, Christmas, New Year – that he came looking for tips, but were flattered by the invitation and out of curiosity decided to take it up.

On the morning of the ceremony, Olivia, the *mali*, Balvinder

207

Singh and myself all set off to Village Shahpur Jat in Mr Singh's taxi. It was a bright February morning, and the *mali*'s newly polished buttons glittered in the sunlight.

'This Mr Postman very good man,' said Mr Singh, who had not been invited to the ceremony, but was clearly looking forward to attending none the less.

'Very rich man,' agreed the *mali*. 'For five years he saving shah-al-arhee for daughter's wedding.'

(The *mali* had a unique way of turning simple English words into Hindi or Urdu equivalents: the clay tubs in which he planted his flowers became fellah-i-puts, seedlings were Sid-ud-Dins, while my favourite flower – the hollyhock – became a holi-ul-haq. After you got used to the conventions of his speech, he became readily comprehensible: shah-al-arhee was the *mali*'s rendering of salary.)

The *mali* proved quite correct about Mr Shahiduddin Postman's resources. Shahpur Jat was Mr Postman's ancestral village. It was originally a farming settlement in Haryana but had recently been absorbed into the Delhi suburbs. The small government flat I had been expecting turned out instead to be a large if simple village *haveli*, occupied by Mr Postman's extended family – his three brothers, their children and Mr Postman's old mother.

The marriage was being held in the wide courtyard of the house. Striped awnings had been stretched across the courtyard and ranks of chairs arranged in rows around the walls. Fairy lights and streamers of tinsel hung from the tent posts; spicy smells wafted through the air. In the middle stood a huge tin trunk the size of a Roman sarcophagus, packed full of the wedding presents Mr Postman was giving to his daughter: twenty new *salwar kameez*, piles of crockery, huge copper pots, a sewing machine, an iron and so on.

Our host greeted us at the entrance gate, shaking me by the hand, bowing to Olivia, embracing the *mali* and frowning at Balvinder Singh. Then, like Shah Jehan with the guests at Dara's wedding, Mr Postman took us over to the trunk to admire the presents. Getting the gentle hint, we produced our contribution to his daughter's dowry: a small electric blow-heater.

'For winter,' I said.

'Not only winter,' replied Mr Shahiduddin Postman. 'On this

208

most beautiful radio we will now be listening to Mr Mark Tully Sahib of BBC every day of year.'

Before we had time to correct his mistake, Mr Postman had sat us in a row at the top of the courtyard. He presented the *mali* and myself with a hookah and while we took a preliminary suck, we were introduced to the other guests.

Again I was surprised by the smartness of the gathering. On my right was Dr Adbul Haidar, a rather gloomy assistant lecturer from the Hamdard University in New Delhi; beyond him sat Mr Swaroop Singh, a clerk at the Jawaharlal Nehru University. Both were from the same village as Mr Shahiduddin Postman; both had managed to get educated and to break out of the village on to the lower rungs of academia. Dr Haidar proudly explained that the bride, Mr Postman's daughter, was a rare creature – a Muslim girl who had been educated up to the tenth class.

'Most of our children in willage Shahpur Jat are being literate,' said Dr Haidar. 'We are a very forward-looking willage. But,' and here he lowered his voice, 'the groom's family are Jats. They are very backward farmer-people.'

As we were talking, out of the corner of my eye I could see Balvinder Singh stumbling back from the cooking-corner of the tent, holding a plate piled high with hot pakoras. As he walked he was stuffing them into his mouth.

'This man is a friend of Mr Postman?' asked Dr Haidar.

'Up to a point,' I said.

'This is animal-man,' replied Dr Haidar rather harshly.

Dr Haidar went off to talk to Mr Postman and I got into conversation with Mr Bhajan Lal, the *Pradhan* (headman) of the village. Mr Lal's English was even less fluent than my Hindi, so we chatted, ungrammatically, in his tongue. Thanks to our twice weekly lessons, Olivia and I had now become confident enough in Hindi for the practice of it to become enjoyable rather than tiresome – if only because people were so surprised to hear any non-Indian speak even the most stumbling version of it. Mr Lal was no exception.

LAL Sahib! You are speaking Hindi!

WD A little.

LAL Oh, sahib! Truly this is day among days! What is your good name, sahib?'

WD (confident now; a phrase I knew) My name is William.

LAL Oh thankyou Mr Will-Yums Sahib. Where are you learning this beautiful Hindi?

WD In Delhi. A *munshi* comes to our house . . .

LAL In Delhi! Heaven be praised . . .

As we chattered, other villagers crowded around and asked the usual round of Indian questions: where were we from? How did we know Mr Shahiduddin Postman? What was our mother tongue? Were we Muslims? How many Muslims were there in Scotland? One particularly persistent gentleman was clearly using us as a punchbag for his English. His conversation had a curiously circular quality:

'I am Hindu, sahib.'

'Really?'

'But I am not looking like Hindu.'

'No.'

'I am looking like Sikh gentleman.'

'Yes.'

'But I *am* Hindu.'

'Good.'

'Although I am not looking like . . .'

We had been at the wedding a full hour before I began to be curious about the whereabouts of the bride and groom.

'Would you like to see the bride?' asked Dr Haidar.

'She is already here?'

'Yes, yes,' replied Dr Haidar. 'Of course. She is in ladies' department.'

I was led into a shuttered room off the courtyard. It was nearly dark, but in the half-light you could just make out four or five women fussing around a surprisingly elderly-looking girl trussed up in a red Rajasthani costume.

'This is Muslim wedding in Hindu ambulance,' explained Dr Haidar.

'What is a Hindu ambulance?' I asked.

'This is the feeling of Hinduism,' replied Dr Haidar.

'I don't understand,' I said.

'You see our bride is wearing a red Hindu dress,' said Dr Haidar, 'and also her hands painted with swirls of henna, like a Hindu

210

bride. Also there is a large ring in her nose. This is what we call Hindu ambulance.'

I looked at the bride. Her face was cast downwards but even in the half-light you could see that the poor girl looked terrified.

'She has fair complexion,' said Dr Haidar. 'But she is little shy.'

'Isn't she rather old?' I whispered.

'Mr Shahiduddin is well off by village standards, but still he is not a very rich man,' replied Dr Haidar. 'For this wedding he would have to save for many years. During this time his daughter is not growing any younger.'

'But she must be nearly forty,' I said.

'The salary of our government servants,' explained Dr Haidar quietly, 'is parlous in the extreme.'

There came the sound of shouting outside.

'Hurry!' said Dr Haidar. 'The groom is here.'

Wishing the bride good luck, we pushed our way through the milling crowds of guests and out under the entrance arch of the *haveli*. We arrived just in time to see the first members of the brass band – a trombone and a tuba – come round the corner of the lane. Making no concessions to the concept of melody, the band members blasted away at their instruments as loud as they could.

'Very beautiful music,' said Balvinder Singh, who had appeared by my side, and was now wobbling his head from side to side in rapt appreciation. 'Tip-top beautiful.'

The band formed two lines around the entrance of the house. On the nearby rooftops street urchins were dancing frantically to the music. The noise got louder and louder, faster and faster, and less and less tuneful. The groom's party – green-turbanned farmers from Haryana – appeared around the corner of the lane and formed a circle outside the entrance of the house. A few stumbled as they walked, indicating the cause of the delay.

'I am thinking that maybe these gentlemen have been to one English Wine Shop,' said Dr Haidar, speaking in that slightly sanctimonious tone that Muslims sometimes adopt when discussing alcohol.

As Dr Haidar spoke a party of sweepers appeared in the lane, coming from the opposite direction to the marriage party. They

211

Wedding band

were a dirty-looking crew of dark-skinned rag-pickers; each carried a sack-load of rubbish on his back. Mr Shahiduddin Postman darted out from the crowd and with a set of violent curses sent the unfortunate untouchables scurrying off the way they had come. At that moment, with a final fanfare from the brass band, the groom appeared: a sallow-looking youth on a mangy white stallion supporting a young boy in front of him. The groom was wearing white pyjamas and a pill-box hat. Around his neck hung a garland of silver tinsel. Like his bride-to-be, he looked absolutely miserable.

'This is our custom,' said Dr Haidar. 'We think that a groom must look little bit shy.'

'He certainly doesn't look as if he is enjoying himself much.'

'Maybe he is thinking that today he will loose his freedom. After this day he will be having to obey his wife.'

212

'I thought Muslim men were always the unchallenged heads of their households.'

'This thing is not true,' said Dr Haidar. 'In all countries, irrespective of religion, behind the scenes the women are ruling the men. How long have you been married?'

'One year.'

'After a while you will understand,' said Dr Haidar, shaking his head gloomily.

The band stopped, and a group of the groom's more drunken friends broke into song. Their chosen melody was a paean of praise to a local politician, Mr Devi Lal, then the Chief Minister of Haryana. The song, which had become popular at the last election, went something like this:

> Devi Lal, leader of the farmers,
> Will make blossoms bloom in Fall.
> Before such a leader,
> all enemies will cower,
> While Devi Lal stands tall.
> Devi Lal, leader of the farmers,
> Will make buffaloes rich in milk,
> He'll give everyone a tractor,
> A record cotton-crop,
> There's no doubt about it: Devi Lal's tip-top.

There then followed a curious little pantomime, apparently also dictated by tradition. The bride's younger sister, herself no babe-in-arms, confronted the terrified groom and demanded an offering before he and his party would be admitted to the house. Though the groom looked as if he longed to get the whole thing over and done with, he obeyed the dictates of tradition and refused.

'Before you come in, first you must pay,' repeated the bride's sister.

One of the groom's party produced a fifty-rupee note. The sister folded her arms and shook her head. Another flutter of notes was produced: two hundred rupees more.

'We cannot accept less than seven hundred rupees,' said the sister.

Slowly, a few more notes appeared: 300, 400, 550, 650 – finally

213

700 rupees had been collected. The sister stood back, and the groom, followed by his drunken friends and hangers-on, pushed on into the courtyard. I thought a religious ceremony must now follow, but I was mistaken. The bargaining had not finished. The groom and his close family took their places, cross-legged, on the matting beside the trunk of wedding gifts. Facing them sat Mr Shahiduddin Postman and his brothers. In between the two families sat the village *qazi* and two other bearded *maulvis*.

'What are they doing?' I asked Dr Haidar.

'This moment we call the *mihr*,' he replied. 'The groom's family must settle how much money they will pay the bride if the marriage is a failure and ends in divorce.'

This slightly depressing bout of bargaining – which had been brushed over so quickly in the *Shah Jehan Nama* – took at least a quarter of an hour. The marriage which followed it took a fraction of the time – about three minutes. There was a short reading from the Quran and the solemn recitation of the Offer and Acceptance. Then the groom signed a piece of paper which was passed to Mr Shahiduddin Postman and four witnesses for countersignature. It was only when everyone rose to their feet, shook hands and made a beeline for the cooking tent – where, it emerged, Balvinder Singh had been for the last half-hour – that I realized that the ceremony was over. During the entire marriage the bride had remained in her darkened room.

'What about the bride?' I asked Dr Haidar.

'She is still in the ladies' department.'

'And when will she come out?'

'Later. She cannot come into gents' department until the marriage is over.'

As Dr Haidar spoke I remembered the miniature of Dara Shukoh's wedding from the Windsor Castle *Shah Jehan Nama*. Now I realized what had been so odd about it: amid all the festivities and celebrations there had been no sign whatsoever of the bride around whom the whole affair was revolving.

'So the bride does not play any part in the marriage?' I asked.

'No. At least not an active part.'

'And still she will not have met her husband?'

'No. But she will meet him soon enough,' said Dr Haidar. He

214

shook his head gloomily. 'Now they are husband and wife they must spend the rest of their life together.'

One day in the middle of February I made an appointment to meet Dr Jaffery at the Red Fort. Dr Jaffery knew the building as well as anyone and I much looked forward to going around it with someone who had studied it for so many years.

With the note confirming our appointment, Dr Jaffery sent me a photocopy of the *Mirza Nama* – 'The Book of the Perfect Gentleman'. This short manuscript, which was only rediscovered in a private library at the turn of the century, spells out the sort of behaviour that was expected of a young Mughal gentleman in Delhi about 1650. I would not properly be able to understand the Mughals' palace, said Dr Jaffery, unless I first read through their book of etiquette.

The *Mirza Nama* was an extraordinary document. It revealed an unrepentantly superficial world where life revolved around the minutiae of outward appearances and public display. What was vital in a young *mirza* (or gentleman) were the clothes and manners which covered him; the wholeness or corruption of the man within was of no interest or relevance. The most important thing – of course – was being seen with the right people, and the *Mirza Nama* opens with a salutary warning: 'He [the *mirza*] must not speak to every unworthy person, and should regard men of his own class as the only [fit] companions [for him].' He should not 'joke with every good-for-nothing fellow'. The key was to draw as firm a distinction as possible between the *mirza* and ordinary folk. Thus the young gallant should never ever be seen walking on foot, and should at all times carry funds enough 'for the expenses of a palanquin' which he should regard as 'the best of all conveyances'.

If, while on his litter, the *mirza* should pass through a bazaar and see something which appeals to him 'he should not make any difficulty about the price, and ought not to buy like a common trader.' This distaste for the subject of money should also guide his behaviour if another gentleman was impudent enough to enquire about his income: '[In such a situation the *mirza*] should try to get the topic changed; if not he should leave the house to its owner and run away as fast as his feet can carry him. He should not look back.' Nor should a gentlemen ever discuss that most unfashionable subject religion, lest some fanatic 'cause him bodily injury' (still good advice in Delhi today).

It was also important for any aspiring young gallant to give good parties. Towards this end the *mirza* should make a point of smoking scented tobacco blended with hashish; precious gems – emeralds and pearls – should be ostentatiously crushed into his wine. As far as conversation was concerned, there was one golden rule: a gentleman should avoid telling shaggy-dog stories. Moreover if any of his guests 'begins a long story, the *mirza* should not attend it, because [such stories] are styled "the prison house of conversation".'

Literary accomplishment was to be valued: all aspiring gentlemen were expected to know by heart the *Gulistan* (The Rose Garden) and *Bustan* (The Orchard) of Sa'di; but more important still was grammatical correctness: 'In society the *mirza* should [always] try to guard against the shame of committing any mistake in conversation, for such incorrectness in speech is considered a great fault in a gentleman.' It was even acceptable to chant or recite a verse or two in public if the young *mirza* had 'beauty and a good voice'; but he should not do so too often or at length for fear – heaven forbid – that he be mistaken for a professional poet or singer. (The *mirza*, moreover, 'should never trust any well-clothed person who pretends to be an author . . .')

Having your own original opinions was clearly a major flaw in a *mirza* and, just to be on the safe side, the *Mirza Nama* offers a few acceptable opinions for the young gentleman to learn by heart and adopt as his own. Among flowers and trees he should admire the narcissus, the violet and the orange. He should eat his fill of watermelon ('the best of all fruits') and 'rice boiled with spices should be preferred by him to all other eatables.' A gentleman 'should not make too much use of tobacco' but 'should recognize the Fort in Agra as unequalled in the whole world [and] . . . must think of Isfahan as the best town in Persia'; if he insists on travelling he should visit 'Egypt because it is worth seeing'.

Finally, the *Mirza Nama* advises the young gallant on the tricky

216

matter of dress. Brightly coloured coats, shirts and trousers should be tailored to a tight fit; an elaborately decorated scarf should encircle his waist and hold a dagger: 'With a monthly salary of one hundred rupees let him allot ten rupees for the belt and the embroidered badge . . . if he spends fifty rupees on a fur it will not be prodigality.' But things could be taken to excess. While it was vital to be well turned out, the young gallant should beware of imitating those fops who spent their time building huge and elaborate turbans: men like Mirza Abu Said, a great *amir* under Shah Jehan, who was so fastidious in the construction of his head-wraps that the Imperial Durbar had usually finished by the time he had finished tying it all together.

'In India,' concludes the *Mirza Nama*, a gentleman 'should not expect intelligence and good behaviour from those who put big turbans on their heads.'

The Red Fort is to Delhi what the Colosseum is to Rome or the Acropolis to Athens: it is the single most famous monument in the city. It represents the climax of more than six hundred years of experimentation in palace building by Indo-Islamic architects, and is by far the most substantial monument – and in its day was also by far the most magnificent – that the Mughals left behind them in Delhi. Viewed from the end of Chandni Chowk, the sight is superb: a great rhubarb-red curtain wall pierced by a pair of magnificent gates and fortified by a ripple of projecting bastions, each one topped with a helmet-shaped *chattri*.

Dr Jaffery had with him a proof of the new translation of Inayat Khan's *Shah Jehan Nama* while I had brought a leather-bound copy of Bernier's *Travels*. Both contained good accounts of the founding of the New City. Before we looked at the Fort, we sat in a *chai* shop, sipping hot tea and reading out loud from Inayat Khan's chronicle. Like the *Mirza Nama*, the *Shah Jehan Nama* worships superficial, shiny things – gifts, uniforms, jewels – and deliberately ignores the darkness and corruption which lay at the heart of the court. Where it differs from the *Mirza Nama* is in the richness of the fawning which curdles every sentence: reading Inayat Khan's

217

chronicle you experience a sensation like drowning under a sea of the sweetest, stickiest honey.

> Several years before the thought came to His Majesty's omniscient mind that he should select some pleasant sight on the banks of the River Jumna . . . where he might found a splendid and delightful edifice. In accordance with the promptings of his noble nature, he envisioned that streams of water should be made to flow through the proposed fort and that its terraces should overlook the river.

For all its oily sycophancy, the *Shah Jehan Nama* probably gives the authentic flavour of the enterprise: Shah Jehan's town, like Shah Jehan's court chronicle, was there to glorify the ruler. The Emperor wanted to raise a city as a memorial to his rule; for, as the contemporary historian Qandhari observed: 'A good name for Kings is achieved by means of lofty buildings . . . that is to say, the standard of the measure of men is assessed by the worth of their buildings.'

In their different ways, both book and buildings were part of a great Imperial Mughal ego-trip.

Making our way through the crowds – great busloads of excited if baffled-looking Rajasthani villagers –- Dr Jaffery and I passed over the moat and through the outer gate, part of the indecorous additional defences erected outside Shah Jehan's fort by Aurangzeb. Without adding much to the defensive capabilities of the palace, these outworks succeeded in masking the original work of Shah Jehan 'like a veil over a beautiful bride,' as Dr Jaffery put it.

Leaving the legacy of Aurangzeb behind us, we took in the original façade. Ahead of us towered the great octagonal bastions of Shah Jehan's Lahore Gate, an impregnable wall of solid sandstone overlaid by some restrained detailing: blind arcades of cusped arches, a delicate *jharokha*, and a pair of carved lotus flowers floating on the sandstone spandrels of the great horseshoe arch.

From the gate we passed into the covered bazaar, and after running a gauntlet of salesmen (all offering the same smudged postcards printed on blotting paper) emerged into the open in front of the *Naqqar Khana*, the House of the Drums. On passing under the building a cacophony of kettle drums and trumpets would once have announced the arrival of any important visitor. According to

Bernier, who regularly visited the fort over the six years that he spent in and around Delhi:

> To the ears of a European newly arrived, this music sounds very strangely, for there are ten to twelve hautboy, and as many cymbals, which [all] play together. On my first arrival it stunned me so as to be insupportable: but such is the power of habit that the same noise is now heard by me with pleasure; in the night particularly, when in bed and afar, on my terrace, this music sounds in my ears as solemn, grand and melodious.

Before the British destroyed the surrounding buildings in 1857, the *Naqqar Khana* gave on to an enclosed courtyard leading up to the *Diwan-i-am*, the forty-pillared Hall of Public Audience, the site of the Imperial Durbars. Today the original effect is entirely lost. Both *Diwan-i-am* and *Naqqar Khana* stand as isolated buildings, marooned in wide seas of green grass. Dr Jaffery could still point out the faded murals which filled niches of the Drum House – pictures of Central Asian plants, he thought, put there to remind the Mughals of their TransOxianan homelands – but the painted and gilt ceiling of the audience hall has entirely disappeared, along with the awnings, the Kashmiri carpets, the solid silver railings and the magnificent Peacock Throne which, with its twelve pillars of emerald supporting a golden roof topped with two gilt peacocks ablaze with precious stones, was arguably the most dazzling seat ever constructed.

To flesh out the red sandstone skeleton – to recreate within the cusped ribs of the cadaver the durbars of Shah Jehan – I again opened Dr Jaffery's copy of Bernier. Standing in front of the Audience Hall, I read the Frenchman's description of the scenes which had taken place within, then a Delhi commonplace, a tiresome chore for the nobles:

> Every day about noon [the monarch] sits upon his throne, with some of his sons at his right and left, while the eunuchs who stand about the royal person flap away the flies with peacock tails or agitate the air with large fans . . . Immediately under the throne is an enclosure, surrounded by silver rails, in which are assembled the whole body of Omrahs, the Rajahs and the Ambassadors, all standing with their

eyes bent downwards, and their hands crossed. At a greater distance from the throne are the inferior nobles, also standing in the same posture of profound reverence. The remainder of the entire courtyard is filled with persons of all ranks, high and low, rich and poor . . .

Whenever a word escapes the lips of the King . . . however trifling its import, it is immediately caught by the surrounding throng; and the Chief Omrahs, extending their arms towards heaven, as if to receive benediction, exclaim Wonderful! Wonderful! He has spoken wonders! Indeed there is no Mughal who does not know and does not glory in repeating the Persian proverb:

If the monarch says the day is night,
Reply – 'of course: the moon and stars shine bright.'

These Imperial durbars were Inayat Khan's favourite material, giving him ample occasion to tug his forelock and fill the pages of the *Shah Jehan Nama* with paeans to the generosity of his Imperial paymaster. Day after day, like some fatuous television game-show host, Inayat Khan lists the presents given and received:

On Sunday the 17th of Rabi'I [20 March 1650] the festival of Nauroz [New Year] was celebrated in the most splendid and sumptuous style as the ocean of royal bounty and munificence broke into surging billows . . . At this auspicious assembly, from the foaming waves of kindness and munificence, Prince Buland Iqbal received a gorgeous robe of honour with a vest; a dagger studded with precious diamonds and sapphires and incised ornament and a girdle studded with diamonds . . .

And so on and on and on.

The *Diwan-i-am* was as far into the Imperial Palace as most nobles would ever go. Only the most privileged would hope to cross from here into the inner enclosure, where amid streams, paradise gardens and pavilions, lay the zenanas of the women and the private apartments of the Great Mogul. Bernier, in his role as imperial

220

surgeon, did make it into the zenana complex, but was not much the wiser afterwards:

> Who is the traveller who can describe from ocular observation the interior of that building? I have sometimes gone into it when the King was absent from Delhi and once pretty far I thought, for the purpose of giving my advice in the case of a great lady so ill that she could not be moved to the outward gate; but a *Kachemire* shawl covered my head, hanging like a large scarfe down to my feet, and a eunuch led me by the hand, as if I had been a blind man.
>
> You must be content, therefore, with such a general description as I have received from some of the eunuchs. They have informed me that the *seraglio* contains beautiful apartments, more or less spacious and splendid according to the rank and income of the females. Nearly every chamber has its reservoir of running water at the door; on every side are gardens, delightful alleys, shady retreats, streams, fountains and grottoes.

Miniatures still survive showing this part of the palace decked in all its splendour with shady silk awnings of brilliant scarlet, gilded cupolas shining atop the *chattris* and, lying open to pavilions, the *Hayat Baksh* or Life-Bestowing Paradise Garden, planted with cypress, mangoes, apricots and sweet-smelling *nargis, kuzah* and *gulal*. Through everything runs the bubbling runnel of the canal, the *Nahr-i-Bihisht* or River of Paradise, punctuated by pools, carefully carved water-chutes and groups of free-flowing fountains.

Today the inner enclosure should still be the climax of the fort, but the sight of it produces only a sensation of severe anticlimax. As Dr Jaffery pointed out, the British of the last century must take much of the blame for this. At the back of the fort they diverted the Jumna and laid in its place a main road so that the delicate Mughal pavilions look out, not on to the source of the Waters of Paradise, but on to Mahatma Gandhi Marg, the most noisy and polluted stretch of the Delhi Ring Road.

Inside the walls, in a similarly enlightened spirit, the conquerors destroyed most of the courtyards of the palace, leaving – and that grudgingly – little in the inner enclosure except the Pearl Mosque

Pearl Mosque

and a single string of pavilions spaced out also on the Jumna battlements. Even the Mughal gardens were uprooted and replaced with sterile English lawns. In the place of the marble fantasies they tore down, the British erected some of the most crushingly ugly buildings ever thrown up by the British Empire – a set of barracks that look as if they have been modelled on Wormwood Scrubs. The barracks should have been torn down years ago, but the fort's current proprietors, the Archaeological Survey of India, have lovingly continued the work of decay initiated by the British: white marble pavilions have been allowed to discolour; plasterwork has been left to collapse; the water channels have cracked and grassed over; the fountains are dry. Only the barracks look well maintained.

The Mughal buildings which remain – a line of single-storey pavilions, the Emperor's private apartments and the zenana buildings – stand still in their marble simplicity; but without their carpets, awnings and gorgeous trappings they look strangely uncomfortable: cold and hard and white, difficult to imagine back into life. Today,

222

as the pavilions lie empty and neglected, they look like ossified tents – silk turned to stone. The Emperor is dead; the courtiers have dispersed. The whole structure has crumbled. The gorgeous canopies have rotted, the bamboo supports have snapped. The dazzling inlay of precious stones was long ago picked out with daggers.

Most infuriating of all is the Mumtaz Mahal, the Palace of Jahanara Begum. Once the most magnificent of the zenana buildings, it was the only one to be the exclusive residence of a single woman. The privacy made it perfect for the reception of forbidden lovers – which made Roshanara Begum all the more jealous that such facilities should be given to her sister Jahanara while being refused to her. Nevertheless, with all the spies at work in the palace, even here secrecy was impossible. Shah Jehan soon came to hear of Jahanara's orgies, and according to Bernier, resolved to surprise his daughter *in flagrante* with one of her secret paramours:

> The intimation of Shah Jehan's approach was too sudden to allow her [Jahanara Begum] the choice of more than one place of concealment, so the affrighted gallant sought refuge in the capacious cauldron used for the baths. The King's countenance denoted neither surprise or displeasure; he discoursed with his daughter on ordinary topics, but finished the conversation by observing that her skin indicated a neglect of her customary ablutions, and that it was proper she should bathe. He then commanded the eunuchs to light a fire under the cauldron, and did not retire until they gave him to understand that his wretched victim was no more.

This, of all the Fort's pavilions, should be haunted by ghosts, yet today it is converted into a grubby little museum lacking any atmosphere or mystique. The ruins of so many Indian palaces – Mandu, for example, or the great Hindu capital of Hampi – still retain an aura of great dignity about them in their wreckage, but in the Red Fort that aura is notable by its absence. Instead, what remains, despite the completeness of the walls and the outer gates, is a peculiar emptiness, a hollowness at the very heart of the complex. For all the marble, for all the inlay, for all the grand memories glimpsed through finely perforated *jali* screens, the final impression is sad, almost tawdry.

The sycophants have drifted away to find new lords to flatter; what they left behind them now looks merely empty and vainglorious.

That week Olivia and I visited Dr Jaffery's family *haveli* in the walled city for the first time. He had been very nervous about inviting us.

'You should not make friends with an elephant keeper,' he had said, 'unless you first have room to entertain an elephant.'

'Doctor, I wish you would explain your aphorisms sometimes.'

'My friend: I am referring to you. You are a European. You come from a rich country. I am a poor scholar. It is unwise for us to become close because I cannot afford to entertain you in the style to which you are accustomed.' Dr Jaffery frowned: 'I am a simple man. I live in a simple house. You will be disgusted by my simple ways.'

'Don't be silly, doctor. Of course I won't.'

'So if I invited you to my house you would not be upset by the simple food I would serve?'

'Nothing would give me greater pleasure.'

'In that case you and your wife must come and eat some simple dervish dishes with me and my family.'

It was now early March and Ramadan had just begun. With its overwhelmingly Hindu population, New Delhi was quite unchanged by the onset of the Muslim month of fasting, but the Old City had been transformed since our last visit. There were now far fewer people about: many streets were deserted but for groups of tethered goats fattening for their slaughter on Idul-Zuha. Those Muslims who were out on the streets looked bad-tempered: they had not eaten or drunk since before dawn, and were in no mood for smiles or pleasantries. Even the endlessly patient bicycle rickshaw drivers muttered curses under their breath as they drove us uphill through the narrowing funnel of tightly-packed houses.

Dr Jaffery's house lay a short distance from the Turkman Gate, off the narrow Ganj Mir Khan. A steep flight of steps off the street led to a first-floor courtyard dotted with pots of bougainvillaea. Here we were met by Fardine, Dr Jaffery's nephew.

Fardine was a tall, good-looking boy, about sixteen years old;

like his uncle he was dressed in white *kurta* pyjamas. Dr Jaffery was still giving lectures at the college, Fardine said. Would we like to come upstairs and help him fly his pigeons until Dr Jaffery arrived for *iftar*, the meal eaten at sunset each day during Ramadan?

He led us up four flights of dark, narrow stairs, before disappearing up a rickety ladder out on to the roof. We followed and emerged on to a flat terrace with a magnificent view over Old Delhi. To the right rose the three swelling domes of the great Jama Masjid; to the left you could see the ripple of small semi-domes atop the ancient Kalan Masjid. In between the two mosques, in the great arc of roofs and terraces which surmounted the houses of Shahjehanabad, I saw for the first time that secret Delhi which lies hidden from those who only know the city from ground level. From Dr Jaffery's rooftop you could look out, past the anonymous walls which face on to the Old Delhi lanes, and see into the shady courtyards and the gardens which form the real heart of the Old City.

In the last hour before the breaking of the Ramadan fast, the courtyards and rooftops were filling with people. Some were lying on charpoys, snoozing away the last minutes before their first meal for thirteen hours. Others sat out on carpets beneath the shady trees enjoying the cool of the evening. Nearby, little boys were playing with brightly coloured diamond-shaped kites which they flew up into the warm evening breeze. They pulled sharply at the strings, then released the kites so that they flew in a succession of angular jerks, higher and higher into the pink evening sky. While most of the fliers were quietly attempting to raise their kites as high as possible into the heavens, some of the boys were engaged in battles with their neighbours. They locked strings with the kites of their enemies and attempted, by means of the ground glass glued on their strings, to cut their opponents' kites free.

Yet, on the rooftops, the kite fliers were easily outnumbered by the pigeon fanciers – the *kabooter baz* – who stood on almost every terrace, hands extended into the air calling to their pigeons: *Aao! Aao! Aao!* (Come! Come! Come!) Above them, the sky was full of the soft rush of beating wings, clouds of pigeons dipping and diving in and out of the domes and through the minarets. The flocks whirled and wheeled, higher and higher, before nose-diving suddenly down towards their home terrace on the command of their

225

Kabooter baz

flier. Some came to rest on the bamboo pigeon frames – horizontal
slats of trellising raised on a pole – that several of the fliers had
raised above their roofs.

226

In England the mention of pigeon fanciers brings to mind Geordies and flat caps and Newcastle Brown Ale. In Delhi the sport has very different associations. It is remembered as the civilized old pastime of the Mughal court. Its laws were codified by Abu'l Fazl in the *A'in-i-Akbari* and its delights and dangers were illustrated by the Mughal miniaturists. Its arts were mastered by, among others, the last of the Great Moguls, the Emperor Bahadur Shah Zafar. It is still one of the great passions of the Old Delhi-wallahs, and one of the many habits which distinguishes them from their Punjabi neighbours in the New City.

Fardine took us to the edge of his terrace, where his own pigeons were kept in a large coop. He opened the wire-mesh door and scattered some grain on the floor. Immediately the pigeons began to strut and flutter out, billing and cooing with pleasure. As they emerged from their coop, Fardine pointed out the different varieties in his collection.

'These are the *Shiraji*,' he said pointing to two birds with reddish wings and black chests. 'They are the fighter pigeons. This is a very good pair: they have won many battles. And you see these?' He was now pointing at some large pigeons, coloured very light blue-grey. 'These are the *Kabuli Kabooter*. They are the strongest pigeons in Delhi. They are not very fast but they can fly very high for two to four hours – sometimes more. And these red ones: they are *Lal Khal*, along with the *Avadi Golay* they are the fastest of all *kabooter*.'

With a swift movement he picked up one of the *Lal Khals* and kissed it on its head. Then, turning it over, he pointed at the miniature bracelets he had fixed to its ankles. 'Look!' he said. 'They wear *ghungroos* like a dancer!'

Fardine took out a tin can from a cupboard beside the coop. In it was grain mixed with *ghee* (clarified butter). This was obviously the pigeons' favourite delicacy: at the sight of the tin can, the pigeons leapt in the air and fluttered above us waiting to dive down on the first grains; others landed flirtatiously on Fardine's arms and shoulders. The boy threw the sticky grain up into the air and the pigeons swooped down after it. The birds on Fardine's shoulders manoeuvred their way down to the edge of the can where they sat on its rim, greedily pecking at the grains. Others sat on Fardine's open palm eating from his hand.

227

When the birds had eaten their fill, Fardine stood back and shouted: 'Ay-ee!' Immediately with a great flutter of wings the pigeons rose into the air and circled above the terrace. When Fardine whistled the birds shot off in the direction of the Jama Masjid; another whistle and they returned. Fardine waved his arms and the birds rose high into the air; at the cry of *'Aao! Aao! Aao!'* they obediently returned. With another flutter of wings, the birds came in to land on their coop.

'These tricks are easy to learn,' said Fardine shrugging his shoulders. 'But to become a master – a *Khalifa* – can take twenty years of training. A master can teach his pigeons to capture another man's flock and drive it home like a herd of sheep. He can make his birds fly like an arrow – in a straight line, in single file – or can direct them to any place he likes, in any formation. There are perhaps five thousand *kabooter baz* in Delhi, but there are only fifty *Khalifa*.'

As Fardine spoke, there was a sudden report, like a loud explosion. Seconds later the muezzin of a hundred Delhi mosques called the Faithful to prayer with a loud cry of 'Allaaaaah hu-Akbar!' The sun had set. The fast was over. It was time for the *iftar*.

Dr Jaffery was prostrated on a prayer carpet, finishing his evening *namaaz*. Fardine went to join him. Uncle and nephew knelt shoulder to shoulder, hands cupped, heads bowed in the simple position of submission.

When he had finished, Dr Jaffery rose to his feet, brushed the dust off his pyjamas and came over to Olivia and me. He welcomed us, then added: 'You looked at us strangely while we were praying. Do you never pray?'

'I used to,' I said, embarrassed. 'Now . . . I am not sure what I believe in, whether I'm an agnostic or . . .'

'You make God sound so complicated,' said Dr Jaffery, cutting in. 'God is simple. To follow him is not so difficult. Just remember the advice of Rumi: "Follow the camel of love."'

'But follow it where?' I said.

'To wherever it leads,' replied Dr Jaffery. 'God is everywhere. He is in the buildings, in the light, in the air. He is in you, closer to you than the veins of your neck.'

'But . . .'

'If you honour him and believe God is one you will be all right,' said Dr Jaffery. 'Come. The *iftar* is ready.'

He led us into the house and introduced us to his two nieces, Nosheen and Simeen. They were pretty girls, about sixteen and seventeen, dressed in flowery *salwar kameez*.

A sheet had been spread out on the ground, and around it had been placed a square of long hard bolsters. The *iftar* meal was laid in its centre. We sat down and Dr Jaffery handed us a plate of dates: traditionally the delicacy with which Muslims break the Ramadan fast. There followed a succession of delicious Delhi kebabs rounded off with fruit *chaat*: a kind of spicy fruit salad. While we ate, Dr Jaffery talked of the (then) impending break-up of the Soviet Union:

'The Iranians are already broadcasting to Central Asia in Turkish,' he said. 'There will be a revival of Timurid Empire. Just you see. Before long there will be an embassy of Samarkand in Delhi.'

After we had finished everyone lay back on the bolsters. Dr Jaffery's nieces begged him to tell us one of his Mullah Nasir-ud-Din stories and eventually he obliged.

He told how, on one of his visits to Delhi, the legendary Mullah Nasir-ud-Din arrived in the city in the middle of Ramadan. The mullah was very hungry and when he heard that the Emperor was providing a free *iftar* to anyone who came to the Red Fort he immediately tied up his donkey and went along. However he was so dirty from his ride that the Master of Ceremonies placed him in a distant corner, far from the Emperor, and at the end of the queue for food.

Seeing he would not be served for several hours, the mullah went off back to the caravanserai in which he was staying. He washed and dressed in a magnificent embroidered robe topped with a great gilt turban, then returned to the feast. This time he was announced by a roll of kettle drums and a fanfare of trumpets bellowing from the *Naqqar Khana*. The Master of Ceremonies placed him near the Great Mogul and a plate of freshly grilled lamb was

229

put before him. But Mullah Nasir-ud-Din did not eat. Instead he began to rub the lamb all over his robe and turban.

The Mogul said: 'Eminent Mullah. You must be a foreigner from a distant and barbarous land! I have never seen such manners in my life before!' But Mullah Nasir-ud-Din was unrepentant. He replied: 'Your Highness. This gown got me fed. I think it deserves its portion too, don't you?'

After the story was finished, Nosheen and Simeen said goodnight and disappeared upstairs to bed. But Fardine, Olivia and I sat up with Dr Jaffery sipping tea and chatting until well after midnight. At first Dr Jaffery told more Mullah Nasir-ud-Din stories, but after a while the conversation became more serious.

I asked the doctor about Dara Shukoh and Aurangzeb, and soon the doctor was telling us about the civil war and the accounts given of it by Bernier and Manucci.

Throughout the 1650s the power and influence of Dara Shukoh continued to rise.

In the Mughal court great importance was always given to small details of protocol and privilege: the colour of a turban, the number of jewels in a noble's dagger, the place he was assigned in the Red Fort: all these things had significance as subtle indicators to an *omrah*'s place in the ranking of the empire.

It was with a succession of such hints that Shah Jehan let it be known that his eldest son bathed in an ever-brighter glow of Imperial approval. Nobles attending the court were ordered to go first to the apartments of Dara Shukoh and there make their morning obeisance before going on to the *Diwan-i-khas* to greet Shah Jehan. Elephant fights were staged whenever Dara wished; his retainers were allowed to hold gold and silver maces in the durbar hall; Dara himself was assigned a small throne immediately beside that of his father. On two occasions Shah Jehan went so far as to declare Dara his desired successor, while adding that the matter rested in the hands of Allah.

Meanwhile the Emperor ordered that Aurangzeb should remain – unrewarded – on gruelling campaign against the empire's enemies in the Deccan. It was against this background that the crisis of September 1657 was played out.

The emergency had a most unexpected cause. Shah Jehan's extraordinary sexual appetites were always a matter of some speculation in the Imperial City, both to travellers and to native Delhiwallahs. Many contemporary writers comment on Shah Jehan's legendary appetites: the Emperor's lust for his daughter Jahanara, his penchant for seducing the wives of his generals and relations, and the numbers of courtesans invited into the palace to quench the monarch's thirst when his expansive harem proved insufficient. Manucci's writings are full of more or less fanciful speculation on this matter:

> All the world knows that the Mohammedans, following the example of their master, Mohammed, are very licentious; wherefore the men among them do not content themselves with a few wives, but seek every method of gratifying themselves in this particular.
>
> Shah Jehan, not contenting himself with the women he had in his palaces, forfeited the respect of his nobles by intrigues with their wives . . . [Moreover] for the greater satisfaction of his lusts, Shah Jehan ordered the erection of a large hall adorned through out with great mirrors. All this was made so that he might obscenely observe himself with his favourite women. It is impossible to explain satisfactorily the passion that Shah Jehan had in this direction.

While the passing of time did nothing to lessen the Emperor's appetites, it apparently did nothing either to improve his performance. It was rumoured that as the monarch's virility grew less reliable he developed a habit of taking substantial quantities of aphrodisiacs. Whether they worked or not, the potions had a serious and potentially fatal side-effect: 'these stimulating drugs,' wrote Manucci, 'brought on a retention of urine . . . for three days Shah Jehan was almost at death's door.'

Jahanara Begum moved into Shah Jehan's apartments to nurse the Emperor herself. The gates of the palace were closed. In the city it was rumoured that the Emperor was already dead. In the Chandni Chowk shopkeepers boarded up their premises, buried their treasure and prepared for a long period of unrest. Meanwhile spies in the Red Fort reported the developments to each of Shah Jehan's four sons, all of whom assumed that the long-awaited succession battle was now imminent. Each began to gather troops and to borrow money from usurers.

The first to make a move was Shah Shuja, the Emperor's second son and viceroy of Bengal. Collecting a large army, he marched it across the width of northern India, supported on his flank by a flotilla of ships advancing slowly down the Ganges. In a battle before the walls of Agra, Shah Shuja was defeated by the Imperial army commanded by Dara's twenty-five-year-old son, Sulaiman Shikoh.

Shah Jehan had now recovered from his illness and was able to move to Agra and join in the victory celebrations. These festivities were, however, soon cut short when news arrived that the Emperor's third and fourth sons, Aurangzeb and Murad Baksh, had joined forces and were heading north. Their army was about half the size of Dara's, although highly trained and confident. But Aurangzeb was rarely prepared to rely on military prowess alone. He opened up a correspondence with the more pliable officers among Dara's army and with promises of rewards secretly won over a sizeable proportion of his opponent's force.

Despite the April heat, the rebel army made fast progress through Central India and by the end of the month had reached a position near Ujjain. Crossing the last barrier, a narrow but fast-flowing river, the rebel army drew up on the plain of Samugarh a few miles from Agra. It was 29 May 1657. Facing them were the battalions of Dara Shukoh, among them Dara's junior artilleryman Niccolao Manucci:

> When placed in the field our army looked like a lovely city adorned with beautiful tents flying innumerable flags of all colours . . . Prince Dara amidst his squadron appeared like a crystal tower, resplendent as a sun shining over the land. All around him rode many squadrons of Rajput cavalry whose armour glittered from afar. In front went many ferocious war elephants clad in shining steel with tusks encrusted with gold and silver.

232

The vast army numbered around 100,000 cavalry and 25,000 musketeers as well as divisions of war elephants and camel-artillery. Nevertheless, for all the glitter and gold, Manucci was not over-confident: 'The greater number of soldiers that Dara had enlisted were not very warlike; they were butchers, barbers, blacksmiths, carpenters, tailors and such like. It is true that on their horses and with their arms they looked well at a review; but they knew nothing of war.'

The day of the battle dawned a hot May morning. On the insistence of Khalil Ullah Khan, one of Aurangzeb's agents in the Imperial army, Dara made a decision to leave his strong defensive position and open the attack. Soon after nine o'clock his army lumbered forward. Aurangzeb's musketeers held their fire until the last minute, then discharged their entire artillery. The Rajputs who had been in the lead took the full force of the barrage; the new conscripts behind them turned and fled.

But Dara did not waver. He pressed on, encouraging his army from the top of his great caparisoned war elephant. Around him the Rajputs regrouped. The superior numbers of the Imperial army stood them in good stead: within a few minutes, Dara's forces had broken through the rebels' artillery and put to flight the infantry. It was then that Aurangzeb's cunning saved the day for the rebels. His agents within the Imperial army managed to assassinate three of Dara's generals as they sat exposed on their elephants. One, Ram Singh Rathor, was controlling the left wing. When his Rajputs saw that their leader had fallen, they began to give way.

Seeing his opportunity, Khalil Ullah Khan rode up to Dara and advised him to dismount from his war elephant and ride over to take charge of the wavering left wing. In the panic of the moment, the prince agreed. With Dara no longer visible on his elephant a rumour spread that he had been killed. Aurangzeb seized the moment and pressed forward. By noon, Dara's poorly disciplined troops had given way 'like dark clouds blown by a high wind'. The battle was lost.

Dara fled back to Agra and set off on the road to Delhi without daring to face his father. On hearing the news of the battle, Shah Jehan prepared to ambush Aurangzeb as he entered the Agra Fort – but his plan was betrayed by Aurangzeb's sister and ally,

Roshanara Begum. The rebels besieged the fort, sent in troops to rescue Roshanara, then left the old monarch locked into the harem, a prisoner in his own palace.

Later, while the rebel army celebrated their victory, Aurangzeb invited Murad Baksh to his tent and there got him drunk. When he had fallen asleep, Aurangzeb quietly chained up his brother in silver fetters and sent him off to Delhi in a covered elephant howdah. On his arrival, Murad was thrown into a dungeon in Selimgarh, opposite the Red Fort. There he was force-fed poppy-water, an extract of opium guaranteed to leave the drinker crippled and quite insane within the space of a few months.

In a brief campaign, Aurangzeb had seized the empire, imprisoned his father, and had begun hunting down and murdering his three brothers. Now, although Shah Jehan still lived, Aurangzeb decided to have himself crowned. For this ceremony he chose the beautiful pleasure garden of Shalimar, about five miles north of Old Delhi.

Although few Delhi-wallahs know of its existence, the garden of Shalimar still survives today. I went there one spring evening with my diary under my arm, looking for a peaceful place to write.

Bernier describes Shalimar as 'handsome and noble . . . although not to be compared to Fontainebleau, Saint Germain or Versailles.' He is right: by both Mughal and French standards it is a large but hardly dramatic garden. There is a single Shahjehani-style pavilion, a few dry water channels and fine surrounding wall. But though simple, Shalimar is still very atmospheric: it is overgrown and forgotten, heavily haunted by djinns. It is a good place to sit and watch the sun go down.

I came to the garden by way of the village which has grown up on its edge. The villagers were sitting on their charpoys, sucking lengths of sugarcane. One lady crouched under the leathery flanks of a water buffalo, gently pulling at the beast's udders, shooting warm jets of frothy milk into a battered tin pail. Nearby, a cart horse had just been released from its harness and was busy munching at its fodder; the up-ended cart stood to one side. I wound my way through this village scene, then quite suddenly I was no longer in an Indian village, but instead in a Mughal garden. The dusty cart-track had become a lawn; the village houses had given way to straight, symmetrical lines of bottle-palms; in the borders the lilies and irises were in full bloom – wonderful swathes of azure and magenta leading on into the *char-bagh*.

I realized then quite what an intrusion any Mughal garden is into the Indian scene. Hindus revere nature but never feel any need to marshal or mould it into a design of their own: a banyan tree will almost be encouraged to spread its drooping creepers into the middle of any village market, or to block any backwoods track. It is revered for itself; however it develops, that end is regarded as a sort of perfection. As in nature, so in architecture: Hindu palaces seem to grow organically of their own will: a hall here, a shrine there, a sudden inexplicable curve in the curtain wall somewhere else.

The Muslim tradition is quite different. Inheriting the Greek love of order and logic, Islamic gardens – like their buildings – are regimented into lines of perfect symmetry; balance and design is all; nothing is left to impulse or chance. With these qualities, the Mughal gardens dotted around the subcontinent are as alien to the Indian environment as the Brighton Pavilion is to the English south coast, or the Chinese Pagoda to Kew. Outside the garden, all is delightful chaos; inside, reflecting the central concept of Islam, spontaneity is crushed by submission to a higher order.

As if they had subconsciously realized this, a little party of Muslims had taken up their station on a carpet by the edge of the garden. Here an elderly mullah was nodding his turban as he instructed a party of young novices on the Koran and the *Hadiths*, the sayings of the Prophet. Books were spread out on the ground. The murmur of chanting voices carried above the far-distant thunder of the Grand Trunk Road, the old Mughal highway linking the farms of the Punjab with the bazaars of Delhi. In the undergrowth around them, village women were heading back home, carrying on their heads great bundles of firewood for their cooking-hearths. There was that all-pervasive evening scent of cut grass and jasmine.

I came across the garden's central pavilion quite by chance, stumbling on it as I followed a dried water-course. It is now so overgrown with vines and creepers that it has half returned to the jungle. The plasterwork has peeled to reveal the red sandstone underneath; and in places that sandstone has in turn crumbled away to reveal the intricate brickwork that lies at the core of the structure.

As the sun began to go down, I wandered happily through the ruins until I came across a band of Timurid star-vaulting in one of the side chambers. Here a few fragments of painted stucco still remained and on these were painted a tangle of trailing flowers: roses, tulips and irises, some cut, some growing from the ground, others emerging from cornucopias – ancient symbols of fertility and plenty, merging and tangling with the real creepers of the jungle.

Perhaps partly because of the decay, the garden had retained the atmosphere of enclosure and secrecy – that feeling of shutting out the world beyond – essential to any walled pleasure garden. It was just this conspiratorial atmosphere that Roshanara Bagh and the Red Fort both now lack.

I walked on, past mango trees, sisam and jamun to the garden wall. This faces out on to a flooded water meadow full of grazing buffaloes. An elderly herder in white pyjamas was sitting to one side. Around him swooped two hoopoes. It was spring and the hoopoes were dipping and diving, circling each other, so that the black and white of their zebra-underwings melted into the scarlet of their crests. Behind me, over by the pavilion, the colour on the red-stone pillars grew more vivid as the evening light slipped down their sides. Suddenly there was a loud screech, and on the roof a wild peacock appeared. I opened my diary and started scribbling.

But as I sat with my legs dangling over the edge, looking out on to the quiet water meadow, the anarchy of Delhi seemed far away and I began to see why in all the most sensible cultures, Paradise was envisaged as a walled pleasure garden. Before I came to India, I had not realized that the English word 'paradise' was borrowed from the ancient Persian words *pairi* (around) and *daeza* (a wall). The word was brought west by Xenophon, who introduced it into Greek when describing the fabulous garden built by the Persian Emperor Cyrus at Sardis; from the Greek *paradeisoi* it passed into Latin as *paradisum*; and hence into Middle English as *paradis*.

Now, sitting in the Shalimar Garden, it was very easy to see why the Persian word for an enclosed garden had become an English synonym for bliss.

The day after the Shalimar crowning ceremony, Aurangzeb again gathered his army and headed north after Dara Shukoh. But it was not until August 1659, a year and a half after Dara's defeat, that Aurangzeb finally captured him. Fleeing across the western deserts, abandoned by all but his immediate family, Dara was eventually betrayed by Jiwan Khan, a local chieftain whom Dara had personally saved from death only a few years before. Like Murad before him, Dara was seized, manacled and sent to Delhi in a closed howdah.

Just before he entered the city, he was transferred to a 'miserable and worn out animal, covered with filth'. Holding his young son in front of him in a sort of cruel parody of his wedding procession, he was humiliatingly marched publicly down the full length of the new Chandni Chowk. Bernier, who was in Delhi that day, witnessed the procession. Dara was dressed in 'dirty cloth of the coarsest texture, and his sorry turban was wrapped around with a muffler like that worn by the meanest of people.' Half-way down the great boulevard a fakir shouted up to Dara that previously he had always been generous to the poor; but now he understood that Dara had nothing to give. Hearing the man, Dara stripped off his sackcloth cloak and threw it down. But Aurangzeb's troops forbade the holy man to accept the gift. Dara, they said, no longer had any right to give anything to anyone.

A few days later a group of nobles keen to impress Aurangzeb broke into the quarters where Dara was being kept, a small garden outside the walls of Shahjehanabad towards Nizamuddin. Dara seized a kitchen knife and tried to defend himself, but the thugs overpowered him. They threw him to the ground and beheaded him in front of his son. The prince's head was cleaned, wrapped in a turban and presented to Aurangzeb on a golden dish. The new Emperor called for lights, examined the face, then thrust at it three times with a sword. He said: 'Behold the face of a would-be king

237

and Emperor of all the Mughal realms. Take him out of my sight.'

No one was more pleased about Dara's demise than Roshanara Begum. She had begged Aurangzeb not to spare Dara, and now that she heard of his end she threw a great party in the Imperial harem. At this gathering she persuaded Aurangzeb that it would be an amusing joke to send the head to their father in his palace-prison in Agra. It was duly dispatched the following morning with Aurangzeb's chief eunuch, I'tibar Khan. '[The eunuch] waited until the hour Shah Jehan had sat down to dinner,' wrote Manucci.

> When he had begun to eat, I'tibar Khan entered with the box and laid it before the unhappy father, saying: 'King Aurangzeb, your son sends this *plat* to your majesty to let you see that he does not forget you.' The old Emperor said: 'Blessed be God that my son still remembers me.' The box having been placed upon the table, he ordered it with great eagerness to be opened. But on withdrawing the lid, he discovered the face of Prince Dara. Horrified, he uttered a cry and fell on his hands and face upon the table, and, striking against the golden vessels, broke some of his teeth and lay there apparently lifeless.
>
> Jahanara Begum and the other women present began to wail, beat their breasts, tear their hair and rend their garments . . . But the eunuch I'tibar Khan made a report to King Aurangzeb of what had passed, with all the details, whereby he and Roshanara Begum received great delight.

The unnatural act of Dara's murder and the treacherous overthrow of Shah Jehan acted like a curse upon Delhi. Never again did it match that apex of prosperity that it reached during the brief nine years that Shah Jehan ruled from the Red Fort.

Aurangzeb spent as little time as possible in the city, preferring to continue his campaigns from Aurangabad, his own foundation in the Deccan. Delhi had lived by the court and when the court disappeared, the city emptied like a basin of water whose plug had been removed. Travellers began to describe the city as being like a ghost town: 'The city appears to be a desert when the King is absent,' wrote the French traveller Jean de Thévenot. 'If there have been four hundred thousand Men in it when the King was there,

there hardly remains the sixth part in his absence.'

But it was not just the absence of the Emperor. Aurangzeb's rule proved harsh and repressive. Spies were everywhere; men never knew whom they could trust. All the things that had made Delhi an amusing and lively city were one by one forbidden. Dancing women and courtesans were forced to marry. Prostitution was banned, as was wine-drinking, hashish-smoking and the playing of music.

More serious were Aurangzeb's actions against non-Muslims. His fundamentalist outlook led him to destroy Hindu temples across the empire. He imposed a special tax on all Hindus and executed Guru Teg Bahadur, the ninth of the great teachers of the Sikhs. The religious wounds he opened up have never again entirely healed; but at the time they literally tore the country in two. From the fissures between the two religions, there emerged whispers of sorcery, of strange succubuses, of unrest among the city's djinns. In the wilds of Rajasthan a naked army of shaven-headed Hindu *sadhus* was rumoured to be marching on Delhi, led by an old sorceress. Early reports had the *sadhus* sweeping the Mughal army in front of them – until, so it was said, Aurangzeb deployed strange magic against them.

It was the golden age of the fakirs. Their activity amazed and baffled even the sceptical Bernier: 'They tell any person his thoughts, cause the branch of a tree to blossom and to bear fruit within an hour, hatch an egg in their bosom within fifteen minutes, producing what ever bird may be demanded, and make it fly around the room.'

Later, when Aurangzeb ordered the decapitation of the naked fakir Sarmad, an Armenian Jew who had converted to Islam, the sage allegedly picked up his head and walked up the steps of the Jama Masjid. There he said a final set of prayers before departing to the heavens.

Meanwhile in the court, the dam-burst of treachery unleashed by Aurangzeb left the principal players wading deeper and deeper into the darkness. Roshanara Begum, the Lady Macbeth of Delhi, had taken over the position vacated by Jahanara Begum: chief of the Imperial Harem. She gathered about her a vast retinue and used to enjoy making pompous processions through the streets of

Delhi. But then, during the monsoon of 1661, she made her fatal mistake.

Aurangzeb had been struck down with a fever, and it was believed that he was beyond recovery. Believing this to be the case, Roshanara stole the Imperial seal and used it to forge an order that proclaimed Aurangzeb's nine-year-old youngest son to be the next Emperor in preference to the rightful heir. This switch was intended to enable Roshanara to retain her influence by stepping in as the child's regent. But at this awkward moment, Aurangzeb suddenly recovered. He discovered from his eunuchs what Roshanara had been up to, and, despite her support for him over many years, he disgraced her. Later, after she was caught red-handed in an orgy with nine lovers in her Red Fort harem apartments, Aurangzeb arranged for his sister to be discreetly poisoned. She died in great pain, 'swollen out like a hogshead, leaving behind her the name of great lasciviousness'. She was buried under the pavilion she had built in the Roshanara Gardens.

With his sister poisoned, Aurangzeb was now able to trust no one. In his old age he marched to and fro, viciously putting down rebellions, trying to impose his harsh regime on his unwilling subjects. On his death in 1707 the empire fragmented. Yet the Mughal line never quite died out.

'It was all great-grandfather Aurangzeb's fault,' said Pakeezah Sultan Begum, rearranging her cardigan. 'If it wasn't for him we'd still have the empire.'

The Crown Princess angrily seized a book held out by one of the other staff at the library. 'Please be stamping this for me, Highness.'

Pakeezah Begum took the plastic stamp, wetted it on the ink-pad and firmly stamped the return-by date on the leaf at the front.

'Tell the boy to bring this back on the 20th of March or there will be a fine of five rupees.' The woman took the book and moved away, but the Princess had not finished: 'Oh, and Mrs Bannerji?' she said. 'Please bring me some more tea. These cups are both *stone cold*.'

240

Mrs Bannerji nervously took the cups and muttered an apology: 'Sorry, Highness.'

'They know who I am, so these people give me respect,' said Pakeezah when Mrs Bannerji had disappeared. 'We are colleagues and we are working together. But they know my ancestral chain so they are not trying it on too much.'

'Do many people in Delhi know who you are?' I asked.

'The old Delhi-wallahs know. Also some other people guess. Last weekend I went to a wedding and one lady came up and said: "You are different from these people." I was not wearing any special clothes, but this lady – she was from an old Lucknow family – could see by my manners that I was not a common person.'

Pakeezah nodded her head: 'I find it is the little things which give you away if you are royalty: how you eat, how you talk, how you welcome people. Small and subtle things. But important. Although we now live with the common people we don't have their habits.'

Mrs Bannerji brought two new cups of tea and placed them beside Pakeezah Begum's big, black bakelite telephone. Pakeezah thanked her: 'Now that's what I call a *nice* cup of tea,' she said.

'Do you think you would have made a good Empress?' I asked, nibbling a biscuit.

'If I was Empress I would be a constitutional Empress only,' said Pakeezah, drawing herself up. 'I would be like your Queen: not having so much power but maintaining my dignity and status. Probably I would have an elected Prime Minister beneath me,' she said. 'Democracy is a good thing for modern times.'

Pakeezah looked at her watch: it was just after five o'clock. She said: 'We can't talk here – library is closing now. Perhaps you would come to my home. Then you could meet my mother. She knows our family history better than I.'

The Princess gathered her things together and wrapped a tatty shawl over her sari and cardigan. I followed her as she waddled out of the library.

'Whatever glory my ancestors had,' she continued, 'that is gone now. My family should accept that fact. We have no official royal status. We have nothing.'

We wandered past the Delhi Gate and on through the crumbling streets of Old Delhi; as we went, Pakeezah stared sadly around her.

241

'Look what this so-called government has done to my city,' she muttered. 'My ancestors built the most beautiful city in the world. They had the finest food, the finest way of living, the most lovely gardens, the finest dress. Everything was perfect in Delhi when they were ruling. Now no one is maintaining anything. These people have become so careless. They are not proud of their past.'

We turned off the main road at the Faiz Bazaar and wandered through dirty back lanes towards Daryaganj.

'This area used to contain big *havelis*,' explained Pakeezah. 'It was the home of all the great *omrahs* and poets from my ancestor's court. So many famous families used to be living here. Now working-class people from all-over have come in. Naturally their way of living is very different from ours.'

A squatting beggar wailed at us from his place beside an open sewer. Pakeezah Begum frowned. 'I think we should move to another area, but my mother says the family should stay here. Daryaganj is near the Fort. My mother says if we can't live inside the Fort at least we should live in its suburbs.'

The house consisted of a small corner of an old, much-partitioned *haveli*. It had a little courtyard off which led three simple, white-washed rooms. In one of these, perched on a bedstead, sat the senior-most descendant of Genghis Khan, Tamerlane, Babur and Shah Jehan. She had been paralysed for thirty years. For all this time the bedstead had been her throne. Beneath it, two geese were pecking at some grain.

Sahabzadi Qamar Sultan, born in the first year of the twentieth century, was wrapped up in an all-enveloping white *salwar kameez*. She chewed *paan* from an elaborately incised silver box. She was very old and very deaf. Her old-fashioned courtly Urdu was difficult to understand and her daughter translated for me.

'He's writing a book about our Delhi,' Pakeezah shouted into her mother's ear.

'I'm sorry?' whispered the old woman.

Pakeezah repeated what she had said. This time the old Princess smiled and said something to her daughter.

'She says welcome. May God bless you and may you have a long life.'

'Thank you,' I said. 'May your mother also have a long life.'

'She's already ninety-one,' said Pakeezah.

242

I asked exactly how they were related to the Great Moguls. I had expected the women to be fairly distant cousins of the Emperors. I was quite wrong.

According to the old Princess, she was the granddaughter of Fateh-ul-Mulk, the heir apparent of the last Mogul Emperor, Bahadur Shah Zafur II. Fateh-ul-Mulk had been poisoned in a court intrigue well before 1857, but his six-year-old son, the Princess's father, had survived both this and the Mutiny.

When the British took the Old City after the Seige of Delhi, the child had been smuggled out of the fort and hidden in the jungle around Mehrauli. Later, when tempers had cooled, her father, Mirza Farkunda Zamal, had been awarded a pension by the penitent British authorities; he was even given a seat of honour at the first Delhi Durbar in 1877. According to my scribbled sums, the old Princess would have been conceived when her father was forty-nine.

'Neither my brothers or sister or I have any children,' said Pakeezah when her mother had finished telling the story. 'Our only nephew died of typhoid thirty years ago. He was just fourteen. When we pass away the direct line will end.'

'Does your mother not have any brothers or sisters?' I asked.

'She had a younger sister. She was extremely beautiful, but she had no children because she was married to a djinn.'

'You're being serious?'

'Of course. My aunt was satisfied with her djinn and refused to marry. They lived together in their own apartment. The djinn used to support her – to give her money and so on.'

'Could anyone else see this djinn?'

'No, but my mother could see the presents the djinn brought her.'

'You really believe this?' I asked.

'Why not?' said Pakeezah Begum.

We talked of Partition and the how the old princess had thrown the last family heirlooms – a series of beautiful inlaid jade daggers – down the *haveli* well, in case the police arrested them for possessing offensive weapons. We talked of the old Princess's meeting with Jawaharlal Nehru when he whispered into her ear: 'Sister, if ever you need *anything*, just let me know.' We talked of the hard times after Independence, of how the old princess had refused to take the charity of the government. After this, Pakeezah's brothers went

243

Humayun's Tomb

to Pakistan while her younger sister emigrated to England: she now lived in Wembley where her husband worked in a biscuit factory making shortbread. And we talked of the Red Fort and how Pakeezah had cried the first time she went around it as a schoolgirl.

'In the fort I saw the finest set of buildings in the world – but no one was caring for them. They were all falling apart. My ancestors brought such sophisticated culture to India – but they have just let it disintegrate. In time it will just disappear and no one will ever know.'

It was getting late and the old Princess was visibly tiring. It was time for me to go. I said my goodbyes to the head of the House of Timur; Pakeezah offered to lead me back through the labyrinth of Daryaganj to the Faiz Bazaar. As we walked she told me how she had always resisted her brother's attempts to persuade her to emigrate to Pakistan.

'I always felt Pakistan would be a very unstable country,' said Pakeezah. 'And anyway. My sixth sense told me to stay here. Delhi is our home.' She shrugged: 'For all its faults we love this city.'

Then, after a pause, she added: 'After all, we built it.'

EIGHT

As soon as you awoke you knew it was going to be hot.

The sun had just appeared over the treeline, as blond as clarified butter but powerful none the less, hinting at the furnace-heat to come. Soon the kites were circling the thermals, a great helix of wide-winged birds sailing the vectors in sweeping corkscrew spirals. By late morning the air was on fire; to open the door on to the roof terrace was to feel in your face a blast of heat as strong as that from a blazing kiln. Noon came like a white midnight: the streets were deserted, the windows closed, the doors locked. There was no noise but for the sullen and persistent whirr of the ceiling fans.

The heat had sprung up quite suddenly: the change from late winter to high summer – six months of European weather – was compressed into little more than a Delhi fortnight. The previous autumn, the muggy monsoon heat had begun to diminish on the very day following the festival of Dusshera. In the same way the change of season and the onset of the sledgehammer-heat of summer was exactly marked by another Hindu holiday – the spring festival of Holi. One day everyone was laughing and singing in the Delhi gardens, covering each other with pink powder and coloured Holi-water; the next they had imprisoned themselves in the silent air-conditioned purdah of their bedrooms and offices, waiting patiently for the reprieve of evening.

The rising mercury changed everything. In the gardens the annuals shrivelled and died. The earth cracked; the lawns became bald and bleached. The tar on the roads glistened like liquid quicksilver.

People became tired and listless. Fruit decayed: an uneaten mango, firm at breakfast, could be covered with a thin lint of mould by evening. Water shot boiling from the cold taps. There was no relief except to shower with bottles of cold water from Mrs Puri's fridge.

Added to the morning procession of salesmen were melon sellers and juice boys, cool water vendors (50 paise a glass) and great caravans of ice cream wallahs. In the Old City men set up small roadside stalls around big red earthenware pots containing *jal jeera,* a dark, spicy, green liquid which burns the mouth but cools the body: a more primitive yet more effective coolant than anything on offer in the new town.

Unconsciously, we adapted our routine to suit the new conditions. We rose at five-thirty and breakfasted outside on fresh mangoes. After a light lunch we would siesta in our bedroom, and not emerge until sunset. The balmy evenings were the compensation for the unpleasantness of the day. At six p.m. we would call Mr Singh to take us to swim in one of the hotel pools or maybe to wander among the old tombs in the Lodhi Gardens; as we passed, black bats would flit through the ruins like departed spirits.

Later we would sit outside on the terrace reading and drinking cold beer by candlelight; translucent green geckos would hoover up the mosquitoes from around the flames as we read. Sometimes, on the nights when there were power cuts and the ceiling fans ceased to whirr, we would drag our mattresses outside and sleep under the stars.

As the sun grew more fierce, our complexions darkened and Olivia's freckles sprang into prominence. I thought them beautiful, but they clearly alarmed Mr Singh who was not used to my wife's Celtic colouring. One morning, while driving through the Old City, he turned quite suddenly into the Meena Bazaar near the Jama Masjid. Without any explanation, he jumped out and approached one of the Ayurvedic healers who for centuries have sat on the roadside here, surrounded by the ingredients of their trade: live iguanas whose fried juices are said to cure impotence; ginseng for philtres used to spread or extinguish the fires of love; tree bark to ward off a woman's menopause; the bringraj herb from the high Himalayas said to conquer baldness or thicken the beard of the most effete Sikh.

As I sat in the hot taxi I could see Balvinder Singh haggling with one of the healers. Eventually Balvinder handed over a pocketful of change and the healer gave him a small pot of white powder. On returning to the car, to my surprise Balvinder solemnly handed the pot to me.

'For madam,' he said earnestly.

'Thank you,' I said. 'But what is it?'

'Medicine,' said Balvinder. 'To cure Mrs William.'

'Of what?'

'Her face,' said Balvinder, drumming his fingers on his cheek-bones. 'This powder will cure Madam's pox.' He pointed to the sky: 'Indian sun. Very bad for Britisher ladies.'

I looked baffled; my friend looked embarrassed.

'Sahib,' he whispered. 'This powder will make Mrs William's skin white again.'

One evening in mid-April, Dr Jaffery and I were walking down the Chandni Chowk heading towards the doctor's rooms in the Ghazi-ud-Din Medresse. It was the end of Ramadan and the Old City, funereal for the last month, had sprung back to life with a vengeance. Fairy lights were hung over many of the mosques and houses. As we walked we had to negotiate our way through thick crowds clustering around the sweet shops and the sewing machines of the *derzis* (tailors):

'This is the day we call *al-vida*,' said Dr Jaffery. 'It means "the goodbye". It is the last Friday of our fast.'

We passed Gunthe Wallah's, the old Mughal sweet shop, once – so legend has it – patronized by Shah Jehan's chief elephant. The elephant had been leading a procession down the Chandni Chowk but had halted outside Gunthe Wallah's and had refused to move on towards the Red Fort, despite the frantic proddings of its mahout, until it was first allowed to consume a box of Gunthe Wallah's best *mithai*. Now, although there were no signs of any elephants, the

shop was besieged by crowds of equally persistent villagers competing with each other to be served. To help cope with the demand, the shop assistants had arranged a line of trestles outside the shop, each one piled high with the Gunthe Wallah's stickiest and most sickly sweets.

Nearby other shops had set up trestles loaded with silk saris and embroidered *salwars*, high-heeled shoes and embroidered mosque hats, trinkets and bracelets, jewellery and decorations. The owners of the roadside *dhabas* had placed steaming cauldrons full of saffron-coloured biryani rice outside their doors; from inside came wafts of grilling kebabs. To one side, a Sikh was doing a roaring trade in posters of Saddam Hussein. Despite the Iraqi president's failure to win the Gulf War, Saddam was still regarded as something of a hero by the Delhi Muslims, although this failed to explain why the pin-up most popular in the city was that which showed Saddam dressed in full Austrian costume: *lederhosen*, braces, Tyrolean hat, knobbly knees and all.

Dr Jaffery and I passed by a cluster of black-chadored ladies spooning ice cream under their veils.

'Today all the village people come into Delhi to buy presents for *Id*,' said the doctor. 'For us it is like your Christmas Eve. The feast will probably be held tomorrow.'

'Why only probably?' I asked.

'It depends on the moon,' replied the doctor. 'Tonight the Moon Committee will meet in the Jama Masjid. If they judge that the New Moon can be clearly seen, then it will be *Id*. If not – if there is too much cloud cover – we will have to fast for one more day.'

After the hot, dusty bustle of the Chandni Chowk, Dr Jaffery's simple white cell was marvellously cool and welcoming. The thick stone walls, the domed ceiling and the bamboo blinds on the arched windows controlled the temperature as efficiently as any air conditioning system. After Dr Jaffery had finished his evening prayers we ate a simple *iftar* together: dates, grapes and a plate of curried lamb. As we ate, Dr Jaffery promised to give me a ring the following morning to confirm that the festival was going to be celebrated.

'And if it is cancelled?'

'Then I will not ring,' said the doctor, raising his eyebrows. 'Do

249

you not know the story of the Persian warrior who was marching to battle?'

'I don't,' I said. 'Tell me.'

'The warrior was carrying a bow but no arrows. On the road he met a friend who asked why he had not brought any ammunition. "How will you fight?" asked his friend. "I will use the arrows sent by the enemy," he replied. "But what if no arrow comes?" "Then," replied the bowman, "there will be no war." In the same way, if there is no call from me there will be no *Id* prayers.'

While we were talking, from outside in the courtyard there came the sudden sound of excited shouting. We left our food and went to the door. On the opposite side of the quadrangle, silhouetted figures were standing on the roofs, whooping and jumping about. One figure was letting off a Roman candle.

'What's happening?' I asked.

'Look!' said Dr Jaffery. 'Over there! The new moon.'

I looked in the direction Dr Jaffery was pointing. There, suspended just above the domes and minarets of the old city, a perfect silver crescent could be seen shining out over the rooftops.

'The fast is over,' said Dr Jaffery. 'Everyone will be relieved. Although –' and here he lowered his voice '– a few of the more pious mullahs will pretend to weep and to be unhappy. They will say "Ramadan is the month of blessings. Now the angels will not bless us for another year." But secretly these people will be happy, too. No one likes to fast.'

The following morning there was a cool breeze blowing down from the hills; the sky was the colour of attar of roses. Woken by Dr Jaffery's dawn call, I went to see the *Id* prayers at the Jama Masjid.

Mr Singh and I drove through the wide streets of New Delhi, empty now but for a few pilgrims washing under the public pumps near the shrine of Nizamuddin. We headed up the Ring Road towards Old Delhi, and as we drove the avenues began to fill with bicycle rickshaws, all heading in the same direction. By the time we reached the Red Fort we had hit a traffic jam. It was barely six in the morning. Leaving Mr Singh near the Fort, I jumped out and joined the throng of figures, all dressed in new white homespun.

All the ages of man and all the races of Islam seemed to be

250

represented: moustachioed Arabs, dark-skinned Somalis, small South Indians in *lungis*, huge Delhi businessmen bulging out of their pyjamas, prodigiously bearded Afghans swathed in shawls like Old Testament prophets – all of them surging up through the Meena Bazaar towards the Jama Masjid steps.

As they walked, some threw *Id* alms to the cripples, lepers and Bangladeshi refugees who lined the way like a guard of honour, palms extended, heads bowed. As you passed you could hear them murmuring '*Ya Allah! Ya Allah!*' Mixed in with the beggars sat the occasional hawker eager to empty his stock of mosque caps or rosary beads before the holy month had ended.

The tide of Muslims washed on, up into the mosque. We had all arrived early – the prayers were not due to start for another half-hour – but already the vast courtyard was three-quarters full. Seven or eight thousand figures had taken up position kneeling on prayer carpets, so that as you walked in through the great red-stone gate you were confronted by rank upon rank of white-clad backs topped with brightly coloured turbans or embroidered mosque-caps.

To get a better view, I climbed the narrow staircase leading to the balcony at the top of the east wall. This platform was also fast filling up, but I managed to edge my way along the wall-walk to the shade of a *chattri* at the south-east corner. Here, a group of young Muslim girls in new mirror-work costumes were sitting cross-legged under the watchful eye of their father; each one wore a tinsel hairband plaited into her pigtails. Choosing a space on the edge of the wall, a respectful distance apart from the girls, I dangled my legs over the edge and took in the spectacle unfolding below.

I have always thought that Hinduism is at its most sympathetic and comprehensible in the countryside: a simple roadside shrine, a sacred river, a holy spring – these things are the life-blood of that great religion. In the same way, Islam has always been an urban faith, ill at ease with the wilderness; its civilization has always flourished most successfully in the labyrinths of the ancient bazaar towns of the East. Certainly there can be no doubt that Islam looks at its most impressive in a great urban cathedral mosque, especially on an occasion like *Id*.

From all directions people were still pouring out of the maze of the Old City and heading towards one of the three gates of the Jama

251

Masjid – three seething crocodiles of humanity heading towards the same walled courtyard. Within minutes the last remaining areas of pink stone flooring were covered with bodies and had turned homespun-white. The mosque was now packed full, but still crowds were pouring in. Finding the courtyard full, latecomers were taking up their stations in perfectly straight ranks first on the steps, then in the roads leading up to the mosque, then out in the gardens and bazaars beyond. Five minutes before the prayers were due to start, the waves had nearly stilled. Twenty or thirty thousand people were kneeling down facing westwards, patiently waiting for the final prayers of Ramadan. Had I taken up my station on the same day two, three or even four hundred years earlier the same spectacle would have presented itself, completely unchanged.

Then the Imam began to speak.

For thirty minutes Imam Bukhari – the direct descendant of the mullah Shah Jehan called from Bukhara to inaugurate his new mosque on 23 July 1656 – addressed the faithful through the minaret's loudspeakers. His Urdu was difficult to understand, but his message was clearly political – there were frequent references to America, Israel, Kashmir and Rajiv Gandhi. Overhead, flights of pigeons wheeled through the minarets, cutting over the heads of the congregation towards the Red Fort. One of the girls beside me began to fidget, and her father tried to retain her interest by pointing out Delhi landmarks visible from our turret. Bukhari reached his climax and, with a final burst of electronic feedback, the sermon rasped to a close.

Then the prayers began. The congregation stood up and raised their open palms to their ears. They bent double, and from the front prayer aisle came the distant cry: *Allah hu-Akbar!* God is Great! *Bismillah e rehman e rahim!* In the name of God most generous and merciful! The faithful knelt down and placed their heads on the ground: *La Allah illah Allah, Muhammad Resul-allah!* There is no God but God and Muhammad is the Seat of God! Over and over again, for twenty-five minutes, the heads rose and fell before the final triumphant cry of *Allah hu-Akbar!* Then, to mark the end of the service, three enormous thunder-flashes were let off in the rear gatehouse. The sound ricocheted off the walls of the Red Fort and echoed back; a plume of purple smoke rose into the morning air.

252

Everyone stood up. The worshippers headed off in their own directions, and the ordered chequerboard shattered. Suddenly patches of pink sandstone were again visible in the courtyard. The crowd flowed out through the gates and the pink patches grew. All around, men were embracing and wishing each other '*Id Mubarak.*'

The little girls in my *chattri* were standing expectantly around their father who was distributing *Idi* – their long-awaited *Id* pocket money. Below, in the Meena Bazaar, the *dhabas* had begun to fill with feasting families, all wolfing down piles of biryani rice, extra-large *cajra* puris and a special *Id* sweet named *peni* (made with minced carrots but surprisingly tasty.)

I sat in a *dhaba* in the shade of a tarpaulin, nibbling *Id* sweets and watching the festive crowds milling all around me. It was only nine o'clock. But already it was becoming unbearably hot.

During the sweltering *Id* of 1333, a camel caravan could be seen winding its way through the narrow passes and defiles of the Hindu Kush. On the principal camel sat an irascible Muslim judge. He had been travelling for eight years and was now heading south towards Delhi, the capital of the Sultan of Hindustan.

Sheikh Abu Abdullah Muhammed ibn Abdallah ibn Muhammed ibn Ibrahim al-Lawati, known to his friends by the diminutive Ibn Battuta, had left his birthplace of Tangier in the early June of 1325. He was then only twenty-one, a callow aristocrat fresh from law school. Resolving to 'quit all my friends and tear myself away from my home', he headed off along the North African coast in the direction of Mecca, driven onwards by what he described as 'an overmastering impulse from within'. At the beginning of his journey he suffered badly from homesickness. 'I set out alone,' he wrote, 'finding no companion to cheer the way with friendly intercourse, and no party of travellers with whom to associate myself.' By the time he arrived in Tunis he was so 'affected by loneliness that I could not restrain my tears and wept bitterly.'

Since then, however, the Moroccan had completed his pilgrimage and visited Palestine, East Africa, Khorasan and Byzantium. He had married several times, bought himself a small harem of slave girls, and gained a reputation as a traveller and a teller of interesting tales. No longer was Ibn Battuta inexperienced or vulnerable. Instead his diaries had begun to assume something of the knowingness of incipient middle age; at times, indeed, he was in danger of becoming priggish and opinionated. As with many later European voyagers, travel in this part of the world, far from broadening the mind, seemed instead to lead to a blanket distrust of anyone of a different creed, colour or class.

Thus while Ibn Battuta was tolerably enamoured of a pretty Greek slave girl he had bought in Ephesus, he wrote that the filthy freedmen of her accursed race were 'swine eaters', drinkers of intoxicating liquors and 'enemies of Allah'. Provincial Muslims, so he discovered to his horror, could sometimes behave almost as badly. The beautiful and promiscuous Muslim women of the Maldives, for example, he thought shockingly immodest, and though Battuta frequently 'ordered them to wear clothes . . . I met with little success.'

China was even worse: 'I was sorely grieved that heathendom had so strong a hold over [this rich country],' he wrote after a few weeks in Qanjanfu. 'Whenever I went out of my house I used to see any number of revolting things. It distressed me so much that I used to keep indoors and go out only in case of necessity.'

Expecting little good to come out of any country even partially populated by non-Muslims, Ibn Battuta had few expectations of India. The Hindus, he knew, at least refrained from eating pigs (unlike the Chinese or the disgusting Christians of Byzantium), but he had heard that they had other habits the very thought of which made him swoon. 'The Hindus venerate oxen,' he wrote, 'and it is said that they actually drink the oxen's *urine* when they fall sick.' Later, on witnessing a *sati* (the immolation of a Hindu widow), Ibn Battuta was so shocked he nearly fell off his camel.

As he rode down the narrow goat-trails of the Khyber Pass, Battuta would have known that the Delhi Sultanate was violent frontier country, constantly in a state of war with the pagan Mongols to the north and the infidel Hindus to the south. In this connection he mentions one of his friends, Malik Warna, who chose to move to India from the then far more peaceful and civilized country of Afghanistan. Battuta clearly thought his decision extraordinary: 'Warna was an excellent man, with a liking for hunting, falcons, horses, slaves, servants and rich and kingly robes ... Of course India is no place for a man of his character.' 'A man is honoured in that country,' he continues, 'according to what may be seen of his actions, conduct and zeal, since no one in India knows anything of family or lineage.'

It was, in short, no place for a gentlemen. But more worrying even than India's lack of blue-blooded Arab families, was the prospect of its tyrannical Sultan, the blood-thirsty parricide Muhammed bin Tughluk.

Stories of Tughluk's excesses were common across the width of Asia. A Chancellor of the Exchequer who had failed to prevent thieves penetrating his treasury was summarily beaten to death. A mystic who refused to retract a statement accusing Tughluk of tyranny had his mouth held open by skewers while excrement was poured down his throat. Worst of all was the fate that befell a captured rebel general: he was flayed alive 'and when he had been flayed his flesh was cooked with rice and sent to his sons and family.'

Ibn Battuta soon felt the deadening hand of Tughluk's rule. Having passed from the Mediterranean to the Indus without attracting the attention of a single government official, Battuta, like so many subsequent travellers, crossed the Indian frontier only to find himself caught up in an impenetrable web of bureaucracy: no sooner had they set foot on the east bank of the Indus than intelligence officials 'wrote to Delhi informing the king of our arrival and giving him all the details concerning us.' The traveller was then grilled by the corrupt Indian border officials: 'Their custom was to take a quarter of everything brought in by the merchants and to exact a duty of seven dinars for every horse.' None of this was at all to the Moroccan's taste: 'The idea of having my baggage searched was most disagreeable to me. There was nothing valuable in it, though it seemed a great deal in the eyes of these people.'

Battuta put up with all this for he had reason to believe that the Sultan would amply reward him for his efforts. Delhi may have been a relatively unsophisticated frontier town, a vast barracks-metropolis built to defend Islam's boundary with the Mongols and Hindus, but it was still very much a land of opportunity: an ambitious Muslim could achieve great wealth and prominence there in very little time. Ibn Battuta was always one to try his luck. After all, as he wrote in his diary: 'Muhammed bin Tughluk was especially well known in his generosity to foreigners for he preferred them to the peoples of India. He singles them out for favour . . . [especially] Arabs for whom he has a particular affection.'

Formalities completed, Battuta again mounted his camel. Beating off an ambush by 'eighty infidels on foot', he and his train headed off on the last stage of his journey through the burning plains of the Punjab towards the mighty Indian capital and the palace of the Sultan.

Few maps of modern Delhi bother to mark Begampur. It lies engulfed amid the new colonies that have recently sprung up along the way to Mehrauli, a small enclave of mud-walled, flat-roofed village life besieged by a ring of high-rise apartments. The smart metalled road which links the new colonies to Aurobindo Marg gives out a few hundred feet before you get to the village. Bouncing along the rubble track, you arrive in the midst of a dust storm of your own creation.

I saw Begampur for the first time on a hot evening in early May. As the dust began to subside, shafts of late afternoon light could be seen raking down the village streets. Beyond the flour mill, the rim of the horizon was on fire; mynas and parakeets were calling to roost.

Wandering from house to house I asked for directions to the ruins of the palace. The villagers shrugged their shoulders: what palace? Finally, turning a corner, I saw what I was looking for.

Lying amid waste land to one side of the village, there rose the jutting silhouette of a cyclopean wall. It was flanked on one side by a great domed hall, supported on a quadrant of megalithic arches, each one at least twelve feet thick; to its side the palace wall rose upwards with a colossal, almost Romanesque massiveness.

The walls of both palace and hall were completely undecorated; there was none of the intricate sculptural filigree normally embroidered on the stonework of early Islamic buildings. This puritanical,

256

megalithic masonry was the chosen style of Muhammed bin Tughluk. From here, the grim *Hazar Ustan* or Thousand Pillared Palace,
Tughluk ruled the largest and most powerful empire India had
known since the time of Ashoka, one and a half millennia previously. From here he controlled a web of spies and informers that
ran from Madurai to Attock, from the beaches of Malabar to the
mangrove swamps of Bengal.

Climbing up several flights of narrow, twisting stairs, I reached
the Sultan's penthouse pavilion with its view over the rooftops of
Begampur. Ibn Battuta describes arriving at this place through a
succession of now-vanished gates and courtyards, each surrounded
by cohorts of trumpeters and guards. It was the second court that
contained the infamous corps of executioners.

'Tughluk was far too free in shedding blood,' writes Battuta.
'Every day hundreds of people – chained, pinioned and fettered –
were brought to [the sultan's hall] and those who were for
execution were executed, those for torture tortured, and those for
beating beaten. It was but seldom that the entrance to his palace
was without a corpse. One day as I arrived at the palace my horse
shied at the sight of a white fragment on the ground. I asked what
it was and one of my companions said: "It is the torso of a man
who was [this morning] cut into three pieces."'

To enter into the third court, the visitor had to receive the written
permission of the Sultan. Only the most distinguished visitors were
admitted: 'The third gate opens into the Thousand Pillars,' noted
Battuta.

> It is here that the Sultan holds his audiences ... [He] sits
> cross-legged on a throne above a great dais while one hun-
> dred élite guards stand on either side carrying shields,
> swords and bows ... [When all the functionaries have
> assembled] fifty elephants are brought in. Each is adorned
> with silken cloths and has its tusks shod with iron for the
> greater efficacy of killing criminals. These elephants are
> trained to make obeisance to the Sultan and incline their
> heads, and when they do so the Chamberlain cries in a loud
> voice: *'Bismillah!'*
> Then the musicians and dancers come in. The first to

257

enter are the daughters of the infidel Indian kings who have been taken captive during that year. After they have sung and danced, the sultan presents them to the *amirs* and the distinguished foreigners.

Eventually the time came for Battuta's own audience with the Sultan. Battuta presented the gifts he had brought from Khorasan; and in return he was given the post of *Qazi* (or judge) and presented with two villages, a pension of twelve thousand dinars and a house in which to live. He was terrified of the Sultan, but for his own safety decided the best policy was to cling to the Tughluk's fingertips 'and every time he said any encouraging word to me I kissed his hand, until I had kissed it seven times.'

It is obvious from his writings that Battuta was most impressed by what was to be for eight years his adopted city. Delhi then consisted of five or six distinct districts dotted between the banks of the Jumna and the plains around the old Hindu fort of Lal Kot. Several of these settlements had recently been united into a single city called Jahanpanah (The Refuge of the World) by a great loop of wall forty miles long. Its total population was just under half a million.

'Delhi,' writes Batutta, is a 'vast and magnificent city, uniting beauty with strength. It is surrounded by a wall that has no equal in the world, and is the largest city in India, nay in the entire Muslim Orient.'

Other authorities fill out the Moroccan's picture: 'The houses are built of stone and brick, and the roofs are of wood,' noted the Arab geographer al-Umari in his encyclopaedic *Masalik-ul-Absar Fi Mamalik-ul-Amsar* ('The Visions of the Kingdoms'). 'There are great monasteries, large open spaces, and numerous baths. There are also about two thousand small mosques and hermitages. Gardens extend on three sides of the city in a straight line for twelve thousand paces.'

The domes of one of Jahanpanah's finest buildings, its great cathedral mosque, lay just a little to the south of the pavilion where I was now sitting. Rising up above the rooftops of Begampur, the mosque – a great ripple of egg-shaped cupolas arranged around a shady cloister garth almost as broad as that in the Old

Mosque at Begampur

Delhi Jama Masjid — dwarfed the village that lay scattered all around it.

The building had certainly seen better days. From my rooftop I could see that one side of the prayer hall roof had collapsed. The once gleaming whitewash was dark and smoke-blackened; in places the plaster had fallen away to reveal the messy rubble-walling beneath. Goats grazed on the grass growing unkempt between the paving stones. But despite the decay, the mosque still somehow retained a profound and venerable grandeur. Its strength lay in its simplicity. Its pillars were just rectangular blocks of mousy-grey ashlar; its capitals plain but for a fringe of simple water-leaf scallops. There was no colour, little ornament, no distraction. Yet the utter simplicity of the individual parts focused attention on the balance and harmony of the whole: the rhythm of the arches, the rise and fall of the cupolas, the austere curves of the domes. Unerringly, the

259

eye was drawn towards the towering *ivan* punctuating the middle of the west wall.

In its clarity and purity of form, the mosque reminded me of the best early Cistercian architecture – that brief and precious half-century before the original ascetic urge began to give way to the worldly frivolity of the Later Middle Ages, the period that produced the great Chapter House at Fountains and the original dark-stone nave at Rievaulx.

All around my rooftop pavilion could be seen other fragmentary remains of the Jahanpanah which Ibn Battuta would have known: a series of fragile mediaeval islands standing out amid the sea of modern sprawl.

Turning a quarter circle away from the mosque towards the setting sun, through the early evening heat haze I could see the distant silhouette of the Qutab Minar, the tower of victory built by the first Sultan immediately after he had driven the Hindus from Delhi in 1192. The tower still stands above the walls of the old Hindu fortress, a tapering cylinder rising up 240 feet in four ever-diminishing storeys like a fully extended telescope placed lens-down on a plateau in the Aravalli hills. The tower is a statement of arrival, as boastful and triumphant as the Tughluk buildings around me were understated and austere.

Turning to the north-east, I could just make out the lines of the walls of Siri, the first completely new city to be built by the Muslim conquerors in the Delhi plains. But the greatest of the ruins of medi-aeval Delhi, the great fort of Tughlukabad, lay some six miles due east of my rooftop, virtually invisible now in the gathering darkness.

As the sun began to set behind the Qutab Minar, I made up my mind to explore sometime soon what was once the most enormous complex of fortifications in all Islam. But with the growing ferocity of the Delhi heat it became increasingly easy to find excuses to put off ever leaving the house at all.

The sky turned the colour of molten copper. The earth cracked like a shattered windscreen. April gave way to May and every day the heat grew worse.

Hot sulphurous winds began to rake through the empty Delhi avenues. The walls of the houses exuded heat like enormous ovens. The rich fled to the hill stations and the beggars followed them. The activity of those Delhi-wallahs that remained in their city slowed to a snail's pace.

One Delhi-wallah of whom this was not true was our unfortunate *mali*. At the beginning of May, Mrs Puri's businessman son decided to build a 'Japanese' garden facing on to his veranda. From the early hours of the morning the unfortunate *mali* could be seen labouring away, pouring with sweat — despite the heat he still insisted in wearing his thick serge uniform — as he constructed a sort of miniature Mount Fuji in the corner of the front lawn.

Sadly, this exercise in horticultural Orientalism proved too much for the *mali*. After a heroic week of earth moving, he went down with heatstroke. He retired to his charpoy leaving Mrs Puri's lawn resembling an open-cast coal mine; on one side a slag heap drifted on to the driveway, blocking access to or from the house. The inconvenience these excavations caused was second only to that created by the dust storms. In Delhi the high summer is enlivened by the advent of the *Lu*, the hot desert wind which in May begins to blow in from Rajasthan, bringing with it much of the Thar Desert. Burning grit rains down on the city then blows gusting through the grid of scorching streets. At the road junctions, spiralling dust-devils replace the absent beggars. Up in the sky, the sun hangs like a red disc behind the veil of sand.

Inside our flat, small drifts of this sand began to blow in under the doors and through the cracks in the window frames. All this proved a formidable challenge to our sweeper, a delightful Rajasthani lady named Murti. Murti is beautiful, charming and intelligent. She has many talents. Sadly, sweeping is not one of them.

Every morning she arrived at our door and spent five minutes flustering around with her hand-broom. Clouds of dust would fly up into the air, drift around the flat for a while, then settle on the beds and desk and chairs. There it remained. Dusting was a particular bugbear of Murti's, rarely attempted and never with any success. But Olivia, a model employer, believed it would be churlish to point this out. After Murti had completed her statutory five minutes

261

of dust re-distribution, my wife waved her a cheery goodbye. 'Jolly good, Murti,' she would say. 'That's enough for today.'

This pantomime went on happily until the first week of May, when Mrs Puri appeared one morning unannounced at our door, intent on doing a spot-check of her property. She took one look at the sand dunes drifting around our sitting-room and shook her head.

'What is this?' she said, drawing a circle in the sand with her stick.

Olivia began to explain about not wanting to upset Murti, but Mrs Puri raised her hand.

'Mrs William,' she said firmly. 'I am thinking you are not understanding the management of these people.'

'But . . .'

'If Murti is not doing her duty properly then you must be telling her to do it again.'

'But Murti hates sweeping,' said Olivia.

'Then,' said Mrs Puri, rapping her stick on the floor. 'Then she must be made to enjoy it.'

While all this was going on in our flat, something was clearly up at International Backside. Balvinder Singh was in high spirits. Despite the terrible heat, for a month now his conversation had gradually been becoming even more venal than normal.

'You like this one, Mr William?' he would ask as we passed some pretty Punjabi girl along Lodhi Road.

'What do you mean?'

'That young lady. Standing by traffic light. She with long hair.'

'I'm a married man, Mr Singh.'

'Me too. Same thing, no problem. You like?'

'She's okay. Bit young.'

There would be a pause.

'You know something, Mr William?'

'What?'

'She going kissing Lodhi Garden.'

'But the girl's only about ten.'

'Maybe,' Mr Singh would whisper. 'But Lodhi Garden is Love Garden.'

I had learned by now that an upsurge in Mr Singh's libido was usually brought on by some other outside circumstance. It was not until the middle of May that I discovered what it was that had so stimulated my friend. One morning I called International Backside and Balvinder said he would be around in five minutes. When he finally appeared, it was in a brand new Ambassador taxi. By the time I had come downstairs and made it over the *mali's* trenchworks, Balvinder had polished the bonnet so bright he could curl his moustache in the reflection.

'Balvinder,' I said. 'Congratulations!'

Mr Singh beamed with pride.

'Many months I have been saving,' he said. 'Now big loan has been granted by Bank of Punjab.'

'Well done,' I said.

'Before every time you tell me: very old car, very smell, very dirt.'

'Balvinder, I would never . . .'

'Now new car. You not complaining.' Balvinder briskly opened the door and indicated that I should get in. 'Yesterday Sikh temple going with family. First going God, *puja* doing. Afterwards whisky and German Beer drinking, taxi-stand party having. No smell, no dirt, no problem!'

'I didn't know you were religious, Balvinder,' surprised by his admission that he had been to the gurdwara.

'I going Sikh temple one time one year. Tip-top special occasion only,' he muttered.

'And what have you done with the old car?'

'Brother Gurmack Singh giving.'

'You really gave it away?'

'Almost giving. Seventy thousand rupees only.'

Balvinder inserted the gleaming new key into the ignition.

'Look!' he said, gesturing towards the instrument panel. 'All new design.'

This was perhaps stretching the point. The Ambassador was, without doubt, fresh from the factory. It had sparkling white antimacassars, new footmats and a splendid technicolour Guru Nanak pasted over its glove compartment. A garland of freshly picked marigolds hung from the mirror. But for all that, in its basics it was indisputably the same Indian-made version of the 1956 Morris Oxford that had lorded it over the roads of India for some thirty-odd years now. I tentatively suggested as much to Balvinder.

'No, no, Mr William,' he replied. 'All new computer design. Look – computer system.'

Balvinder turned the key, then pressed a button. The dashboard lit up, miraculously illuminated from behind. There was a hushed silence before Balvinder whispered: 'Mr William, this vehicle computer product of Indian Space Programme. It driving speed-of-light.'

And so we set off towards Tughlukabad, Balvinder doing his best to prove his point.

Rays from the rising sun were shining through the thick under-growth of the jungle as we drove past. Keols, invisible in the forest canopy, were calling to each other in their incessant woody voices. Then, quite suddenly, we were out of the jungle and into the day-light and the walls of the great fortress, as solid and immobile as stone elephants, were rising up all around us.

Tughlukabad is the most uncompromisingly militaristic ruin in Delhi, perhaps in all India. Ring after ring of rough-hewn stone walls thunder their way across the open plain on the deserted south-eastern edge of the city. As at Begampur there is a complete absence of decoration or of any aesthetic consideration. Instead, massive blocks of stone are simply piled high, block upon block, until the towers reach up, in some places to a height of nearly thirty metres.

But with the Mongol hordes massing in the Hindu Kush, the Tughluks could take no chances. The whole spreading fortress was surrounded not just by a moat, but by a deep artificial lake. Dams were built linked by causeways to a series of smaller outpost forts. The flood waters were controlled by a succession of carefully engin-eered sluice-gates and locks. To take the complex, the Mongol

Ghiyas-ud-Din Tughluk's Tomb in Tughlukabad

hordes would have had to abandon their steppe ponies and turn aquatic before they could even reach the outer defences.

I climbed up through one of the thirteen gates and clambered over the piles of collapsed masonry blocking the way to the top of the citadel. Even today, seven hundred years after it was built, the vast walled enclosure is still an impressive sight. But at the time of the Tughluks, when the gridded lines of now-collapsed rubble were bustling streets and bazaars, armouries and elephant stables, all rising up from the glittering waters of the lake, then the sight must have been breathtaking. Ibn Battuta was lucky enough to see it in its prime:

> The walls which surround this city are simply unparalleled. There is room inside the wall for horsemen and infantry to march from one end of the town to the other . . . Inside Tughlukabad is the great palace whose tiles the Sultan has gilded. When the sun rises they shine with a brilliant light that makes it impossible to keep one's eyes fixed upon it. The Sultan deposited within this town a vast store of wealth. It is said that he constructed a tank and poured into it molten gold so that it became one vast molten block.

From where I was standing, far below me I could see a separate miniature fort linked to the mother fortress by an umbilical causeway. Here, in the midst of the most defensible position in all Tughlukabad lies the tomb of Ghiyas-ud-Din Tughluk, the father of Sultan Muhammed and the creator of this impregnable complex.

The tomb is an almost pyramidal cube of red sandstone whose almost absurdly thick inward-battering walls are topped by a dome of solid white marble. Like a miniature expression of the whole, the tomb is defended on all sides by its own set of machicolated walls, built as if to keep the Angel of Death at bay; they represent perhaps the most elaborate set of defences ever raised to protect a corpse. Nothing could be further removed from the graceful garden-tombs of the Great Moguls than this warrior's memorial, as narrowly militaristic as theirs were elegant and sophisticated. One breathes silky refinement; the other still rings with the clank of rusty chain-mail.

This enclosure is the key to the entire complex. It demonstrates the extent of the Tughluks' obsession with defence, and highlights the essentially militaristic nature of their Sultanate. The Damascene geographer al-Umari confirms what is implied by the tomb: that Delhi, for all its bazaars and shrines and fine architecture, was above all a barracks: 'The army [of Delhi] consists of 900,000 horsemen. These troops consist of Turks, the inhabitants of Khata, Persians and Indians. They have excellent horses, magnificent armour and fine costumes. The Sultan also has 3000 elephants and some 20,000 Turk *mamluks* (warrior slaves).'

I tramped through the ruins of Tughlukabad trying in my mind to fill the deserted barracks with Turkish *mameluks* and Persian cavalry officers. I thought of them studying the Military Manual of Fakhr-i-Mudabbir, the *Adab al-harb Wa'l-Shaj'a*, which was written at about the time Tughlukabad was being built. The manual is not only one of the most interesting documents to come out of the Sultanate, it is also one of the most precious keys we have to the concerns that meant most to the war-obsessed *amirs* of Tughluk Delhi.

Climbing up on to a high bastion, I looked down over the shimmering interior of the fort and thought of the words that must once have been a set text for the cavalrymen stationed here:

The sword was invented by Jamshed, the first of monarchs and its terror and majesty are greater than those of all other weapons. It is for this reason that when a Kingdom has been taken by force of arms, it is said to have been taken by the sword.

As to the different kinds of swords there are many sorts: Chini, Rusi, Rumi, Firangi, Shahi, Hindi and Kashmiri. Of these the Hindi sword is the finest, and of all Hindi swords, that known as the *mawj-i darya*, the waves of the sea, is the most lustrous.

The bow was the pre-eminent weapon given by Jibrail to Adam in Paradise. It will never be superseded in this world or the next and in Paradise the blessed will practise archery.

When choosing a bow you should try to acquire above all others the mountain bow of Ghazna. It is made of horn and its aim is straight.

The Indian bow – the *kaman-i Hindavi* – is made of cane. Its arrows do not travel very far but at a short distance it inflicts a very bad wound. The head of the arrow used with it is usually barbed and if lodged inside the flesh, the shaft is liable to break off. This leaves the head, which is usually poisoned, in the flesh. It is impossible to extract.

The bows of Central Asia use horse hide as the bowstring. It is a poor material. Use instead a bowstring of rhinoceros hide, for it will snap asunder the bowstrings of all other bows to which the sound reaches whether these are made of the hide of wild ox, the horse, or even the flanks of a young nilgai.

What Tughlukabad was to the military of fourteenth-century Delhi, the suburb of Hauz Khas was to the savants. For while Tughluk

Delhi was first and foremost a barracks-town, it was not entirely without culture or civilization. Educated refugees fleeing the Mongol conquests of Samarkand and the Central Asian university towns had taken shelter in the city in their thousands and there they acted as an intellectual leaven to the warrior slaves who had dominated Delhi since its conquest.

At Hauz Khas a beautiful tank had been excavated by the Sultan Iltutmish and the artists and intellectuals slowly collected around its banks. On one of its sides stood the most elegant set of buildings ever erected by the Tughluks.

The Hauz Khas *medresse* was a college whose academic reputation was as wide as the Sultanate itself. Its principal hall, which still stands, is as long and as narrow as a ship, with delicately carved kiosks and balconies projecting out over the lake. Contemporary memoirs are as full of praise for the building's beauty as they are for the work which took place within its walls: 'Its magnificence, proportions and pleasant air makes it unique among the buildings of the world,' wrote the chronicler Barni. 'Indeed it could justifiably be compared to the palaces of ancient Babylon. People come from East and West in caravan after caravan just to look at it.'

The excitable Delhi poet Mutahhar of Kara went even further: 'The moment I entered this blessed building,' he writes, 'I saw a soul-animating courtyard as wide as the plain of the world. Its fragrance possessed the odour of amber, and hyacinths, basils, roses and tulips were blooming as far as the eye could reach. Nightingales were singing their melodious songs and . . . [their voices blending] with the debates and discussions of the students.'

More impressive still was the menu in the college dining-room, something which the salivating Mutahhar singles out for special praise: 'Pheasants, partridges, herons, fish, roasted fowl, grilled kids, fried loaves, brightly-coloured sweets of different kinds and other good things were heaped everywhere in large quantities.' Pomegranate syrup prepared with a mixture of sorrel was served as a drink and betel nuts were brought in on gold and silver dishes after the meal. As they ate, the students sat cross-legged on carpets brought from as far away as Shiraz, Damascus and the Yemen.

The curriculum of the college centred on Muslim jurisprudence and Quranic studies, but Delhi had a reputation for astronomy and medicine and it is probable that these were also taught at the Hauz Khas. Medicine was a particular interest of the Tughluk Sultans, and Sultan Muhammed's nephew Firoz Shah founded no fewer than seventy dispensaries and a *Shifa Khana* (or Central Hospital) where free food, drink and medicine were supplied to the sick at the expense of the treasury.

The doctors of the college and the hospital practised a highly sophisticated offshoot of classical Greek medicine that would have been immediately recognizable to Hippocrates or Galen; it was known, after its Greek origins, as *Unani* (Ionian) *Tibbia*. The secrets of *Unani* medicine were originally passed from the Byzantine Empire to Sassanid Persia by heretic Nestorian Christians escaping the oppressive Orthodoxy of Constantinople. The exiles set up a medical school at Jundishapur, south of modern Teheran, where their arcane and esoteric formulae were stolen by the Arabs during the early conquests of Islam.

Adapted in Baghdad and Cairo, cross-fertilized with the ancient medical practices of Pharaonic Egypt, Sumeria, Assyria and Babylon, *Unani* medicine was finally codified into a cohesive system by the great Arab scholar Ibn Sina (or Avicenna as he was known in the mediaeval west). Thus refined, the medicine passed to Central Asia and into the syllabuses of the universities of Samarkand and Tashkent. Thence it was finally brought to India in the thirteenth century by refugees fleeing Genghis Khan – at about the same time as Abelard was lecturing to his students at the new university of Paris.

While western medicine has always tended to concentrate on the elimination of germs, the *Unani* doctors tried not to lose sight of the patient as a whole being; they conceived of therapy in the original Greek sense of healing, at once taking into account physical, mental and spiritual well-being. *Unani* medicine emphasized aiding the body's inbuilt ability to heal itself and its ethics forbade any treatment which, while curing a specific ailment, harmed the soundness of the body as a whole. Treatment was not merely a matter of prescribing herbal medicines, but a whole regimen which controlled the diet and the life-style. For this reason *Unani* hospitals were equipped with the best cooks, and, in the case of the sixth-century Bait al-Hikmah in Baghdad, a whole troupe of singers and musicians as well.

All these elaborations were built on the basic Hippocratic theory of the Four Humours. The theory postulates the presence in the human body of blood, phlegm, yellow bile and black bile. Each person's unique mixture of these substances determines his temperament: a predominance of blood gives a sanguine temperament; a predominance of phlegm makes one phlegmatic; yellow bile, bilious (or choleric); and black bile, melancholic. As long as these humours are in balance, the human system is healthy; it is imbalance which can result in disease. A *Unani* physician attempts to diagnose the imbalance and restore each individual to his proper equilibrium. As no two humours are identical, no two people are treated in exactly the same manner.

While *Unani* medicine has completely died out in the area where it was born and developed, I had not been surprised to find that – like almost every other tradition which has ever come to Delhi – it still survived intact in the alleys of the Old City. There are now some 1500 hakims still practising their Byzantine medicine in Delhi, and they appear to do a thriving business. *Unani* medicine is regarded every bit as seriously as conventional western treatment and it is quite distinct from the dubious folk-medicine offered to passers-by by roadside fakirs, or Balvinder Singh's freckle-destroying friends in the Meena Bazaar.

The centre of the modern *Unani* hakims is still around Ballimaran, the Street of the Cat Killers, where the doctors moved when the area was first built in the late 1640s. Under the Mughals, Ballimaran was an aristocratic enclave full of large and airy *havelis*. But for centuries now – like the rest of Old Delhi – the area has been in slow decay. Boys with wicker baskets full of bricks and masonry hurry past; the streets stink and run with mud and excrement. Yet behind the grubby façades, if you know where to look, you can still find the *Unani* doctors, practising in exactly the way they always have.

Their surgeries are wonderful. Inside dark, vaulted rooms whose mahogany shelves are heavy with jars, bottles and vials, elderly white-bearded men can be seen feeling the pulse of heavily-veiled women; behind, in the shadows, their assistants are busy decanting liquids like mediaeval alchemists: white powders are mixed with grey crystals then, slowly, crystal by crystal, dissolved in a vat of bubbling, frothing liquid.

270

The air of the mediaeval is quite appropriate: the techniques these hakims practise are more or less identical to those once taught in the fourteenth-century Hauz Khas *medresse*.

Then, in the second week of May, a friend of ours – a classical dancer named Navina – fell down a flight of stairs. When we went over a week later, she told us she was being treated for an inflamed tendon on her knee. Her doctor was a hakim near the Turkman Gate. If we were interested, she said, we would be welcome to come along and watch him treat her.

In high summer the hakim's surgery closed at 10.30 AM, so Olivia and I went over to our friend soon after breakfast. We all drove up to Old Delhi together. On the way Navina told us about a friend of hers, an American girl who for many years had suffered from excruciating headaches and backaches. She had consulted innumerable doctors in the west, but beyond prescribing pain-killers no one had been able to help her; as a result the girl had begun to resign herself to her condition. Then Navina had taken the girl to see her hakim. Abdul Jamil Khan had felt her pulse and examined the base of her spine. Straight away he asked whether she had had a serious accident when she was small. The girl nodded: when she was six she had been badly thrown by a horse. The hakim prescribed a strict diet and treated her with his own herbal massage oils. Within a month she was cured.

Hakim Abdul Jamil's surgery consisted of one very small room leading off a lane near the Old Delhi Kalan Masjid. The room was divided in two by a curtain. To one side a line of very ill and miserable looking Old Delhi-wallahs sat on low stools; from beyond the far side came the whistle of a boiling kettle and the occasional ring of metal on metal. We queued for half an hour before the hakim was able to see us. Bicycle rickshaws trundled past with a frantic ringing of bells. An old goat came up and nuzzled itself against my thigh. Finally the curtain was drawn back and the three of us – Olivia, Navina and myself – were ushered in.

The hakim was a plump, middle-aged Muslim gentleman. He wore a white *kurta* top over a checked *lungi*; he was barefoot and he

271

kept his beard close-clipped. He was leaning back against a bolster; beneath him a frayed reed mat acted as makeshift carpeting. All around the hakim – in trays, on top of cupboards, stretched out over long mahogany bookshelves – stood line upon line of cork-stoppered jars, phials and bottles. All these jars contained ground and powdered herbs of different colours and consistencies. In an enamel tray in front of the hakim lay a collection of surgical instruments which looked as if they might have escaped from the Roman artefact room in the British Museum.

Without rising from his position, Abdul Jamil Khan greeted us and indicated that we should be seated. Navina sat on a bench in front of the hakim and extended her arm. The hakim took it, and shutting his eyes placed his three fingers on the arteries below her wrist.

The taking of the pulse, I knew, was the principal form of *Unani* diagnosis. Every hakim is trained to recognize the slightest and most subtle variations not only in the speed but in the strength and movement of the pulse: by the fourteenth century, Delhi doctors had sub-classified many thousands of different pulse types which they named after the movements of different animals: the snake and leech pulse could be picked up by the pressure of the index finger; the crow, the lark and the frog could be sensed by the middle finger; the swan, the pigeon and the cock by the ring finger. For two minutes, Hakim Abdul Jamil concentrated on Navina's right wrist; then, without speaking he took her left arm and, shutting his eyes again, concentrated on that. Finally he released her.

'Navina,' he said. 'You have been eating cauliflower again.'

Navina nodded guiltily.

'If you are to get better you must do what I say. For two weeks please listen: eat nothing except cucumber and marrows.'

As he spoke, he pulled out from one side an electric ring; from the other he took a fire-blackened cauldron. He switched the ring on and placed the cauldron on top.

'This is the wonderful bit,' said Navina, hitching up her skirt as far as her knee. 'The cauldron contains the hakim's special herbal concoction. He steams my knee with it.'

The mixture was soon boiling. Placing a kind of cotton tent flap over both the cauldron and Navina's leg, the hakim slowly lifted and lowered the lid of the cauldron releasing into the room whiffs of aromatic herbs. The noise of the opening and closing of the lid created the metallic ringing we had heard from beyond the curtain in the waiting-room.

'It's absolutely wonderful,' said Navina. 'Immediate relief.'

'What is in the cauldron?' I asked the hakim.

'*Dawa* [medicine],' replied the hakim evasively.

'But what sort of medicine?'

'Wild herbs. I collect them all myself.'

'From where?'

'Everywhere. The ridge. Over the Jumna. The hills . . . Badrinath, Kedarnath.'

'But what sorts of herbs . . .'

'He won't tell you,' said Navina. 'It is his family's great secret.'

'All special herbs,' said the hakim, smiling mischievously. 'My father was telling me. His father told him . . .'

'Anyway it seems to do the trick,' I said.

'I am not the healer,' said the hakim, piously raising both his palms. 'I am only the instrument through which it comes.'

We thanked Abdul Jamil and left the shop.

Stepping outside, the blank white glare of the sun hit us like a cudgel on the back of our heads.

The incessant heat, day after day, week after week, made everyone bad-tempered. After the euphoria of buying his new car had died down, Balvinder Singh, never one to hold back on an expletive at the best of times, increasingly began to splutter along in a state of semi-permanent fury. He swore at innocent passers-by, shouted graphic insults at rival drivers and hooted his horn as if his life depended on it: BEEP BEEP! Oh Bloody Fuck! BEEP BEEP BEEP BEEP! You Hindu Bloody Donkey Chap! BEEP! Dog! BEEP BEEP! Sister-Fucker! BEEP BEEP BEEP BEEP BEEP! Bloody Fuck Nonsense!

As the summer progressed, I was sometimes equally irritable and did not always take kindly to Mr Singh's barbs.

273

'Yeh! Mr William: why you no smelling?'

'What did you say, Balvinder?'

'Why you no smelling?'

'That's not very polite.'

'Mr William. Please answer. Why you not *smelling*?'

'Well, if you must know, I had a bath this morning. And I always make a point of applying a little under-arm deodorant.'

'No, no, Mr William. Maybe you are uncomfortable in this here hot weather. Normally you smell a lot.'

'Did you just say I normally smell a lot?'

'Oh yes, Mr William,' said Balvinder, shaking his head emphatically. 'But these days your face is very sad.'

Realizing at last what he had been getting at, my expression changed to a broad grin.

'That's better,' said Mr Singh. 'Now at last you are smiling.'

One other change brought about by the hot weather was noticed by Mrs Puri.

'Mr William,' she said one morning in her customary forthright manner. 'You are going bald.'

'Only a little bit, Mrs Puri,' I said defensively, knowing she was speaking the truth. The humiliating retreat of my hairline had been going on for five or six years now and was beginning to turn into a rout.

'Mr William,' said Mrs Puri, her brow furrowing. 'You should not be going bald at your age.'

'In my country it's quite common,' I said, searching for excuses. 'I'm twenty-five now. It's not unusual for the Scots to begin to thin out a bit at that age.'

'Well,' said my landlady. 'Your people should be putting on turbans. Then this would not happen.'

'I don't think that would make much difference,' I said. 'At least in my case.'

'Well, if you're not going to wear a turban then you should at least go to Nizamuddin,' said Mrs Puri. 'The saint there is very good at solving all sorts of calamities. Mark my words. Your baldness will be reversed in a jiffy.'

274

Nizamuddin is a Muslim village not very far from Mrs Puri's house, on the edge of Lutyens's city. In contrast to the broad, tree-lined avenues of Imperial Delhi around it, Nizamuddin is a warren of mediaeval shrines, mosques, mausoleums and dervish monasteries, all clustering around the tomb of Shaykh Nizam-ud-Din Auliya, the greatest of all Indian Sufis.

Shaykh Nizam-ud-Din was a contemporary of Ghiyas-ud-Din Tughluk. He withdrew from the world and preached a simple message of prayer and renunciation. He promised his followers that by loosening their ties with the flesh and with the world they could purge their souls of evil and move towards direct experience of God. According to the Shaykh, the first step of Sufism was not related to Friday prayers or empty rituals, but with the mastery of the maxim: 'Whatever you do not wish to be done to yourself, do not wish it to happen to others; wish for yourself what you wish for others also.'

Nizam-ud-din ate little, saying he could not swallow food when so many starving people slept in the streets or in the corners of mosques around him. Anything he was given he distributed to the poor, irrespective of whether they were Hindu or Muslim. At a time when almost all Muslims – including Ibn Battuta – believed that non-Muslims were enemies of Allah and thus damned to an eternity in hell-fire, Nizam-ud-Din preached a gentler doctrine of reconciliation, maintaining that 'every community has its own path and faith and way of worship.' It was not just his tolerance of other religions that made Nizam-ud-Din popular with non-Muslims: Hindus, Buddhists and Christians all found echoes of their own faiths in his teachings.

The Shaykh believed that following the mystical thread towards individual communion with God involved a long and hard struggle until the individual ego had been totally annihilated. He likened his own role among his disciples to that of a well-mannered host towards a group of simple guests. Some of the guests had never been in a house before and needed to be taught to use a chair and how to make simple conversation. Others worried continually about when and where they would be served food. The duty of the host was to calm them down after their journey and to demonstrate to them by his own patient example that there were other chambers where cooks were preparing a feast and where, in due time, they too would eat. Because they could not see the cooks, many were fearful that they did not exist. It was the duty of the host to persevere with these guests, to prepare them, and to teach them the rules of etiquette so that they would know how to tackle the feast when it was finally served.

Nizam-ud-Din was never afraid to be controversial. He believed strongly in the power of music and poetry to move devotees towards spiritual ecstasy and hence towards greater love of God. In this he came into conflict with the orthodox mullahs of the Delhi mosques. Jealous of his following, they summoned him before the Sultan and charged him with heresy. The saint managed to preach his way out of the trap that was laid for him, but it was not the last time he would come into conflict with Sultan Ghiyas-ud-Din Tughluk.

Nizam-ud-Din was in the middle of a project to provide his Sufi monastery with a tank to collect rainwater when the Sultan announced his plan to build Tughlukabad. All labourers working on private projects were to report immediately to the foreman at the designated site. According to tradition, Nizam-ud-Din was unable to stop his workmen going off to build the new fort, but calmly prophesied that before long the whole complex would be abandoned, providing shelter only to shepherds and nomadic Gujjars. So it is today. The Tughluks have gone; Tughlukabad is a ruin; only Nizamuddin remains.

Every Thursday night, huge crowds still gather before the tomb of the Shaykh to pray for anything from baldness cures to a change of government, and to hear the *qawwalis* (sacred love hymns) being sung in honour of the saint. Traditionally, this is the time that dervishes whirl: overcome at hearing the hymns sung in praise of their saint, they fall into a trance, rise to their feet and spin like a child's top. The whirling dervish is a phenomenon as old as Sufism itself: the same spectacle is shown in Persian miniatures dating from the tenth century – orange-robed monks, hands raised to heaven, faces uplifted in ecstasy. It was something I longed to see for myself: even more, in fact, than I longed for the return of my once-golden locks.

I had often visited friends living in the modern suburb of

276

Nizamuddin East, but had never had occasion to visit the crumbling old village which clustered around the shrine on the other side of the road. On my first visit one warm Thursday night in early May, I persuaded Dr Jaffery to accompany me.

The Sufi enclave was a revelation. Surrounded by rings of shanty huts, the settlement led through a warren of ever-narrowing lanes and alleys, past crumbling tombs and collapsing mosques, deeper and deeper into the past. The further Dr Jaffery and I went into the vortex of vaulted passageways, the less and less sign there was first of the twentieth century, with all its noise and cars and auto-rickshaws, then of the nineteenth and eighteenth centuries with their blank-faced late Mughal town houses. By the time we ducked under a narrow arch and emerged into the daylight of the central enclosure, we were back in the Middle Ages; the legacy of the Tughluk period was lying all around us.

On the veranda of the Shaykh's tomb sat the surviving male members of Nizam-ud-Din's family. Wearing frock coats and full beards, they sat nodding into their Qurans or noting down donations in their ledgers. All around milled the devotees: pilgrims, dervishes and *sannyasin*, labourers and merchants, scholars and soldiers, opium addicts, petty thieves . . . Some sat cross-legged on the cool marble floor; others joined the queue to enter the tomb. As they stood waiting, a dervish in a light woollen tunic fanned them with a large shield-shaped *pankah* embroidered in gold with sacred *kufic* calligraphy. In one corner sat a *qalander* – a holy fool – deep in animated conversation with an invisible djinn. He sat squatting on his calves, nodding and smiling, lifting his hands in protestation, twitching his head from side to side. To one side, sitting beside a brazier of billowing incense, another dervish was calmly sharpening a pair of skewers with a whetstone and making as if to run them through his cheeks. He was an amazing figure: barefoot, with naked legs, a saffron frock pulled over his torso and a beehive-shaped turban wrapped around a gold busby on his head.

'Come,' said Dr Jaffery, taking me gently by the shoulder. 'We must pay our respects to the Shaykh.'

We joined the queue of pilgrims, and soon passed under the cusped arch and into the velvety warmth of the shrine.

The tomb exuded the same thick, hushed, candlelit air of extreme sanctity that hangs over venerated shrines all over the world: the atmosphere reminded me immediately of the tomb of Saint James in Compostela or the Holy Sepulchre in Jerusalem. The interior was narrow and claustrophobic. In the centre, under a painted dome, was a marble cot covered in a thick velvet canopy like an enormous four-poster bed; from its front beam hung suspended a pair of ostrich eggs. Between the canopy and the raised marble tomb-cover, pilgrims had piled a mountain of rose garlands on to a crimson drape, so that now the material lay almost invisible beneath the wind-fall of petals.

The pilgrims, all men – women were excluded from the interior shrine – slowly circled around the balustrade, heads bowed, hands cupped in invocation, stopping every so often to murmur prayers or recite mantras. Outside, through the latticed grilles, you could see the dark shapes of barren ladies clawing at the rear of the tomb. Some tied threads through the *jali* screen: each string a reminder to the Shaykh to provide the woman with the longed-for male heir.

278

Dr Jaffery murmured a prayer and we left the tomb behind an old blind guru who was being led slowly forward by a young disciple. The guru's eyes were clouded blue almonds. As he walked, he tapped a dark teak walking stick held in his free hand.

Outside in the courtyard there was a sudden roll of drum beats. The *qawwali* singers had struck up a hymn: 'Salaam!' they sang, 'Salaam Khwaja Nizamudeeeeen!'

There were six *qawwals*, all dressed in high-necked Peshwari waistcoats, all sitting cross-legged in a line in front of the tomb. Two had harmoniums; two had small *tabla* drums. Two had no instruments but instead clapped and sang. One of the singers was a toothless old man with a gravelly voice; he was dark and heavily-bearded and narrow-eyed like one of the Magi in Van Eyck's *Adoration of the Lamb*. He was accompanied by the quavering treble of his young grandson.

Within minutes, the crowd milling around the shrine had settled in a semi-circle around the musicians. Everyone was listening intently, overtaken by the music. The *qawwals* picked up momentum, singing faster and faster, louder and louder. As they reached the climax of each verse, the two singers raised their hands in the air and the stones in the old man's rings glinted in the light. Then the hymn began to wind down, until just the boy was singing in his soft, high voice accompanied only by the barest of bass drones from the harmonium. The singing stopped. There was a fraction of a second of complete silence. Then with a great battering of *tablas*, the singers built up to the final verse. Over and over again they repeated the name of the saint: Nizam-ud-Din! NIZAM-UD-DIN! NIZAM-UD-DIN!

At the edge of the crowd, the two *pankah*-wallahs were slowly, hypnotically waving their fans in time to the chant. All around, the devotees began to sway with a distant look in their eyes as if they were on the verge of a trance. Seeing this the *qawwals* extended their song and attempted another climax. Their voices rose to new heights of passion, but the moment had been lost. There was no trance; the climax had somehow just been missed. The song ended, and a barely tangible shiver of disappointment passed through the crowd.

Later, sitting in a *dhaba* with Dr Jaffery, I remarked on how many of the devotees had been Hindus and Sikhs. Dr Jaffery shrugged his shoulders. 'Hindus and Sikhs also have their dreams which they wish the saint to make reality,' he said. 'That is one level. Also you do not have to be a Muslim to beg the saint's help in deeper matters. Many Hindus, like us, are impatient for the divine. They want to see in this life a glimpse of the face of God.'

'But the face of God that they would glimpse would be very different from the face you would see, wouldn't it?'

'Naturally,' said the doctor. 'Who is to say what is the true face of the God?' He swung his prayer beads around his index finger.

'Jalal-ud-Din Rumi used to tell a story about a far distant country, somewhere to the north of Afghanistan. In this country there was a city inhabited entirely by the blind. One day the news came that an elephant was passing outside the walls of this city.

'The citizens called a meeting and decided to send a delegation of three men outside the gates so that they could report back what an elephant was. In due course, the three men left the town and stumbled forwards until they eventually found the elephant. The three reached out, felt the animal with their hands, then they all headed back to the town as quickly as they could to report what they had felt.

'The first man said: "An elephant is a marvellous creature! It is like a vast snake, but it can stand vertically upright in the air!" The second man was indignant at hearing this: "What nonsense!" he said. "This man is misleading you. I felt the elephant and what it most resembles is a pillar. It is firm and solid and however hard you push against it you could never knock it over." The third man shook his head and said: "Both these men are liars! I felt the elephant and it resembles a broad *pankah*. It is wide and flat and leathery and when you shake it it wobbles around like the sail of a dhow." All three men stuck by their stories and for the rest of their lives they refused to speak to each other. Each professed that they and only they knew the whole truth.

'Now of course all three of the blind men had a measure of insight. The first man felt the trunk of the elephant, the second the leg, the third the ear. All had part of the truth, but not one of them had even begun to grasp the totality or the greatness of the beast they had encountered. If only they had listened to one another and meditated on the different facets of the elephant, they might have realized the true nature of the beast. But they were too proud and instead they preferred to keep to their own half-truths.

'So it is with us. We see Allah one way, the Hindus have a different conception, and the Christians have a third. To us, all our different visions seem incompatible and irreconcilable. But what we forget is that before God we are like blind men stumbling around in total blackness . . .'

While the doctor was telling his story, the waiters had brought us our shami kebabs. Now, while we ate, I questioned the doctor on Sufism and the teachings of Nizam-ud-Din and Jalal-ud-Din Rumi. Pushing his plate to one side, Dr Jaffery slowly explained to me all I wanted to know.

During the early centuries of the Christian era from the outskirts of Antioch to the wastes of the Sinai, hermits and ascetics could be found all over the deserts of the Levant, sitting in caves or on dung heaps, isolated on top of pillars or scavenging the wastelands for locusts and honey. Punishing the flesh, they sought salvation in the desert.

When this area was conquered by the armies of Islam in the early seventh century, many of the hermits converted to the new religion and helped inspire a more elusive and mystical strand in Islam, a reaction to the severe and orthodox certainties then being crystallized in the Quran. Impatient for Paradise, these Muslim mystics – known as Sufis, dervishes or fakirs – turned their backs on the world in the hope of achieving some tangible, mystical experience of God.

As orthodox Islam spread, through Persia, into the Himalayas and out through the Hindu Kush to Sind and India, Sufism spread alongside it, reacting with local mystical beliefs so as to take in elements of Hinduism, Tantrism and the wild shaman-cults of the Eastern Himalayas. In an attempt to induce illumination, Indian Sufis suspended themselves upside down in wells for periods of forty days, eating nothing. Others lived on a diet of snakes and scorpions, smoking hashish, and carrying maces in order to inflict wounds upon themselves. Some rubbed ashes over their bodies and went about naked, even in the Himalayan snows. One sect, influenced by Hindu *sadhus,* used to pierce their genitalia with lead bars attached to huge rings, a physical guarantee of their vows of celibacy.

Others, less extreme, followed purer, more philosophical paths in search of union with the Divine. They retired to Sufi monasteries and spent their lives performing spiritual exercises. These more respectable Sufi sects managed to achieve considerable influence: 'It is well known,' wrote the fourteenth-century Delhi poet Isami, 'that it is only through that fakir's blessing that a King or an Emir can come to power . . . When a Sufi leaves a country, that country suffers untold miseries. This is a proven fact.'

Stories of their powers multiplied, and the boundary between truth and fiction, never strong in India, lost its clarity. Who did not know of Shah Jalal who made a daily flight from eastern India to Mecca on a flying camel in order to say his morning *namaz* (the camel, it was said, always brought him back in time for an early breakfast). Or of Shah Madar of Jaunpur, the patron saint of jugglers, who liked to wing his way around the subcontinent on a piece of wall; he never ate and his curses could cover a man with blisters.

In recent years, with the rise of Islamic fundamentalism, the unorthodox Sufis have been persecuted and banned in many Muslim countries. Only in India and Pakistan do their numbers increase and their cults grow ever more popular and elaborate.

For some the Sufi path is still a method for achieving pure union with God. In Old Delhi there are still several *khanqahs* where groups of Sufis follow simple, monastic lives: eating little, owning no possessions, depriving themselves of sleep, living only to pray and repeat over and over again the ninety-nine names of Allah: 'I try to say His name 24,000 times each day,' claimed one very elderly Sufi I was taken to see by Dr Jaffery. 'I feel very comfortable when I am reciting. I sit quiet and meditate with my eyes closed and mouth shut . . . sometimes, when I am lucky, I suddenly feel as if my heart is filled with light.'

More commonly, modern Sufis hold spiritual surgeries, giving out charms, amulets and herbal medicines mainly to simple villagers, whom they charge for their services. Most seem to have little grasp either of homoeopathic medicine or the basics of Sufi philosophy; many are transparent frauds. In Delhi today there may be as many as a hundred such dervishes. Pir Syed Mohammed Sarmadi is one of the most notorious. A hugely fat Sufi with a mountainous turban, an elephantine girth and a great ruff of double chins, he operates one of the most profitable faith-healing businesses in India. One of Sarmadi's forebears was beheaded by the Mughal Emperor Aurangzeb after he wandered into the Imperial presence stark naked, shrieking out Sufi poetry. Sarmadi launched his healing business, in a lean-to attached to his ancestor's tomb, after claiming to have received a vision of his martyred great-grandfather wandering the Delhi streets, head in hand.

Every day he sits cross-legged in his surgery between ten and five, with a short break for a kebab at lunch. It is a small room, and Sarmadi fills a great deal of it. Its walls are lined with powders and sacred texts, framed monograms of Arabic calligraphy and pictures of the Ka'ba at Mecca. There is a continuous queue of folk waiting to see him, and Sarmadi keeps the queue moving. Each petitioner gets about two minutes of his time. The pilgrim will come in, sit down, and explain his problem. Sarmadi will listen, breaking his concentration only to clean his fingernails or to gob into his golden spittoon. When the supplicant has said his piece, Sarmadi will wave his peacock fan and blow over the petitioner, recite a bit of the Quran, write out a charm or a sacred number, and place it in an amulet. He will then dismiss the supplicant, having first received his fee of fifty rupees, a week's wage for an Indian labourer.

Finally, before leaving, the petitioner will hand another twenty rupees to an elderly eunuch who stands outside the surgery with a goatskin full of water. On receipt of the money, the eunuch will pour the water into a drain which runs under the beheaded Sufi's grave. This, the supplicant is told, has the same merit as personally washing and anointing the dead man's body. On a good day, Sarmadi may have as many as two hundred supplicants.

I once complained to Dr Jaffery that so many of the Sufis in Old Delhi appeared to be blatant fakes. The doctor said he agreed with me, although he added: 'But William, my friend, you must remember one thing. Fake Sufis are like any other kind of counterfeit. Forgeries only exist because real gold is so incredibly valuable . . .'

That summer, after the inferno heat of the day had given way to the gentler warmth of the evening, Olivia and I often used to walk to Nizamuddin. There we would listen to the *qawwalis* and talk to the pilgrims.

It did not take long to realize that the great majority of the pilgrims to the shrine regarded Nizam-ud-Din not as a long dead saint, but as a living Shaykh, whose help and advice could still be readily consulted. Once, sitting listening to *qawwalis*, I asked Dr Jaffery whether this was a general view.

'The saints do not die,' he said. 'Your body – my body – it will decompose. But this does not happen to the saints. They merely disappear behind a veil.'

'But how can you know this?' I asked.

'Just use your eyes! Look around you,' said Dr Jaffery. 'In this enclosure there lies the tomb of one Emperor – Muhammed Shah

Rangila – and one Princess – Jahanara. Over the road lies the mausoleum of another Emperor – Humayun. These tombs are more magnificent than the tomb of Nizam-ud-Din, but who goes to see them? Only tourists in charabancs. They laugh and eat ice creams and when they come to the tomb chamber they never think to remove their shoes.

'But this place is different. No one is called to Nizam-ud-Din's tomb. It is the cenotaph of a poor man who died penniless. Yet every day thousands come, and they bring with them their tears and their innermost desires. There must be something which keeps them coming, six hundred years after Nizam-ud-Din left his body. Everyone who comes here instinctively feels the presence of the saint.'

After I got to know the *pirzadas* who looked after the shrine – all of them direct male descendants of Nizam-ud-Din's elder sister – they began to tell me stories of people who had seen their ancestor in different parts of his old monastery.

'You can only see Nizam-ud-Din if you are pure in heart,' explained Hassan Ali Shah Nizami, as we sat together one evening on the veranda of the tomb. 'It depends on the intensity of your devotion. Some see him sitting on his tomb. Others see him walking around the shrine. To others he appears in dreams. There are no hard and fast rules. Since he left his earthly body he is not bound by our limitations.'

'Have you ever seen him?' I asked.

'Not with my eyes,' replied Nizami. 'But sometimes when I am trying to cure someone or to exorcize an evil djinn and I call on his name I can feel his presence . . . It is as if I am a flute: on my own I am nothing. But Nizam-ud-Din knows how to blow through me and – how do you say it? – to produce through me a pure note of healing.'

Nizami told me a story to illustrate how jealously Nizam-ud-Din still looks after his shrine. For centuries it has been a custom that only the *pirzadas* are allowed to clean the tomb of their forebear. One night the custodian on duty wanted to see a play that was being performed nearby, so he delegated the task of cleaning the tomb to a friend. When the *pirzada* returned he saw his friend lying flat on his face with the broom still in his hand. He called some of his colleagues and together they dragged the man out of the shrine, and revived him by pouring water over his face. Later, the man told how he had begun to sweep the shrine when a powerful beam of light emerged from the tomb and struck him down. He was terrified and could remember nothing. The other *pirzadas* immediately cleaned the shrine themselves then performed rituals to beg the forgiveness of their angry ancestor.

To the *pirzadas* and dervishes who gathered in Nizamuddin, the most extraordinary supernatural incidents were everyday, almost mundane: the dervishes would tell me – deadpan – that they had been granted the stigmata ('mystical wounds from the Prophet's fingers') the previous week, or maybe that they had seen an army of heavily-armoured demons marching across the heavens the night before. The tone in which they related these visions was exactly the same as that in which they might have listed the bus schedule to Lucknow or the names of the films being shown at the Regal in Connaught Place.

One evening I spent several hours questioning the *pirzadas* and dervishes about the djinns. As we talked a large group collected around us and everyone added stories about their own experiences with the invisible spirits.

'You can't see the wind. In the same way you can't see a djinn,' one dervish remarked. He was a heavily bearded Bengali; at his side he wore a long, curved scimitar.

'The only people who can see the djinns are the great saints and the high Brahmins,' agreed a second dervish, a Gujarati from Ahmedabad.

'They can live anywhere: in somebody's house or in the air.'

'And the female ones can take on the form of any living creature. They can be a donkey, a rat, a beautiful woman . . .'

'A snake.'

'A goat.'

'A jackal.'

'A black dog or a water buffalo.'

'The great djinns are said to ride around the world on eagle's wings.'

'The Caliph Haroun al-Rashid used to learn songs and airs from the poets among the djinns. They took an oath of fidelity to him and helped him build his great palace on the banks of the Euphrates . . .'

One matter which caused a degree of controversy was the question of whether djinns were Muslim or not.

'Djinns are a form of the devil. They cannot be Muslim,' said one Sufi, a huge Afghan.

There were murmurs of disagreement. All the rest shook their heads. Some of the dervishes stroked their beards.

'You are wrong,' said the scimitar-wearing Bengali. 'The djinns are capable of salvation. The Prophet was sent to them as well as to us. The Quran says that some of them will enter the great garden of Paradise.'

'Some djinns are Muslim. Others are Hindus,' added the Gujarati dervish.

'It is true,' agreed another. 'And the Muslim djinns live in mosques.'

'They give *namaz* and perform all the rituals of the faith,' said a Pakistani from Hyderabad. 'They have Allah written in their hearts. You will not find any pagan ones wherever the voice of the *azan* travels.'

'The Hindu djinns live in jungles. Also they are liking ruins: old temples, cemeteries, cremation grounds, caravanserai . . .'

'Some hide in the feet of big trees.'

'But a great saint can capture and convert even the Rajas among the Hindu djinns,' said the Gujarati. 'They can make use of their power for their own ends.'

'Who?' I said. 'Who can do this today?'

'In Sindh there is one man,' said the Pakistani. 'His name is Sayyid Raiz Attar. He lives in the desert near Hyderabad. He has captured many djinns and used them to help him build his monastery.'

'In Delhi there is also a great Sufi who has the knowledge of the secret of the djinns,' said the Bengali. 'He performs wonders with the powers of his djinns. It is said that he is one of the greatest of all the dervishes in India.'

'What's he called?' I asked.

'His name,' said the Bengali, 'is Pir Sadr-ud-Din.'

'It is a miracle,' said Mr Ravi Bose, wiping the sweat off his brow. Since seven o'clock Mr Bose and I had been waiting for Sadr-ud-Din. We were standing in the narrow shade of the dervish's shrine near the Turkman Gate of the Old City. It was a boiling May morning and dry, gritty winds from the desert were raking through the narrow lanes. We were very hot, and Sadr-ud-Din was nearly three hours late.

'Really I am telling you. It was nothing but a miracle,' continued Mr Bose. 'The dervish came to my house and within *ten minutes* he had found the djinns – the whole family of them.'

'You could see these djinns?' I asked.

'No, but Pir Sadr-ud-Din was seeing them as plain as it was day. His Holiness says that the djinns were black colour, of most ugly complexion, and that some were gents and some were ladies. There were two hundred and eight in all.'

'Two hundred and eight is rather a lot of djinns isn't it?' I said. 'I mean: where were they all?'

'Hiding in various parts of the house,' replied Mr Bose. 'Sadr-ud-Din was saying that fifty-two of them were under the stairs, fifty-two more were in the attic, and that the rest were in the kitchen.'

While we had been waiting, Mr Bose had treated me to his life history. He had revealed that he was a specialist in electro-plating. He was an educated man, so he said; he had a small car, a big house and two children. His life had been without problems – until, that is, the business with the sweeper-lady.

The previous month he had become sure that the sweeper was stealing from him, and he had been forced to throw her out. As she went, she had put a curse on his household – had filled his home with black magic and hordes of malignant djinns. Soon his children had begun to sicken, his business had gone into decline, and his wife had packed her bags and walked out. He was not a superstitious man, he said, but he had to do something. It was one of his Muslim employees who had put him in touch with Sadr-ud-Din.

'So did Sadr-ud-Din manage to get rid of your djinns?' I asked.

'Why not?' replied Mr Bose. 'He did some rituals. We purchased a kilo of curds and Sadr-ud-Din boiled them in a frying pan. Suddenly there appeared a pungent smell. This indicated that the devils were expediting Mr Sadr-ud-Din's requests and were vacating the premises as per instructions.'

His Holiness Sadr-ud-Din Mahboob Ali Shah Chisti finally appeared shortly before ten a.m. He was a large man, with big feet and a firm handshake; he had a saturnine face and he beamed a rotting-red betel-nut grin. He wore a high-necked Peshwari waistcoat and on his head he had placed a loose red and white *keffiyeh*. Without a word, he took a key out of his pocket, and opened the door of the shrine. A steep flight of steps disappeared down into the earth.

The Sufi plunged into the darkness. Like ferrets into a burrow, we followed. It was several minutes before our eyes adjusted to the darkness. We were in a cavern. The walls were covered in plaster, worked into the shape of domes and blind arches. In some of these arches, shallow niches had been excavated and in these Sadr-ud-Din had placed flickering candles and incense sticks. In the centre of the cavern was a tomb, and around the tomb a canopy. Sadr-ud-Din was sitting cross-legged underneath it with his eyes closed. Finally he indicated that I should speak.

'Tell me,' I said, 'about the djinns.'

Sadr-ud-Din paused before answering. For two whole minutes the candles flickered in silence.

'The djinns are composed of vapour or flame,' said Sadr-ud-Din. 'They were created by Allah at the time of Shaitan [Satan], many centuries before the birth of Adam. Every year their numbers increase. There are male and female djinns and the female ones are very beautiful.'

'Do you have power over the djinns?' I asked.

'I do.'

'Have you captured a djinn?'

'Yes.'

I waited. He did not speak. The candles flickered.

'How do you capture a djinn?' I asked.

'It is a great secret. The art was first discovered by Solomon and passed on to the dervishes of his time, long before the age of the Prophet Muhammad. Even today the great dervishes still keep this secret. They cannot pass it on to anyone but another master dervish.'

289

'In that case,' I said, 'how do you become a great dervish?'

There was another long pause.

'If you are to become a great dervish,' he said eventually, 'you must first learn to leave your body. Sometimes you must pray for many years before you master the technique. Only then can you ascend directly to God.'

'You have done this?' I asked.

'I first left my body when I was sixteen,' replied Sadr-ud-Din. 'My *Pir* made me spend forty-one days fasting, up to my neck in the Jumna. Twice a day he took me out of the water, for an hour each time, and he would give me a glass of orange juice. After that my *Pir* led me to a graveyard. Again he made me fast for forty-one days. Then he took me to a mountain top. This time I fasted for twenty-one days.

'On the last day of the fast I left my body and ascended towards a light in the sky. The light was God. It was a huge light, like many suns, but I could not see its centre for it was covered with a cloak. . . . Now every time when I fast and leave my body I see a little more of this light. When people come to me with their problems I talk to the light, and I ask for the success of their petition.'

Again, Sadr-ud-din stopped. Shadows danced around the guttering candles.

'God has given me power,' said the dervish. 'Now I can finish any problem. I can capture djinns and cast out devils. I can cure headaches, mend broken limbs, restore milk to the breasts of a dry woman.' His eyes gleamed in the candlelight.

'Nothing,' he said, 'nothing is beyond me.'

On his travels, Ibn Battuta always made a point of visiting the most famous Sufis and dervishes in every town that he passed through.

At Konya in Turkey he paid homage to the tomb of Jalal-ud-Din Rumi. In Hebron he saw the monumental wall of a mosque that the djinns had built at the command of Solomon. In Alexandria he stayed with the Sufi master Shaykh al-Murshidi. According to Battuta, al-Murshidi 'bestowed gifts miraculously created at his word. Parties of men of all ranks used to come to see him. Each one of them would desire to eat some flesh or fruit or sweetmeat at his cell, and to each he would give what he suggested, though it was frequently out of season.'

Taking a siesta on the Shaykh's roof, Battuta had a dream of being carried on the wings of a great bird which flew him east towards Mecca and then on past the Yemen to the furthest Orient. Coming down from the roof, he was amazed to find that the Shaykh already knew of his dream. The Shaykh then went on to interpret it, prophesying exactly the route Battuta was to take to the east. Later, another Egyptian Sufi named Burhan-ud-Din foretold for him the names of the dervish masters he would meet on the way. Although at that time he had had no plans to travel a step further than Mecca, wishing only to complete the *hajj* pilgrimage, Ibn Battuta did in due course travel on to China and quite accidently stumbled across each of the three Sufi masters that Burhan-ud-Din had named.

Nevertheless, despite Ibn Battuta's fascination with the netherworld of the dervishes, on his arrival in Delhi – at least at first – more worldly considerations seem to have dominated the Moroccan's thoughts. He had, after all, done remarkably well for himself. At a time when the average Hindu family lived on about five dinars a month, Sultan Muhammed bin Tughluk had awarded Ibn Battuta a stipend of 12,000 dinars a year and appointed him to the important post of Delhi *Qazi*. Battuta, it seems, was not remotely qualified for the job. He had never before acted as a sitting judge and had not practised law in any capacity since he left Mecca several years previously.

But Battuta was never one to look a gift horse in the mouth. He appears to have shrugged off his lack of qualifications and settled down happily to a life which offered him some considerable comforts. During his first seven months in the Indian capital, he did not get around to hearing a single legal case. Instead he directed his energies into getting married yet again – this time to Hurnasab, the daughter of a prominent Sultanate nobleman – and spending some four thousand dinars doing up and enlarging his house near the Qutab Minar. He regularly attended the court and sometimes went hunting with the Sultan. He even managed to persuade the Sultan to pay off the debts that he had incurred on a spending binge in the Delhi bazaars. It was all very agreeable and must have made a nice change from the demanding, uncomfortable and often dangerous business of travelling around the mediaeval Middle East on camelback.

While Ibn Battuta had – at first – no reason to feel anything but gratitude to the Sultan, most of the people in Delhi felt very differently. On his succession, the Sultan had embarked on a series of ludicrously ill-considered reforms. These included an attempt to double the tax revenue from the villages around Delhi (which caused a devastating famine) and an attempt to introduce a token copper currency on the Chinese model (which ended with massive forgeries and the virtual bankruptcy of the exchequer). The humiliating failure of these schemes only made Tughluk more brutal. According to the chronicler Zia-ud-Din Barni, 'when the Sultan found that his orders did not work so well as he desired, he became still more embittered against his people and began to cut them down like weeds.'

Like many other tyrants in similar situations, Tughluk's first response was to increase the powers of the secret police. Ibn Battuta, who was not initially in the firing line (and anyway rather approved of ruthless government) was most impressed:

> It was the custom [of Tughluk] to set alongside every *amir*, great or small, a *mamluk* [slave] to spy upon him and keep him informed of all that *amir* did. He also placed slave girls in their houses [to act as spies]. These girls passed on their information to the sweepers, and the sweepers in turn passed it on to the head of the intelligencers who then informed the Sultan. [In Delhi] they tell a story of a certain *amir* who was in bed with his wife and wished to have intercourse with her. She begged him by the head of the Sultan not to do so, but he would not listen to her. The following morning the Sultan sent for him and had him executed.

It was only much later that Battuta made a wrong move and felt personally the darker side of Tughluk's rule. In 1341, eight years after he had arrived in Delhi, Battuta made the mistake of visiting Shaykh Shihab ud-Din. The Shaykh was the most politically radical

292

of the Sufis in Delhi. Earlier Tughluk had punished him for his insolence by plucking out his beard. After this Shihab-ud-Din had retired to a farm near the banks of the Jumna and there dug himself a large underground house complete with 'chambers, storerooms, an oven and a bath'. Battuta's association with the troglodyte clearly came to the ears of the secret police, for when the Shaykh was later arrested – for refusing to obey the Sultan's orders that he should emerge from his subterranean shelter – Battuta was also put under guard:

'[The Sultan] had thoughts of punishing me and gave orders that four of his slaves should remain constantly beside me in the audience hall. When this action is taken with anyone, it rarely happens that he escapes. I fasted five days on end, reading the Quran from cover to cover each day, and tasting nothing but water. After five days I broke my fast, and then continued to fast for another four days on end.'

Only after the Shaykh had been cruelly tortured and executed did the Sultan relent and release Ibn Battuta. Thanking Allah for sparing him, Battuta gave away everything he owned, swapped clothes with a beggar and for five months became a dervish himself, taking up quarters in a cave outside the gates of Lal Kot.

Ibn Battuta was not alone in his experience. All through Delhi innocent men were increasingly being picked up by Tughluk's secret police. Things got worse and worse, and the Delhi-wallahs responded to the oppression in the only way they could. Every day they took to writing notes 'reviling and insulting' the Sultan and threw them anonymously into the audience hall of the *Hazar Ustan*. This proved the final straw. In a fit of fury, Tughluk decided to destroy Delhi. He gave orders that the capital was immediately to be moved to Daulatabad, seven hundred miles to the south. The city's entire population of half a million was given just three days to pack up and leave.

'The majority complied with the order, but some of [the populace] hid in their houses,' wrote Ibn Battuta. '[After the deadline had run out] the Sultan ordered a search to be made, and his slaves found two men in the streets, one a cripple, the other blind. They were brought before him and he gave orders that the cripple should be flung from a mangonel and the blind man dragged from Delhi to Daulatabad, a distance of forty days' journey. He fell to pieces on the road and all that reached Daulatabad was his leg.'

Among those who were expelled from Delhi was the grandfather of the great Delhi poet Isami: 'My grandfather then lived in the secluded retirement of his house,' wrote Isami in his *Shah Nama-i Hind*.

He had already distributed his ancestral estate among his sons and now hardly ever came out of his house except for Friday prayers.

My grandfather was ninety when the Emperor turned him out of Delhi. Sitting [fast asleep] in his litter, he reached Tilpat before some of those who enjoyed access to him removed the cover of his palanquin. The blessed old man looked out and when he beheld thickets of gorse and groves of trees on all sides, he enquired of the servants where he was. He was amazed to find himself in such a strange place, surrounded by thick woods and wild animals.

When the servants heard this, they heaved a sigh of grief and said: 'O Sir! You were asleep when the Deportation Police arrived. They ordered us to leave this city for Daulatabad, along with all the common people. There is no possibility of going back to Delhi.'

When the grand old man heard this he heaved a sigh and died on the spot. His death – which was really a deliverance from his sorrows – was mourned by all. Wailings and lamentations broke out in every direction and men and women fell to lacerating their faces and pulling out their hair.

On the third day, after burying the old man by the side of the road, the caravan set off. It was an irksome journey over very hot soil, under a burning sun. [Women in purdah] who had hardly ever walked around a garden were compelled to travel through strange parts. Many expired. Babies suckled on the breast died for want of milk and adults died of thirst. Some were walking barefoot and their bleeding feet painted the road like an idol-house. Out of that caravan only one in ten reached Daulatabad.

Delhi was left like a paradise without its houris and its

houses were reduced to the abode of djinns. Later, it was
all set on fire.

On either side of the road an avenue of ancient banyan trees
extended off in a straight line into the distance. The trunks of the
trees were thick and gnarled and the long aerial roots hung down
over the road like the legs of giant wooden spiders. Sometimes they
dropped so low that the root-ends brushed the roof of the car.

It was early in the morning but already there were crowds of
villagers out on the roads: goatherds in loincloths, driving their
flocks before them; a party of labourers in Congress hats and
billowing white dhotis; three travelling musicians wearing crimson
gowns, each holding a long, curving stringed instrument: either a
veena or a *sarangi*. Beyond the trees, in the far distance, you could
see the eerie shapes of the Deccani hills: a line of grey ramparts
rising and falling in a dragon's-back of wind-eroded outcrops. In
Hindu legend, these great lumps of Jurassic granite were said to be
the lumber discarded by the gods after the creation of the world.

I saw the crumbling tombs before I saw the ruined city. Quite
suddenly there were hundreds of them, dotting the scrub on either
side of the avenue: a wilderness of overgrown mausolea, some
domed, some roofed with cones, others surmounted with neat
brickwork pyramids. They were quite alone now, surrounded only
by low bushes of silvery camel-thorn. This, I realized, is what the
tombs of Delhi must have looked like a hundred years ago, before
Lutyens spun them all into the web of his new city.

Then, round a corner, the black crag of Daulatabad came into
view, rising up precipitously from the plains. The rock is probably
the greatest natural fortress in India. It rises from a square base,
three sides towering vertically upwards in sheer, unscalable cliff
faces, while the fourth side rises less suddenly at a steep, though
not perpendicular, angle. What nature left undone on that fourth
face, man has completed. Four semi-circular rings of grim Tughluk
ramparts swing outwards from the rock face like successive tiers
of an amphitheatre. The walls are slightly smaller than those of

Tughlukabad, but are built from an impervious jet-black granite that makes them look just as formidable.

Here, as in Delhi, the Tughluks could not afford to take any chances. While their Maratha enemies in this part of India did not possess the military might of the Mongols, they made up for their deficiencies by sheer ingenuity. Centuries earlier, one clan of Marathas had perfected a technique for scaling the cliff faces that protected the hill forts of Central India: they trained giant monitor lizards – which in the Deccan grow to over five feet long – to climb straight up sheer rock faces; and so firm and fast was the lizards' grip on the cliff's cracks and crevices, that the Maratha assault troops were able to tie ropes around the reptiles' bodies and clamber up behind them.

Perhaps to prevent their enemies using this technique, the Tughluks dug a deep moat around the rock's central citadel; the one crossing point was bridged by a leather step-ladder which was drawn up at night. Further up the Tughluks maintained and renovated the old defences dug centuries before by the troglodyte Rajas of Deogir: a Rider Haggard-like maze of dark tunnels – the only possible way to the hilltop – all but one of which ended in a deep crevasse. This warren was barred by retractable stone slabs and an iron trapdoor that could be fired red hot; the whole complex could then be sealed and filled with smoke so as to asphyxiate anyone within.

This gaunt citadel was the end of the road for those Delhi-wallahs who succeeded in making the seven-hundred-mile forced march into Maharashtra. On their arrival they found an impregnable but unwelcoming fortress; by their own labour they built within the walls a home from home, a New Delhi in the Deccan.

Ibn Battuta's memories of Daulatabad were dominated by the monstrous rats he saw in the dungeons of the citadel ('they are bigger than cats – in fact cats run away and cannot defend themselves against them'), but Isami gives a more coherent account of the city.

Although only one tenth of the population of Delhi reached Daulatabad, they were still able to turn it into a fertile and prosperous land. Uneven places were levelled and made flat. The whole area around the city and suburbs was transformed into a series of interesting gardens and mansions. Plants grew to such an extent that the heavenly bodies looked down on it with pleasure. People of every sort and from all parts of India flocked there in order to reside.

Like the Punjabi refugees who transformed Delhi after 1947, the uprooted newcomers worked hard to rebuild their lives in their new home. Yet at Daulatabad little now remains to bear witness to their labours. The whole city is a ruin, uninhabited, deserted and quite forgotten. It does not even enjoy the dubious immortality of a place in the tourist brochures.

What moved me most as I walked around the empty ruins was the extent to which the homesick exiles had tried to rebuild here the Delhi that they lost. The whole project was one enormous exercise in nostalgia. The Daulatabad Jama Masjid was an almost exact copy of the Qu'wwat-ul Islam mosque at the base of the Qutab Minar. The ramparts were scaled-down versions of the walls of Tughlukabad. The tombs around the city were exact replicas of those that ringed the outskirts of Delhi.

After circling the lower town I climbed up, through the dark labyrinth – lit for me by a guide with a burning splint – to the top of the citadel. It was there, looking out over the plain, that I noticed in the far distance, beyond the city walls, amid the grey stippling of the thorn scrub, a well-maintained walled garden still shaded by a bright green grove of fig and mulberry trees.

The enclosure proved to be a small Chisti *khanqah* – a dervish monastery – the only inhabited building in the whole echoing emptiness of old Daulatabad, once the largest and most powerful city in all India. As at Nizamuddin, the shrine of the penniless dervish had survived – maintained and venerated – while the palaces of his rich and powerful contemporaries had decayed into roofless ruins. The enclosure had originally been constructed by one of Nizam-ud-Din's disciples, Shaykh Baha-ud-Din Chisti, and like its model in Delhi contained a tomb and a mosque, both sharing a shady courtyard and reached by way of a steep step well.

It was now a quiet and peaceful place. I sat in the whitewashed courtyard, beneath a fluttering flag, watching the old dervish who

297

maintained the *dargah* going about his devotions and giving out *ta'wiz* (amulets) to the occasional pilgrims. When not otherwise engaged, he held animated conversations with the white fan-tailed pigeons that he kept in a wooden coop behind the tomb. The shrine was completely silent but for the gentle cooing of the old man's doves, the fluttering of the flags and the distant ringing of goat bells on the scorched mountainside beyond.

Before I left, I went into the tomb to pay my respects to the dead Shaykh. The old dervish blessed me, then placed a peacock feather on the tomb and touched it on first one, then the other of my shoulders. Afterwards we talked about Baha-ud-Din: how the saint had been expelled from Delhi by Sultan Muhammed bin Tughluk, how he had walked to Daulatabad and how he had built the *dargah* up from nothing, preaching to the Muslim exiles and converting the local Hindus.

It was from this dervish that I heard for the first time the name of Khwaja Khizr.

It was not human effort, said the dervish, but the supernatural agency of Khwaja Khizr that built the step well of Baha-ud-Din.

In accordance with the dictates of the Chisti tradition, Shaykh Baha-ud-Din chose to build his *khanqah* outside the walls of the city. Like Nizam-ud-Din he wanted to be near enough to the city for the people to come out and listen to him, but far enough away to be outside the wranglings of city politics. 'My room has two doors,' Nizam-ud-Din had said. 'If the Sultan comes in through one, I will leave by the other.'

Remembering this, Baha-ud-Din chose a distant and barren corner of the Daulatabad plain for his retreat. He assembled the bricks and the mortar, but soon realized that there was no one willing to help him build his *khanqah*, nor any water nearby to drink once the retreat had been finished. Undaunted, he shut his eyes and prayed three times to Khwaja Khizr, the Green Sufi who guards the Waters of Life. When Baha-ud-Din awoke, the bricks and mortar had disappeared; in their place – fully built – stood the step well brim full of fresh, cool spring water. To this day, said the dervish, the well had never dried out, nor the water turned sour.

It was a story I did not really dwell upon until a few weeks later when I came across Khwaja Khizr's name a second time, this time in Delhi. I was rereading the *Muraqqa'-e Dehli* when Khizr's name turned up in a passage on the Hauz-i-Shamsi, the artificial lake built by the Sultan Iltutmish outside Lal Kot. Not far from the Hauz, near the Mehrauli Idgah, maintained the *Muraqqa*, was the Makhan-i Khizr (House of Khizr). There, at any time, one could summon up Khwaja Khizr, the Green Sufi, and have an interview with him – if you knew the right invocations and performed the correct rites. Looking through the other books on my shelf I found that the *Shah Jehan Nama* also refers to a Khwaja Khizr Ghat on the Jumna near the Red Fort. Clearly the Green Sufi was once a well-known figure in Delhi myth and legend.

Intrigued, I disappeared for days into the Nehru Library to follow up all the references I could find to Khwaja Khizr. The Green One, it turned out, was once celebrated throughout Islam. He was said to be the unseen guide and protector of all Sufis, a mysterious figure who would rescue dervishes lost in the billowing sands of the Sinai or drowning in the Nile or the Oxus. He appeared in the wilderness and to those who deserved it, he imparted his God-given knowledge.

There was disagreement among Islamic scholars about when he lived. Sometimes he was called a contemporary of Abraham who left Babel alongside the Patriarch; at other times a friend of Moses who helped guide the tribes of Israel through the Red Sea. Some believed he was a cousin and contemporary of Alexander of Macedon and that he commanded the Greek rearguard at Issus. Other authorities were more specific: they said that Khizr was the great-grandson of Shem son of Noah, that he was immortal and that his body was miraculously renewed every five hundred years. He wore a long white beard and one of his thumbs had no bone in it. He was always dressed in green and was called Khizr (Arabic for green) because wherever he knelt and prayed the soil instantly became covered with thick vegetation. He was still alive, maintained medi-aeval Islamic writers, a wanderer over the earth. If three times appealed to he would protect the pure in heart against theft, drown-ing, burning, snakes and scorpions, kings and devils. He flew

299

through the air, lived on a diet of water parsley and talked the languages of all peoples. Sometimes he travelled by river, balanced on a large fish. He lived on an island or a green carpet in the heart of the sea, but he had a house in Jerusalem and prayed once a week on the Mount of Olives. He could make himself invisible at will.

Khwaja Khizr's fame spread from the Sufis of the Sultanate to the Hindus of North India who quickly realized that Khizr was really an incarnation of Vishnu. In the Punjab the Green One used to be worshipped as a river god and in many temples he was depicted sailing down the Indus on the back of a large fish. In Sindh he was known as the Raja Khidar, God of Boatmen; any Sindhi who travelled by river or sea – and all those descending into a well – propitiated him by feeding Brahmins, distributing parched gram and lighting candles on well-heads in his honour. In the bazaars of Gujarat he was said to haunt the markets in the early morning and fix the rates of grain, which he also protected from the Evil Eye. In Baroda he was invoked to cure headaches.

When you try to begin to cut back through the jungle of myths that have sprung up wherever the feet of Khwaja Khizr have rested, you inevitably arrive back at the Quran. Jalal-ud-Din Rumi and most other commentators believed that Khizr was the unnamed teacher in Surah XVIII who acts as a guide to Moses and attempts to teach him patience. Yet if you look further, you find that the Quran was only a brief stopping point for the Green One.

For the story in Surah XVIII is in turn based on earlier legends collected in the Alexander Romances, the body of Middle Eastern myths that grew up around the memory of Sikander – Alexander the Great. In these stories Khizr appears as the sage who presided over the Waters of Life and the Well of Immortality. He guided the Macedonian through the darkness of the Wasteland in his vain search for the Blessed Waters, but although he took Alexander to the very brink of the well, the Macedonian hesitated and failed to drink, thus losing his chance for ever. The Romance bears an unmistakable resemblance to the later mediaeval legends of the Holy Grail and may well have been one of their principal inspirations.

The Syriac Alexander Romance dates from the early centuries of the Christian era, yet even this is not the origin of the Khizr myth. For the relevant parts of the Alexander Romance are in turn borrowed from one of the most ancient poems in the world: the Sumerian Epic of Gilgamesh.

The Gilgamesh Epic survives today in a version discovered in the library of Ashurbanipal in Nineveh, but it was originally written down much earlier, probably around 2600 BC, soon after the invention of writing. In these stories, Khizr is known by the name Utnapishtim, the Survivor of the Flood. At the end of the poem, Gilgamesh goes on a quest through the Darkness and over the Waters of Death in search of the sage who alone knows the secret of immortality. Utnapishtim − Khizr − shows him where to find the plant which will enable him to escape death, but no sooner has Gilgamesh found it than it is seized and stolen by a serpent.

The story of Khizr in the Gilgamesh Epic may later have provided the anonymous writers of the Book of Genesis with the idea of another serpent who interfered with the eating of another plant and thus stole from Adam mankind's last hope of immortality. Khizr is thus not only one of the very first characters in world literature, he is also one of the most central: he may have inspired the Fall. What interested me, however, was that the same character was still remembered by a dervish at Daulatabad, and that when the *Muraqqa'-e Dehli* was written in the eighteenth century, Khizr was also remembered in Delhi. What I now wanted to know more than anything was whether the Khizr tradition − inconceivably ancient as it was − was still alive in Delhi today. To find out I knew exactly what to do.

I called Mr Singh and asked him to take me up to Old Delhi. Half an hour later we were parked outside Dr Jaffery's rooms in the Ghazi-ud-Din Medresse.

'Of course I know Khizr,' said Dr Jaffery. 'He is the prophet who guides lost dervishes in the desert. He appears when you have no food and takes you to safety.'

'And people still see him?'

301

'There are stories,' said Dr Jaffery. 'But then there are always stories in this city.'

'Please,' I said. 'Tell me a story about Khizr.'

'Well – I have a friend who is a dervish. He has a shrine near Okhla. One day he was walking along the banks of Jumna when he tripped. His foot slipped and he fell into the river. The Jumna is very fast flowing at that point and everyone who was watching thought he would drown. Then my friend called out three times the name of Khizr. Immediately, so he says, he felt someone pulling at his shirt, pulling him back towards the river bank. He could not see anything, but one of the people watching on the banks said they saw a green shape – solid like a log, but moving like a man – hanging on to his shirt, and pulling him in to land. To this today that dervish is certain that it was Khizr who saved him.'

I showed Dr Jaffery the reference to the Makhan-i Khizr in the *Muraqqa'-e Dehli* and, putting on his glasses, he studied it carefully. Eventually Dr Jaffery put the book down.

'I know this place,' he said. 'But I haven't been there since I was a child. I was taken there by my grandfather long before Partition. I've no idea if it's still there.'

'What are you doing now?' I asked.

'Marking essays.'

'Leave them for an hour,' I begged. 'Please.'

Dr Jaffery frowned. He hesitated, then relented. He put on his jacket and led the way out of the room.

We drove straight down to Mehrauli. It was the hottest part of the day and clouds of scorching dust were billowing in through the car windows; by the time we got to the Qutab Minar the backs of both our shirts were wet with sweat. At the Qutab, we left the main road and turned right towards the ancient village of Mehrauli. We passed under the great dome of Adham Khan's tomb and veered round, following the lines of the walls of Lal Kot, the original Hindu fortress which fell to the Muslims in 1192.

Off the metalled road we entered a different world: a maze of narrow, dusty lanes clogged with pack donkeys and herds of goats; children washed under hand pumps by the roadside. Then, still following Dr Jaffery's directions, we pulled out beyond the outskirts of Mehrauli and entered the scrub. Spiky thorn bushes and orange

302

gulmohar trees lined our way. After a mile or so, out of the bush reared the whitewashed walls of a mosque: the Mehrauli Idgah.

'It's somewhere around here,' said Dr Jaffery. 'An Afghan dervish was looking after the Khizr *Khana* when my grandfather brought me – but that was over fifty years ago.'

We left the car and followed a winding footpath leading downhill from the Idgah into the jungle. The undergrowth grew thicker. Ahead of us a pair of babblers hopped along the path. Through the trees, we could still see the walls of Lal Kot rising up in the distance and all around, under the trees and deep in the undergrowth, there were piles of masonry – temple pillars, brackets, grave platforms – overgrown with vines and flowering creepers.

Suddenly Dr Jaffery was pointing ahead: 'Look! Look!'

At the bottom of the valley, nestled into the crook of the hill, stood a small whitewashed *dargah*, surrounded by a wall. There were only two or three buildings: a cook-house, a courtyard, a prayer room, and, over the grave of the saint, a small Lodhi-period *chattri*. To one side, surrounded by a low balustrade, was an old round well.

'This,' said Dr Jaffery, 'is where the dervish lived.'

We left our shoes at the gate and walked in. Sitting cross-legged on a reed mat was a small, dark-skinned Sufi with a goatee beard. He was young, lean, wiry and half-naked, wearing nothing but a *lungi* and an emerald green shawl. He had covered his torso with coconut oil and his skin glistened in the sunlight.

Dr Jaffery said '*Asalaam alekum*' and, squatting down in front of the dervish, explained what we were looking for. Without a word the dervish got up and walked over to the *chattri*. From a nail on one of the uprights he took a single key, and indicated we should follow him. Then he darted straight up the steep rock face above the shrine, Dr Jaffery and myself following as best we could. We reached the top just in time to see the dervish dive down into a narrow crevice. I went over to where he had been standing. A flight of steps cut into the rock led downwards. At the bottom was the mouth of a cave. A metal grille covered the entrance and the dervish was turning his key in the lock. I tripped down the stairs and followed the dervish into the Makhan-i Khizr.

The interior was plain and whitewashed. A reed mat was placed

303

in the centre of the cave, facing on to an arched *mihrab* cut into the far wall. In between the mat and the niche stood a plate of coals.

'This is what the dervishes stare into when they meditate,' said Dr Jaffery.

'So the cave is still used?'

Dr Jaffery asked the dervish. The dervish muttered a reply in a language I did not understand.

'Certainly,' said the doctor. 'This gentleman says that he is the guardian of the cave. Sufis who wish to enter a deep trance come here and spend forty-one days in prayer.'

'And does Khizr appear to them?' I asked.

Again Dr Jaffery translated my question to the man.

'He says many dervishes have tried,' replied Dr Jaffery, 'but he knows no one who has succeeded in summoning Khizr for many years now. He says the dervishes of today are less powerful than in former times.'

'Why is that?' I asked.

'This generation is not interested in spiritual attainment,' said Dr Jaffery. 'Too many dervishes like to fool simple villagers and take money from them. They pretend to fast but secretly they go off and eat *naan* and chicken tikka. It is a much easier path than that which leads to God. Some dervishes can still produce djinns but they are unable to call up Khizr. That takes a greater power. We live in an age of spiritual decay.'

'What the Hindus call the *Kali Yuga*?' I asked.

'Exactly. The Hindus believe that in history there have been epochs of creation and epochs of destruction. An empire is built up and then, without warning, it quite suddenly falls apart. They say that now we are in a cycle of decay – that we are too sinful and that everything is cracking up.'

'What do you think?' I asked.

Dr Jaffery shrugged his shoulders. 'I don't know,' he said. 'Maybe the Hindus are right. Maybe this *is* the age of Kali. The dark age, the age of disintegration . . . All the signs are there . . .'

The disintegration of the empire of Muhammed bin Tughluk came quite suddenly – almost, in fact, without warning.

Following the débâcle of the shifting of the capital from Delhi to Daulatabad, one by one the various provincial governors rose up against the Sultan and declared themselves independent. In 1335 no less than fifteen separate rebellions broke out. Tughluk pursued the rebel governors, marching and counter-marching up and down the country, beheading one, flaying another alive, ordering a third to be cut to pieces by his war elephants. As he passed through the rebellious provinces he harried and burned great tracts of his own kingdom.

'He laid the country to waste,' wrote the chronicler Zia-ud-Din Barni, 'and every person that fell into his hands he slew. Many inhabitants fled and took refuge in the jungles, but the Sultan had the jungles surrounded and every individual that was captured was killed.'

In the middle of this terror, Tughluk decided to send an embassy to China. As his ambassador he chose Ibn Battuta, the man whom he had nearly executed only a few months before. Battuta was still living as a dervish when the Sultan's emissaries arrived before his cave.

> The Sultan [had] sent me saddled horses, slave girls and boys, robes and a sum of money. I put on the robes and went to him. I had a [simple] tunic of blue cotton which I wore during my retreat, and as I took it off I upbraided myself [for leaving the religious life and succumbing to the lure of the world].
>
> I duly presented myself before the Sultan who showed me greater favour than ever before. He said to me: 'I have sent for you to go as my ambassador to the Emperor of China, for I know your love of travel.'

In due course a grand caravan set off from Delhi. At the head went the ambassador and his companions, followed by one thousand mounted bodyguards and a long train of camels carrying gifts for the Emperor of China: one hundred concubines, one hundred Hindu dancing girls, gold candelabras, brocades, swords and gloves embroidered with precious seed pearls. Behind the camels came the

305

most valuable gifts of all: no less than one thousand thoroughbred Turkestani horses.

The fate of Ibn Battuta's embassy showed quite how bad things had become in Tughluk's Sultanate. Less than a hundred miles south of Delhi, the caravan ran into an army of rebellious Hindus. In the skirmish that followed, Ibn Battuta, the new ambassador, was separated from his servants and captured: 'Forty infidels carrying bows in their hands came upon me and surrounded me. I was afraid that they would shoot me if I fled from them, and I was wearing no armour. So I threw myself to the ground and surrendered, as they do not kill those who do that. They seized me and stripped me of everything that I was carrying except a tunic, shirt and trousers.'

Battuta eventually managed to escape and rejoin his embassy, but it was as if the whole expedition was cursed. At Calicut on the Malabar Coast, Battuta loaded his treasures on to four large dhows, then lingered on the shore for Friday prayers. Suddenly a violent storm sprang up; the clumsy dhows grounded and broke up, drowning the slaves, the troops and the horses. Ibn Battuta found himself stranded on the shore with ten dinars in his pocket and a simple prayer rug on the ground before him. Everything else he owned was lost. Not daring to return to Delhi and face the wrath of the Sultan, he continued on to China as a private traveller. By the time he finally returned to Morocco and settled down in Fez to write his memoirs, he had been travelling for 29 years and covered some 75,000 miles, about three times the distance logged by Marco Polo.

Sultan Muhammed bin Tughluk continued to march around his slowly shrinking kingdom for another nine years. Then during the monsoon of 1351, he contracted malaria on campaign against a confederacy of rebels. While still recovering from his fever, the Sultan ate a plate of bad fish.

'The fish did not agree with him,' wrote Barni. 'His illness returned and the fever increased. His army was in great trouble for they were a thousand *kos* distant from Delhi, deep in the desert, and severely threatened by the enemy. On the 21st of Muharram 1351, Muhammed bin Tughluk departed this life on the banks of the Indus, fourteen *kos* from Thatta.'

During his lifetime, the Sultan had built himself a massive tomb of red sandstone. This he erected in the very centre of Jahanpanah, the new city of Delhi he had first built, then destroyed. The tomb stands today. It is a fine sight – a rectangular plinth of grey ashlar crowned by a prism of finely dressed Agra sandstone. The tomb is topped by a high, curving dome the shape of a Phrygian cap. Six hundred years after it was built the tomb hardly shows any sign of decay and ruination – only the gold finial on the tip of the dome has disappeared – but it does not contain the body of Sultan Muhammed bin Tughluk. On his death the hated monarch was brought back to Delhi and quietly secreted within the Tughluk mausoleum opposite the fortress of Tughlukabad. There he remains, in between his father and his father's favourite pet dog. His tomb was instead given to an impoverished mendicant named Kabir-ud-Din Awliya.

Of this wandering Sufi who, cuckoo-like, occupies the most sumptuous tomb to be built in Delhi before the coming of the Mughals, nothing is now known.

Towards the end of May it became clear that the normal crowds of Sufis who came to listen to the *qawwalis* in Nizamuddin were being supplemented by hoards of mendicants, pilgrims and dervishes from outside Delhi. On making enquiries, I was told that pilgrims were on their way to the greatest dervish festival in all Islam – the annual *Urs* (or death memorial) of the Sufi saint Khwaja Moin-ud-Din Chisti in the Rajasthani town of Ajmer. The *Urs* took place on the nights leading up to the last full moon of May, and this year, despite the terrible heat, 500,000 pilgrims were expected.

A heavy stink of spice and urine and dust and cooking hung over the transit camp in Old Delhi where the pilgrims were being lodged. From a canvas mosque came the cries of the camp muezzin; everywhere dervishes could be seen pottering about, praying, chatting, unrolling their bedding and cooking their breakfast – thousands of wild men with staring eyes, straggling beards and unkempt hair. The different Sufi orders were distinguished by different colours – the Chistis (in whose ecstatic trances may lie the origin of the

English word jester) wore yellow, while the followers of Hussein wore red, the colour of martyrdom. Some of the pilgrims had narrow eastern eyes and wispy beards; others, Pathans, were big men with mutton-chop whiskers and sharp, hawk-like features. The transit camp was a wonderful sight and on impulse I bought a ticket for the night bus to Ajmer, determined to see more.

We set off at nine. The rickety old bus juddered out of the camp with its cargo of dervishes screeching out their prayers as if the journey to Ajmer was to be their last. Squashed beside me was a shepherd, a nomad from Kashmir named Boob Khan. He had a henna-dyed beard and a turquoise turban; he was tall and lean and we conversed through an interpreter, a jeweller named Afzal Abdullah. Boob Khan said that he was going to Ajmer to pray for the welfare of his family; he had been three times before, and on each occasion his prayers had been answered: 'On one occasion a sick person was healed. On another I came out of a financial crisis. I ask Moin-ud-Din [the Sufi saint] and he asks God and ultimately we get what we desire. The saint is the beloved of God and through him we get what God might refuse.'

'Can't you just ask the saint in Kashmir?' I said. 'Why go all the way to Ajmer?'

'Moin-ud-Din knows I am coming from a far country,' replied Boob Khan. 'And because of this he pays more attention to my requests.'

It was a boiling May night. The bus was hot and sticky and few of the pilgrims in the bus got much sleep. We were unloaded at the bus station in Ajmer just before noon, and had to walk the final kilometre to the shrine.

The *dargah* was packed. Tens of thousands of devotees from all over India and beyond were milling around. Ecstatics and madmen were shrieking to themselves, beating their foreheads against the stone railings on the tomb. Blind beggars stumbled around with their alms bowls. Women discreetly suckled young babies under the folds of their saris.

We bought punnets full of roses to throw on the saint's grave, and gave an offering to the man who looked after the pilgrims' shoes while they prayed. After we had paid our respects at the

Qawwali singers

tomb of the saint, the jeweller asked me if I had asked Moin-ud-Din for anything in particular.

'No,' I replied.

'There must be something you want,' he said.

'Only to see a dervish whirl.'

'Then ask him for that.'

I shrugged my shoulders, embarrassed.

'Well, I will ask him if you will not.'

I spent the rest of the afternoon touring the *dargah* with Boob Khan. We visited the white marble mosque built by Shah Jehan and the great cauldrons, twenty feet wide, in which the *pirzadas* were cooking food for the poor pilgrims. We saw a female *qalander* weeping before the tomb of a saint and another girl, barely twenty, rolling around the marble pavement, twitching and writhing.

'She has an evil djinn,' explained a *pirzada* who was leaning against a pillar nearby.

'You will exorcize it?' I asked.

'No need,' explained the *pirzada*. 'Moin-ud-Din will do it automatically. If she spends one night in front of the tomb by morning the djinn will have fled.'

By six o'clock darkness had fallen and the musicians – two harmoniums, three drummers and a vocalist – had begun to strike up the *qawwalis*. A large crowd had gathered, sitting cross-legged under a canvas awning. Perhaps it was the numbers and the claustrophobia, but the atmosphere was completely different from the *qawwalis* I had watched week after week in Nizamuddin. The volume was louder, and the bass boom of the *tabla* drums echoed around the tent, hitting the listener almost physically in the chest. The crowd joined in the hymns, clapping and singing and shouting.

Then quite suddenly a Sufi at the far side of the crowd was seized by a shaking fit, throwing his head from side to side, eyes wide and staring; but he remained anchored to the ground, and before long his fit had passed. The first batch of hymns finished and the crowd dispersed. Boob Khan went off in search of supper. I hung around the tomb, talking to the jeweller.

At eight-thirty the band went back to work. This time the crowd was smaller, but the singing was just as spirited. The drums clattered and the voice of the singer rose to a falsetto. The hymn gathered momentum and the volume rose. Suddenly there was a crack, and I looked to my left. A few feet away there knelt a dervish in a yellow *salwa kameez*. Although still on his knees, he had fallen forward so that his forehead had slammed against the marble, and he lay there quivering and moaning, apparently in pain. I was about to get up and help, but was restrained by the jeweller: 'He is in *wajd* [a trance],' he told me. 'Watch.'

Almost as he spoke, the dervish rose to his feet and stood up. For a few seconds he stood transfixed, like a rabbit caught in the glare of headlights. He was shaking slightly, but appeared rooted to the spot. Then, slowly, he turned around so as to face the shrine. From where I was sitting I could see his eyes; his pupils had disappeared, up into the eyelids, and the eyeballs were pure white. He pointed to the shrine, then sunk to his knees in a position of *namaz*; after that he lay flat. Then, suddenly he rose again, jumping about, dancing madly, fantastically, and through the music you could hear him crying out: 'Allah . . . Allah . . . Allah . . .'

He began bowing from the waist like a Chinese courtier; only then did he begin to turn. As the music rose to its climax and the crowd clapped, encouraging him on, he turned faster and faster, his skirts flying out, spinning round and around on a single axis

310

screaming loudly: 'Ha! Ha! Ha!' Finally, he fell down and curled up into an embryonic ball.

'You see,' said the jeweller. 'You should not have been sceptical.'

'What do you mean?'

'That *wajd* was for you,' said the jeweller. 'Moin-ud-Din always answers the prayers of pilgrims.'

NINE

IT WAS JULY NOW, and the monsoon was late.

Day after day the sun pulsed down through a beaten-bronze sky; the heat assaulted you like a mugger the second you stepped out of the shade. The nights, now almost as hot as the days, provided little relief. No one in Delhi was able to sleep. Conversations became abrupt; tempers were short. Rumours proliferated: in the bazaars people muttered that a drought was developing in Rajasthan; that water shortages were spreading throughout North India; that this year the rains would again prove inadequate for the needs of the parched and thirsty land. Everyone agreed – as they did every year – that it had to be the hottest summer in living memory.

Delhi has always suffered the worst heat of any major Indian city. The Great Moguls, remembering their nomadic ancestors, overcame the problem by moving their entire court to the cool of Kashmir for the duration of the summer. The business of governing the empire could then be comfortably conducted lying on Persian rugs beside the rills of a pleasure garden, or in a canoe on a fishing expedition in the Dal Lake.

At first the British resisted this tradition. With starched shirt-fronts and starch-stiff upper lips they stayed stubbornly in the Delhi Civil Lines, dressing every night for dinner in full evening dress as if the integrity of the Empire depended on it. Ingenious Heath Robinson methods of heat control were devised to make their stay less unpleasant. Sir Thomas Metcalfe, William Fraser's successor as

Delhi Resident, tunnelled a room under the Jumna; he found that the river kept the room several degrees cooler than anywhere else in the house.

Later, a British inventor in Delhi patented the Thermantidote, a strange device in which a *pankah*-wallah turned a large fan, not unlike the propeller of a Sopwith Camel. This would suck air through a curtain of wet hay, hurl it into the house, and make the interior smell like a horse-box. But by the mid-nineteenth century the British seem to have agreed that, even with the aid of the Thermantidote, Delhi was best avoided in high summer. From then on, the majority of the British inhabitants of the city therefore decamped to Simla in April, and stayed there for the duration of the hot weather.

Late that summer, as the plains of North India were transformed into one vast shimmering heat haze, Olivia and I bowed to tradition and followed the ghosts of the memsahibs – and much of the modern Delhi middle class – up into the cool of the old Imperial summer capital. Rejecting the aeroplane, we did what Delhi-wallahs have done now for a century: we took the Himalyan Queen as far as Kalka then changed on to the narrow-gauge miniature railway which winds its way up the steep slopes to Simla.

The little train looked like something out of a child's toy box: the old carriages were of wood, painted kingfisher blue; they seated only ten people each. The engine was newer – it dated from the time of the Second World War – and made a noise like a London taxi. Accompanied by a great deal of hooting, the train jarred into life and chugged uphill at a speed little faster than walking pace, turning corner after corner in an ever-widening ripple of uphill curves. We stopped at an Edwardian station with high Swiss gables overhung with flowering creepers; in the window-boxes there were primroses and sunflowers. The temperature dropped. Leaves widened, colours brightened. The relief was immediate. After three months of sledgehammer heat it was like coming up for air.

A group of rowdies further down the train began to cheer; in my carriage, a pair of army officers and their wives chattered happily in the time-warped 1930s diction that still survives in the better Indian regiments:

'Shalini, my dear, you're sitting on my hat.'

314

'Tiger said to me – "Old boy," he said, "if you're going to go Up the Country, you've got to do it in style . . ."'

'Good old Tiger! Trust a Tollygunge man.'

As evening drew in, we turned a bend and caught a first glimpse of Simla's bungalows and country houses rising up from among the deodars of the ridge. Crowning the top of Summer Hill stood Viceroy's Lodge, a familiar silhouette of Edwardian towers and pinnacles, a Scotch Baronial stronghold looking strangely at home only a couple of hundred miles from Tibet. Through an open window I felt the first drops of rain blowing into the carriage. The sky darkened and the hillsides grew grey; a wave of nostalgia crept up on me: this was not the torrential tropical rain of the Indian plains, but the familiar, hesitant, half-hearted drizzle of home.

To Kipling, Simla was a place of illicit romance. In story after story of *Plain Tales from the Hills*, the same plot repeats itself. After the sweltering boredom of the plains, the young officer goes up to Simla, where, bowled over by the sudden glut of young English beauties, he falls in love with a Mrs Hauksbee or a Mrs Reiver: 'He rode with her and walked with her, and picknicked with her, and tiffined at Peliti's with her, till people raised their eyebrows and said "Shocking!"'

Today it takes a great leap of the imagination to see the old summer capital as it was seen by the Victorians: to feel the sexual frisson they must have felt when they set out on their first promenade to Scandal Point. But there is no mistaking the shadow of the departed English. It lies everywhere: in the shooting sticks and riding whips in the shop windows; in the net-curtained bungalows named 'Pine Breezes' and 'Fair View'; in the crumbles and custards on the boarding-house menus.

Yet it was all counterfeit. Simla was and has always been an idealized, picture-postcard *memory* of England, all teashops, village churches and cottage gardens – the romanticized creation of addled exiles driven half-mad by the Delhi heat. It looked as if it has been built from paintings on the tops of tins of shortbread. You kept asking yourself: what on earth was this strange half-timbered English village doing here in the middle of the Himalayas?

The oddest place of all was the Gaiety Theatre. It was once *the* place for amateur theatricals and remains unaltered since the last

315

British sailed for home. Olivia and I spent a happy morning studying the production photographs, images of plays which must have been outdated well before they were performed in 1937: men with false moustaches kneeling down to propose marriage to comely girls in flapper hats, while outside conspiratorial housemaids delayed the vicar in the front hall. Sometimes it was difficult to tell the names of the actors from those of the parts. Did names like Major Trail, Miss Mold and Miss Dunnett ever really exist outside the pages of Agatha Christie?

Olivia and I returned down to Delhi through the burning plains three days later. We arrived after midnight on one of those suffocating late summer nights when the heat exudes from the walls and the roads, and the air seems used and stale, composed of exhalations only. Overhead, the red moon shone behind clouds of heavy, windborne dust. We paid off the rickshaw and walked towards the front gate. As we drew near, in the dim light we could see that an elaborate tent had been erected inside the garden and a line of trestles set up to one side. Mrs Puri had obviously been entertaining. But it was late at night and I didn't stop to ask myself why our landlady would suddenly have taken to entertaining out of doors in high summer.

I only discovered what had happened in our absence the following morning.

At nine o'clock I went downstairs as usual to fetch the milk. Outside Mrs Puri's flat, twenty pairs of shoes and slippers were scattered by the door. The sitting-room had been completely cleared of furniture and white sheets had been spread out on the bare floor. Around the wall, sitting back against bolsters, was a group of large Punjabi women, all frantically fanning themselves and talking in hushed voices about the monsoon:

'It gets later and later each year . . .'

'We used to get such *lovely* rains, but nowadays . . .'

'It's this ozone layer that is doing it . . .'

'What to do?'

Mrs Puri, wearing a white *salwar*, was sitting slightly apart from this group with her back to me. Her head was drooping. She was

316

not joining in the conversation. Walking into the kitchen, I asked Ladoo what was happening.

'It's Mr Puri,' he said.

'What about him?'

Ladoo looked suddenly serious. *'Khatam hogia,'* he said. 'He died on Sunday.'

'Mr Puri's *dead*? How?'

'He died in his sleep. They cremated him on Monday evening. *Mataji* [Mrs Puri] took his ashes to the Ganges herself.'

'And these people?' I pointed to the sitting-room.

'These are the mourners.'

That evening a party of Sikh priests arrived from the gurdwara. They built a small shrine at one end of Mrs Puri's sitting-room and placed a huge bound copy of the Sikh holy book – the *Guru Granth Sahib* – under a canopy in the centre. Then they began singing a series of sad and plaintive mourning hymns, each verse rising to a prolonged wail of grief.

Olivia and I took our places quietly at the back. For a moment I did not recognize our landlady sitting opposite us at the far side of the room: she seemed to have shrunk somehow, to have disappeared into herself. She sat silently in a corner, hunched under her veil, suddenly small and vulnerable. The formidable *grande dame* who had kept us all in order for ten months was unrecognizable in her grief. At the end of the service we went up to Mrs Puri and said how very sorry we were.

'He was an old man,' she said simply. 'It is bad for us but good for him. This is life.'

'He will be reincarnated now?' I asked.

'This is what the Gurus tell us,' said Mrs Puri. 'But these things are myths. Who is to say? Many have gone that way but none have returned.' She raised her hands in a gesture of helplessness. Then she added something that took us both by surprise.

'I would have liked you to have been here for the cremation,' she whispered. 'You should have been there. You are part of our family now.'

All week the priests sang their hymns, the relations fanned themselves and Mrs Puri looked more and more exhausted. As the week dragged on, she sunk lower and lower on her bolster, sometimes falling fast asleep during the chanting. She had not had a single night's sleep since her husband died.

Among Sikhs there is a tradition that mourning should continue for a full seven days after a cremation. On the third day, the *Akand Parth* (the chanting of the *Guru Granth Sahib*) begins. It continues night and day for ninety-six hours without a break until every verse of the sacred book has been sung. When, on the seventh day, the chanting is over, a final service of farewell is held; it is called the *Antim Ardas*.

The day before the service, an army of half-naked workmen began constructing an enormous marquee the full length of the public lawn opposite the house. A cathedral of bamboo staves rose from the holes bored into the solid earth; above that was wrapped a superstructure of brightly coloured homespun. The shrine containing the *Guru Granth Sahib* was moved on to a high dais at the end of the tent, and beneath it was placed a framed and garlanded portrait of Mr Puri flanked by pictures of Guru Nanak and Guru Tegh Bahadur. Vases of tuberoses and frangipani were placed on either side of the pictures, filling the tent with their mesmeric scent.

The morning of the *Antim Ardas*, the weather changed quite suddenly and it dawned strangely overcast and heavy. Sulphurous red thunderheads rose up in the south-east. At noon there was a brief dust storm; then, very gradually, the sky darkened even further to turn the colour of essence of damsons.

The rain came just as lunch was finishing. A breeze rose, the trees shivered and for the first time in Delhi in many months it began to spit: the first of the pre-monsoon showers. *Ayahs* (nannies) rushed out on to the roof terraces to rescue their washing. Children playing hopscotch in the road gave up their game; raindrops wiped clean the dust they had carefully marked out in squares. There was a distant peal of thunder. But in the event it turned out only to be a brief shower. The first of the rainy season clouds floated on northwards and the service started at three o'clock as planned.

A large party of Sikh priests had already taken up position on

318

the dais. Behind the book sat two *granthis*; one held a horsetail fly-whisk, the other waved a container full of billowing incense. Both men ministered to the big bound book as if it were some living dignitary. To one side sat four other elderly Sikhs: a singer with a fine high tenor voice, a harmomium player and two drummers. The band quietly struck up a series of sad, slow dirges, and the marquee began to fill with people. Men sat on the left, women on the right. Most of the congregation consisted of the Puris' Sikh neighbours, but at least twenty or thirty Hindus also turned up. Irrespective of faith, when the mourners entered the tent they walked up to the dais and prostrated themselves almost flat before the picture of Guru Nanak.

Soon, despite the rain water dripping incessantly from the leaky tent, two or three hundred people were sitting cross-legged on the floor. The hymns wound their way through minor keys. The climax of each verse was beautifully held by the singer, while a descant harmony was added by the harmonium player. The congregation were visibly moved; turbanned heads shook slowly from side to side in time with the music:

> Wahe Guru,
> Wahe Guru,
> Wahe Guruji-o!
> Wahe Guru!
>
> Sat nam,
> Sat nam,
> Sat namji-o!
> Sat nam!

The hymn drew to a close and one of the priests gave an address; everyone stood up, then they all prostrated themselves before the *Guru Granth Sahib*. Prayers were said for Mr Puri, his widow and his children and grandchildren. There was a last chant of 'Wahe Guru!' and the family filed slowly out led, with great dignity, by Mrs Puri. They lined up at the entrance to the tent to say goodbye to the guests. At the end of the line was our landlady. As we drew near we could see her eyes were red and her cheeks were still wet.

319

Taking my hand, she mumbled, very quietly: 'Thank you very much for coming.'

We had now been in Delhi for nearly eleven months. The monsoon proper had arrived in Bombay and would soon be in the capital. Already the air was heavy and sticky with a terrible damp-heat. The thick pall of gloom cast over the household by Mr Puri's death made up our minds. We longed for home, for our friends and our families. Although it was the most unpleasant time of year in Delhi, the Scottish Borders were now at their best: the harebells were out on the Lammermuirs and the gannets would soon be nesting on the Bass Rock. It was time for a proper break. Olivia booked us two tickets back to Britain at the end of the month.

Before we could go, however, I had to complete my research. As soon as the *Antim Ardas* was over, I headed back to the Nehru library and began sifting through the bottom layers of Delhi's historical stratigraphy.

It soon became clear that trying to disentangle the history of pre-Muslim Delhi was like penetrating deeper and deeper into a midsummer dust storm: the larger landmarks stood out, but the details were all obliterated.

Prithviraj Chauhan was the twelfth-century Rajput chieftain who lost Delhi to the Muslims. He enlarged the walls of Lal Kot, the Delhi fort of the Rajputs, but other than those walls he left no other testament or record. All we know of the man comes from a very late mediaeval epic, the *Prithvi Raj Raso*, written by the Rajasthani bard Chand Bardai.

In the epic, Chauhan is depicted as the archetypal heroic gallant who elopes with the daughter of a neighbouring chieftain, Jai Chand, sweeping her up on to the back of his stallion while her father looks impotently on. A year later (in 1191) when the Muslim warlord Muhammed of Ghor descended from Central Asia with his Turkish cavalry, Prithviraj repulsed and defeated the invading army, but chivalrously released Muhammed whom he had captured. In 1192 the treacherous Turk returned with a far larger force and defeated Prithviraj at the battle of Taraori, Jai Chand having obstinately failed to come to the aid of his son-in-law.

Muhammed proved in victory to be less magnanimous than Prithviraj. The Rajput was beheaded; his fort of Lal Kot was beseiged and captured, then burned to the ground. The Qu'watt-ul-Islam, the first mosque in India, was raised from the shattered masonry of Delhi's sixty-seven Hindu temples; thus was Islam brought to the subcontinent.

Before the Chauhans, Lal Kot was controlled by another Rajput clan, the Tomars. Again, one name survives: Raja Anangpala Tomar. Later bardic historians maintain that Anangpala founded the fort of Lal Kot in the year 1020 and that he installed within it the enigmatic metal pillar which still stands, gleaming and unrusted, beneath the Qutab Minar. The Tomar's name is still preserved at Anangpur, a village six miles to the south of the Qutab, where a massive, pre-Muslim dam of shining quartzite still straddles a narrow valley. Near the structure, heavily overgrown, lie pillars from long-destroyed temples and a few barely-visible ramparts of a primitive hill fort. But of the purpose of the dam or the character and qualities of its builder, nothing is now remembered, and scholars dispute happily among themselves the value of different pieces of mutually contradictory evidence – ambiguous references in late, highly corrupted religious texts; the evidence of place names; stray finds by archaeologists; the odd almost unreadable inscription.

And then, quite suddenly, on the very edge of the dark abyss of prehistory, ancient Delhi is dramatically spotlit, as if by the last rays of a dying sun. The light is shed by the text of the greatest piece of literature ever to have come out of the Indian subcontinent: the *Mahabharata*, the great Indian epic.

While its equivalents in the west – the *Odyssey, Beowulf* or the *Nibelungenlied* – have died out and are only remembered now by the most bookish of scholars, the story of the *Mahabharata* is still the common property of every Hindu in the subcontinent, from the highly educated Brahmin scientist down to the untouchable roadside shoe-black. Recently, when a 93-episode adaptation was shown on Indian television, viewing figures never sank beneath 75 per cent and rose to a peak of 95 per cent, an audience of some 600 million people. In villages across India, simple Hindu peasants prostrated themselves in front of their village television screens for two hours every Sunday morning. In the towns the streets were deserted; even the beggars seemed to disappear. In Delhi, government meetings had to be rescheduled after one memorable Sunday morning when almost the entire cabinet failed to turn up to an urgent briefing.

The *Mahabharata* is more than worthy of its fame. Even in translation it retains the narrative and moral power of a Shakespearian tragedy, but with the action grafted on to the Indian equivalent of the world of Homer. The epic occupies roughly the same place in the Indian national myth as that held in Britain by tales of King Arthur, but for Hindus the *Mahabharata* also retains the religious significance of the New Testament: included within it is the *Bhagavad Gita*, the most subtle, wise and sacred of all Hindu religious texts.

The *Mahabharata* opens in a hermitage on the edge of the Naimisa Forest. There a group of *rishis* are preparing for the night when the bard Ugrasravas arrives on the threshold. The *sadhus* invite the bard to join them on the condition that he amuses them with tales of his travels. Ugrasravas tells them that he has just returned from the great battlefield of Kurukshetra and agrees to tell the story of the apocalyptic war which reached its climax on those plains. He introduces the epic by emphasizing its sacred power.

'A Brahmin who knows all the four *Vedas* [the Hindu Old Testament] but does not know this epic, has no learning at all,' he says. 'Once one has heard this story no other composition will ever again seem pleasing: it will sound as harsh as the crow sounds to one who has heard the song of the cuckoo. From this supreme epic comes the inspiration of all poets: no story is found on earth that does not rest on this base. If a man learns the *Bharata* as it is recited, as it once fell from the lips of Vyasa — what need has that man of ablutions in the sacred waters of Pushkar?'

In sheer length, the epic is still unrivalled. It consists of some 100,000 Sanskrit *slokas* (stanzas), eight times the length of the *Iliad* and *Odyssey* put together, four times the length of the Bible; quite simply it is the longest composition in the world. Yet miraculously, even a generation ago, it was common to find wandering storytellers who knew the whole vast epic by heart: they would sit in the coffee houses or on the steps of the Delhi Jama Masjid and recite the entire poem without a break over the course of seven days and seven nights.

Even today, when the wandering bard has followed the Indian lion into near-extinction – killed off, in the case of the epic, by Hindi movies and national television – it is just possible, in very remote places, to find men who still know the epic. A friend of mine, an anthropologist, met one such wandering story-teller in a little village of Andhra Pradesh. My friend asked him how he could remember so huge a poem. The bard replied that in his mind each stanza was written on a pebble. The pile of pebbles lay before him always; all he had to do was to remember the order in which they were arranged and to read the text from one pebble after another.

In the form in which it survives today, the *Mahabharata* is a colossal miscellany of Hindu religious discourses, folk tales and legends. But all these diversions are built up around a central story of almost minimalist simplicity.

The epic tells the tale of two groups of semi-divine cousins who vie for control of Upper India – the Bharata, from which the poem takes its name. One branch of the family, the Kauravas, rule from Hastinapura; the others, the Pandavas, from the great city of Indraprastha. When the Kauravas cheat the Pandavas out of their kingdom through a rigged game of dice, the latter are forced to spend twelve years in exile wandering in the wild forests at the foothills of the Himalayas. At the end of the thirteenth year, when the Kauravas refuse to return Indraprastha to their cousins as agreed at the end of the game of dice, the two sides prepare for war. When the last battle – the Hindu Ragnarok – finally takes place on the field of Kurukshetra, the world is all but destroyed by Pasupata, the Ultimate Weapon, given to the Pandavas by Lord Shiva. But after eighteen days of horrific slaughter, the Kauravas are defeated and the good rule of the Pandavas is re-established.

The site of Indraprastha – the Pandavas' great capital, the Indian Troy – was marked until very recently by the village of Inderpat. The settlement was cleared away in the construction of Lutyens's Delhi, but until then it had survived since prehistory beside the (much later) ruins of Purana Qila, the early Mughal fortress built by the Emperor Humayun in the late sixteenth century. According to the *Mahabharata*, the great city which once stood there – the very first of all the innumerable cities of Delhi – was simply unparalleled anywhere, either in the world of men or the world of the Gods. '[It resembled] a new heaven,' wrote Vyasa,

> made strong by moats that were like oceans and surrounded by a wall that covered the sky . . . Dread-looking double gates hung on towers that rose up into the clouds. The walls were covered with spears and javelins of many kinds, surpassingly sharp and smoothly turned as though with double-tongued snakes . . .
>
> [Inside] the fortress was a well-laid plan of streets . . . that shone with beautiful white buildings. This lovely and beautiful place was packed with treasure as if it was the seat of the God of Riches. There did the Brahmins assemble, the wisest scholars of the sacred Vedas who knew all tongues of the earth. From all regions merchants too came to that city to seek their fortune, and artisans [skilled in] all crafts came to live there.
>
> Lovely gardens surrounded the city with mango and rose-apple trees, breadfruit and oleanders, palms and jasmine, all charming to behold and blossoming and bending under the burden of their fruit. The trees were always in flower and swarmed with birds of all kinds . . . There were pleasure hillocks and tree-shaded lotus ponds filled with pure water, alive with wild geese and ducks, doves and cakravaka birds . . .

The finest of all the town's buildings was the Great Hall, the master-piece of Maya, the architect of the gods. Fetching precious stones and crystal building materials from the far north, Maya built:

> . . . a peerless hall, celestial, beautiful, studded with precious stones which became famous in the Three Worlds [Earth, the Heavens and the Underworld]. The Hall – which had solid golden pillars – measured ten thousand cubits in circumference. Radiant and divine, it shimmered like Fire, challenging even the luminous splendour of the Sun. Eight thousand armed Raksasas [demons] – red-eyed, sky-going, terrifying – guarded and protected the hall. It stood covering

the sky like a mountain or a monsoon cloud, long, wide, smooth, faultless . . . not even the Hall of Krishna or the Palace of Brahma possessed the matchless beauty imparted [to that building] by Maya . . .

Indeed so superb was the hall, that when Duryodhana, the chief of the Kauravas came to see it, he was seized with bitter jealousy: 'I am burning,' he told one of his brothers, 'and drying up like a small pond in the hot season.'

[Duryodhana] saw divine designs that he had never seen before, even in the City of the Elephant [Hastinapura] . . .

One time the prince came, in the middle of the hall, upon a crystal slab and thinking it was water he raised his robe; again, seeing a pond filled with crystalline water and adorned with crystalline lotuses, he thought it was land and fell with his clothes on. When they saw this, the servants laughed merrily and gave him clean robes . . . Another time he tried a door which appeared to be open, and hurt his forehead [on the *trompe l'oeil*] . . .

The more I read of the *Mahabharata* – especially those sections dealing with Indraprastha – the more I longed to know how far the descriptions were factual, or if they were simply the product of Vyasa's imagination. After all, in the Aegean, Heinrich Schliemann and Sir Arthur Evans had managed to prove that both Mycenae and Minoan Knossos had a firm basis in fact; and there seemed no reason to assume that the *Mahabharata* was any less historical than the *Iliad*, or that Indian bards were any more inventive than their Greek counterparts.

But it was not easy to discover the truth. Indian archaeological excavations receive little attention outside the studies of those scholars who participate in them, and for this reason it took some time to track down the archaeologist whose life work was dedicated to researching the historical truth behind the *Mahabharata*. Leafing through the annual reports of the Archaeological Survey of India, I found out that twenty years ago a small section of the site of Indraprastha had been dug by the distinguished Indian archaeologist Professor B.B. Lal. It turned out that Lal had also, a little earlier, dug the site of the Kauravas' capital, Hastinapura.

325

As luck would have it, the professor happened to be passing through Delhi. He was staying beside the site of his old excavation, at the Archaeological Rest House within the ruins of the Purana Qila. But, as I discovered when I rang him, Professor Lal was busy completing an excavation report. He had a publishing deadline and said he could not see me for some time. Finally, one hot, sticky afternoon, three days before we were due to fly back to London, the telephone rang. It was the professor. He said that he was able to fit me in for a few minutes if I could come round to the Purana Qila immediately. I jumped into a taxi and went straight over.

Professor B.B. Lal was a small, neat, well-groomed man in a light safari suit. He sat at his desk under a slowly-turning fan. Behind him were ranks of bookshelves; on either side he was flanked by glass cabinets full of pottery shards and old bones.

Time was short, so I got straight to the point: quite simply, how historical did he think the *Mahabharata* was?

The professor smiled, took off his glasses and began polishing them. He said: 'Let me tell you a story.

'Nearly forty years ago, in 1955, I happened to take the Kalka Mail from Calcutta to Delhi. When the train stopped at Allahabad there was a great commotion on the platform: people were desperately trying to climb into the train, there were police everywhere, women were crying . . . Anyway; the train pulled out and I didn't discover what had happened until the following morning. The Kumbh Mela [the great gathering of *sadhus* held once every decade] was being celebrated near Allahabad. Hundreds of holy men had massed and were marching down to the water to bathe when suddenly the elephants carrying the Naga Sadhus had run amok; in the ensuing panic hundreds were killed.

'Many years later I was directing an excavation near Allahabad and, as is the custom, towards the end of the dig we held a musical evening for the staff and labourers working on the site. In the middle of the concert, one of the labourers got up with his *veena* and sung a ballad he had composed about the 1955 Kumbh Mela.

The basic story was recognizable but he had added a lot of *masala* [spice], and the numbers had all got exaggerated.

'The idea intriged me so I investigated in the villages round about, and discovered two other versions of the same ballad circulating. Each singer had told the story in his own way, each one had added lots of *masala* – but the basic story was still recognizable in all the versions; there was a kernel of truth despite all the elaborations.'

'And you think the same is true of the *Mahabharata*?'

'Exactly – although if so many details had been altered in forty years in the Kumbh Mela story, think how much the *Mahabharata* must have been confused in its gestastion. The most ancient text that survives mentions the Parthians, Romans and Huns, so it cannot be earlier than about AD 400. But the *Mahabharata* describes events which must have taken place centuries previously, perhaps around 900 BC. That means there were 1300 years during which the story could have been inflated out of all proportion to the original events.'

The professor picked up a pencil from his desk and twirled it in his fingers.

'In the text of the *Mahabharata* it says that the epic started off as a poem called *Jaya* – Victory – with only 8800 verses. Then it became the *Bharata*, with 24,000 *slokas*, before being transformed into the Great Bharata – the *Mahabharata* – with 100,000 stanzas. For all we know, before the *Jaya* the poem might well have started off as an even smaller, simpler ballad such as the one the labourer sung at our musical evening.'

'So are you saying you can't believe anything that you read in the text of the epic?'

'No, I'm not saying that,' replied Profesor Lal. 'But what *is* clear is that you can't rely on the text *alone*. The only way to deal with the problem – speaking as an archaeologist – is to look at the *Mahabharata* sites themselves.'

'And they have survived?'

'Not only that: they have kept the same names. Look on the map. There is still only one Hastinapura and one Kurukshetra. That much is certain.'

Professor Lal leaned back in his chair and stretched his arms.

'Back in the early 1950s I began to carry out a survey of all the

327

places mentioned in the *Mahabharata* as well as a few which local tradition strongly associated with the epic – in all about forty sites. What I discovered by excavation was that the *lowest* levels in *all* these sites shared an identical material culture, and that every single one of them was definately in existence at around about 1000 BC. Moreover, all the sites yielded quantities of one very distinctive type of pottery known as Painted Grey Ware.'

By chance, I had seen some examples of Painted Grey Ware only a week previously while I was wandering around the National Museum in Janpath. In what was certainly the least interesting gallery in the whole museum – the one that contained the collection of broken shards, arrowheads and shattered terracotta fragments from Indian prehistoric sites – one case stood out.

The Painted Grey Ware spotlit in that display case was extraordinary stuff: eggshell thin – almost translucent – and wonderfully delicate. In some of his writings, Professor Lal has compared it on stylistic grounds to a set of shards found at Thessaly in northern Greece. But to my non-specialist eye the pots seemed strikingly similar to the superb pottery found at neolithic sites in the Greek Cyclades. The Cycladic culture which produced this extraordinary pottery also produced the beautiful marble figurines whose simple lines, shield-shaped faces, strange, abstract postures and almost elemental simplicity inspired both Henry Moore and Brancusi when, entirely independently, they both saw Cycladic figurines in museums – Brancusi in the Louvre, Moore in the British Museum. The result was sculptures like Moore's great *Moon Head* and Brancusi's oval *Beginning of the World*.

Partly because of their influence on twentieth-century art, the Cycladic figurines and their related pottery statuettes look to us today strangely modern. The same is true of Painted Grey Ware: the superb elliptical profiles of the bowls directly recall Brancusi's *Beginning of the World*, while the abstract patterns that cover their surfaces would have appealed to Matisse. It was lovely to imagine the Pandavas eating off this simple yet superb pottery in the great hall of Indraprastha, but I still did not see how the discovery of this pottery in all the *Mahabharata* sites could be taken to prove the historicity of the epic conclusively. I said this to Professor Lal.

'You're quite right,' he said. 'There is no direct and unimpeachable archaeological proof you can produce to establish the historical accuracy of the *Mahabharata*. But the fact that all those diverse sites were, unequivocally, in existence at the same time, sharing the same material culture, is circumstantial evidence of a kind. And when you combine it with other evidence, you do begin to build up a picture.'

'What other evidence?' I asked.

'Well – when we were excavating at Hastinapura a very interesting thing happened. On the dry side of the mound a lot of Painted Grey Ware was turning up, but on the side facing the river there was nothing. I could not understand this and kept asking myself why.

'Then on my camp bed one night I remembered what was written in the *Mahabharata*: that many generations after the Battle of Kurukshetra, when Nicaksu was King, Hastinapura had been abandoned after a Ganges flood swept it away. After that the people of Hastinapura had gone off to live at Kausambi. I realized that what must have happened was that the Ganges had swept away half the site; and that only on the dry side of the mound – that facing away from the river – had the Painted Grey Ware levels survived intact.

'This idea came to me at about one o'clock in the morning. I woke up my colleagues and, together with four *chowkidars* each carrying petromex lights, we went back to the site there and then armed with pickaxes and shovels. We examined all the rain gullies and, thanks to some good luck, in one cutting we found the boundary: on one side there was a thick deposit of mud and slush; on the other, the undisturbed Painted Grey Ware layers. The same pattern turned up in our main trenches soon afterwards. After this we took borings in the ancient bed of the Ganges and sure enough we found a huge conglomerate of washed-out habitation material. The Painted Grey Ware site at Hastinapura *was*, unequivocally, destroyed by a flood, just as the *Mahabharata* had said.

'Later we dug some trenches at Kausambi – the site near Allahabad that the people of Hastinapura are said to have moved to. Sure enough in the lowest levels there, we found the same late degenerate form of PGW that we had been digging up at the top of the pre-flood levels of Hastinapura. Short of uncovering an inscription, that is the clearest archaeological evidence that you

could hope for to confirm the *Mahabharata* text. It is a very nice –
and very rare – example of archaeology exactly corroborating literary texts.'

'And what about Indraprastha?' I asked. 'Did you manage to
confirm the *Mahabharata* text there as well?'

'Ah,' said Professor Lal, his face falling slightly. 'Well, when we
dug in Purana Qila we did find continuous deposits from the
Mughal period, right down through the Sultanate and the Rajput
levels to the Buddhist and pre-Buddhist period . . .' He broke off:
'Rather than me trying to describe it all to you why don't I just
show you? Come on.'

We got up and left the office. It was now late evening and the
great red sun was setting over the ramparts and cupolas of Purana
Qila. We walked briskly along a track towards the Humayun Gate
of the Fort, passed the Sher Mandal, and then turned left off the
track towards a steeply sloping gully. On one side, a wall of earth
rose up thirty feet from the dry bed of what must once have been
a small stream. The earth wall was as clearly stratified as the rings
of a tree.

'Look!' said the professor. 'The whole history of Delhi is there!
That wall represents continuous occupation for three thousand
years. At no time was this area ever deserted.'

'People just carried on epoch after epoch? Despite all the burn-
ings, killings and invasions?'

'In most sites you would expect at least brief periods when people
moved away from a place. But Delhi was always occupied. There
was never, ever a break. At the top of the wall you have the twentieth century. There are the Mughal levels . . . that is the Sultanate
period . . . and down there at the bottom: those are the Painted
Grey Ware levels.'

'Indraprastha?' I said.

The professor shrugged: 'Yes and no. You see, all we found in
the PGW layers was one small mud structure. I think the main part
of the city must probably have been to the south – through the
Humayun Gate towards Humayun's Tomb.'

'Where the Zoo and Sundernagar are now?'

'Exactly: all around that area – particularly near the Jumna –
we have picked up basketfuls of Painted Grey Ware.'

'So the site is still there awaiting future archaeologists?'

'If they ever manage to raise the money – yes. But these days who is going to give funds for a proper ten-year excavation?'

'But the palaces and gates and towers . . . wouldn't every university in the world compete to donate money for a site of that importance?'

'You won't find many palaces in the PGW layers,' said Professor Lal.

'What do you mean? In the *Mahabharata* . . .'

'Poetic licence,' said the professor. 'The archaeological evidence shows that the Painted Grey Ware culture was really fairly primitive – basically it was a rural, pastoral economy. At Hastinapura they had iron and copper implements, a few tools made of bone. Some glass ornaments, good wheel-turned pottery . . .'

'But the buildings?' I asked. 'What would the great hall of Indraprastha have been like?'

'If it ever existed it would have been wattle and daub.'

'Wattle and daub?'

'You get some mud-brick walls, earthern ramparts, the odd structure of kiln-fired bricks, but generally speaking PGW structures are almost always wattle and daub.'

'Any use of marble?'

The professor shook his head: 'Stone is very rare in this area and they didn't have the resources to move it very far. To date no PGW layer has come up with any stone buildings.'

'What about paintings? The *trompe l'oeil* which fooled Duryodhana?'

'No – nothing like that. Just monochrome geometric amd floral ornament on pottery. No human figures. The material culture described in the text is that of the fourth century AD, not the ninth century BC.'

The professor turned and began walking back to the Rest House. 'The Indraprastha of the *Mahabharata*,' he said, 'was basically created by the pen of a poet.'

'And destroyed,' I said, 'by the trowel of an archaeologist.'

Professor Lal smiled: 'If you like,' he said.

So, I thought: the Kauravas and the Pandavas turned from demi-gods into cave men, the great war reduced to a tribal feud fought with sticks and stones. Indraprastha's towers of amethyst had crumbled into dull palisades of mud brick and sharpened stakes; an apparently impregnable city of the imagination, built of couplets and rhymes and ingenious metres, had been breached by the archaeologist's pickaxe and shovel. After nearly a year's research into Delhi's history it seemed that I had finally reached the end of the trail.

Olivia and I packed up our flat in a gloom. Power cuts had now become increasingly frequent, and whenever the fans ground to a halt the heat forced us to give up piling our things into boxes, and sit, virtually immobile, until the power returned. True, it was certainly a little less hot than before – the sun was masked with cloud and the temperature had dropped several degrees from the peak of the heat at the end of June – but if anything the weather was now more unpleasant because of the humidity in the air. Everywhere you went, people were talking of nothing but the imminence of the monsoon.

'Oh, the rains we used to get when I was a child in the Punjab!' said Mrs Puri when we went downstairs to say goodbye. 'But today you never know. If it's a good monsoon all the common people go mad and dance around. And if it doesn't break the servants become quite impossible.'

On the day before our flight, I took our parakeets up to Old Delhi to Dr Jaffery; his nieces had kindly promised to look after them while we were away. After we had said goodbye, Balvinder Singh drove me to the travel agent to pick up our tickets for the next day. When I returned from the shop clutching the folder, Balvinder asked what I was holding.

'Air tickets,' I said. 'We're going back to England tomorrow, Balvinder.'

'Going Ing-land?'

'Yes.'

'Oh Mr William.'

'What Balvinder?'

'You not coming back?'

I was flattered – and somewhat surprised – to find that Balvinder seemed saddened by the prospect of our departure.

'Don't worry,' I said. 'We'll be back in a couple of months.'

'Oh Mr William,' said Balvinder. 'You must come back soon.'

'We'll be back at the very beginning of October.'

'Oh Mr William. Sooner, sooner.'

This really was very touching.

'I can't come sooner than October, Balvinder,' I said.

'Maybe you come end September.'

It did sound as if he genuinely was going to miss us.

'Well I suppose . . . yes . . . there is no reason we couldn't come at the end of September.'

'*Acha*,' said Balvinder Singh. 'Then you do one thing.'

Balvinder pulled the car into the side of the road, whipped out a notebook from his glove compartment and began scribbling into it.

'You bring for me one ITT in-car hifi, one Sony Walkman, one Phillips Video Cassette, two bottles Johnny Walker Black Label, one crate Carlsberg Extra Tasty . . .'

Balvinder tore the sheet from the notebook and handed it to me. 'Payment,' he said, 'on delivery, cash on nail, no problem.'

Early the following morning, woken by the distant rumbling of thunder, I lay awake thinking over everything I had read about ancient Delhi. Then it dawned on me that of course Indraprastha *wasn't* the beginning of Delhi's history after all. There was one ancient myth connected with the city that claimed to predate even the legends of the *Mahabharata*.

As I lay there, unable because of the heat to get back to sleep, I remembered reading in Carr Stephen's classic 1876 study *The Archaeology and Monumental Remains of Delhi* that a tradition had been maintained in the city – at least until Carr Stephen's own day – explaining why the Pandavas chose to build Indraprastha where they did. According to this tradition, the site of Delhi was already sacred many millennia before the *Mahabharata*.

The legend relates that once upon a time, at the end of the Duvaparyyoga, soon after the creation of the world, Brahma, the Creator, suffered a fit of divine amnesia and forgot all the *Vedas* and sacred scriptures. In order to remember them, the God peformed a series of yogic exercises and austerities, before diving into the Jumna. Soon afterwards, during the monsoon when the waters were in full spate, the flooded river miraculously threw up the sacred texts on the right bank of the river, not far from where the Jumna hits the foothills of the Aravallis. The place where the scriptures were washed up was named Nigambodh Ghat, the Bank of Sacred Knowledge.

It was for this reason that the Pandavas chose to build Indraprastha where they did, and for this reason also (here the tradition diverges from the 'official' text of the *Mahabharata*) that after the Battle of Kurukshetra, the five brothers returned to Indraprastha and performed the great *Das Ashwamedha Yuga* – the Imperial Ten Horse Sacrifice – at Nilli Chattri on the Nigambodh Ghat.

The Ghat remains, but I had never gone to see it. Our flight did not leave until evening; we still had plenty of time to visit this, the site hallowed by tradition as being the most ancient in all Delhi.

It dawned a dark and threatening morning. Great purple thunderheads were scudding low over the domes of the Old City. A storm was clearly threatening: the trees were being tossed around, the leaves were rustling, but still the humidity seemed near the point of saturation. Above, the hawks and vultures circled lower and lower, as if their aerial spirals were being pressed downwards by some invisible hand in the sky. Occasionally there was a blue crackle of lightning followed by a distant boom from the south-east: a soft cloud-collision announcing the coming storm.

We drove up the Ring Road, the motorway which for much of its length follows the old course of the Jumna. Driving up the dry riverbed was like looking at a section of Professor Lal's stratigraphy: on the way we drove through millennia of Delhi's history, the detritus of city after city spaced out on the old river bank. Leaving Lutyens's broad twentieth-century avenues we passed by the Purana Qila, the early Mughal addition to Delhi's bastions; after that we passed the shattered domes of Feroz Shah Kotla; then the magnificent walls of the Red Fort with their great ribbed *chattris*; and finally we drove under the walls of Salimgarh, the old Bastille of Delhi. Passing beyond all of these, we headed up towards the site of William Fraser's first house.

But before we got there we took a right turn and drove into a grove of ancient neem trees. All around saffron-clad *sadhus* were squatting by the road, their dreadlocks dishevelled by the rising wind. Some of the holy men had small portable primuses on which they were attempting to brew tea; others sat swinging their prayer beads on their index fingers, puffing mesmerically at their *chillums* (hashish pipes).

We walked past the mendicants and passed into the Nigambodh Ghat cremation ground – an expanse of tin-topped pavilions, each raised over a broad stone hearth. Here, only ten days previously, Mr Puri had been cremated by his family. But it was early still and all that now smoked amid the ashes of the hearths were sticks of incense tended by one or two early-rising widows. On one side, a party of sweepers were doing their best to clear up the detritus – garlands of marigolds, lumps of charcoal, broken clay pots which had once contained offerings for the *sadhus* – but the blustery breeze blew away as much as the sweepers could gather.

Beyond, through a line of arches, down a flight of steps, we could just see the black ooze of the Jumna, now – at the end of the hot season, on the very eve of the rains – in its very darkest incarnation. The closer we came, the filthier it looked: a black swathe of suspended mud as heavy and sluggish as crude oil. But beauty and sanctity lie in the eyes of the beholder and the believer. At the bottom of the steps a *sadhu* was sitting, arms outstretched, shouting out his prayers to the River Goddess Jumna. He was, I realized with a start, actually *worshipping* the ooze below him.

Hindus believe that all rivers, irrespective of their beauty or cleanliness, deserve special homage as givers of life and fertility. They are the veins of Mother Earth, just as the mountains are her muscles and the forests are her long and lovely tresses. The red sediment carried from the hills during the monsoon is the Earth Mother's menstrual flow. The Jumna, one of India's seven most sacred rivers, is no exception. She is the daughter of the Sun and the sister of Yama, God of Death. Once, under the influence of alcohol, Balaram the brother of Krishna attempted to rape her; when she resisted the divine drunkard tied her to his plough and dragged her across North India – irrigating the fertile plains of the Doab as he did so. Finally he dumped her into the Ganges near Allahabad.

Attractive enough to awaken Balaram's lust, the Jumna's dark complexion has never troubled the normally colour-conscious Hindus. In the Golden Age of the Guptas (the fifth and sixth centuries AD) when it became common for statues of the two sisters, Ganga and Jumna, to be placed at the doors of temples, Jumna was depicted as a beautiful Dravidian girl with a delicately curved, almost Semitic nose and thick, curly hair. In the Delhi National Museum there is a pair of fine idols of the two goddesses brought from Ahichchhatra, one of the *Mahabharata* sites. Ganga stands on a crocodile and looks like a lovely long Punjabi girl: she is tall and thin and her long tresses are tied into a plait. Jumna, who stands on a tortoise, is unmistakably a Tamil – she has huge, sensuous lips, tight, curly locks and a diaphanous bodice which barely succeeds in enclosing her enormous breasts; of the two sisters she is by far the most attractive.

As Olivia and I stood looking out on the sun rising slowly above the dark ooze of the holy river, one of the *doms* who tended the burning ghat appeared through the arch behind us. On his head he carried a shallow bowl of human ashes. Slowly, reverently, he made his way down the steps, then jumped into one of the two boats tied at the bottom. Walking to the far end, he cast off and waited for the dinghy to drift into the current. When he was out in the flow he gently tipped the ashes into the river, like King Arthur returning Excalibur to the lake. For a moment the white ash swirled milky on the surface, then it sank; only the black charcoal floated. Circling slowly in the eddies, it was gently swept off downstream towards the Ganga.

When the *dom* returned to the bank I asked him for directions to the Nili Chattri, the temple that was said to mark the site of the Ten Horse Sacrifice. He pointed downstream several hundred yards and said that he would take us in his boat. We got in. The *dom* – an Indian Charon on an Indian Styx – took the oars and pushed off.

It was at this point that it finally began to rain. At first it was no more than a shower, but soon the murky water around us burst into a ripple of concentric circles. On the bank a *dhobi* (laundryman) squatting over his slapping-stone, stopped dead as if amazed by the water suddenly falling from the heavens. The *sadhus* sitting cross-legged along the edge of the ghats looked up expectantly at the sky.

In the boat we were now passing the spires of a group of small riverside temples. The oars dipped and splashed on the choppy waters; we headed on downstream to the southern edge of the Nigambodh Ghat. Then the *dom* pulled slowly in towards the bank. He jumped out, pulled the prow on to the lowest of the steps and pointed up the ghats.

At the top of the steps, surrounded by a grove of neem trees, was a dark and ancient temple, its plasterwork stained by centuries of monsoon rain. In the centre of its inner sanctuary, enclosed by a quadrant of black stone pillars, stood Shiva's phallic symbol, the *lingam*; it was resting on a white marble *yoni*, its female receptacle. A copper pot had been raised on a tripod so that it dripped Jumna water out of a hole in its base down on to the egg-shaped *lingam* stone. The water then ran, through the *yoni*, on to the floor and out towards the river.

As we stood there in the half-light, a saffron-clad *sadhu* with a beehive topknot and a thick black beard appeared out of the darkness towards the rear of the temple. His face was lit by a single flickering oil lamp.

'*Namaskar*,' he said, raising his hands in the Hindu gesture of welcome. He had the triple-mark of Shiva drawn on his forehead; his eyes were as dark as the waters of the Jumna. Then he saw what we were looking at, and said, in Hindi: 'This *lingam* was raised by the Pandava brothers.'

'When?' I whispered.

'After the *Das Ashwamedha Yuga*,' said the *sadhu*. 'This *lingam* marks the site.'

In fact the *lingam* looked early mediaeval; it certainly wasn't prehistoric. Yet the *sadhu*'s words showed that the oldest legend in Delhi was still current. The story of the Nigambodh Ghat and the founding of Indraprastha *had* survived to the present day.

Standing there in the dark temple, as the rain lashed down on the ghats, I realized that of course it must have been the *sadhus* here on the banks of the Jumna who had preserved this most ancient of Delhi legends: the story of the Ten Horse Sacrifice and, long epochs before that, the tale of the sacred *shastras* emerging from the river flooded by the monsoon cloudburst. It was a wonderful legend: the mythical story of Delhi's first birth linked with the un-deniable fact of its annual rebirth in the monsoon rains.

Indraprastha had fallen; six hundred years of Muslim domination had come and gone; a brief interruption by the British was almost forgotten. But Shiva, the oldest living God in the world, was still worshipped; Sanskrit – a language which predates any other living tongue by millennia – was still read, still spoken. Moreover, the *sadhus* and *rishis* – familiar figures from the *Mahabharata* – remained today, still following the rigorous laws of India's most ancient vocation: giving up everything to wander the face of the earth in search of enlightenment; renouncing the profane in the hope of a brief glimpse of the sacred. In these wet and dishevelled figures sitting cross-legged under the neem and banyan trees of the river bank lay what must certainly be the most remarkable Delhi survival of all.

We left an offering for the temple keeper amid the small pile of marigold petals at the base of the *lingam*.

Then we walked slowly back through the warm rain towards the boat. At the bottom of the steps a drenched *sannyasi* was leaping about, dancing like a madman, his arms outstretched towards the heavens. Above him, the branches of the neem trees shook fantastically in the wind. There was a forked flash of lightning followed, almost immediately, by a sharp whipcrack of thunder.

The water was now coming down in great rushing torrents. Instantly it drenched us to the skin, before pouring down the steps of the ghat and splashing into the river at the bottom.

With a noise like a bursting dam, the world slowly dissolved into a great white waterfall.

Glossary

Acha Good
Allah hu-Akbar! God is Great! (Muslim prayer)
Amir Muslim nobleman (lit. 'rich')
Asalaam alekum Peace be upon you (Muslim greeting)
Avadi Golay Fast-flying pigeon from Lucknow
Avatar Incarnation
Ayah Nanny
Azan The Muslim call to prayer
Bahot Very
Bait al-Hikmah Renowned mediaeval hospital in Baghdad
Baksheesh A tip or offering
Bandh Closed or on strike; also a dam
Barsati A top floor flat (lit. 'rain shelter')
Bhagavad Gita Crucial section in the *Mahabharata* when Krishna persuades a faltering Arjuna to fight in the great battle of Kurukshetra, telling him that he must do his duty and that anyway all is illusion. The *Gita* is the most holy text in all Hinduism.
Bharat India (in Hindi and Sanskrit)
Bidi Cheap Indian cigarette (made from tobacco dust wrapped in a leaf)
Biryani Fancy rice dish
Bogie Hinglish (qv) word for railway carriage
Burqa Tent-like covering of Muslim women (extended version of the chador, qv)
Burra Sahib Big man (lit. 'Great Sir')
Bustan The Orchard (a famous Persian poem by Sa'di)
Caravanserai Lodging house for mediaeval merchants throughout Islam
Chador Muslim woman's veil (lit. 'sheet'). Can involve anything from a headscarf or sack to a fully fledged tent (see *burqa*).
Chai Tea
Chajja Long outward-jutting eave on a Mughal or Sultanate building designed to give maximum shade
Chamcha Sycophant (lit. 'spoon')
Champa Frangipani
Chapatti Disc of unleavened bread
Char-bagh Garden of Persian inspiration divided into four parts by irrigation runnels
Charpoy Rope-strung bed on which the population of rural India spend much of their lives (lit. 'four feet')
Chattri A domed Mughal kiosk supported on pillars, often used as decorative feature to top turrets and minarets (lit. 'umbrella')
Chela Daughter, disciple, follower or slave
Chillum Hashish pipe
Chota hazari Bed tea (lit. 'little breakfast')
Chowkidar Watchman, guard or groundsman
Chunar Plaster
Dargah Muslim Sufi shrine
Das Ashwamedha Yuga The Ten Horse Sacrifice, only to be performed by maharajas, great kings and emperors. At the end of the *Mahabharata* the Pandavas perform the *Das Ashwamedha Yuga* (according to some on the banks of the Jumna near Indraprastha).
Dawa Medicine
Dervish Muslim holy man or mystic; same as a fakir or Sufi
Derzi-wallah Tailor
Dhaba Roadside restaurant
Dharna A peaceful protest (usually involving a long period spent sitting outside the house or office of a person considered to be responsible for some injustice)
Dhobi Laundryman
Dhoti Traditional loin-wrap of Hindu males
Diwali Hindu festival of lights

Diwan-i-am Hall of Public Audience in the Red Fort

Diwan-i-khas Hall of Private Audience in the Red Fort

Djinn An invisible spirit, composed of flame, often (though not necessarily always) mischievous. The djinns are referred to in the Quran and were introduced into India by the Muslims, but are now believed in by both Hindus and Muslims. Same word (though with slightly different connotations) as 'genie'.

Dom Untouchable responsible for cremations and cremation grounds; Hindu equivalent of undertaker

Durbar A courtly levee or reception at an Indian palace

Dusshera Hindu festival celebrating Lord Ram's victory over the demon Ravanna

Fakir Muslim holy man or mystic: same as a dervish or Sufi

Galee Abuse

Ghazal Urdu or Persian love lyric

Ghee Clarified butter

Godown Warehouse or storeroom

Gora White man

Golay Racing pigeon

Granthi Sikh reader (or official) in a gurdwara (qv)

Gulistan The Rose Garden (a famous Persian poem by Sa'di)

Gulmohar Orange-red flower which blooms in the hottest period of the summer (lit. 'Peacock Flower')

Gunda Hired thug

Gurdwara Sikh temple (lit. 'the Guru's doorway')

Hadiths The Traditions of the Prophet Muhammad; sayings and injunctions not included in the Quran

Hajj The Muslim pilgrimage to Mecca

Hajji One who has been thereon

Hakim Muslim doctor practising ancient Greek or *Unani* (qv) medicine

Haveli Courtyard house

Hayyat Baksh The 'Life Giving' Garden in the Red Fort

Hazar Ustan The Hall of a Thousand Pillars

Hijra Eunuch

Hinglish Modern Indian English

Holi Hindu spring festival; the occasion is normally celebrated by the throwing of coloured water and the consumption of a great deal of hashish and opium

Hookah Waterpipe or hubble-bubble

Howdah Seat carried on an elephant's back, usually canopied

Id The two great Muslim festivals: Id ul-Fitr marks the end of Ramadan, while Id ul-Zuha (or Bakr-id) commemorates the delivery of Isaac. To celebrate the latter a ram or goat is slaughtered, as on the original occasion recorded in the Old Testament.

Idgah Open-air mosque used biannually for Id prayers. Idgahs are normally very large and are designed to take the overspill from the proper mosques on the Id festivals.

Iftar Meal eaten at sunset during the Ramadan fast

Inshallah God willing

Ivan High entrance portal normally bounded by a pair of minarets; same as a *pishtaq*

Jalebi Sticky Indian sweet made by deep-frying sugar syrup

Jali Lattice-work stone screen

Jamevar Antique Kashmiri shawl

Jataka Buddhist legend

Jawan Police constable (lit. 'young man')

Jaya Victory

Jharokha Projecting window or balcony

Jizya Quranic tax imposed on non-Muslims

Jhuggi Shanty settlement

Jungli Wild, unrefined

Kabooter Pigeon

Kabooter baz Pigeon flier

Kalidasa Great classical Sanskrit poet and playwright; lived first millennium B C in Ujjain, Central India.

Kali Yuga The age of Kali; an epoch of destruction and disintegration

Karkhana Factory

Keffiyeh Arab headcloth

Khalifa Official at a cock or partridge fight (lit. 'Caliph')

Khanqah Dervish monastery

Khitmagar Bearer, table-servant

Khoon Blood

Kirpan Sikh ceremonial sword

Kos The Mughal mile (about 2½ British miles). The measure is still used in remote parts of rural India.

Kshatriya The warrior caste

Kucha Alley
Kufic Arabic calligraphy used for monumental purposes
Kurta Long, loose Indian shirt worn with pyjama bottoms; traditional Delhi garb
Langoor Free kitchen; food alms given by Sikhs at a gurdwara
Langur Type of monkey
Lathi Bamboo staff used by Indian police to control crowds
Lingam The phallic symbol associated with Lord Shiva in his role as Divine Creator
Lu The hot desert wind which blows in from Rajasthan during midsummer
Lungi Sarong-style loin-wrap; simplification of the dhoti
Mahabharata The great Indian epic; the *Iliad*, *Odyssey* and Bible of the subcontinent, all combined into the longest single literary composition on earth, 100,000 stanzas long.
Mahal Palace
Mahar Severance fee paid to a Muslim woman by her husband in the event of a divorce
Maidan A park or common in the centre of an Indian city
Mali Gardener
Mameluk Warrior slave
Masala Spicy
Masjid Mosque
Mataji Lit. 'Respected Mother'
Maulvi Quranic scholar
Medresse Islamic theological college and seminary
Mehfil An evening of courtly Mughal entertainment, normally including dancing, the recitation of poetry and the singing of *ghazals* (qv).
Mithai Sweets
Mohalla Sub-division of a Mughal city: a group of residential lanes, entered through a single gate.
Muezzin Muslim prayer leader. In the old days used to chant the prescribed prayers from minarets five times a day. An endangered species since the advent of the cassette recorder.
Munshi Teacher, clerk or secretary
Murqana Stalactite-type decoration over mosque doorway
Mushaira Mughal literary evening
Naan Type of bread, cooked in a tandoor

Namaste Hindu greeting (lit. 'I bow to you')
Namaz Muslim prayers, traditionally offered five times daily
Naqqar Khana Drum House
Nastaliq Type of Urdu script
Nautch Type of dance performance popular in the early nineteenth century
Nihang Sikh guard, dedicated to protecting the faith
Nulla Ditch
Omrah Mughal nobleman
Paan An Indian delicacy and digestive. It consists of a folded leaf containing (among other goodies) betel nut, a mild stimulant.
Padshah Emperor
Pakora Indian fritter: cheese or vegetables coated in batter and deep-fried
Pandit Brahmin (lit. 'scholar'); origin of the English word 'pundit'
Pankah Fan
Pankah-wallah Man engaged to operate said fan before the advent of electricity
Pirzada Official at a Sufi shrine. Often the descendant of the saint around whose tomb the shrine is built.
Pradhan Village headman
Puja Hindu prayers (lit. 'adoration')
Pujari One who prays (i.e the Brahmin in charge of a temple or a Hindu wedding ceremony)
Pukka Proper, civilized, refined; opposite of *jungli* (qv)
Qalander Ecstatic mystic or Holy Fool, usually itinerant; often mentally unstable
Qawwali Devotional verses sung at Sufi shrines with the intention of increasing the fervour of devotees and transporting them into a state of trance or *wajd* (qv)
Qawwals The group of musicians who sing *qawwalis*
Qazi Muslim judge
Ramadan Muslim month of fasting, normally some time around March
Ramayana The great Sanskrit epic telling the story of Lord Ram's rescue of his wife Sita from the clutches of the demon Ravanna who lives on the island of Lanka (lit. 'Ram's Road')
Rangila Colourful; nickname of the Emperor Muhammed Shah (1720–48) one of the more decadent of the Mughals
Rath Chariot
Rishis Hindu holy men, hermits and

teachers who lived long ago in the foothills of the Himalayas; similar to modern *sadhus*

Sadhu Hindu holy man

Salwar kameez Long tunic and matching loose trousers favoured mainly by girls in North India and by both sexes in Pakistan and Afghanistan

Samosa Curried puff pastry triangle. Delicious

Sannyasi One who has shed his worldly ties and become a wanderer

Sanskrit Indo-European language (lit. 'Purified') probably brought to India by the Aryans during the second millennium BC. The sacred tongue of Hinduism, it is still used by Brahmins for their worship.

Sarangi Violin-type musical instrument played with a bow

Sati Old Hindu custom of widow-burning; now illegal and largely discontinued, but for the odd case in Rajasthan

Sepoy Indian soldier in the service of the East India Company

Seraglio Harem

Shaitan Muslim name for Satan

Shaykh Head dervish in a Sufi monastery or *khanqah* (qv)

Sherwani Long Muslim frock coat

Shikar Hunting

Shikastah Old-fashioned classical Urdu script

Shish Mahal 'Palace of Mirrors', found in the Red Fort and in the larger Indian forts and *havelis*

Sikh Follower of the religion founded by Guru Nanak in the Punjab in the fifteenth century – a sort of compromise between Islam and Hinduism. Sikhs believe in one God and are opposed to idol worship. They are hard-working and, though they make up less than 1% of India's population, are both prominent and unmistakable: in obedience to Guru Nanak's command, observant Sikh men never cut their hair, and sport a turban and a long beard.

Sitar Indian instrument not dissimilar to an elongated lute

Sloka Stanza in a Sanskrit composition

Sufi Muslim holy man or mystic; same as a dervish or fakir

Syce Groom, stable lad

Tabla Type of drum

Tambura Another type of drum

Ta'wiz Sufi charm

Teh khana, Tykhana Underground cool house, much favoured in Mughal palaces

Tiffin Luncheon; originally eighteenth-century English slang, but still in use in Delhi

Tiffin tins Set of metal containers in which a commuter carries his home-cooked luncheon to his office

Tikka Caste-mark worn by Hindu women on their forehead; also a popular preparation of tandoori chicken

Titar Partridge

Tonga Two-wheeled horse-drawn taxi-carriage

Unani Greek (Ionian)

Urdu National language of Pakistan, almost identical to the Hindustani spoken today in Delhi. The language developed as a compromise between Persian and the different Indian languages in use in the Mughal army. (Its name is a reference to this military background and derives from the same root as the English 'horde'.) In the eighteenth century, Urdu developed into a language of great beauty, but few residents of Delhi can still speak this fine courtly version of the tongue.

Urs Annual festival held in Sufi shrines to commemorate the death of the founding Shaykh

Vedas The oldest Hindu religious texts; the four Vedas form the Hindu equivalent of the Old Testament

Veena Indian lute

Wajd Mystical trance

Wallah Man

Yoni Hindu vaginal symbol; usually represented cupping the Shiva *lingam* or phallus

Zenana Women's part of a Muslim household; the harem

Select Bibliography

General

Michael Alexander, *Delhi and Agra: A Traveller's Companion* (London, Constable, 1987)

Maheshwar Dayal, *Rediscovering Delhi: The Story of Shahjehanabad* (New Delhi, S. Chand, 1982)

H.C. Fanshawe, *Delhi Past and Present* (Reprint edn: New Delhi, Vintage Books, 1992)

R.E. Frykenberg (ed.), *Delhi Through the Ages* (Delhi, Oxford University Press, 1986)

Gordon Hearn, *The Seven Cities of Delhi* (Calcutta, Thacker, Spink, 1928)

H.K. Kaul (ed.), *Historic Delhi* (Delhi, Oxford University Press, 1985)

Sir Sayyid Ahmad Khan, *Asar al-Sanadid* trans. R. Nath as *Monuments of Delhi: A Historical Study* (New Delhi, Ambika Publications, 1979)

Y.D. Sharma, *Delhi and Its Neighbourhood* (New Delhi, Archaeological Survey of India, 1974)

Khuswant Singh, *Delhi: A Portrait* (New Delhi, Oxford University Press, 1983)

Percival Spear, *Delhi: A Historical Sketch* (Oxford, Oxford University Press, 1937)

Percival Spear, *Delhi: Its Monuments and History* (Bombay, Oxford University Press, 1945)

Chapter Two

Pranay Gupte, *Mother India: A Political Biography of Indira Gandhi* (New York, Charles Scribner's Sons, 1992)

Inder Malhotra, *Indira Gandhi: A Personal and Political Biography* (London, Hodder and Stoughton, 1989)

Mark Tully, *From Raj to Rajiv: Forty Years of Indian Independence* (London, BBC, 1988)

Mark Tully and Satish Jacob, *Amritsar: Mrs Gandhi's Last Battle* (London, Jonathan Cape, 1985)

Chapter Three

Ahmed Ali, *Twilight in Delhi* (London, Hogarth Press, 1940)

Maulana Abdul Kalam Azad, *India Wins Freedom* (New York, Longmans, 1960)

Alan Campbell-Johnson, *Mission With Mountbatten* (London, Robert Hale, 1951)

Nirad C. Chaudhuri, *Thy Hand Great Anarch!* (London, Chatto and Windus, 1987)

Michael Edwardes, *The Last Years of British India* (London, Cassell, 1963)

Trevor Royle, *The Last Days of the Raj* (London, Michael Joseph, 1989)

Pavan K. Verma, *Mansions at Dusk: The Havelis of Old Delhi* (New Delhi, Spantech, 1992)

Chapter Four

Charles Allen, *Plain Tales from the Raj* (London, Andre Deutsch, 1975)

Robert Byron, 'New Delhi', *Architectural Review*, 69, January 1931

Philip Davies, *Splendours of the Raj: British Architecture in India 1660–1947* (London, John Murray, 1985)

Nigel B. Hanklin, *Hanklyn-Jankin, A Stranger's Rumble-Tumble Guide to Some Words, Customs and Quiddities Indian and Indo-British* (New Delhi, Banyan Books, 1992)

Christopher Hussey, *The Life of Sir Edwin Lutyens* (London, Country Life, 1950)

Robert Grant Irving, *Indian Summer:*

Lutyens, Baker and Imperial Delhi (New Haven, Yale University Press, 1981)

Thomas R. Metcalf, An Imperial Vision (Oxford, Oxford University Press, 1989)

Jan Morris with Simon Winchester, Stones of Empire: The Buildings of the Raj (Oxford, Oxford University Press, 1983)

Clayre Percy and Jane Ridley, The Letters of Edwin Lutyens (London, Collins, 1985)

Gavin Stamp, 'Indian Summer', Architectural Review, 159, June 1976

Sir Henry Yule, Hobson Jobson (London, John Murray, 1904)

Chapter Five

C.F. Andrews, Zaka Ullah of Delhi (Cambridge, Heffer, 1924)

Mildred Archer, Between Battles: The Album of Colonel James Skinner (London, Al-Falak and Scorpion, 1982)

Mildred Archer, 'Artists and Patrons in Residency Delhi, 1803–1858', in R.E. Frykenberg, Delhi Through the Ages (Delhi, Oxford University Press, 1986)

Mildred Archer and Toby Falk, India Revealed: The Art and adventures of James and William Fraser 1801–35 (London, Cassell, 1989)

C.A. Bayly, Rulers, Townsmen and Bazaars: North Indian Society in the Age of British Expansion 1770–1870 (Cambridge, Cambridge University Press, 1983)

Alex Cain, The Cornchest for Scotland (Edinburgh, National Library of Scotland, 1986)

Emily Eden, Up the Country (Reprint edn: London, Virago, 1983)

Fanny Eden, Tigers, Durbars and Kings: Fanny Eden's Indian Journals 1837–1838 ed. Janet Dunbar (London, John Murray, 1988)

James Forbes, Oriental Memoirs 4 vols. (London, White, Cochrane, 1813)

William Franklin, 'An Account of the Present State of Delhi', Asiatik Researches, 4, 1795

James Baillie Fraser, Military Memoirs of Lieut-Col. James Skinner, 2 vols. (London, Smith, Elder, 1851)

Narayani Gupta, Delhi Between Two Empires 1803–1931: Society, Government and Urban Growth (New Delhi, Oxford University Press, 1981)

Christopher Hibbert, The Great Mutiny (London, Allen Lane, 1978)

Denis Holman, Sikander Sahib (London, Heinemann, 1961)

Victor Jacquemont, Letters from India (1829–32) 2 vols. trans. Catherine Phillips (London, Macmillan, 1936)

M.M. Kaye (ed.), The Golden Calm: An English Lady's Life in Moghul Delhi. Reminiscences by Emily, Lady Clive Bayley, and by her father, Sir Thomas Metcalfe (London, Webb and Bower, 1980)

Lady Maria Nugent, Journal of a Residence in India 1811–1815 2 vols. (London, 1839)

Ralph Russel (ed.), Ghalib: The Poet and his Age (London, George Allen and Unwin, 1972)

Pavan K. Verma, Ghalib: The Man, The Times (New Delhi, Penguin, 1989)

Stuart Cary Welch (ed.), The Emperor's Album (New York, Metropolitan Museum, 1987)

Chapter Six

Mozaffar Alam, The Crisis of Empire in Mughal North India: Awadh and the Punjab, 1707–48 (New Delhi, Oxford University Press, 1986)

Stephen P. Blake, Shahjahanabad: The Sovereign City in Mughal India 1639–1739 (Cambridge, Cambridge University Press, 1991)

Dargah Quli Khan, The Muraqqa'-e Dehli trans. Chander Shekhar (New Delhi, Deputy Publications, 1989)

Ralph Russel and Khurshid ul-Islam, Three Mughal Poets (New Delhi, Oxford University Press, 1991)

S.K. Sharma, Hijras: The Labelled Deviants (New Delhi, Gian Publishing House, 1989)

Percival Spear, The Twilight of the the Mughuls: Studies in Late Mughul Delhi (Cambridge, Cambridge University Press, 1951)

Chapter Seven

Catherine B. Asher, Architecture of Mughal India (Cambridge, Cambridge University Press, 1992)

François Bernier, *Travels in the Mogul Empire, 1656–68* ed. Archibald Constable, trans. Irving Brock (Reprint edn: Delhi, S. Chand, 1972)

Sir Richard Burn (ed.), *The Cambridge History of India Vol. IV: The Mughul Period* (Cambridge, Cambridge University Press, 1937)

Zahiruddin Farukhi, *Aurangzeb and his Times* (Bombay, D.B Tarapovevala, 1935)

William Foster (ed.), *Early Travels in India 1583–1619* (Reprint edn: New Delhi, Oriental Books Reprint Corporation, 1985)

Bamber Gascoigne, *The Great Moghuls* (London, Jonathan Cape, 1971)

Gavin Hambly, *Cities of Mughul India* (New York, G.P Putnam's Sons, 1968)

Mirza Kamran, 'The *Mirza Nama* (The Book of the Perfect Gentleman) of Mirza Kamran with an English translation', ed. and trans. Maulawi M. Hidayat Husain, *Journal of the Asiatic Society of Bengal*, NS 9, 1913

Inayat Khan, *The Shah Jehan Nama* ed. W.E Begley and Z.A Desai (New Delhi, Oxford University Press, 1990)

Ebba Koch, *Mughal Architecure* (Munich, Prestel-Verlag, 1991)

Elizabeth B. MacDougall and Richard Ettinhausen (eds), *The Islamic Garden* (Cambridge, Mass., Harvard University Press, 1976)

Niccolao Manucci, *Storia do Mogor* trans. William Irvine 4 vols. (Reprint edn: Calcutta, Editions Indian, 1965)

Elizabeth B. Moynihan, *Paradise as a Garden in Persia and Mughal India* (New York, George Braziller, 1979)

Kalika-Ranjan Qanungo, *Dara Shukoh* (Calcutta, M.C. Sarkar, 1935)

Constance M. Villiers Stuart, *Gardens of the Great Mughals* (London, 1913)

Chapter Eight

Julian Baldick, *Mystical Islam: An Introduction to Sufism* (London, I.B. Tauris, 1989)

Zia-ud-Din Barni, *Ta'rikh-i Firuz Shahi* in Sir H.M. Elliot and John Dowson (ed. and trans.), *The History of India as told by its own Historians* vol. 3 (London, Trubner, 1871)

Ibn Battuta, *Travels in Asia and Africa 1325–1354* (London, Routledge and Kegan Paul, 1929)

E.A.T.W. Budge, *The History of Alexander the Great, Being the Syriac Version* (London, John Murray, 1889)

William Crooke, *The Popular Religion and Folklore of Northern India* 2 vols. (Reprint edn: Delhi, Munshiram Manoharlal, 1968)

Simon Digby, *Warhorse and Elephant in the Delhi Sultanate: A Study in Military Supplies* (Karachi, 1971)

Simon Digby, 'Qalanders and Related Groups' in Y. Friedmann (ed.), *Islam in India* Vol.1 (Jerusalem, Magna Press, 1984)

Ross E. Dunn, *The Adventures of Ibn Battuta: A Muslim Traveller of the 14th Century* (London, Croom Helm, 1986)

H.A.R. Gibb, *The Travels of Ibn Battuta* 3 vols. (Cambridge, Cambridge University Press, 1971)

Sir Wolseley Haig (ed.), *The Cambridge History of India Vol. III: Turks and Afghans* (Reprint edn: Delhi, S. Chand, 1987)

A.M. Hussain, *The Rise and Fall of Muhammed bin Tughluq* (London, Luzac, 1938)

Abdu'l Malik Isami, *Futuhu's Salatin or The Shah Nama-i-Hind* 3 vols. trans. A.M Hussian (Aligarh, Asia Publishing House, 1967–77)

K.S. Lal, *The Twilight of the Sultanate* (Bombay, Asia Publishing House, 1963)

Bruce B. Lawrence, *Notes From a Distant Flute: The Extant Literature of Pre-Mughal Indian Sufism* (Teheran, Imperial Iranian Academy, 1978)

S.B.P. Nigam, *Nobility Under the Sultans of Delhi* (Delhi, Munishiram Manoharlal, 1968)

Khaliq Ahmad Nizami, 'A Medieval Indian Madrasah', in K.A. Nizami, *Studies in Medieval Indian History and Culture* (Allahabad, Kitab Mahal, 1966)

Khaliq Ahmad Nizami, *Some Aspects of Religion and Politics in India during the Thirteenth Century* (New Delhi, Idarah-i Adabiyat-i Delli, 1974)

346

Ishtiaq Husian Qureshi, *The Administration of the Sultanate of Delhi* (Lahore, Muhammed Ashraf, 1942)

Saiyid Athar Abbas Rizvi, *A History of Sufism in India* 2 vols. (New Delhi, Munshiram Manoharlal, 1978)

Jalal-ud-Din Rumi, *The Mathnawi* ed. and trans. R.A. Nicholson (London, Luzac, 1925–40)

Annemarie Schimmel, *I Am Wind, You Are Fire: The Life and Work of Rumi* (Boston, Shambhala, 1992)

Idries Shah, *The Way of the Sufi* (London, Jonathan Cape, 1963)

Idries Shah, *The Sufis* (London, Octagon Press, 1964)

Christine Troll, *Muslim Shrines in India* (New Delhi, Oxford University Press, 1989)

Sin-Leqi-Unninni, *Gilgamesh* trans. John Gardiner and John Maier (New York, Vintage Books, 1985)

Anthony Welch and Howard Crane, 'The Tughluqs: Master Builders of the Sultanate', in *Muqarnas* vol. 1 (New Haven, Yale University Press, 1983)

Chapter Nine

D.P. Agrawal and Dilip K. Chakrabarti (ed.), *Essays in Indian Prehistory* (Delhi, Agam Prakashan, 1976)

Bridget and Raymond Allchin, *The Rise of Civilisation in India and Pakistan* (Cambridge, Cambridge University Press, 1983)

Walter A. Fairservis, *The Roots of Ancient India: The Archaeology of Early Indian Civilisation* (New York, Macmillan, 1971)

D.H. Gordon, *The Prehistoric Background of Indian Culture* (Bombay, Bhulabhai Memorial Institute, 1958)

S.P. Gupta and K.S. Ramachandran (ed.), *Mahabharata: Myth and Reality* (Delhi, Agam Prakashan, 1976)

J.P. Joshi, 'The Mahabharata and Indian Archaeology', in B.M. Pandey and B.D. Chattopadhyaya (ed.), *Archaeology and History* (Delhi, Agam Kala Prakashan, 1987)

David Kinsley, *Hindu Goddesses: Visions of the Divine Feminine in the Hindu Religious Tradition* (Berkeley, University of California Press, 1986)

B.B. Lal, 'Excavations at Hastinapura and Other Explorations in the Upper Ganga and Sutlej Basins 1950–52', *Ancient India*, 10–11, 1954–5)

Vettam Mani, *Puranic Encylopaedia* (Delhi, Motilal Banarsidas, 1975)

Henry Moore, *Henry Moore at the British Museum* (London, British Museum Press, 1981)

Carr Stephen, *The Archaeology and Monumental Remains of Delhi* (Reprint edn: Allahabad, Kitab Mahal, 1967)

Margaret and James Stutley, *A Dictionary of Hinduism: its Mythology, Folklore, and Development, 1500 BC– AD 1500* (London, Routledge and Kegan Paul, 1977)

Vyasa, *The Mahabharata* 3 vols. trans. J.A.B. Van Buitenen (Chicago, University of Chicago Press, 1973–8)

Benjamin Walker, *The Hindu World: An Encylopedic Survey of Hinduism* 2 vols. (London, George Allen and Unwin, 1968)

Index

349

351

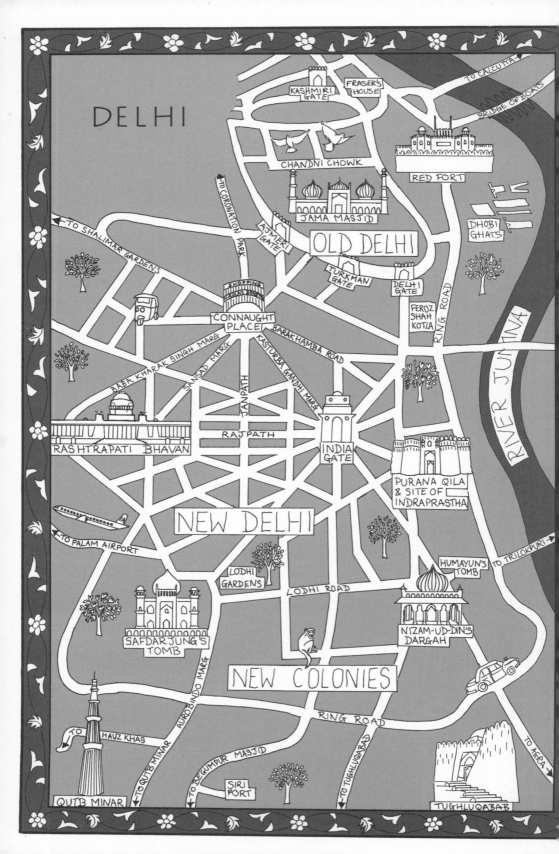